Brian Friel

Brian Friel was born in Omagh, County Tyrone, in 1929. His plays include: *Philadelphia, Here I Come!*, *Faith Healer*, *Translations*, *Making History* and *Dancing at Lughnasa*.

by the same author

BRIAN FRIEL

Plays Two

Dancing at Lughnasa

Fathers and Sons

Making History

Wonderful Tennessee

Molly Sweeney

Introduced by
Christopher Murray

FARRAR, STRAUS AND GIROUX

NEW YORK

Farrar, Straus and Giroux
18 West 18th Street, New York 10011

This collection first published in 1999
by Faber and Faber Limited
3 Queen Square London WCIN 3AU

Published in the United States by Farrar, Straus and Giroux
Printed in the United States of America

A CIP record for this book
is available from the British Library

ISBN 978-0-571-19710-1

14 16 18 20 19 17 15

Contents

Contents

Introduction

Like so many great dramatists from Shakespeare through Ibsen to O'Neill and Miller, whose later plays reveal both a surprising mature flowering and a shapely inclusion of youthful themes, Brian Friel's latest work as represented in this volume is at once a new departure and a return to familiar ground. As he is ever the protean playwright, whose work shifts agilely from political to non-political themes, it is always dangerous to be categorical about phases of development in Friel's drama. And yet 1986, when *Fathers and Sons* had its première, does seem to mark a new and exciting stage of transition. The achievement of *Translations* (1980), with its complex and many-layered linguistic, cultural and political themes, was behind him, so it was time, following the farcical and mischievous *Communication Cord* (1982), to strike out in a new direction.

Not that the process is that simple or automatic. Friel was still closely involved with the Field Day Theatre Company, which he had co-founded in 1980, and was only gradually inching his way to the point where the new kind of play he was to write, best exemplified in *Dancing at Lughnasa* (1990), was to signal a return to the Abbey Theatre. As Friel himself put it in interview with Ciaran Carty: 'A play offers you a shape and a form to accommodate your anxieties and disturbances in that period of life you happen to be passing through. But you outgrow that and you change and grope for a new shape and a new articulation of it.' The artist writes as he must and not by prescription of any kind. The later 1980s thus saw Brian Friel moving away from the preoccupations

which had led to the writing of *Translations* and finding
new release in *Fathers and Sons*. Close personal and
family relationships were to become again his major
theme, the crises that demand a re-evaluation of a man's
or a woman's whole mode of being. For the most part the
plays of this new phase thus find their centre more in
individual trauma than in political crisis, although Friel
was to write one other political play for Field Day, namely
Making History (1988).

In spite of this development towards a non-political
drama, all five plays in this volume are in various ways
history plays. They are occupied with time, memory and
the imminence of death. Looked at in another way they
are plays about collapse of various kinds, historical,
social, moral, psychological. Offsetting collapse is
transcendence, or the search for a mode of living with
dignity which accords with an awareness of the
insufficiency of late twentieth-century criteria of success.
This opposing theme is spiritual, indeed religious, which
appears with quite a positive emphasis in these later plays.

In all five plays, moreover, a powerful theatricalism
operates. Friel writes classically, poetically, in images
which crystallize meaning symbolically; invariably these
images find reflection in Friel's careful and specific stage
directions. His decision to direct the premières of *Molly
Sweeney* (1994) and *Give Me Your Answer, Do!* (1997)
himself may indicate a fear that directors were not always
interpreting his work as he would wish. The texts must be
seen as designed, lit and choreographed by the
playwright. Like Beckett, Friel has a musical concept of
dramatic form; all performance features from dialogue to
dance are included in 'scores' which demand rigorous
attention to pacing, intelligent recognition of pattern,
shifts in mood, and establishment of atmosphere. The
plays are like extended poems, and yet they are 'actorly'.
The roles provided are subtle and deep. The doctor

Shpigelsky, in Friel's version of Turgenev's *A Month in the Country* (1992), says, 'If the mask fits, wear it,' and this should alert the reader to the extent to which irony and sub-text govern the plays in general. The 'private' and 'public' personae are not so patently held apart in the later plays as in *Philadelphia, Here I Come!* (1964). In this regard the later plays are more complex. Clearly, here, as always, Friel's writing is understated but constantly performative; the masks in these plays seem less obvious since they are as likely to be imposed by others as voluntarily assumed by the individual. Nevertheless, the notion of the metaphorical mask is central to the explorations of identity conducted in *Making History* and *Molly Sweeney*. Masks and identities interact productively also in *Wonderful Tennessee* (1993), where the characters seem morally disabled. Seeming is the name of the game; self-possession or repression is equally a brittle pose in these later plays. Of course, the famous dance in Act I of *Dancing at Lughnasa* provides stunning evidence of Friel's theatrical power, but one should also be alert to its less flamboyant, more Chekhovian, and more diverse manifestations elsewhere.

Fathers and Sons liberated Friel from writer's block, which had troubled him following *The Communication Cord*. That play, perhaps, had drawn a line all too boldly underneath the sort of play *Translations* was, namely, an exploration at the deepest level of what Friel now mockingly referred to as national 'pieties'. Yet his future theme had not yet disclosed itself. This was undoubtedly frustrating, for this was the time when Field Day was undertaking a massive cultural revolution. There was even talk of a large-scale anthology of Irish writing which would redraw the map of Irish intellectual history. Perhaps Friel was numbed by the appalling cycle of violence in Northern Ireland at this time. Perhaps he deferred to the Field Day pamphlets which confronted that political situation. In any case, *Fathers and Sons* represents a joyous victory over silence at a difficult period. Although it was offered to Field Day for production it was beyond the resources of that company and was staged instead by the National Theatre, London.

Fathers and Sons, a most adept transformation of Turgenev's 1862 novel into a play text, refuelled Friel's imagination. It sometimes happens that a writer can find in reworking or adapting another writer's work that he/she is thereby gathering nuts for a lean period. We used, perhaps, to look askance at Shakespeare for turning so readily to Holinshed's *Chronicles* or to Plutarch's *Lives* or to the Italian novella for his source material, when we should instead have been taking note of how the dramatic process works: parasitically, one might say, and yet in complex and fructifying ways. Chekhov had already lent resonance to Friel's work in *Aristocrats*, and he had made a version of *Three Sisters* in 1981, but Turgenev was new territory, and the task of adapting a novel set him new problems, for he had not done this before. When a few years later he adapted Turgenev's comedy *A Month in the Country*, Friel set out (in a preface) the notion that the relationship between Chekhov and Turgenev was 'metabiotic'. Metabiosis he defined as 'a mode of living in which one organism is dependent on another for the preparation of an environment in which it can live'. This is a far subtler metaphor than to say one author 'paved the way' for another. In effect, Turgenev prepared an environment in which Friel as Chekhovian artist could live or be reborn. Friel could treat Bazarov ironically. Bazarov is the single-minded activist whose untimely death puts into perspective the family values he so loftily scorned. When he falls in love and is scorned for his pains Bazarov clears a space for others to build more fruitful, less intellectual lives. Scene 4 in Act II of Friel's version has no correlation in Turgenev's novel; it marks a fresh shoot, a stirring of something new in Friel's own oeuvre. The scene depicts 'an annual harvest dance in preparation'. Here, as elsewhere emphasized in Friel's version of Turgenev's text, dance becomes an image of order. Even Pavel claims he was 'an excellent dancer once upon a time'. To Anna's bleak question, referring to Bazarov's absurd death, 'How do you carry on?', Friel's imagery of harvest, dance and the double wedding in the offing creates an idea of order and resilience which challenges the disorder inherent in Bazarov's ironic fall. *Dancing at Lughnasa* was soon to bring such imagery to fuller and more persuasive fruition.

Meanwhile, *Making History* was to be Friel's swan-song for Field Day. By this time Thomas Kilroy had joined the board of Field Day (the only southerner to become a member) and had supplied a challenging play, *Double Cross* (1986), which Friel admired. The ambiguities of that piece, the emphasis on the role-playing that political involvement demands, and the sense that the roots of betrayal lie historically far back in the psyche must have made their mark on Friel when he decided to write a play about Hugh O'Neill, Earl of Tyrone, and sixteenth-century Anglo-Irish relations. Kilroy had already written on this theme in *The O'Neill* (1969, published 1995). In the climate of the Field Day pamphlets, the time was ripe for another, more self-conscious look at the O'Neill story. Both authors relied on Sean O'Faolain's biography *The O'Neill* (1942). But where Kilroy had shown the tragedy of a man divided between loyalty to the old, communal Gaelic world and commitment to the new, modern, European world, Friel focuses on the theatrical possibilities inherent in a man's awareness that he is playing a role in what is about to become history. His play becomes virtually a Pirandellian situation, a debate on how the self, or identity, can be undermined once it is mythologized. Historiography itself becomes deconstructed. It is rather like that moment in *Julius Caesar* when, at the point of Caesar's assassination, Cassius calls on his fellow conspirators ritualistically to bathe their hands in Caesar's blood:

> Stoop then, and wash. How many ages hence
> Shall this our lofty scene be acted over,
> In states unborn, and accents yet unknown!
> (III.i.111–13)

Cassius is aware they are 'making history'. Friel, however, goes a step further in this process by adding the historian Lombard, who is constantly prepared to discuss with O'Neill the limits of the history he, Lombard, is in another sense 'making'. By foregrounding this historian so conspicuously Friel sceptically questions history as a mode of knowing the world. (We are reminded of the ironic name given to the historian in *Aristocrats*, Dr Hoffnung, ever 'hopeful' of finding the complete truth.) Dramatically, O'Neill is paralysed by the awareness of how his freedom is subject to Lombard's propagandist purposes, whereby O'Neill is to figure as hero of the counter-reformation. This becomes O'Neill's 'last battle'. He fears he will be embalmed in 'a florid lie'. Here the effect is of a character in Pirandello quarrelling with the director and struggling against the prison-house of the text. Exploiting to the full this situation (the seeds of which lie as much in his own *Living Quarters* [1977] as in the final pages of O'Faolain's biography of O'Neill), Friel depicts the plight of his failed hero as classically tragic.

But there is another dimension to *Making History* also. In a programme note Friel insisted that 'history and fiction are related and comparable forms of discourse and that an historical text is a kind of literary artifact'. One important result of this conviction is the role accorded Mabel Bagenal in O'Neill's story. In fact, Mabel ran away from

O'Neill, laid public complaint against him, and died in 1595, six years before the crucial date Friel supplies which coincides with the defeat at Kinsale. Friel makes her central to O'Neill's whole tragedy. Indeed here, and in the plays which follow, woman is the measure of all things. Mabel is loyal, a value Friel prizes highly; she is wise and sees further than O'Neill himself into what she calls 'the overall thing' or the wider significance of the war against the English; she is the equivalent of a Muse figure whose power O'Neill as artist recognizes only too late and Lombard sees not at all. In a key scene (I.ii), Mabel and her sister Mary discuss herbs and transplanting in what becomes an allegory of the colonizer and colonized issue, or civilians versus barbarians. (Here one might well compare Seamus Deane's Field Day pamphlet, *Civilians and Barbarians* [1983].) The discussion goes to the core of the play, in just the way Shakespeare's scene in the garden in *Richard II* (III.iv) makes pruning and garden management form the central metaphor for Richard's downfall. Mabel believes in and has the courage to put into practice the idea of inter-marriage/cross-fertilization. She dares to marry outside the tribe which, as Jimmy Jack says in *Translations*, is a dangerous undertaking. This is why O'Neill insists that Lombard should place Mabel at the centre of his history of O'Neill: 'That place is central to me.' But in the myth Lombard is erecting Mabel is peripheral. Friel alone can reinstate her. In so doing he is certainly re-making history, but he is also producing a new myth, poetically conceived, for Anglo-Irish relations. Ten years after *Making History* was premièred its imaginative impatience with monoliths may be seen as, in Friel's term, metabiologically creating the environment for the Good Friday Agreement of 1998.

Dancing at Lughnasa marks a triumphant achievement by a writer at the height of his renewed powers. It has proved to be Friel's most successful play in many years, and has now been filmed. It is to a significant degree autobiographical, as Friel's moving dedication concedes. The boy Michael may to a certain extent be taken as Brian Friel (who was not, however, born out of wedlock), aged seven in 1936. Like all great autobiographical plays, from Strindberg's *The Father* (1887) to O'Neill's *Long Day's Journey into Night* (1956), Friel's *Dancing at Lughnasa* transcends the details of actual experience and creates an alternative or parallel world through the power of art. The claim Friel's play has on our attention lies in its fusion of so much diverse material, mythic and sociological, so many themes, comic and tragic, so many subtle and moving characterizations, in a language lyrical to the point of poetic precision and yet simultaneously in denial of the power of language to delineate the contours of actual experience.

Dancing at Lughnasa is, plainly, a memory play. It may be compared in this regard to Williams's *The Glass Menagerie* (1944). Both plays are set in the year 1936, on the cusp of the Second World War; both have a narrator who speaks for the author and who is also the central consciousness; both explore the pathos of loved ones incapable of side-stepping, as the artist-narrator himself must (though not without guilt), the snares set by family and community. But the differences between the two plays are equally important. The main ones are cultural and anthropological. Where Williams re-enacts the classical American need, as first articulated by Huckleberry Finn, to 'light out for the Territory ahead of the rest' and find a new frontier, Friel re-enacts the Irish awareness that far-off hills are green and going into exile a tragic condition. Further, there is no correspondence in Williams to the rich, ritualistic material of dance and religious celebration which in Friel's play arises from the bringing together of residual Celtic myth and modern

African vibrancy. Father Jack would be unthinkable in Tennessee Williams's St Louis.

Memory is the mother of the Muses; memory is what engenders poetry. On the other hand, as old Hugh says in *Translations*, 'to remember everything is a form of madness'. Selection and compression are necessary to what Friel calls 'the artist's truth', which is subjective. There is an analogy here with Friel's 'making history' in other plays. Experience, or personal history, is also subject to the artist's manipulation for purposes other and perhaps higher than establishment of empirical truth. In 'Self-Portrait', published in 1972, Friel discusses 'a particular memory of a particular day . . . a moment of happiness caught in an album'. But the childhood memory, rather like Gar's sustaining memory in *Philadelphia* of fishing with his father, is blatantly fallacious in the details recalled. Human memory, Friel says, is solipsistically creative: 'The fact is a fiction.' The whole of *Faith Healer* is based on this idea. Friel's aesthetic is in that sense quite the opposite of nostalgic. He does not recall in order unavailingly to bewail the loss of youth (in that delicious self-abuse which is the hallmark of inferior art) but in order to set before the spectator or reader the centrality of each individual's self-made universe. The father who comes to this insight in the short story 'Among the Ruins' reflects: 'The past did have meaning. It was neither reality nor dreams. . . . It was simply continuance, life repeating itself and surviving.' This is the key to Friel's consistent use of memory in his plays. Thus in *Dancing at Lughnasa* Michael finally remembers 'that summer in 1936' as 'simultaneously actual and illusory'.

This simultaneity is extraordinary. The tableau the audience sees just before Michael's final speech is 'lit in a very soft, golden light so that the tableau we see is almost, but not quite, in a haze'. It is this doubleness, this ambiguity, this 'almost but not quite', which lends to the play its hypnotic, absorbing power. It enacts loss and imaginative recovery, age and childhood, the decadence of outworn myth and the vigour of residual ritual, parodic dance and the dance of real joy, the union of the sacred and the secular, homecoming and departure, the past and the future, all the rhythms of life's resilience in the face of injustice, breakdown, lies and double dealing symbolized in those primitive-faced kites doomed never to get off the ground.

Wonderful Tennessee could hardly be more different from *Dancing at Lughnasa*. In some ways it is a bolder, more uncompromising play, closer to Beckett than to Tennessee Williams. A Dublin wit described it as '*Waiting for Godot* meets *The Bacchae*', but this, like a lot of Dublin wit, is clever rather than profound. It implies a gauche inability to control the register or level of dramatic communication, whereas Friel's intertextuality is invariably knowing if not self-reflexive. He is postmodernist at least in that sense: in his adept manipulation of allusion, quotation and style. If there is a clash of styles in *Wonderful Tennessee* it is very deliberate.

There is a very serious purpose underlying *Wonderful Tennessee*. It is, in some respects, a harsh condemnation of contemporary Irish society, what Friel had in 1972 scorned as 'the vodka-and-tonic society' of 'permissive Dublin'. This is the stuff of Hugh Leonard's social satires, for example in *The Patrick Pearse Motel* (1971) or (more profoundly) in *Summer* (1974) . Friel's venture into Leonard's territory is, however, under his own banner: as ever, a palimpsest of social, historical, popular cultural and literary sources. Ballads, tin-pan-alley, negro spirituals, and Roman Catholic hymns vie with aborted stories from a range of traditional motifs to make up a multi-layered text.

Avoiding conventional dramatic plotting, *Wonderful*

Tennessee presents a conflict between a place and a group of people. Out of that conflict certain adjustments and arrivals at decision are made possible among the group. In the course of that process, where no single figure or consciousness dominates or serves as filter of meaning, a range of philosophical, moral and social attitudes is displayed and severely tested. In the end there is a humbling of expectations and a re-charging of moral energies.

This use of a place is poetic in the sense that Seamus Heaney's use of landscape in, say, *Station Island* is poetic: the landscape itself seems spiritually possessed. This is altogether different from the usual use of place on stage, even in Chekhov, where all that is required are signs and synecdoche. In other words, space on stage is basically mimetic, as conveyed semiotically, but is usually also representative: *this* room is all the other possible rooms in society and so is symbolic. Stage design usually tries to combine a sense of the real (the 'lived-in') and the metonymic (the representative). Even where the Greeks and the Elizabethans used a *skene* or physical building as setting the convention was that this structure could assume an identity, a location, at the playwright's will: now Thebes, now Athens, or now the exterior of Macbeth's castle in Scotland, now the interior of King Edward's palace in England. But for *Wonderful Tennessee* Friel uses an adaptation of the Greek *skene* which is also and recognizably an old pier by the sea. The designer for the Abbey production, Joe Vanek, spent a week 'up and down every inlet and pier on the Donegal coast' before designing a set which was 'a kind of fusion of parts of them all'. Yet in Friel's own stage description the stone pier has a history also: 'It was built in 1905 but has not been used since the hinterland became depopulated many decades ago.' From the start, the pier has a presence, a personality; it is like a temple in that its solitude emanates a spiritual atmosphere. It is thus not inert, a mere designation of place, but a living, sacred space. Indeed, at the opening of Act II the morning light 'enfolds' the pier 'like an aureole' or saint's halo. The emptiness and the silence all around are strongly emphasized in the opening stage direction: 'Silence and complete stillness . . . an environment of deep tranquillity and peace'. The conflict in the play is between these established values and the disorder and restlessness of the human party which invades the setting.

For the story of the 'island of otherness', *Oileán Draíochta* (literally, 'Magic Island'), which the pier silently guards, Friel draws on the long tradition of voyage literature ('immram') in early Irish culture, for example *The Voyage of Saint Brendan*. Subtitled *Journey to the Promised Land*, this text was written in Latin *c.* AD 800 and often translated, most recently by John J. O'Meara in 1976. Yet it is the contrast that counts between the meaningful spiritual sea-voyage of Saint Brendan and the absurd non-voyage of Friel's modern would-be pilgrims. At the same time, the fragile Berna (for in Friel's later work women are usually both frail and visionary) understands the purpose of pilgrims to the island: 'To remember again – to be reminded . . . To be in touch again – to attest.' Here there is a link back to *Dancing at Lughnasa* and Michael's account of dancing as being 'in touch with some otherness'. It is perhaps the re-definition of 'only connect' as an answer to twentieth-century alienation. It is a reminder of the sacred at the root of the simplest, most commonplace routines.

But the six characters in *Wonderful Tennessee* are in search of whatever healing from the island which the pier oversees. The island is their 'named destination', as Spain was for Gerry Evans in *Dancing at Lughnasa* and as Abyssinia was to be for Frank in *Molly Sweeney*. In each case the destination is illusory. This party-loving group, so patently 'lost' and 'unhappy', as they declare from first entrance, find themselves challenged by the landscape, where there is 'nothing from here to Boston except a derelict church – without a roof'. The placing of a church here, abandoned and roofless, reinforces the motif of religious starvation. The six characters only slowly make any real connection, among themselves or with this landscape and among these ruins.

Although the waiting for the boatman Carlin who never comes appears to echo Beckett, the contrast is far more significant. In *Waiting for Godot* (1953) the bleakness is emphasized by the repetition in Act II of the pointless routines of Act I. But at the start of Act II of *Wonderful Tennessee* the stage direction calls for a lighting effect for 'a new day', namely, 'a pristine and brilliant morning sunlight that enfolds the pier like an aureole and renovates everything it touches'. The last phrase is significant. In Beckett there is never renovation (compare also *Happy Days* [1961]), but rather repetition and entropy. Friel, however, wishes to suggest, in Joyce's phrase, the sanctification of the ordinary. His characters begin to stir towards renovation. Frank sees and is overwhelmed by seeing the dolphin, whose dance, like Hopkins's windhover, stirred his heart in hiding. Frank's experience brings him into silent alliance with Berna. Then Terry's story, a brief historical excursion into the Ireland of the 1930s, touches everybody. All parody stops. The characters no longer regard the island as Edenic, but rather as readers of Friel will regard the 'gentle island' (title of his 1971 anti-pastoral): as a mirror of Ireland's complex, ambivalent combination of violence and the sacred. Since the island is orientated in the midst of the audience it follows that the audience is involved in the circular process uniting the perspectives from island and pier. Of course, the audience is free, like Angela, to withhold involvement ('What a goddam, useless, endless, unhappy outing this has been!'), but the final rhythms of the play make this difficult, and Angela herself is affected. She breaks with Terry and makes a pledge in altogether another style with George. All of the characters finally imitate at one remove the ritual practices of their forebears. In a sense they find meaning, although this is certainly a tenuous business. The certainty of George's death is perhaps the one fixture on the characters' horizon, and their need for a meaningful future takes its direction from that fact. Although they never get to the holy island there is a sense in which the island comes to them. When they all leave, 'silence and complete stillness' descend again and overcome their departing noise. The pier recovers its divine presence. The poetic idea behind this victory of silence over human noise turns the theatre into a place where, in Peter Brook's terms (in *The Empty Space*), the invisible can again be made visible. Brook calls that 'the holy theatre'. It is what *Wonderful Tennessee* strives to create. It is a far better play than its unhappy failure on Broadway might suggest.

With *Molly Sweeney* Friel narrows down his social and moral preoccupations to focus – as in *Making History* but without any overt politics – on a play of ideas. The basic idea is the one Synge explored in *The Well of the Saints* (1905): the right of the blind to remain blind even when a cure is offered. As Synge presents it, in his high romantic style, the conflict is virtually a class question, between beggars and bourgeoisie, although for Synge the beggars represent the artist in society. In the end, Synge's blind couple assert their right to choose inner darkness over socially approved light, and must pay the price of social exclusion. Friel, whose immediate source is less Synge than Oliver Sacks's essay 'To See and Not See', ignores Synge's broad social and aesthetic argument to centre instead on what one might call the 'Fathers and

Daughters' theme. At the core of *Molly Sweeney* is the story of a woman destroyed by patriarchal interference.

It is debatable, however, to what extent the play may be considered allegorical. Is Molly the Irish Everywoman, or even a version of Cathleen Ní Houlihan, the traditional representation of Ireland in female form, as has been suggested? It is likely, however, that such critical approaches are better suited to the novel (compare Molly Bloom) than to drama. Nevertheless, *Molly Sweeney* is an indirect play, where the drama occurs in the form of narrative, not of action, rather as in the earlier *Faith Healer* (which is undoubtedly allegorical). Reading between the lines, we find Molly's mother prefiguring Molly's own collapse at the hands of a father figure. There are many parallels drawn between Molly's father (a judge, always an ominous parentage in Friel) and her surgeon Mr Rice, who tries, as it were, to father her a second time. Frank, too, while mainly a comic foil for Rice, shares with him a similar 'phantom desire, a fantasy in the head', which propels him into re-making Molly. But whereas her father insisted that Molly had nothing to gain from going through the process of what we may call enlightenment, both Frank and (with less certainty) Mr Rice believe she has 'nothing to lose' by changing her blind world for the so-called normal or sighted world. Is this an allegory pointing out the dangers of technologically backed progress as against tradition or nature? In any case, the coercion undermines Molly mentally and in the end she inhabits neither one world nor the other but a 'borderline country' where she is, though broken and dying, nevertheless 'at home there'. She implies a willed retreat, rather like the blind badgers which Frank foolishly tries to move from their habitat.

Because *Molly Sweeney* is narrated it is a complex memory play. The three narrators, who share only the space provided by the stage in what must be Friel's least

realized location in all of his plays, each recount in turn
the story of the fatal operation, before and after. Their
lack of interaction suggests that they do not see each
other, do not exist for each other, and that only the
audience is privy to this tri-partite memory. The form is
thus far more experimental than *Dancing at Lughnasa*,
controlled by a single memory. It is, of course, the
playwright who, like Sir in *Living Quarters*, summons up
these three dispersed figures and allows their discrete
stories to form a continuous discourse. So abstract is this
idea that the setting must remain unspecified.

In Act II Rice's patterned language, 'And I'll remember
Ballybeg', refers to 'the core, the very heart of the
memory', what he calls his own 'performance'. Once
again, the Frielian idea is presented that memory is
something constructed through which the individual
establishes continuity of identity and thereby a consoling
sense of wholeness. Memory, in short, is redemptive. Rice,
as artist, finds renovation in the achievement of Molly's
brief sightedness: his own 'darkness' is momentarily lifted.
The way Rice projects memory forward ('I'll remember
Ballybeg') has a strange effect of collapsing time itself.
Molly herself is likewise collapsed, sacrificed like Grace in
Faith Healer or even Mabel in *Making History* to male
ambition. Frank provides a parody of Rice's more
authentic ambition. Molly's own memories in the hospital
(was she always narrating from the hospital?) reinstate
the 'Fathers and Daughters' motif. Rice and her father
become the same person; her mother is herself. Memory
and the present coincide. Molly has reached a plateau
where she has won the freedom to let illusion and
actuality intermingle. Yet we are told she is dying. Is Friel
not finally agreeing with Synge that the price of this kind
of freedom, the artist's freedom, is exclusion, is exile?
Though about to die Molly is mistress of her own world
and can admit and exclude those she will. In that way,

although not just in that way, the play is stunningly theatrical.

Further studies of women as at once victims of male power and pregnant with autonomy appear in *Give Me Your Answer, Do!*, directed at the Abbey by Friel himself. Here, too, a father and daughter relationship is bound up with mental disturbance. Here, too, the artist is enmeshed in the paradox of symbiotic mastery and destruction. The novelist Tom Connolly in this play has suffered writer's block ever since his daughter's descent into schizophrenia several years before the play opens, and he finds release at last only through denial of the obvious though meretricious solution. The search begun in *Wonderful Tennessee* for answers in a world now cut off from spiritual authority perhaps reaches its true end here, in the clarity of loyalty and the paradox of winning through losing. These are old Frielian ironies, reminted in a new and assured style. *Give Me Your Answer, Do!* closes the circle first described when Friel, after years of silence, felt enabled to write *Fathers and Sons* and so entered upon a fresh and exciting period of artistic activity. Its successful new production at the Hampstead Theatre in the spring of 1998 argues that, like *Wonderful Tennessee*, there is considerably more to this play than may first meet the eye. Like good music, to which Friel's art always aspires, these plays must be heard (in the mind and in the theatre) more than once before their true power strikes home. Once they are allowed to make their proper impact they haunt the imagination for ever.

Christopher Murray
August 1998

DANCING AT LUGHNASA

In memory of those five brave Glenties women

Characters

Michael, young man, narrator
Kate, forty, schoolteacher
Maggie, thirty-eight, housekeeper
Agnes, thirty-five, knitter
Rose, thirty-two, knitter
Chris, twenty-six, Michael's mother
Gerry, thirty-three, Michael's father
Jack, fifty-three, missionary priest

*Michael, who narrates the story, also speaks the lines of
the boy, i.e. himself when he was seven.*

Act One: A warm day in early August 1936.
Act Two: Three weeks later.

*The home of the Mundy family, two miles outside the
village of Ballybeg, County Donegal, Ireland.*

*Set: Slightly more than half the area of the stage is taken
up by the kitchen on the right (left and right from the
point of view of the audience). The rest of the stage – i.e.
the remaining area stage left – is the garden adjoining the
house. The garden is neat but not cultivated.*
Upstage centre is a garden seat.
*The (unseen) boy has been making two kites in the
garden and pieces of wood, paper, cord, etc., are lying on
the ground close to the garden seat. One kite is almost
complete.*
*There are two doors leading out of the kitchen. The
front door leads to the garden and the front of the house.*

The second in the top right-hand corner leads to the bedrooms and to the area behind the house.

One kitchen window looks out front. A second window looks on to the garden.

There is a sycamore tree off right. One of its branches reaches over part of the house.

The room has the furnishings of the usual country kitchen of the thirties: a large iron range, large turf box beside it, table and chairs, dresser, oil lamp, buckets with water at the back door, etc., etc. But because this is the home of five women the austerity of the furnishings is relieved by some gracious touches – flowers, pretty curtains, an attractive dresser arrangement, etc.

Dress: Kate, the teacher, is the only wage-earner. Agnes and Rose make a little money knitting gloves at home. Chris and Maggie have no income. So the clothes of all the sisters reflect their lean circumstances. Rose wears wellingtons even though the day is warm. Maggie wears large boots with long, untied laces. Rose, Maggie and Agnes all wear the drab, wrap-around overalls/aprons of the time.

In the opening tableau Father Jack is wearing the uniform of a British army officer chaplain – a magnificent and immaculate uniform of dazzling white; gold epaulettes and gold buttons, tropical hat, clerical collar, military cane. He stands stiffly to attention. As the text says, he is 'resplendent', 'magnificent'. So resplendent that he looks almost comic opera.

In this tableau, too, Gerry is wearing a spotless white tricorn hat with splendid white plumage. (Soiled and shabby versions of Jack's uniform and Gerry's ceremonial hat are worn at the end of the play, i.e. in the final tableau.)

Rose is 'simple'. All her sisters are kind to her and protective of her. But Agnes has taken on the role of special protector.

Dancing at Lughnasa was first performed at the Abbey Theatre, Dublin, on 24 April 1990. The cast was as follows:

Kate Frances Tomelty
Maggie Anita Reeves
Rose Bríd Ní Neachtain
Agnes Bríd Brennan
Chris Catherine Byrne
Michael Gerard McSorley
Gerry Paul Herzberg
Jack Barry McGovern

Directed by Patrick Mason
Designed by Joe Vanek
Lighting by Trevor Dawson

This production transferred to the National Theatre in October 1990, with the following changes of cast:

Kate Rosaleen Linehan
Gerry Stephen Dillane
Jack Alec McCowen

Act One

*When the play opens Michael is standing downstage left
in a pool of light. The rest of the stage is in darkness.
Immediately Michael begins speaking, slowly bring up the
lights on the rest of the stage.*

*Around the stage and at a distance from Michael the
other characters stand motionless in formal tableau.
Maggie is at the kitchen window (right). Chris is at the
front door. Kate at extreme stage right. Rose and Gerry
sit on the garden seat. Jack stands beside Rose. Agnes is
upstage left. They hold these positions while Michael talks
to the audience.*

Michael When I cast my mind back to that summer of
1936 different kinds of memories offer themselves to me.
We got our first wireless set that summer – well, a sort of
a set; and it obsessed us. And because it arrived as August
was about to begin, my Aunt Maggie – she was the joker
of the family – she suggested we give it a name. She
wanted to call it Lugh* after the old Celtic God of the
Harvest. Because in the old days August the First was *Lá
Lughnasa*, the feast day of the pagan god, Lugh; and the
days and weeks of harvesting that followed were called
the Festival of Lughnasa. But Aunt Kate – she was a
national schoolteacher and a very proper woman – she
said it would be sinful to christen an inanimate object
with any kind of name, not to talk of a pagan god. So we
just called it Marconi because that was the name
emblazoned on the set.

*Lugh – pronounced 'Loo'. *Lughnasa* – pronounced 'Loo-na-sa'.

7

And about three weeks before we got that wireless, my mother's brother, my Uncle Jack, came home from Africa for the first time ever. For twenty-five years he had worked in a leper colony there, in a remote village called Ryanga in Uganda. The only time he ever left that village was for about six months during World War One when he was chaplain to the British army in East Africa. Then back to that grim hospice where he worked without a break for a further eighteen years. And now in his early fifties and in bad health he had come home to Ballybeg – as it turned out – to die.

And when I cast my mind back to that summer of 1936, these two memories – of our first wireless and of Father Jack's return – are always linked. So that when I recall my first shock at Jack's appearance, shrunken and jaundiced with malaria, at the same time I remember my first delight, indeed my awe, at the sheer magic of that radio. And when I remember the kitchen throbbing with the beat of Irish dance music beamed to us all the way from Athlone, and my mother and her sisters suddenly catching hands and dancing a spontaneous step-dance and laughing – screaming! – like excited schoolgirls, at the same time I see that forlorn figure of Father Jack shuffling from room to room as if he were searching for something but couldn't remember what. And even though I was only a child of seven at the time I know I had a sense of unease, some awareness of a widening breach between what seemed to be and what was, of things changing too quickly before my eyes, of becoming what they ought not to be. That may have been because Uncle Jack hadn't turned out at all like the resplendent figure in my head. Or maybe because I had witnessed Marconi's voodoo derange those kind, sensible women and transform them into shrieking strangers. Or maybe it was because during those Lughnasa weeks of 1936 we were visited on two occasions by my father, Gerry Evans, and for the first time in my life I had a chance to observe him.

*The lighting changes. The kitchen and garden are now
lit as for a warm summer afternoon.*

*Michael, Kate, Gerry and Father Jack go off. The
others busy themselves with their tasks. Maggie makes a
mash for hens. Agnes knits gloves. Rose carries a basket
of turf into the kitchen and empties it into the large box
beside the range. Chris irons at the kitchen table. They
all work in silence. Then Chris stops ironing, goes to the
tiny mirror on the wall and scrutinizes her face.*

Chris When are we going to get a decent mirror to see
ourselves in?

Maggie You can see enough to do you.

Chris I'm going to throw this aul cracked thing out.

Maggie Indeed you're not, Chrissie. I'm the one that
broke it and the only way to avoid seven years' bad luck
is to keep on using it.

Chris You can see nothing in it.

Agnes Except more and more wrinkles.

Chris D'you know what I think I might do? I think I just
might start wearing lipstick.

Agnes Do you hear this, Maggie?

Maggie Steady on, girl. Today it's lipstick; tomorrow it's
the gin bottle.

Chris I think I just might.

Agnes As long as Kate's not around. 'Do you want to
make a pagan of yourself?'

Chris puts her face up close to the mirror and feels it.

Chris Far too pale. And the aul mousey hair. Needs a bit
of colour.

9

Agnes What for?

Chris What indeed. (*She shrugs and goes back to her ironing. She holds up a surplice.*) Make a nice dress that, wouldn't it? . . . God forgive me . . .

Work continues. Nobody speaks. Then suddenly and unexpectedly Rose bursts into raucous song:

Rose 'Will you come to Abyssinia, will you come?
Bring your own cup and saucer and a bun . . .'

As she sings the next two lines she dances – a gauche, graceless shuffle that defies the rhythm of the song.

'Mussolini will be there with his airplanes in the air,
Will you come to Abyssinia, will you come?'

Not bad, Maggie – eh?

Maggie is trying to light a very short cigarette butt.

Maggie You should be on the stage, Rose.

Rose continues to shuffle and now holds up her apron skirt.

Rose And not a bad bit of leg, Maggie – eh?

Maggie Rose Mundy! Where's your modesty! (*Maggie now hitches her own skirt even higher than Rose's and does a similar shuffle.*) Is that not more like it?

Rose Good, Maggie – good – good! Look, Agnes, look!

Agnes A right pair of pagans, the two of you.

Rose Turn on Marconi, Chrissie.

Chris I've told you a dozen times: the battery's dead.

Rose It is not. It went for me a while ago. (*She goes to the set and switches it on. There is a sudden, loud three-second blast of 'The British Grenadiers'.*) You see! Takes aul Rosie! (*She is about to launch into a dance – and the music suddenly dies.*)

Chris Told you.

Rose That aul set's useless.

Agnes Kate'll have a new battery back with her.

Chris If it's the battery that's wrong.

Rose Is Abyssinia in Africa, Aggie?

Agnes Yes.

Rose Is there a war there?

Agnes Yes. I've told you that.

Rose But that's not where Father Jack was, is it?

Agnes (*patiently*) Jack was in Uganda, Rosie. That's a different part of Africa. You know that.

Rose (*unhappily*) Yes, I do . . . I do . . . I know that . . .

Maggie catches her hand and sings softly into her ear to the same melody as the 'Abyssinia' song:

Maggie
'Will you vote for De Valera, will you vote?
If you don't, we'll be like Gandhi with his goat.'

Rose and Maggie now sing the next two lines together:

'Uncle Bill from Baltinglass has a wireless up his –

They dance as they sing the final line of the song:

Will you vote for De Valera, will you vote?'

Maggie I'll tell you something, Rosie: the pair of us should be on the stage.

Rose The pair of us should be on the stage, Aggie!

They return to their tasks. Agnes goes to the cupboard for wool. On her way back to her seat she looks out the window that looks on to the garden.

Agnes What's that son of yours at out there?

Chris God knows. As long as he's quiet.

Agnes He's making something. Looks like a kite. (*She taps on the window, calls 'Michael!' and blows a kiss to the imaginary child.*) Oh, that was the wrong thing to do! He's going to have your hair, Chris.

Chris Mine's like a whin-bush. Will you wash it for me tonight, Maggie?

Maggie Are we all for a big dance somewhere?

Chris After I've put Michael to bed. What about then?

Maggie I'm your man.

Agnes (*at window*) Pity there aren't some boys about to play with.

Maggie Now you're talking. Couldn't we all do with that?

Agnes (*leaving window*) Maggie!

Maggie Wouldn't it be just great if we had a – (*Breaks off.*) Shhh.

Chris What is it?

Maggie Thought I heard Father Jack at the back door. I hope Kate remembers his quinine.

Agnes She'll remember. Kate forgets nothing.

Pause.

Rose There's going to be pictures in the hall next Saturday, Aggie. I think maybe I'll go.

Agnes (*guarded*) Yes?

Rose I might be meeting somebody there.

Agnes Who's that?

Rose I'm not saying.

Chris Do we know him?

Rose I'm not saying.

Agnes You'll enjoy that, Rosie. You loved the last picture we saw.

Rose And he wants to bring me up to the back hills next Sunday – up to Lough Anna. His father has a boat there. And I'm thinking maybe I'll bring a bottle of milk with me. And I've enough money saved to buy a packet of chocolate biscuits.

Chris Danny Bradley is a scut, Rose.

Rose I never said it was Danny Bradley!

Chris He's a married man with three young children.

Rose And that's just where you're wrong, missy – so there! (*to Agnes*) She left him six months ago, Aggie, and went to England.

Maggie Rose, love, we just want –

Rose (*to Chris*) And who are you to talk, Christina Mundy! Don't you dare lecture me!

Maggie Everybody in the town knows that Danny Bradley is –

Rose (*to Maggie*) And you're jealous, too! That's what's wrong with the whole of you – you're jealous of me! (*to*

Agnes) He calls me his Rosebud. He waited for me outside the chapel gate last Christmas morning and he gave me this. (*She opens the front of her apron. A charm and a medal are pinned to her jumper.*) 'That's for my Rosebud,' he said.

Agnes Is it a fish, Rosie?

Rose Isn't it lovely? It's made of pure silver. And it brings you good luck.

Agnes It is lovely.

Rose I wear it all the time – beside my miraculous medal. (*Pause.*) I love him, Aggie.

Agnes I know.

Chris (*softly*) Bastard.

Rose closes the front of her apron. She is on the point of tears. Silence. Now Maggie lifts her hen-bucket and using it as a dancing partner she does a very fast and very exaggerated tango across the kitchen floor as she sings in her parodic style the words from 'The Isle of Capri':

Maggie
'Summer time was nearly over;
Blue Italian skies above.
I said, "Mister, I'm a rover.
Can't you spare a sweet word of love?"'

And without pausing for breath she begins calling her hens as she exits by the back door:

Tchook-tchook-tchook-tchook-tchook-tchook-tchook-tchookeeeeeee . . .

Michael enters and stands stage left. Rose takes the lid off the range and throws turf into the fire.

Chris For God's sake, I have an iron in there!

Rose How was I to know that?

Chris Don't you see me ironing? (*fishing with tongs*) Now you've lost it. Get out of my road, will you!

Agnes Rosie, love, would you give me a hand with this (*of wool*)? If we don't work a bit faster we'll never get two dozen pairs finished this week.

The convention must now be established that the (imaginary) Boy Michael is working at the kite materials lying on the ground. No dialogue with the Boy Michael must ever be addressed directly to adult Michael, the narrator. Here, for example, Maggie has her back to the narrator. Michael responds to Maggie in his ordinary narrator's voice. Maggie enters the garden from the back of the house.

Maggie What are these supposed to be?

Boy Kites.

Maggie Kites! God help your wit!

Boy Watch where you're walking, Aunt Maggie – you're standing on a tail.

Maggie Did it squeal? – haaaa! I'll make a deal with you, cub: I'll give you a penny if those things ever leave the ground. Right?

Boy You're on.

She now squats down beside him.

Maggie I've new riddles for you.

Boy Give up.

Maggie What goes round the house and round the house and sits in the corner? (*Pause.*) A broom! Why is a river like a watch?

Boy You're pathetic.

Maggie Because it never goes far without winding! Hairy out and hairy in, lift your foot and stab it in – what is it?

Pause.

Boy Give up.

Maggie Think!

Boy Give up.

Maggie Have you even one brain in your head?

Boy Give up.

Maggie A sock!

Boy A what?

Maggie A sock – a sock! You know – lift your foot and stab it – (*She demonstrates. No response.*) D'you know what your trouble is, cub? You-are-buck-stupid!

Boy Look out – there's a rat!

She screams and leaps to her feet in terror.

Maggie Where? – where? – where? Jesus, Mary and Joseph, where is it?

Boy Caught you again, Aunt Maggie.

Maggie You evil wee brat – God forgive you! I'll get you for that, Michael! Don't you worry – I won't forget that! (*She picks up her bucket and moves off towards the back of the house. Stops.*) And I had a barley sugar sweet for you.

Boy Are there bits of cigarette tobacco stuck to it?

Maggie Jesus Christ! Some day you're going to fill some woman's life full of happiness. (*moving off*) Tchook-

tchook-tchook-tchook . . . (*Again she stops and throws him a sweet.*) There. I hope it chokes you. (*Exits.*) Tchook-tchook-tchook-tchook-tchookeeeee . . .

Michael When I saw Uncle Jack for the first time the reason I was so shocked by his appearance was that I expected – well, I suppose, the hero from a schoolboy's book. Once I had seen a photograph of him radiant and splendid in his officer's uniform. It had fallen out of Aunt Kate's prayer book and she snatched it from me before I could study it in detail. It was a picture taken in 1917 when he was a chaplain to the British forces in East Africa and he looked – magnificent. But Aunt Kate had been involved locally in the War of Independence; so Father Jack's brief career in the British army was never referred to in that house. All the same the wonderful Father Jack of that photo was the image of him that lodged in my mind.

But if he was a hero to me, he was a hero and a saint to my mother and to my aunts. They pored over his occasional letters. They prayed every night for him and for his lepers and for the success of his mission. They scraped and saved for him – sixpence here, a shilling there – sacrifices they made willingly, joyously, so that they would have a little money to send to him at Christmas and for his birthday. And every so often when a story would appear in the *Donegal Enquirer* about 'our own leper priest', as they called him – because Ballybeg was proud of him, the whole of Donegal was proud of him – it was only natural that our family would enjoy a small share of that fame – it gave us that little bit of status in the eyes of the parish. And it must have helped my aunts to bear the shame Mother brought on the household by having me – as it was called then – out of wedlock.

Kate enters left, laden with shopping bags. When she sees the Boy working at his kites her face lights up with pleasure. She watches him for a few seconds. Then she goes to him.

Kate Well, that's what I call a busy man. Come here and give your Aunt Kate a big kiss. (*She catches his head between her hands and kisses the crown of his head.*) And what's all this? It's a kite, is it?

Boy It's two kites.

Kate (*inspecting them*) It certainly is two kites. And they're the most wonderful kites I've ever seen. And what are these designs? (*She studies the kite faces which the audience cannot see.*)

Boy They're faces. I painted them.

Kate (*pretending horror*) Oh, good Lord, they put the heart across me! You did those? Oh, God bless us, those are scarifying? What are they? Devils? Ghosts? I wouldn't like to see those lads up in the sky looking down at me! Hold on now . . . (*She searches in her bags and produces a small, wooden spinning-top and whip.*) Do you know what this is? Of course you do – a spinning-top. Good boy. And this – this is the whip. You know how to use it? Indeed you do. What do you say?

Boy Thanks.

Kate Thank you, Aunt Kate. And do you know what I have in here? A new library book! With coloured pictures! We'll begin reading it at bedtime. (*Again she kisses the top of his head. She gets to her feet.*) Call me the moment you're ready to fly them. I wouldn't miss that for all the world. (*She goes into the kitchen.*) D'you know what he's at out there? Did you see, Christina? Making two kites!

Chris Some kites he'll make.

Kate All by himself. No help from anybody.

Agnes You always said he was talented, Kate.

Kate No question about that. And very mature for his years.

Chris Very cheeky for his years.

Rose I think he's beautiful, Chris. I wish he was mine.

Chris Is that a spinning-top he has?

Kate It's nothing.

Michael exits left.

Chris Oh, Kate, you have him spoiled. Where did you get it?

Kate Morgan's Arcade.

Chris And I'm sure he didn't even thank you.

Rose I know why you went into Morgan's!

Kate He did indeed. He's very mannerly.

Rose You wanted to see Austin Morgan!

Kate Every field along the road – they're all out at the hay and the corn.

Rose Because you have a notion of that aul Austin Morgan!

Kate Going to be a good harvest by the look of it.

Rose I know you have! She's blushing! Look! Isn't she blushing?

Chris holds up a skirt she is ironing.

Chris You'd need to put a stitch in that hem, Rosie.

Rose (*to Kate*) But what you don't know is that he's going with a wee young thing from Carrickfad.

19

Kate Rose, what Austin Morgan does or doesn't do with –

Rose Why are you blushing then? She's blushing, isn't she? Why-why-why, Kate?

Kate (*sudden anger*) For God's sake, Rose, shut up, would you!

Rose Anyhow we all know you always had a –

Agnes Rosie, pass me those steel needles – would you, please?

Pause.

Chris (*to Kate*) Are you tired?

Kate flops into a seat.

Kate That road from the town gets longer every day. You can laugh if you want but I *am* going to get that old bike fixed up and I *am* going to learn to ride this winter.

Agnes Many about Ballybeg?

Kate Ballybeg's off its head. I'm telling you. Everywhere you go – everyone you meet – it's the one topic: Are you going to the harvest dance? Who are you going with? What are you wearing? This year's going to be the biggest ever and the best ever.

Agnes All the same I remember some great harvest dances.

Chris Don't we all.

Kate (*unpacking*) Another of those riveting Annie M. P. Smithson novels for you, Agnes.

Agnes Ah. Thanks.

Kate *The Marriage of Nurse Harding* – oh, dear! For

you, Christina. One teaspoonful every morning before breakfast.

Chris What's this?

Kate Cod-liver oil. You're far too pale.

Chris Thank you, Kate.

Kate Because you take no exercise. Anyhow I'm in the chemist's shop and this young girl – a wee slip of a thing, can't even remember her name – her mother's the knitting agent that buys your gloves, Agnes –

Agnes Vera McLaughlin.

Kate Her daughter whatever you call her.

Rose Sophia.

Kate Miss Sophia, who must be all of fifteen; she comes up to me and she says, 'I hope you're not going to miss the harvest dance, Miss Mundy. It's going to be just *supreme* this year.' And honest to God, if you'd seen the delight in her eyes, you'd think it was heaven she was talking about. I'm telling you – off its head – like a fever in the place. That's the quinine. The doctor says it won't cure the malaria but it might help to contain it. Is he in his room?

Chris He's wandering about out the back somewhere.

Kate I told the doctor you thought him very quiet, Agnes.

Agnes has stopped knitting and is looking abstractedly into the middle distance.

Agnes Yes?

Kate Well, didn't you? And the doctor says we must remember how strange everything here must be to him after so long. And on top of that Swahili has been his language for twenty-five years; so that it's not that his mind is confused – it's just that he has difficulty finding the English words for what he wants to say.

Chris No matter what the doctor says, Kate, his mind is a bit confused. Sometimes he doesn't know the difference between us. I've heard him calling you Rose and he keeps calling me some strange name like –

Kate Okawa.

Chris That's it! Aggie, you've heard him, haven't you?

Kate Okawa was his house boy. He was very attached to him. (*taking off her shoe*) I think I'm getting corns in this foot. I hope to God I don't end up crippled like poor mother, may she rest in peace.

Agnes Wouldn't it be a good one if we all went?

Chris Went where?

Agnes To the harvest dance.

Chris Aggie!

Agnes Just like we used to. All dressed up. I think I'd go.

Rose I'd go, too, Aggie! I'd go with you!

Kate For heaven's sake you're not serious, Agnes – are you?

Agnes I think I am.

Kate Hah! There's more than Ballybeg off its head.

Agnes I think we should all go.

Kate Have you any idea what it'll be like? – crawling with cheeky young brats that I taught years ago.

Agnes I'm game.

22

Chris We couldn't, Aggie – could we?

Kate And all the riff-raff of the countryside.

Agnes I'm game.

Chris Oh God, you know how I loved dancing, Aggie.

Agnes (*to Kate*) What do you say?

Kate (*to Chris*) You have a seven-year-old child – have you forgotten that?

Agnes (*to Chris*) You could wear that blue dress of mine – you have the figure for it and it brings out the colour of your eyes.

Chris Can I have it? God, Aggie, I could dance non-stop all night – all week – all month!

Kate And who'd look after Father Jack?

Agnes (*to Kate*) And you look great in that cotton dress you got for confirmation last year. You're beautiful in it, Kate.

Kate What sort of silly talk is –

Agnes (*to Kate*) And you can wear my brown shoes with the crossover straps.

Kate This is silly talk. We can't, Agnes. How can we?

Rose Will Maggie go with us?

Chris Will Maggie what! Try to stop her!

Kate Oh God, Agnes, what do you think?

Agnes We're going.

Kate Are we?

Rose We're off! We're away!

Kate Maybe we're mad – are we mad?

Chris It costs four and six to get in.

Agnes I've five pounds saved. I'll take you. I'll take us all.

Kate Hold on now –

Agnes How many years has it been since we were at the harvest dance? – at any dance? And I don't care how young they are, how drunk and dirty and sweaty they are. I want to dance, Kate. It's the Festival of Lughnasa. I'm only thirty-five. I want to dance.

Kate (*wretched*) I know, I know, Agnes, I know. All the same – oh my God – I don't know if it's –

Agnes It's settled. We're going – the Mundy girls – all five of us together.

Chris Like we used to.

Agnes Like we used to.

Rose I love you, Aggie! I love you more than chocolate biscuits!

Rose kisses Agnes impetuously, flings her arms above her head, begins singing 'Abyssinia' and does the first steps of a bizarre and abandoned dance. At this Kate panics.

Kate No, no, no! We're going nowhere!

Chris If we all want to go –

Kate Look at yourselves, will you! Just look at yourselves! Dancing at our time of day? That's for young people with no duties and no responsibilities and nothing in their heads but pleasure.

Agnes Kate, I think we –

Kate Do you want the whole countryside to be laughing at us? – women of our years? – mature women, *dancing*? What's come over you all? And this is Father Jack's home – we must never forget that – ever. No, no, we're going to no harvest dance.

Rose But you just said –

Kate And there'll be no more discussion about it. The matter's over. I don't want it mentioned again.

Silence. Maggie returns to the garden from the back of the house. She has the hen bucket on her arm and her hands are cupped as if she were holding something fragile between them. She goes to the kite materials.

Maggie The fox is back.

Boy Did you see him?

Maggie He has a hole chewed in the henhouse door.

Boy Did you get a look at him, Aunt Maggie?

Maggie Wasn't I talking to him. He was asking for you.

Boy Ha-ha. What's that you have in your hands?

Maggie Something I found.

Boy What?

Maggie Sitting very still at the foot of the holly tree.

Boy Show me.

Maggie Say please three times.

Boy Please-please-please.

Maggie In Swahili.

Boy Are you going to show it to me or are you not?

Maggie (*crouching down beside him*) Now, cub, put your

25

ear over here. Listen. Shhh. D'you hear it?

Boy I think so . . . yes.

Maggie What do you hear?

Boy Something.

Maggie Are you sure?

Boy Yes, I'm sure. Show me, Aunt Maggie.

Maggie All right. Ready? Get back a bit. Bit further. Right?

Boy Yes.

Suddenly she opens her hands and her eyes follow the rapid and imaginary flight of something up to the sky and out of sight. She continues staring after it. Pause.

What was it?

Maggie Did you see it?

Boy I think so . . . yes.

Maggie Wasn't it wonderful?

Boy Was it a bird?

Maggie The colours are so beautiful. (*She gets to her feet.*) Trouble is – just one quick glimpse – that's all you ever get. And if you miss that – (*She moves off towards the back door of the kitchen.*)

Boy What was it, Aunt Maggie?

Maggie Don't you know what it was? It was all in your mind. Now we're quits.

Kate (*unpacking*) Tea . . . soap . . . Indian meal . . . jelly . . .

Maggie I'm sick of that white rooster of yours, Rosie. Some pet that. Look at the lump he took out of my arm.

Rose You don't speak to him right.

Maggie I know the speaking he'll get from me – the weight of my boot. Would you put some turf on that fire, Chrissie; I'm going to make some soda bread. (*She washes her hands and begins baking.*)

Rose (*privately*) Watch out. She's in one of her cranky moods.

Kate Your ten Wild Woodbine, Maggie.

Maggie Great. The tongue's out a mile.

Rose (*privately*) You missed it all, Maggie.

Maggie What did I miss this time?

Rose We were all going to go to the harvest dance – like the old days. And then Kate –

Kate Your shoes, Rose. The shoemaker says, whatever kind of feet you have, only the insides of the soles wear down.

Rose Is that a bad thing?

Kate That is neither a bad thing nor a good thing, Rose. It's just – distinctive, as might be expected.

Rose grimaces behind Kate's back.

Cornflour . . . salt . . . tapioca – it's gone up a penny for some reason . . . sugar for the bilberry jam – if we ever get the bilberries . . .

Agnes and Rose exchange looks.

Maggie (*privately to Rose*) Look at the packet of Wild Woodbine she got me.

Rose What's wrong with it?

Maggie Only nine cigarettes in it. They're so wild one of them must have escaped on her.

They laugh secretly.

Chris Doesn't Jack sometimes call you Okawa, too, Maggie?

Maggie Yes. What does it mean?

Chris Okawa was his house boy, Kate says.

Maggie Dammit. I thought it was Swahili for gorgeous.

Agnes Maggie!

Maggie That's the very thing we could do with here – a house boy.

Kate And the battery. The man in the shop says we go through these things quicker than anyone in Ballybeg.

Chris Good for us. (*She takes the battery and leaves it beside Marconi.*)

Kate I met the parish priest. I don't know what has happened to that man. But ever since Father Jack came home he can hardly look me in the eye.

Maggie That's because you keep winking at him, Kate.

Chris He was always moody, that man.

Kate Maybe that's it . . . The paper . . . candles . . . matches . . . The word's not good on that young Sweeney boy from the back hills. He was anointed last night.

Maggie I didn't know he was dying!

Kate Not an inch of his body that isn't burned.

Agnes Does anybody know what happened?

Kate Some silly prank up in the hills. He knows he's dying, the poor boy. Just lies there, moaning.

Chris What sort of prank?

Kate How would I know?

Chris What are they saying in the town?

Kate I know no more than I've told you, Christina.

Pause.

Rose (*quietly, resolutely*) It was last Sunday week, the first night of the Festival of Lughnasa; and they were doing what they do every year up there in the back hills.

Kate Festival of Lughnasa! What sort of –

Rose First they light a bonfire beside a spring well. Then they dance round it. Then they drive their cattle through the flames to banish the devil out of them.

Kate Banish the –! You don't know the first thing about what –

Rose And this year there was an extra big crowd of boys and girls. And they were off their heads with drink. And young Sweeney's trousers caught fire and he went up like a torch. That's what happened.

Kate Who filled your head with that nonsense?

Rose They do it every Lughnasa. I'm telling you. That's what happened.

Kate (*very angry, almost shouting*) And they're savages! I know those people from the back hills! I've taught them! Savages – that's what they are! And what pagan practices they have are no concern of ours – none whatever! It's a sorry day to hear talk like that in a Christian home, a Catholic home! All I can say is that I'm shocked and disappointed to hear you repeating rubbish like that, Rose!

Rose (*quietly, resolutely*) That's what happened. I'm telling you.

Pause.

Maggie All the same it would be very handy in the winter time to have a wee house boy to feed the hens: 'Tchook-tchook-tchook-tchook-tchook-tchook-tchook-tchookeeee . . .'

> *Father Jack enters by the back door. He looks frail and older than his fifty-three years. Broad-brimmed black hat. Heavy grey top coat. Woollen trousers that stop well short of his ankles. Heavy black boots. Thick woollen socks. No clerical collar. He walks – shuffles quickly – with his hands behind his back. He seems uneasy, confused. Scarcely any trace of an Irish accent.*

Jack I beg your pardon . . . the wrong apartment . . . forgive me . . .

Kate Come in and join us, Jack.

Jack May I?

Maggie You're looking well, Jack.

Jack Yes? I expected to enter my bedroom through that . . . what I am missing – what I require . . . I had a handkerchief in my pocket and I think perhaps I –

Chris (*taking one from the ironing pile*) Here's a handkerchief.

Jack I thank you. I am grateful. It is so strange: I don't remember the – the architecture? – the planning? – what's the word? – the lay-out! – I don't recollect the lay-out of this home . . . scarcely. That is strange, isn't it? I thought the front door was there. (*to Kate*) You walked to the village to buy stores, Agnes?

Kate It's Kate. And dozens of people were asking for you.

Jack They remember me?

Kate Of course they remember you! And when you're feeling stronger they're going to have a great public welcome for you – flags, bands, speeches, everything!

Jack Why would they do this?

Kate Because they're delighted you're back.

Jack Yes?

Kate Because they're delighted you're home.

Jack I'm afraid I don't remember them. I couldn't name ten people in Ballybeg now.

Chris It will all come back to you. Don't worry.

Jack You think so?

Agnes Yes, it will.

Jack Perhaps . . . I feel the climate so cold . . . if you'll forgive me . . .

Agnes Why don't you lie down for a while?

Jack I may do that . . . thank you . . . you are most kind . . .

He shuffles off. Pause. A sense of unease, almost embarrassment.

Kate (*briskly*) It will be a slow process but he'll be fine. Apples . . . butter . . . margarine . . . flour . . . And wait till you hear! Who did I meet in the post office! Maggie, are you listening to me?

Maggie Yes?

Kate You'll never believe it – your old pal, Bernie O'Donnell! Home from London! First time back in twenty years!

Maggie Bernie . . .

Kate Absolutely gorgeous. The figure of a girl of eighteen. Dressed to kill from head to foot. And the hair! – as black and as curly as the day she left. I can't tell you – a film star!

Maggie Bernie O'Donnell . . .

Kate And beside her two of the most beautiful children you ever laid eyes on. Twins. They'll be fourteen next month. And to see the three of them together – like sisters, I'm telling you.

Maggie Twin girls.

Kate Identical.

Maggie Identical.

Kate Nora and Nina.

Rose Mother used to say twins are a double blessing.

Maggie Bernie O'Donnell . . . oh my goodness . . .

Kate And wait till you hear – they are pure blond! 'Where in the name of God did the blond hair come from?' I asked her. 'The father. Eric,' she says. 'He's from Stockholm.'

Agnes Stockholm!

Rose Where's Stockholm, Aggie?

Kate So there you are. Bernie O'Donnell married to a Swede. I couldn't believe my eyes. But the same bubbly, laughing, happy Bernie. Asking about everybody by name.

Maggie goes to the window and looks out so that the others cannot see her face. She holds her hands, covered with flour, out from her body.

Chris She remembered us all?

Kate Knew all about Michael; had his age to the very month. Was Agnes still the quickest knitter in Ballybeg? Were none of us thinking of getting married? – and weren't we wise!

Rose Did she remember me?

Kate 'Rose had the sweetest smile I ever saw.'

Rose There!

Kate But asking specially for you, Maggie: how you were doing – what you were doing – how were you looking – were you as light-hearted as ever? Every time she thinks of you, she says, she has the memory of the two of you hiding behind the turf stack, passing a cigarette between you and falling about laughing about some boy called – what was it? – Curley somebody?

Maggie Curley McDaid. An eejit of a fella. Bald as an egg at seventeen. Bernie O'Donnell . . . oh my goodness . . .

Pause.

Agnes Will she be around for a while?

Kate Leaving tomorrow.

Agnes We won't see her so. That's a pity.

Chris Nice names, aren't they? – Nina and Nora.

Kate I like Nora. Nice name. Strong name.

Agnes Not so sure about Nina. (*to Chris*) Do you like Nina for a name?

Chris Nina? No, not a lot.

Kate Well, if there's a Saint Nina, I'm afraid she's not in my prayer book.

Agnes Maybe she's a Swedish saint.

33

Kate Saints in Sweden! What'll it be next!

Rose Mother used to say twins are a double blessing.

Kate (*sharply*) You've offered us that cheap wisdom already, Rose.

Pause.

Chris You've got some flour on your nose, Maggie.

Maggie When I was sixteen I remember slipping out one Sunday night – it was this time of year, the beginning of August – and Bernie and I met at the gate of the workhouse and the pair of us off to a dance in Ardstraw. I was being pestered by a fellow called Tim Carlin at the time but it was really Brian McGuinness that I was – that I was keen on. Remember Brian with the white hands and the longest eyelashes you ever saw? But of course he was crazy about Bernie. Anyhow the two boys took us on the bar of their bikes and off the four of us headed to Ardstraw, fifteen miles each way. If Daddy had known, may he rest in peace . . .

And at the end of the night there was a competition for the Best Military Two-step. And it was down to three couples: the local pair from Ardstraw; wee Timmy and myself – he was up to there on me; and Brian and Bernie . . .

And they were just so beautiful together, so stylish; you couldn't take your eyes off them. People just stopped dancing and gazed at them . . .

And when the judges announced the winners – they were probably blind drunk – naturally the local couple came first; and Timmy and myself came second; and Brian and Bernie came third.

Poor Bernie was stunned. She couldn't believe it. Couldn't talk. Wouldn't speak to any of us for the rest of the night. Wouldn't even cycle home with us. She was

right, too: they should have won; they were just so
beautiful together . . .

And that's the last time I saw Brian McGuinness –
remember Brian with the . . .? And the next thing I heard
he had left for Australia . . .

She was right to be angry, Bernie. I know it wasn't fair
– it wasn't fair at all. I mean they must have been blind
drunk, those judges, whoever they were . . .

*Maggie stands motionless, staring out of the window,
seeing nothing. The others drift back to their tasks:
Rose and Agnes knit; Kate puts the groceries away;
Chris connects the battery. Pause.*

Kate Is it working now, Christina?

Chris What's that?

Kate Marconi.

Chris Marconi? Yes, yes . . . should be . . .

*She switches the set on and returns to her ironing. The
music, at first scarcely audible, is Irish dance music –
'The Mason's Apron', played by a ceili band. Very fast;
very heavy beat; a raucous sound. At first we are aware
of the beat only. Then, as the volume increases slowly,
we hear the melody. For about ten seconds – until the
sound has established itself – the women continue with
their tasks. Then Maggie turns round. Her head is
cocked to the beat, to the music. She is breathing
deeply, rapidly. Now her features become animated by a
look of defiance, of aggression; a crude mask of
happiness. For a few seconds she stands still, listening,
absorbing the rhythm, surveying her sisters with her
defiant grimace. Now she spreads her fingers (which are
covered with flour), pushes her hair back from her face,
pulls her hands down her cheeks and patterns her face
with an instant mask. At the same time she opens her*

mouth and emits a wild, raucous 'Yaaaah!' – and immediately begins to dance, arms, legs, hair, long bootlaces flying. And as she dances she lilts – sings – shouts and calls, 'Come on and join me! Come on! Come on!' For about ten seconds she dances alone – a white-faced, frantic dervish. Her sisters watch her.

Then Rose's face lights up. Suddenly she flings away her knitting, leaps to her feet, shouts, grabs Maggie's hand. They dance and sing – shout together; Rose's wellingtons pounding out their own erratic rhythm. Now after another five seconds Agnes looks around, leaps up, joins Maggie and Rose. Of all the sisters she moves most gracefully, most sensuously. Then after the same interval Chris, who has been folding Jack's surplice, tosses it quickly over her head and joins in the dance. The moment she tosses the vestment over her head Kate cries out in remonstration, 'Oh, Christina –!' But her protest is drowned. Agnes and Rose, Chris and Maggie, are now all doing a dance that is almost recognizable. They meet – they retreat. They form a circle and wheel round and round. But the movements seem caricatured; and the sound is too loud; and the beat is too fast; and the almost recognizable dance is made grotesque because – for example – instead of holding hands, they have their arms tightly around one another's neck, one another's waist. Finally Kate, who has been watching the scene with unease, with alarm, suddenly leaps to her feet, flings her head back, and emits a loud 'Yaaaah!'

Kate dances alone, totally concentrated, totally private; a movement that is simultaneously controlled and frantic; a weave of complex steps that takes her quickly round the kitchen, past her sisters, out to the garden, round the summer seat, back to the kitchen; a pattern of action that is out of character and at the same time ominous of some deep and true emotion.

*Throughout the dance Rose, Agnes, Maggie and Chris
shout – call – sing to each other. Kate makes no sound.*

*With this too loud music, this pounding beat, this
shouting – calling – singing, this parodic reel, there is a
sense of order being consciously subverted, of the
women consciously and crudely caricaturing
themselves, indeed of near-hysteria being induced. The
music stops abruptly in mid-phrase. But because of the
noise they are making the sisters do not notice and
continue dancing for a few seconds. Then Kate notices
– and stops. Then Agnes. Then Chris and Maggie. Now
only Rose is dancing her graceless dance by herself.
Then finally she, too, notices and stops. Silence. For
some time they stand where they have stopped. There is
no sound but their gasping for breath and short bursts
of static from the radio. They look at each other
obliquely; avoid looking at each other; half smile in
embarrassment; feel and look slightly ashamed and
slightly defiant. Chris moves first. She goes to the radio.*

Chris It's away again, the aul thing. Sometimes you're
good with it, Aggie.

Agnes Feel the top. Is it warm?

Chris Roasting.

Agnes Turn it off till it cools down.

Chris turns it off – and slaps it.

Chris Bloody useless set, that.

Kate No need for corner-boy language, Christina.

Agnes There must be some reason why it overheats.

Chris Because it's a goddamn, bloody useless set – that's
why.

Rose Goddamn bloody useless.

Kate Are wellingtons absolutely necessary on a day like this, Rose?

Rose I've only my wellingtons and my Sunday shoes, Kate. And it's not Sunday, is it?

Kate Oh, dear, we're suddenly very logical, aren't we?

Maggie (*lighting a cigarette*) I'll tell you something, girls: this Ginger Rogers has seen better days.

Kate It's those cigarettes are killing you.

Maggie (*exhaling*) Wonderful Wild Woodbine. Next best thing to a wonderful, wild man. Want a drag, Kitty?

Kate Go and wash your face, Maggie. And for goodness' sake tie those laces.

Maggie Yes, miss. (*at window*) Where's Michael, Chrissie?

Chris Working at those kites, isn't he?

Maggie He's not there. He's gone.

Chris He won't go far.

Maggie He was there ten minutes ago.

Chris He'll be all right.

Maggie But if he goes down to the old well –

Chris Just leave him alone for once, will you, please?

Maggie shrugs and goes out the back door. Pause.

Kate Who's making the tea this evening?

Agnes Who makes the tea every evening?

Chris (*at radio*) The connections seem to be all right.

Kate Please take that surplice off, Christina.

38

Chris Maybe a valve has gone – if I knew what a valve looked like.

Kate Have you no sense of propriety?

Chris If you ask me we should throw it out.

Agnes I'd be all for that. It's junk, that set.

Rose Goddamn bloody useless.

Kate (*to Agnes*) And you'll buy a new one, will you?

Agnes It was never any good.

Kate You'll buy it out of your glove money, will you? I thought what you and Rose earned knitting gloves was barely sufficient to clothe the pair of you.

Agnes This isn't your classroom, Kate.

Kate Because I certainly don't see any of it being offered for the upkeep of the house.

Agnes Please, Kate –

Kate But now it stretches to buying a new wireless. Wonderful!

Agnes I make every meal you sit down to every day of the week –

Kate Maybe I should start knitting gloves?

Agnes I wash every stitch of clothes you wear. I polish your shoes. I make your bed. We both do – Rose and I. Paint the house. Sweep the chimney. Cut the grass. Save the turf. What you have here, Kate, are two unpaid servants.

Rose And d'you know what your nickname at school is? The Gander! Everybody calls you the Gander!

Maggie runs on and goes straight to the window.

Maggie Come here till you see! Look who's coming up the lane!

Agnes Who's coming?

Maggie I only got a glimpse of him – but I'm almost certain it's –

Agnes Who? Who is it?

Maggie (*to Chris*) It's Gerry Evans, Chrissie.

Chris Christ Almighty.

Maggie He's at the bend in the lane.

Chris Oh, Jesus Christ Almighty.

The news throws the sisters into chaos. Only Chris stands absolutely still, too shocked to move. Agnes picks up her knitting and works with excessive concentration. Rose and Maggie change their footwear. Everybody dashes about in confusion – peering into the tiny mirror, bumping into one another, peeping out the window, combing hair. During all this hectic activity they talk over each other and weave around the immobile Chris. The lines overlap:

Kate How dare Mr Evans show his face here.

Maggie He wants to see his son, doesn't he?

Kate There's no welcome for that creature here.

Rose Who hid my Sunday shoes?

Maggie We'll have to give him his tea.

Kate I don't see why we should.

Maggie And there's nothing in the house.

Kate No business at all coming here and upsetting everybody.

Rose You're right, Kate. I hate him!

Maggie Has anybody got spare shoelaces?

Kate Look at the state of that floor.

Maggie Maybe he just wants to meet Father Jack.

Kate Father Jack may have something to say to Mr Evans. (*of the ironing*) Agnes, put those clothes away.

Agnes does not hear her, so apparently engrossed is she in her knitting.

Maggie My Woodbine! Where's my Woodbine?

Rose He won't stay the night, Kate, will he?

Kate He most certainly won't stay the night in this house!

Maggie Have you a piece of cord, Aggie? Anybody got a bit of twine?

Kate Behave quite normally. Be very calm and very dignified. Stop peeping out, Rose!

Rose (*at window*) There's nobody coming at all.

Silence. Then Agnes puts down her knitting, rushes to the window, pushes Rose aside and looks out.

Agnes Let me see.

Rose You imagined it, Maggie.

Chris Oh God.

Rose He's not there at all.

Agnes (*softly*) Yes, he is. Maggie's right. There he is.

Rose Show me.

Kate Has he a walking stick?

Rose Yes.

Kate And a straw hat?

Rose Yes.

Kate It's Mr Evans all right.

Agnes Yes. There he is.

Chris Oh sweet God – look at the state of me – what'll I say to him? – how close is he?

Rose I couldn't look that man in the face. I just hate him – hate him!

Kate That's a very unchristian thing to say, Rose. (*as Rose rushes off*) There's no luck in talk like that!

Chris Look at my hands, Kate – I'm shaking.

Kate catches her shoulders.

Kate You are not shaking. You are perfectly calm and you are looking beautiful and what you are going to do is this. You'll meet him outside. You'll tell him his son is healthy and happy. And then you'll send him packing – yourself and Michael are managing quite well without him – as you always have.

Chris does not move. She is about to cry. Kate now takes her in her arms.

Of course ask him in. And give the creature his tea. And stay the night if he wants to. (*firm again*) But in the outside loft. And alone. Now. I brought a newspaper home with me. Did anybody see where I left it?

Chris now rushes to the mirror and adroitly adjusts her hair and her clothes.

Agnes Where is he, Maggie?

Maggie In the garden.

Kate Agnes, did you see where I left the paper?

Maggie It's on the turf box, Kate.

Kate reads the paper – or pretends to. Agnes sits beside the radio and knits with total concentration. Maggie stands at the side of the garden window. Gerry Evans enters left, his step jaunty, swinging his cane, his straw hat well back on his head. He knows he is being watched. Although he is very ill at ease the smile never leaves his face. Chris goes out to the garden where they meet. Gerry has an English accent.

Gerry How are you, Chrissie? Great to see you.

Chris Hello, Gerry.

Gerry And how have you been for the past six months?

Chris Thirteen months.

Gerry Thirteen? Never!

Chris July last year; July the seventh.

Gerry Wow-wow-wow-wow. Where does the time go? Thirteen months? Phew! A dozen times – two dozen times I planned a visit and then something turned up and I couldn't get away.

Chris Well, you're here now.

Gerry Certainly am. And that was a bit of good fortune. Last night in a bar in Sligo. Bump into this chappie with a brand new Morris Cowley who lets slip that he's heading for Ballybeg in the morning. Ballybeg? Something familiar about that name! So. Here I am. In the flesh. As a matter of interest. Bit of good luck that, wasn't it?

Chris Yes.

Gerry He just let it slip. And here I am. Oh, yes, wonderful luck.

Chris Yes.

Pause.

Maggie Looks terrified, the poor fella.

Kate Terrified, my foot.

Maggie Come here till you see him. Aggie.

Agnes Not just now.

Maggie I'm sure he could do with a good meal.

Kate I'll give him three minutes. Then if she doesn't hunt him, I will.

Gerry You're looking wonderful, Chrissie. Really great. Terrific.

Chris My hair's like a whin-bush.

Gerry Looks lovely to me.

Chris Maggie's going to wash it tonight.

Gerry And how's Maggie?

Chris Fine.

Gerry And Rose and Kate?

Chris Grand.

Gerry And Agnes?

Chris Everybody's well, thanks.

Gerry Tell her I was asking for her – Agnes.

Chris I would ask you in but the place is –

Gerry No, no, some other time; thanks all the same. The

old schedule's a bit tight today. And the chappie who gave me the lift tells me Father Jack's home.

Chris Just a few weeks ago.

Gerry All the way from Africa.

Chris Yes.

Gerry Safe and sound.

Chris Yes.

Gerry Terrific.

Chris Yes.

Gerry Lucky man.

Chris Yes.

Gerry uses the cane as a golf club and swings.

Gerry Must take up some exercise. Putting on too much weight.

Kate He's not still there, is he?

Maggie Yes.

Kate Doing what, in God's name?

Maggie Talking.

Kate Would someone please tell me what they have to say to each other?

Maggie He's Michael's father, Kate.

Kate That's a responsibility never burdened Mr Evans.

Chris A commercial traveller called into Kate's school last Easter. He had met you somewhere in Dublin. He had some stupid story about you giving dancing lessons up there.

Gerry He was right.

Chris He was not, Gerry!

Gerry Cross the old ticker.

Chris Real lessons?

Gerry All last winter.

Chris What sort of dancing?

Gerry Strictly ballroom. You're the one should have been giving them – you were always far better than me. Don't you remember? (*He does a quick step and a pirouette.*) Oh, that was fun while it lasted. I enjoyed that.

Chris And people came to you to be taught?

Gerry Don't look so surprised! Everybody wants to dance. I had thousands of pupils – millions!

Chris Gerry –

Gerry Fifty-three. I'm a liar. Fifty-one. And when the good weather came, they all drifted away. Shame, really. Yes, I enjoyed that. But I've just started a completely new career, as a matter of interest. Never been busier. Gramophone salesman. Agent for the whole country, if you don't mind. 'Minerva Gramophones – The Wise Buy'.

Chris Sounds good, Gerry.

Gerry Fabulous. All I have to do is get the orders and pass them on to Dublin. A big enterprise, Chrissie; oh, one very big enterprise.

Chris And it's going all right for you?

Gerry Unbelievable. The wholesaler can't keep up with me. Do you see this country? This country is gramophone crazy. Give you an example. Day before yesterday; just west of Oughterard; spots this small house up on the side of a hill. Something seemed just right about it – you know? Off the bike; up the lane; knocks. Out comes this enormous chappie with red hair – what are you laughing at?

Chris Gerry –

Gerry I promise you. I show him the brochures; we talk about them for ten minutes; and just like that he takes four – one for himself and three for the married daughters.

Chris He took four gramophones?

Gerry Four brochures!

They both laugh.

But he'll buy. I promise you he'll buy. Tell you this, Chrissie: people thought gramophones would be a thing of the past when radios came in. But they were wrong. In my experience . . . Don't turn round; but he's watching us from behind that bush.

Chris Michael?

Gerry Pretend you don't notice. Just carry on. This all his stuff?

Chris He's making kites if you don't mind.

Gerry Unbelievable. Got a glimpse of him down at the foot of the lane. He is just enormous.

Chris He's at school, you know.

Gerry Never! Wow-wow-wow-wow. Since when?

Chris Since Christmas. Kate got him in early.

Gerry Fabulous. And he likes it?

Chris He doesn't say much.

Gerry He loves it. He adores it. They all love school

nowadays. And he'll be brilliant at school. Actually I intended bringing him something small –

Chris No, no; his aunts have him –

Gerry Just a token, really. As a matter of interest I was looking at a bicycle in Kilkenny last Monday. But they only had it in blue and I thought black might be more – you know – manly. They took my name and all. Call next time I'm down there. Are you busy yourself?

Chris Oh, the usual – housework – looking after his lordship.

Gerry Wonderful.

Chris Give Agnes and Rose a hand at their knitting. The odd bit of sewing. Pity you don't sell sewing-machines.

Gerry That's an idea! Do the two jobs together! Make an absolute fortune. You have the most unbelievable business head, Chrissie. Never met anything like it.

She laughs.

What are you laughing at?

Maggie You should see the way she's looking at him – you'd think he was the biggest toff in the world.

Kate Tinker, more likely! Loafer! Wastrel!

Maggie She knows all that, too.

Kate Too? That's all there is.

Maggie Come over till you see them, Agnes.

Agnes Not just now.

Gerry You'd never guess what I met on the road out from the town. Talk about good luck! A cow with a single horn coming straight out of the middle of its forehead.

Chris You never did!

Gerry As God is my judge. Walking along by itself. Nobody near it.

Chris Gerry –

Gerry And just as I was passing it, it stopped and looked me straight in the eye.

Chris That was no cow you met – that was a unicorn.

Gerry Go ahead and mock. A unicorn has the body of a horse. This was a cow – a perfectly ordinary brown cow except that it had a single horn just here. Would I tell you a lie?

Chris laughs.

Go ahead. Laugh. But that's what I saw. Wasn't that a spot of good luck?

Chris Was it?

Gerry A cow with a single horn? Oh, yes, that must be a good omen. How many cows like that have you ever met?

Chris Thousands. Millions.

Gerry Stop that! I'm sure it's the only one in Ireland; maybe the only one in the world. And I met it on the road to Ballybeg. And it winked at me.

Chris You never mentioned that.

Gerry What?

Chris That it winked at you.

Gerry Unbelievable. That's what made it all so mysterious. Oh, yes, that must be a fabulous omen. Maybe this week I'm going to sell a gramophone or two after all.

Chris But I thought you –?

Gerry Look! A single magpie! That's definitely a bad omen – one for sorrow. (*using his stick as a gun*) Bang! Missed. (*mock serious*) Where's my lucky cow? Come back, brown cow, come back!

They both laugh.

Kate They're not *still* talking, are they?

Maggie Laughing. She laughs all the time with him. D'you hear them, Aggie?

Agnes Yes.

Kate Laughing? Absolutely beyond my comprehension.

Agnes Like so many things, Kate.

Kate Two more minutes and Mr Evans is going to talk to me. Laughing? Hah!

Gerry Thinking of going away for a while, Chrissie.

Chris Where to?

Gerry But I'll come back to say goodbye first.

Chris Are you going home to Wales?

Gerry Wales isn't my home any more. My home is here – well, Ireland. To Spain – as a matter of interest. Just for a short while.

Chris To sell gramophones?

Gerry Good God, no! (*Laughs.*) You'll never believe this – to do a spot of fighting. With the International Brigade. A company leaves in a few weeks. Bit ridiculous, isn't it? But you know old Gerry when the blood's up – bang-bang-bang! – missing everybody.

Chris Are you serious?

Gerry Bit surprised myself – as a matter of interest.

Chris What do you know about Spain?

Gerry Not a lot. A little. Enough, maybe. Yes, I know enough. And I thought I should try my hand at something worthy for a change. Give Evans a Big Cause and he won't let you down. It's only everyday stuff he's not successful at. Anyhow I've still to enlist . . . He's still watching us. He thinks we don't see him. I wouldn't mind talking to him.

Chris He's a bit shy.

Gerry Naturally. And I'm a stranger to him practically . . . does he know my name?

Chris Of course he knows your name.

Gerry Good. Thanks. Well, maybe not so good. He's a very handsome child. With your eyes. Lucky boy.

'Dancing in the Dark' softly from the radio.

Maggie Good for you, Aggie. What did you do to it?

Agnes I didn't touch it.

Kate Turn that thing off, Aggie, would you?

Agnes does not.

Gerry You have a gramophone! I could have got it for you wholesale.

Chris It's a wireless set.

Gerry Oh, very posh.

Chris It doesn't go half the time. Aggie says it's a heap of junk.

Gerry I know nothing about radios but I'll take a look at it if you –

Chris Some other time. When you come back.

Pause.

Gerry And Agnes is well?

Chris Fine – fine.

Gerry Of all your sisters Agnes was the one that seemed to object least to me. Tell her I was asking for her.

Chris I'll tell her.

They listen to the music.

Gerry Good tune.

Suddenly he takes her in his arms and dances.

Chris Gerry –

Gerry Don't talk.

Chris What are you at?

Gerry Not a word.

Chris Oh God, Gerry –

Gerry Shhh.

Chris They're watching us.

Gerry Who is?

Chris Maggie and Aggie. From the kitchen window.

Gerry Hope so. And Kate.

Chris And Father Jack.

Gerry Better still! Terrific!

He suddenly swings her round and round and dances her lightly, elegantly across the garden. As he does he sings the song to her.

Maggie (*quietly*) They're dancing.

Kate What!

Maggie They're dancing together.

Kate God forgive you!

Maggie He has her in his arms.

Kate He has not! The animal! (*She flings the paper aside and joins Maggie at the window.*)

Maggie They're dancing round the garden, Aggie.

Kate Oh God, what sort of fool is she?

Maggie He's a beautiful dancer, isn't he?

Kate He's leading her astray again, Maggie.

Maggie Look at her face – she's easy led. Come here till you see, Aggie.

Agnes I'm busy! For God's sake can't you see I'm busy!

Maggie turns and looks at her in amazement.

Kate That's the only thing that Evans creature could ever do well – was dance. (*Pause.*) And look at her, the fool. For God's sake, would you look at that fool of a woman? (*Pause.*) Her whole face alters when she's happy, doesn't it? (*Pause.*) They dance so well together. They're such a beautiful couple. (*Pause.*) She's as beautiful as Bernie O'Donnell any day, isn't she?

Maggie moves slowly away from the window and sits motionless.

Gerry Do you know the words?

Chris I never know any words.

Gerry Neither do I. Doesn't matter. This is more

important. (*Pause.*) Marry me, Chrissie. (*Pause.*) Are you listening to me?

Chris I hear you.

Gerry Will you marry me when I come back in two weeks?

Chris I don't think so, Gerry.

Gerry I'm mad about you. You know I am. I've always been mad about you.

Chris When you're with me.

Gerry Leave this house and come away with –

Chris But you'd walk out on me again. You wouldn't intend to but that's what would happen because that's your nature and you can't help yourself.

Gerry Not this time, Chrissie. This time it will be –

Chris Don't talk any more; no more words. Just dance me down the lane and then you'll leave.

Gerry Believe me, Chrissie; this time the omens are terrific! The omens are unbelievable this time!

They dance off. After they have exited the music continues for a few seconds and then stops suddenly in mid-phrase. Maggie goes to the set, slaps it, turns it off. Kate moves away from the window.

Kate They're away. Dancing.

Maggie Whatever's wrong with it, that's all it seems to last – a few minutes at a time. Something to do with the way it heats up.

Kate We probably won't see Mr Evans for another year – until the humour suddenly takes him again.

Agnes He has a Christian name.

Kate And in the meantime it's Christina's heart that gets crushed again. That's what I mind. But what really infuriates me is that the creature has no sense of ordinary duty. Does he ever wonder how she clothes and feeds Michael? Does he ask her? Does he care?

Agnes rises and goes to the back door.

Agnes Going out to get my head cleared. Bit of a headache all day.

Kate Seems to me the beasts of the field have more concern for their young than that creature has.

Agnes Do you ever listen to yourself, Kate? You are such a damned righteous bitch! And his name is Gerry! – Gerry! – Gerry! (*Now on the point of tears, she runs off.*)

Kate And what was that all about?

Maggie Who's to say?

Kate Don't I know his name is Gerry? What am I calling him? – St Patrick?

Maggie She's worried about Chris, too.

Kate You see, that's what a creature like Mr Evans does: appears out of nowhere and suddenly poisons the atmosphere in the whole house – God forgive him, the bastard! There! That's what I mean! God forgive me!

Maggie begins putting on her long-laced boots again. As she does she sings listlessly, almost inaudibly:

Maggie
"Twas on the Isle of Capri that he found her
Beneath the shade of an old walnut tree.
Oh, I can still see the flowers blooming round her,
Where they met on the Isle of Capri.'

Kate If you knew your prayers as well as you know the

words of those aul pagan songs! . . . She's right: I am a righteous bitch, amn't I?

Maggie
'She was as sweet as a rose at the dawning
But somehow fate hadn't meant it to be,
And though he sailed with the tide in the morning,
Still his heart's in the Isle of Capri.'

She now stands up and looks at her feet.

Now. Who's for a fox-trot?

Kate You work hard at your job. You try to keep the home together. You perform your duties as best you can – because you believe in responsibilities and obligations and good order. And then suddenly, suddenly you realize that hair cracks are appearing everywhere; that control is slipping away; that the whole thing is so fragile it can't be held together much longer. It's all about to collapse, Maggie.

Maggie (*wearily*) Nothing's about to collapse, Kate.

Kate That young Sweeney boy from the back hills – the boy who was anointed – his trousers didn't catch fire, as Rose said. They were doing some devilish thing with a goat – some sort of sacrifice for the Lughnasa Festival; and Sweeney was so drunk he toppled over into the middle of the bonfire. Don't know why that came into my head . . .

Maggie Kate . . .

Maggie goes to her and sits beside her.

Kate And Mr Evans is off again for another twelve months and next week or the week after Christina'll collapse into one of her depressions. Remember last winter? – all that sobbing and lamenting in the middle of the night. I don't think I could go through that again. And the doctor says he doesn't think Father Jack's mind is

56

confused but that his superiors probably had no choice
but send him home. Whatever he means by that, Maggie.
And the parish priest did talk to me today. He said the
numbers in the school are falling and that there may not
be a job for me after the summer. But the numbers aren't
falling, Maggie. Why is he telling me lies? Why does he
want rid of me? And why has he never come out to visit
Father Jack? (*She tries to laugh.*) If he gives me the push,
all five of us will be at home together all day long – we
can spend the day dancing to Marconi.

Now she cries. Maggie puts her arm around her.
Michael enters left.

But what worries me most of all is Rose. If I died – if I
lost my job – if this house were broken up – what would
become of our Rosie?

Maggie Shhh.

Kate I must put my trust in God, Maggie, mustn't I? He'll
look after her, won't he? You believe that, Maggie, don't
you?

Maggie Kate . . . Kate . . . Kate, love . . .

Kate I believe that, too . . . I believe that . . . I do believe
that . . .

Maggie holds her and rocks her.
Chris enters quickly left, hugging herself. She sees the
boy at his kites, goes to him and gets down beside him.
She speaks eagerly, excitedly, confidentially.

Chris Well. Now you've had a good look at him. What
do you think of him? Do you remember him?

Boy (*bored*) I never saw him before.

Chris Shhh. Yes, you did; five or six times. You've
forgotten. And he saw you at the foot of the lane. He

thinks you've got very big. And he thinks you're handsome!

Boy Aunt Kate got me a spinning-top that won't spin.

Chris He's handsome. Isn't he handsome?

Boy Give up.

Chris I'll tell you a secret. The others aren't to know. He has got a great new job! And he's wonderful at it!

Boy What does he do?

Chris Shhh. And he has bought a bicycle for you – a black bike – a man's bike and he's going to bring it with him the next time he comes. (*She suddenly embraces him and hugs him.*)

Boy Is he coming back soon?

Chris (*eyes closed*) Maybe – maybe. Yes! Yes, he is!

Boy How soon?

Chris Next week – the week after – soon – soon – soon! Oh, yes, you have a handsome father. You are a lucky boy and I'm a very, very lucky woman. (*She gets to her feet, then bends down again and kisses him lightly.*) And another bit of good news for you, lucky boy: you have your mother's eyes! (*She laughs, pirouettes flirtatiously before him and dances into the kitchen.*) And what's the good news here?

Maggie The good news here is . . . that's the most exciting turf we've ever burned!

Kate Gerry's not gone, is he?

Chris Just this minute.

Agnes enters through the back door. She is carrying some roses.

He says to thank you very much for the offer of the bed.

Kate Next time he's back.

Chris That'll be in a week or two – depending on his commitments.

Kate Well, if the outside loft happens to be empty.

Chris And he sends his love to you all. His special love to you, Aggie; and a big kiss.

Agnes For me?

Chris Yes! For you!

Maggie (*quickly*) Those are beautiful, Aggie. Would Jack like some in his room? Put them on his windowsill with a wee card – 'ROSES' – so that the poor man's head won't be demented looking for the word. And now, girls, the daily dilemma: what's for tea?

Chris Let me make the tea, Maggie.

Maggie We'll both make the tea. Perhaps something thrilling with tomatoes? We've got two, I think. Or if you're prepared to wait, I'll get that soda-bread made.

Agnes I'm making the tea, Maggie.

Chris Let me, please. Just today.

Agnes (*almost aggressively*) I make the tea every evening, don't I? Why shouldn't I make it this evening as usual?

Maggie No reason at all. Aggie's the chef. (*Sings raucously:*)
  'Everybody's doing it, doing it, doing it.
  Picking their noses and chewing it, chewing it,
  chewing it . . .'

Kate Maggie, please!

Maggie If she knew her prayers half as well as she knows the words of those aul pagan songs . . . (*now at the radio*) Marconi, my friend, you're not still asleep, are you?

Father Jack enters. He shuffles quickly across the kitchen floor, hands behind his back, eyes on the ground, as if he were intent on some engagement elsewhere. Now he becomes aware of the others.

Jack If anybody is looking for me, I'll be down at the bank of the river for the rest of the . . . (*He tails off and looks around. Now he knows where he is. He smiles.*) I beg your pardon. My mind was . . . It's Kate.

Kate It's Kate.

Jack And Agnes. And Margaret.

Maggie How are you, Jack?

Jack And this is –?

Chris Chris – Christina.

Jack Forgive me, Chris. You were only a baby when I went away. I remember Mother lifting you up as the train was pulling out of the station and catching your hand and waving it at me. You were so young you had scarcely any hair but she had managed to attach a tiny pink – a tiny pink – what's the word? – a bow! – a bow! – just about here; and as she waved your hand, the bow fell off. It's like a – a picture? – a camera-picture? – a photograph! – it's like a photograph in my mind.

Chris The hair isn't much better even now, Jack.

Jack And I remember you crying, Margaret.

Maggie Was I?

Jack Yes; your face was all blotchy with tears.

Maggie You may be sure – beautiful as ever.

Jack (*to Agnes*) And you and Kate were on Mother's right and Rose was between you; you each had a hand. And Mother's face, I remember, showed nothing. I often wondered about that afterwards.

Chris She knew she would never see you again in her lifetime.

Jack I know that. But in the other life. Do you think perhaps Mother didn't believe in the ancestral spirits?

Kate Ancestral –! What are you blathering about, Jack? Mother was a saintly woman who knew she was going straight to heaven. And don't you forget to take your medicine again this evening. You're supposed to take it three times a day.

Jack One of our priests took so much quinine that he became an addict and almost died. A German priest; Father Sharpeggi. He was rushed to hospital in Kampala but they could do nothing for him. So Okawa and I brought him to our local medicine man and Karl Sharpeggi lived until he was eighty-eight! There was a strange white bird on my windowsill when I woke up this morning.

Agnes That's Rosie's pet rooster. Keep away from that thing.

Maggie Look what it did to my arm, Jack. One of these days I'm going to wring its neck.

Jack That's what we do in Ryanga when we want to please the spirits – or to appease them: we kill a rooster or a young goat. It's a very exciting exhibition – that's not the word, is it? – demonstration? – no – show? No, no; what's the word I'm looking for? Spectacle? That's not it. The word to describe a sacred and mysterious . . .? (*slowly,*

61

deliberately) You have a ritual killing. You offer up
sacrifice. You have dancing and incantations. What is the
name for that whole – for that –? Gone. Lost it. My
vocabulary has deserted me. Never mind. Doesn't matter
. . . I think perhaps I should put on more clothes . . .

Pause.

Maggie Did you speak Swahili all the time out there, Jack?

Jack All the time. Yes. To the people. Swahili. When
Europeans call, we speak English. Or if we have a – a
visitor? – a visitation! – from the district commissioner.
The present commissioner knows Swahili but he won't
speak it. He's a stubborn man. He and I fight a lot but I
like him. The Irish Outcast, he calls me. He is always
inviting me to spend a weekend with him in Kampala – to
keep me from 'going native', as he calls it. Perhaps when I
go back. If you co-operate with the English they give you
lots of money for churches and schools and hospitals.
And he gets so angry with me because I won't take his
money. Reported me to my superiors in Head House last
year; and they were very cross – oh, very cross. But I like
him. When I was saying goodbye to him – he thought this
was very funny! – he gave me a present of the last
governor's ceremonial hat to take home with – Ceremony!
That's the word! How could I have forgotten that? The
offering, the ritual, the dancing – a ceremony! Such a
simple word. What was I telling you?

Agnes The district commissioner gave you this present.

Jack Yes; a wonderful triangular hat with three enormous
white ostrich plumes rising up out of the crown. I have it
in one of my trunks. I'll show it to you later. Ceremony!
I'm so glad I got that. Do you know what I found very
strange? Coming back in the boat there were days when I
couldn't remember even the simplest words. Not that

anybody seemed to notice. And you can always point, Margaret, can't you?

Maggie Or make signs.

Jack Or make signs.

Maggie Or dance.

Kate What you must do is read a lot – books, papers, magazines, anything. I read every night with young Michael. It's great for his vocabulary.

Jack I'm sure you're right, Kate. I'll do that. (*to Chris*) I haven't seen young Michael today, Agnes.

Kate Christina, Jack.

Jack Sorry, I –

Chris He's around there somewhere. Making kites, if you don't mind.

Jack And I have still to meet your husband.

Chris I'm not married.

Jack Ah.

Kate Michael's father was here a while ago . . . Gerry Evans . . . Mr Evans is a Welshman . . . not that that's relevant to . . .

Jack You were never married?

Chris Never.

Maggie We're all in the same boat, Jack. We're hoping that you'll hunt about and get men for all of us.

Jack (*to Chris*) So Michael is a love-child?

Chris I – yes – I suppose so . . .

Jack He's a fine boy.

Chris He's not a bad boy.

Jack You're lucky to have him.

Agnes We're all lucky to have him.

Jack In Ryanga women are eager to have love-children. The more love-children you have, the more fortunate your household is thought to be. Have you other love-children?

Kate She certainly has not, Jack; and strange as it may seem to you, neither has Agnes nor Rose nor Maggie nor myself. No harm to Ryanga but you're home in Donegal now and much as we cherish love-children here they are not exactly the norm. And the doctor says if you don't take exercise your legs will seize up on you; so I'm going to walk you down to the main road and up again three times and then you'll get your tea and then you'll read the paper from front to back and then you'll take your medicine and then you'll go to bed. And we'll do the same thing tomorrow and the day after and the day after that until we have you back to what you were. You start off and I'll be with you in a second. Where's my cardigan?

Jack goes out to the garden. Kate gets her cardigan.

Michael Some of Aunt Kate's forebodings weren't all that inaccurate. Indeed some of them were fulfilled before the Festival of Lughnasa was over.

She was right about Uncle Jack. He had been sent home by his superiors, not because his mind was confused, but for reasons that became clearer as the summer drew to a close.

And she was right about losing her job in the local school. The parish priest didn't take her back when the new term began; although that had more to do with Father Jack than with falling numbers.

And she had good reason for being uneasy about Rose – and, had she known, about Agnes, too. But what she couldn't have foreseen was that the home would break up quite so quickly and that when she would wake up one morning in early September both Rose and Agnes would have left for ever.

At this point in Michael's speech Jack picks up two pieces of wood, portions of the kites, and strikes them together. The sound they make pleases him. He does it again – and again – and again. Now he begins to beat out a structured beat whose rhythm gives him pleasure. And as Michael continues his speech, Jack begins to shuffle-dance in time to his tattoo – his body slightly bent over, his eyes on the ground, his feet moving rhythmically. And as he dances – shuffles, he mutters – sings – makes occasional sounds that are incomprehensible and almost inaudible. Kate comes out to the garden and stands still, watching him. Rose enters. Now Rose and Maggie and Agnes are all watching him – some at the front door, some through the window. Only Chris has her eyes closed, her face raised, her mouth slightly open; remembering. Michael continues without stopping:

But she was wrong about my father. I suppose their natures were so out of tune that she would always be wrong about my father. Because he did come back in a couple of weeks as he said he would. And although my mother and he didn't go through a conventional form of marriage, once more they danced together, witnessed by the unseen sisters. And this time it was a dance without music; just there, in ritual circles round and round that square and then down the lane and back up again; slowly, formally, with easy deliberation. My mother with her head thrown back, her eyes closed, her mouth slightly open. My father holding her just that little distance away from him so that he could regard her upturned face. No singing, no melody, no words. Only the swish and whisper of their feet across the grass.

I watched the ceremony from behind that bush. But this time they were conscious only of themselves and of their dancing. And when he went off to fight with the International Brigade, my mother grieved as any bride would grieve. But this time there was no sobbing, no lamenting, no collapse into a depression.

Kate now goes to Jack and gently takes the sticks from him. She places them on the ground.

Kate We'll leave these back where we found them, Jack. They aren't ours. They belong to the child. (*She takes his arm and leads him off.*) Now we'll go for our walk.

The others watch with expressionless faces.

Act Two

Early September; three weeks later. Ink bottle and some paper on the kitchen table. Two finished kites – their artwork still unseen – lean against the garden seat.

Michael stands downstage left, listening to Maggie as she approaches, singing. Now she enters left carrying two zinc buckets of water. She is dressed as she was in Act One. She sings in her usual parodic style:

Maggie
  'Oh play to me, Gypsy;
  The moon's high above,
  Oh, play me your serenade,
  The song I love . . .'

She goes into the kitchen and from her zinc buckets she fills the kettle and the saucepan on the range. She looks over at the writing materials.

Are you getting your books ready for school again?

Boy School doesn't start for another ten days.

Maggie God, I always hated school. (*She hums the next line of the song. Then she remembers.*) You and I have a little financial matter to discuss. (*Pause.*) D'you hear me, cub?

Boy I'm not listening.

Maggie You owe me money.

Boy I do not.

Maggie Oh, yes, you do. Three weeks ago I bet you a

penny those aul kites would never get off the ground. And they never did.

Boy Because there was never enough wind; that's why.

Maggie Enough wind! Would you listen to him. A hurricane wouldn't shift those things. Anyhow a debt is a debt. One penny please at your convenience. Or the equivalent in kind: one Wild Woodbine. (*Sings:*)
'Beside your caravan
The campfire's bright . . .'

She dances her exaggerated dance across to the table and tousles the boy's hair.

Boy Leave me alone, Aunt Maggie.

Maggie
'I'll be your vagabond
Just for tonight . . .'

Boy Now look at what you made me do! The page is all blotted!

Maggie Your frank opinion, cub: am I vagabond material?

Boy Get out of my road, will you? I'm trying to write a letter.

Maggie Who to? 'That's for me to know and you to find out.' Whoever it is, he'd need to be smart to read that scrawl. (*She returns to her buckets.*)

Boy It's to Santa Claus.

Maggie In September? Nothing like getting in before the rush. What are you asking for?

Boy A bell.

Maggie A bell.

Boy For my bicycle.

Maggie For your bicycle.

Boy The bike my daddy has bought me – stupid!

Maggie Your daddy has bought you a bicycle?

Boy He told me today. He bought it in Kilkenny. So there!

Maggie's manner changes. She returns to the table.

Maggie (*softly*) Your daddy told you that?

Boy Ask him yourself. It's coming next week. It's a black bike – a man's bike.

Maggie Aren't you the lucky boy?

Boy It's going to be delivered here to the house. He promised me.

Maggie Well, if he promised you . . . (*very brisk*) Now! Who can we get to teach you to ride?

Boy I know how to ride!

Maggie You don't.

Boy I learned at school last Easter. So there! But you can't ride.

Maggie I can so.

Boy I know you can't.

Maggie Maybe not by myself. But put me on the bar, cub – magnificent!

Boy You never sat on the bar of a bike in your life, Aunt Maggie!

Maggie Oh yes, I did, Michael. Oh yes, indeed I did. (*She gathers up the papers.*) Now away and write to Santa some other time. On a day like this you should be out

69

running about the fields like a young calf. Hold on – a new riddle for you.

Boy Give up.

Maggie A man goes to an apple tree with two apples on it. He doesn't take apples off it. He doesn't leave apples on it. How does he do that?

Boy Give up.

Maggie Think, will you!

Boy Give up.

Maggie Well, since you don't know, I will tell you. He takes *one* apple off! Get it? He doesn't take *apples* off! He doesn't leave *apples* on!

Boy God!

Maggie You might as well be talking to a turf stack.

Jack enters. He looks much stronger and is very sprightly and alert. He is not wearing the top coat or the hat but instead a garish-coloured – probably a sister's – sweater. His dress now looks even more bizarre.

Jack Did I hear the church bell ringing?

Maggie A big posh wedding today.

Jack Not one of my sisters?

Maggie No such luck. A man called Austin Morgan and a girl from Carrickfad.

Jack Austin Morgan – should I know that name?

Maggie I don't think so. They own the Arcade in the town. And how are you today?

Jack Cold as usual, Maggie. And complaining about it as usual.

Michael exits.

Maggie Complain away – why wouldn't you? And it is getting colder. But you're looking stronger every day, Jack.

Jack I feel stronger, too. Now! Off for my last walk of the day.

Maggie Number three?

Jack Number four! Down past the clothes line; across the stream; round the old well; and up through the meadow. And when that's done Kate won't have to nag at me – nag? – nag? – sounds funny – something wrong with that – nag? – that's not a word, is it?

Maggie Nag – yes; to keep on at somebody.

Jack Yes? Nag. Good. So my English vocabulary is coming back, too. Great. Nag. Still sounds a bit strange.

Kate enters with an armful of clothes from the clothes line.

Kate Time for another walk, Jack.

Jack Just about to set out on number four, Kate. And thank you for keeping at me.

Kate No sign of Rose and Agnes yet?

Maggie They said they'd be back for tea. (*to Jack*) They're away picking bilberries.

Kate (*to Jack*) You used to pick bilberries. Do you remember?

Jack Down beside the old quarry?

Maggie The very place.

Jack Mother and myself; every Lughnasa; the annual ritual. Of course I remember. And then she'd make the most wonderful jam. And that's what you took to school with you every day all through the winter: a piece of soda bread and bilberry jam.

Maggie But no butter.

Jack Except on special occasions when you got scones and for some reason they were always buttered. I must walk down to that old quarry one of these days.
'O ruddier than the cherry,
O sweeter than the berry,
O nymph more bright,
Than moonshine night,
Like kidlings blithe and merry.'

(*Laughs*.)Where on earth did that come from? You see, Kate, it's all coming back to me.

Kate So you'll soon begin saying Mass again?

Jack Yes, indeed.

Maggie Here in the house?

Jack Why not? Perhaps I'll start next Monday. The neighbours would join us, wouldn't they?

Kate They surely would. A lot of them have been asking me already.

Jack How will we let them know?

Maggie I wouldn't worry about that. Word gets about very quickly.

Jack What Okawa does – you know Okawa, don't you?

Maggie Your house boy?

Jack My friend – my mentor – my counsellor – and yes, my house boy as well; anyhow Okawa summons our people by striking a huge iron gong. Did you hear that

72

wedding bell this morning, Kate?

Kate Yes.

Jack Well, Okawa's gong would carry four times as far as that. But if it's one of the bigger ceremonies, he'll spend a whole day going round all the neighbouring villages, blowing on this enormous flute he made himself.

Maggie And they all meet in your church?

Jack When I had a church. Now we gather on the common in the middle of the village. If it's an important ceremony, you would have up to three or four hundred people.

Kate All gathered together for Mass?

Jack Maybe. Or maybe to offer sacrifice to Obi, our Great Goddess of the Earth, so that the crops will flourish. Or maybe to get in touch with our departed fathers for their advice and wisdom. Or maybe to thank the spirits of our tribe if they have been good to us; or to appease them if they're angry. I complain to Okawa that our calendar of ceremonies gets fuller every year. Now at this time of year over there – at the Ugandan harvest time – we have two very wonderful ceremonies: the Festival of the New Yam and the Festival of the Sweet Cassava; and they're both dedicated to our Great Goddess, Obi –

Kate But these aren't Christian ceremonies, Jack, are they?

Jack Oh, no. The Ryangans have always been faithful to their own beliefs – like these two Festivals I'm telling you about; and they are very special, really magnificent ceremonies. I haven't described those two Festivals to you before, have I?

Kate Not to me.

Jack Well, they begin very formally, very solemnly with the ritual sacrifice of a fowl or a goat or a calf down at the bank of the river. Then the ceremonial cutting and anointing of the first yams and the first cassava; and we pass these round in huge wooden bowls. Then the incantation – chant, really – that expresses our gratitude and that also acts as a rhythm or percussion for the ritual dance. And then, when the thanksgiving is over, the dance continues. And the interesting thing is that it grows naturally into a secular celebration; so that almost imperceptibly the religious ceremony ends and the community celebration takes over. And that part of the ceremony is a real spectacle. We light fires round the periphery of the circle; and we paint our faces with coloured powders; and we sing local songs; and we drink palm wine. And then we dance – and dance – and dance – children, men, women, most of them lepers, many of them with misshapen limbs, with missing limbs – dancing, believe it or not, for days on end! It is the most wonderful sight you have ever seen! (*Laughs.*) That palm wine! They dole it out in horns! You lose all sense of time!

Oh, yes, the Ryangans are a remarkable people: there is no distinction between the religious and the secular in their culture. And of course their capacity for fun, for laughing, for practical jokes – they've such open hearts! In some respects they're not unlike us. You'd love them, Maggie. You should come back with me!

How did I get into all that? You must stop me telling these long stories. Exercise time! I'll be back in ten minutes; and only last week it took me half an hour to do number four. You've done a great job with me, Kate. So please do keep nagging at me. (*He moves off – then stops.*) It's not Gilbert and Sullivan, is it?

Kate Sorry?

Jack That quotation.

Kate What's that, Jack?

Jack 'O ruddier than the cherry / O sweeter than the berry' – no, it's not Gilbert and Sullivan. But it'll come back to me, I promise you. It's all coming back. (*Again he moves off.*)

Kate Jack.

Jack Yes?

Kate You are going to start saying Mass again?

Jack We've agreed on next Monday, haven't we? Haven't we, Maggie?

Maggie Yes.

Jack At first light. The moment Rose's white cock crows. A harvest ceremony. You'll have to find a big gong somewhere, Kate.

He leaves. Pause. Kate and Maggie stare at each other in concern, in alarm. They speak in hushed voices.

Kate I told you – you wouldn't believe me – I told you.

Maggie Shhh.

Kate What do you think?

Maggie He's not back a month yet.

Kate Yesterday I heard about their medicine man who brought a woman back from death –

Maggie He needs more time.

Kate And this morning it was 'the spirits of the tribe'! And when I mentioned Mass to him you saw how he dodged about.

Maggie He said he'd say Mass next Monday, Kate.

Kate No, he won't. You know he won't. He's changed, Maggie.

Maggie In another month, he'll be –

Kate Completely changed. He's not our Jack at all. And it's what he's changed into that frightens me.

Maggie Doesn't frighten me.

Kate If you saw your face . . . of course it does . . . Oh, dear God –

Maggie now drifts back to the range. Kate goes to the table and with excessive vigour wipes it with a damp cloth. Then she stops suddenly, slumps into a seat and covers her face with her hands. Maggie watches her, then goes to her. She stands behind her and holds her shoulders with her hands. Kate grasps Maggie's hand in hers.

Maggie All the same, Kitty, I don't think it's a sight I'd like to see.

Kate What sight?

Maggie A clatter of lepers trying to do the Military Two-step.

Kate God forgive you, Maggie Mundy! The poor creatures are as entitled to –

She breaks off because Chris's laughter is heard off. Kate jumps to her feet.

This must be kept in the family, Maggie! Not a word of this must go outside these walls – d'you hear? – not a syllable!

Chris and Gerry enter left. He enters backways, pulling Chris who holds the end of his walking stick.

Throughout the scene he keeps trying to embrace her. She keeps avoiding him.

Gerry No false modesty. You know you're a great dancer, Chrissie.

Chris No, I'm not.

Gerry You should be a professional dancer.

Chris You're talking rubbish.

Gerry Let's dance round the garden again.

Chris We've done that; and down the lane and up again – without music. And that's enough for one day. Tell me about signing up. Was it really in a church?

Gerry I'm telling you – it was unbelievable.

Chris It was a real church?

Gerry A Catholic church as a matter of interest.

Chris I don't believe a word of it.

Gerry Would I tell you a lie? And up at the end – in the sanctuary? – there were three men, two of them with trench-coats; and between them, behind this lectern and wearing a sort of military cap, this little chappie who spoke in an accent I could hardly understand. Naturally I thought he was Spanish. From Armagh, as it turned out.

Chris I'm sure he couldn't understand you either.

Gerry He described himself as the recruiting officer. 'Take it from me, comrade, nobody joins the Brigade without my unanimity.'

She laughs – and avoids his embrace.

Chris It's a wonder he accepted you.

Gerry 'Do you offer your allegiance and your loyalty and your full endeavours to the Popular Front?'

Chris What's the Popular Front?

Gerry The Spanish government that I'm going to keep in power. 'I take it you are a Syndicalist?' 'No.' 'An Anarchist?' 'No.' 'A Marxist?' 'No.' 'A Republican, a Socialist, a Communist?' 'No.' 'Do you speak Spanish?' 'No.' 'Can you make explosives?' 'No.' 'Can you ride a motor-bike?' 'Yes.' 'You're in. Sign here.'

Chris So you'll be a dispatch rider?

Gerry imitates riding a motor-bike.

And you leave on Saturday?

Gerry First tide.

Chris How long will you be away?

Gerry As long as it takes to sort the place out.

Chris Seriously, Gerry.

Gerry Maybe a couple of months. Everybody says it will be over by Christmas.

Chris They always say it will be over by Christmas. I still don't know why you're going.

Gerry Not so sure I know either. Who wants salesmen that can't sell? And there's bound to be *something* right about the cause, isn't there? And it's somewhere to go – isn't it? Maybe that's the important thing for a man: a *named* destination – democracy, Ballybeg, heaven. Women's illusions aren't so easily satisfied – they make better drifters. (*Laughs.*) Anyhow he held out a pen to sign on the dotted line and it was only when I was writing my name that I glanced over the lectern and saw the box.

Chris What box?

Gerry He was standing on a box. The chappie was a midget!

Chris Gerry!

Gerry No bigger than three feet.

Chris Gerry, I –

Gerry Promise you! And when we were having a drink afterwards he told me he was invaluable to the Brigade – because he was a master at disguising himself!

Chris Gerry Evans, you are –

Gerry Let's go down to the old well.

Chris We're going nowhere. Come inside and take a look at this wireless. It stops and starts whenever it feels like it.

Gerry I told you: I know nothing about radios.

Chris I've said you're a genius at them.

Gerry Chrissie, I don't even know how to –

Chris You can try, can't you? Come on. Michael misses it badly.

She runs into the kitchen. He follows.

You should see Jack striding through the meadow. He looks like a new man.

Kate (*to Gerry*) Were you talking to him?

Gerry He wants to do a swap with me: I'm to give him this hat and he's to give me some sort of a three-cornered hat with feathers that the district commissioner gave him. Sounds a fair exchange.

Maggie Chrissie says you're great with radios, Gerry.

Gerry I'll take a look at it – why not?

79

Maggie All I can tell you is that it's not the battery. I got a new one yesterday.

Gerry Let me check the aerial first. Very often that's where the trouble lies. Then I'll have a look at the ignition and sparking plugs. Leave it to Gerry.

He winks at Chris as he goes out the front door and off right.

Maggie He sounds very knowledgeable.

Chris It may be something he can't fix.

Kate I know you're not responsible for Gerry's decisions, Christina. But it would be on my conscience if I didn't tell you how strongly I disapprove of this International Brigade caper. It's a sorry day for Ireland when we send young men off to Spain to fight for godless Communism.

Chris For democracy, Kate.

Kate I'm not going to argue. I just want to clear my conscience.

Chris That's the important thing, of course. And now you've cleared it.

Gerry runs on and calls through the window:

Gerry Turn the radio on, Chrissie, would you?

Maggie It's on.

Gerry Right. (*He runs off again.*)

Chris Just as we were coming out of the town we met Vera McLaughlin, the knitting agent. (*softly*) Agnes and Rose aren't back yet?

Maggie They'll be here soon.

Chris She says she'll call in tomorrow and tell them

herself. The poor woman was very distressed.

Kate Tell them what?

Chris She's not buying any more hand-made gloves.

Maggie Why not?

Chris Too dear, she says.

Kate Too dear! She pays them a pittance!

Chris There's a new factory started up in Donegal Town. They make machine gloves more quickly there and far more cheaply. The people Vera used to supply buy their gloves direct from the factory now.

Maggie That's awful news, Chrissie.

Chris She says they're organizing buses to bring the workers to the factory and back every day. Most of the people who used to work at home have signed on. She tried to get a job there herself. They told her she was too old. She's forty-one. The poor woman could hardly speak.

Maggie Oh God . . . poor Aggie . . . poor Rose . . . what'll they do?

Agnes enters the garden. Kate sees her.

Kate Shhh. They're back. Let them have their tea in peace. Tell them later.

They busy themselves with their tasks. Agnes is carrying two small pails of blackberries which she leaves outside the door of the house. Just as she is about to enter the kitchen a voice off calls her:

Gerry (*off*) Who is that beautiful woman!

She looks around, puzzled.

Agnes Gerry?

81

Gerry Up here, Aggie!

Agnes Where?

Gerry On top of the sycamore.

Now she sees him. The audience does not see him.

Agnes Mother of God!

Gerry Come up and join me!

Agnes What are you doing up there?

Gerry You can see into the future from here, Aggie!

Agnes The tree isn't safe, Gerry. Please come down.

Gerry Come up and see what's going to happen to you!

Agnes That branch is dead, Gerry. I'm telling you.

The branch begins to sway.

Gerry Do you think I could get a job in a circus? Wow-wow-wow-wow!

Agnes Gerry –!

Gerry (*sings*) 'He flies through the air with the greatest of ease –' Wheeeeeeeeee!

She covers her eyes in terror.

Agnes Stop it, Gerry, stop it, stop it!

Gerry 'That daring young man on the flying trapeze . . .'

Agnes You're going to fall! I'm not looking! I'm not watching! (*She dashes into the house.*) That clown of a man is up on top of the sycamore. Go out and tell him to come down, Chrissie.

Maggie He's fixing the aerial.

Agnes He's going to break his neck – I'm telling you!

Maggie As long as he fixes the wireless first.

Kate How are the bilberries, Agnes?

Agnes Just that bit too ripe. We should have picked them a week ago.

Chris Is that a purple stain on your gansey?

Agnes I know. I'd only begun when I fell into a bush. And look at my hands – all scrabbed with briars. For all the sympathy I got from Rosie. Nearly died laughing at me. How is she now? (*Pause.*) Is she still in bed?

Chris Bed?

Agnes She wasn't feeling well. She left me and went home to lie down. (*Pause.*) She's here, isn't she?

   Maggie rushes off to the bedroom.

Kate I haven't seen her. (*to Chris*) Have you?

Chris No.

Kate When did she leave you?

Agnes Hours ago – I don't know – almost immediately after we got to the old quarry. She said she felt out of sorts.

Chris And she went off by herself?

Agnes Yes.

Kate To come home?

Agnes That's what she said.

   Maggie enters.

Maggie She's not in her bed.

Agnes Oh God! Where could she –

Kate Start at the beginning, Agnes. What exactly happened?

Agnes Nothing 'happened' – nothing at all. We left here together – when was it? – just after one o'clock –

Chris That means she's missing for over three hours.

Agnes We walked together to the quarry. She was chatting away as usual. I had my two buckets and she had –

Kate Go on – go on!

Agnes And just after we got there she said she wasn't feeling well. I told her not to bother about the bilberries – just to sit in the sun. And that's what she did.

Kate For how long?

Agnes I don't know – five – ten minutes. And then I fell into the bush. And that was when she laughed. And then she said – she said – I've forgotten what she said – something about a headache and her stomach being sick and she'd go home and sleep for a while. (*to Maggie*) You're sure she's not in her bed?

Maggie shakes her head.

Kate Then what?

Agnes begins to cry.

Agnes Where is she? What's happened to our Rosie?

Kate What direction did she go when she left you?

Agnes Direction?

Kate Stop snivelling, Agnes! Did she go towards home?

Agnes I think so . . . yes . . . I don't know . . . Maggie –

Maggie She may have gone into the town.

Chris She wouldn't have gone into town in her wellingtons.

Agnes She was wearing her good shoes.

Kate Are you sure?

Agnes Yes; and her blue cardigan and her good skirt. I said to her – I said, 'You're some lady to go picking bilberries with.' And she just laughed and said, 'I'm some toff, Aggie, amn't I some toff?'

Maggie Had she a bottle of milk with her?

Agnes I think so – yes – in one of her cans.

Maggie Had she any money with her?

Agnes She had half-a-crown. That's all she has.

Maggie (*softly*) Danny Bradley.

Kate What? – who?

Maggie Danny Bradley . . . Lough Anna . . . up in the back hills.

Chris Oh God, no.

Kate What? – what's this? – what about the back hills?

Chris She has some silly notion about that scamp, Bradley. She believes he's in love with her. He gave her a present last Christmas – she says.

Kate (*to Agnes*) What do you know about this Bradley business?

Agnes I know no more than Chris has –

Kate I've often seen you and Rose whispering together. What plot has been hatched between Rose and Mr Bradley?

Agnes No plot . . . please, Kate –

Kate You're lying to me, Agnes! You're withholding! I want the truth!

Agnes Honest to God, all I know is what Chris has just –

Kate I want to know everything you know! Now! I want to –

Maggie That'll do, Kate! Stop that at once! (*calmly*) She may be in the town. She may be on her way home now. She may have taken a weak turn on her way back from the quarry. We're going to find her. (*to Chris*) You search the fields on the upper side of the lane. (*to Agnes*) You take the lower side, down as far as the main road. (*to Kate*) You go to the old well and search all around there. I'm going into the town to tell the police.

Kate You're going to no police, Maggie. If she's mixed up with that Bradley creature, I'm not going to have it broadcast all over –

Maggie I'm going to the police and you'll do what I told you to do.

Chris There she is! Look – look! There she is!

She has seen Rose through the window and is about to rush out to greet her. Maggie catches her arm and restrains her. The four sisters watch Rose as she crosses the garden – Chris and Kate from the window, Maggie and Agnes from the door. Rose is unaware of their anxious scrutiny. She is dressed in the 'good' clothes described by Agnes and they have changed her appearance. Indeed, had we not seen the Rose of Act One, we might not now be immediately aware of her disability. At first look this might be any youngish country woman, carefully dressed, not unattractive, returning from a long walk on a summer day. She walks slowly, lethargically, towards the house. From her right hand hangs a red poppy that she plucked casually along the road. The face reveals nothing – but nothing is being deliberately concealed. She sees Agnes's cans of fruit. She stops beside them and looks at them. Then she puts her hand into one of the cans, takes a fistful of berries and thrusts the fistful into her mouth. Then she wipes her mouth with her sleeve and the back of her hand. As she chews she looks at her stained fingers. She wipes them on her skirt. All of these movements – stopping, eating, wiping – are done not dreamily, abstractedly, but calmly, naturally. Now she moves towards the house. As she approaches the door Agnes rushes to meet her. Instead of hugging her, as she wants to, she catches her arm.

Agnes Rosie, love, we were beginning to get worried about you.

Rose They're nice, Aggie. They're sweet. And you got two canfuls. Good for you.

Agnes leads her into the house.

Agnes Is your stomach settled?

Rose My stomach?

Agnes You weren't feeling well – remember? – when we were at the quarry?

Rose Oh, yes. Oh, I'm fine now, thanks.

Agnes You left me there and you said you were coming home to lie down. D'you remember that?

Rose Yes.

Chris But you didn't come home, Rosie.

Rose That's right.

Agnes And we were very worried about you.

Rose Well . . . here I am.

Chris Were you in the town?

Agnes That's why you're all dressed up, isn't it?

Chris You went into Ballybeg, didn't you?

Pause. Rose looks from one to the other.

Maggie (*briskly*) She's home safe and sound and that's all that matters. Now I don't know about you girls but I can tell you this chicken is weak with hunger. Let me tell you what's on the menu this evening. Our beverage is the usual hot, sweet tea. There is a choice between caraway-seed bread and soda bread, both fresh from the chef's oven. But now we come to the difficulty: there's only three eggs between the seven of us — I wish to God you'd persuade that white rooster of yours to lay eggs, Rosie.

Chris There are eight of us, Maggie.

Maggie How are there —? Of course — the soldier up the sycamore! Not a great larder but a nice challenge to someone like myself. Right. My suggestion is . . . Eggs Ballybeg; in other words scrambled and served on lightly toasted caraway-seed bread. Followed — for those so inclined — by one magnificent Wild Woodbine. Everybody happy?

Chris Excellent, Margaret!

Maggie Settled.

Rose has taken off her shoe and is examining it carefully.

Agnes We'll go and pick some more bilberries next Sunday, Rosie.

Rose All right.

Agnes Remember the cans you had? You had your own two cans – remember? Did you take them with you?

Rose Where to, Aggie?

Agnes Into the town . . . wherever you went . . .

Rose I hid them at the quarry behind a stone wall. They're safe there. I'll go back and pick them up later this evening. Does anybody know where my overall is?

Maggie It's lying across your bed. And you'd need to bring some turf in, Rosie.

Rose I'll change first, Maggie.

Maggie Be quick about it.

Chris How many pieces of toast do you want?

Maggie All that loaf. And go easy on the butter – that's all we have. Now. Parsley. And just a whiff of basil. I don't want you to be too optimistic, girls, but you should know I feel very creative this evening.

Rose moves towards the bedroom door. Just as she is about to exit:

Kate I want to know where you have been, Rose.

Rose stops. Pause.

You have been gone for the entire afternoon. I want you to tell me where you've been.

Agnes Later, Kate; after –

Kate Where have you been for the past three hours?

Rose (*inaudible*) Lough Anna.

Kate I didn't hear what you said, Rose.

Rose Lough Anna.

Chris Kate, just leave –

Kate You walked from the quarry to Lough Anna?

Rose Yes.

Kate Did you meet somebody there?

Rose Yes.

Kate Had you arranged to meet somebody there?

Rose I had arranged to meet Danny Bradley there, Kate. He brought me out in his father's blue boat. (*to Maggie*) I don't want anything to eat, Maggie. I brought a bottle of milk and a packet of chocolate biscuits with me and we had a picnic on the lake. (*to Agnes*) Then the two of us went up through the back hills. He showed me what was left of the Lughnasa fires. A few of them are still burning away up there. (*to Kate*) We passed young Sweeney's house – you know, the boy who got burned, the boy you said was dying. Well, he's on the mend, Danny says. His legs will be scarred but he'll be all right. (*to all*) It's a very peaceful place up there. There was nobody there but Danny and me. (*to Agnes*) He calls me his Rosebud, Aggie. I told you that before, didn't I? (*to all*) Then he walked me down as far as the workhouse gate and I came on home by myself. (*to Kate*) And that's all I'm going to tell you. (*to all*) That's all any of you are going to hear.

She exits, her shoes in one hand, the poppy in the other. Michael enters.

Kate What has happened to this house? Mother of God, will we ever be able to lift our heads ever again . . .?

Pause.

Michael The following night Vera McLaughlin arrived and explained to Agnes and Rose why she couldn't buy their hand-knitted gloves any more. Most of her home knitters were already working in the new factory and she advised Agnes and Rose to apply immediately. The Industrial Revolution had finally caught up with Ballybeg.

They didn't apply, even though they had no other means of making a living, and they never discussed their situation with their sisters. Perhaps Agnes made the decision for both of them because she knew Rose wouldn't have got work there anyway. Or perhaps, as Kate believed, because Agnes was too notionate to work in a factory. Or perhaps the two of them just wanted . . . away.

Anyhow, on my first day back at school, when we came into the kitchen for breakfast, there was a note propped up against the milk jug: 'We are gone for good. This is best for all. Do not try to find us.' It was written in Agnes's resolute hand.

Of course they did try to find them. So did the police. So did our neighbours who had a huge network of relatives all over England and America. But they had vanished without trace. And by the time I tracked them down – twenty-five years later, in London – Agnes was dead and Rose was dying in a hospice for the destitute in Southwark.

The scraps of information I gathered about their lives during those missing years were too sparse to be coherent. They had moved about a lot. They had worked as cleaning women in public toilets, in factories, in the Underground. Then, when Rose could no longer get work, Agnes tried to support them both – but couldn't. From then on, I gathered, they gave up. They took to drink; slept in parks, in doorways, on the Thames Embankment. Then Agnes died of exposure. And two days after I found Rose in that grim hospice – she didn't recognize me, of course – she died in her sleep.

Father Jack's health improved quickly and he soon recovered his full vocabulary and all his old bounce and vigour. But he didn't say Mass that following Monday. In fact he never said Mass again. And the neighbours stopped enquiring about him. And his name never again appeared in the *Donegal Enquirer*. And of course there was never a civic reception with bands and flags and speeches.

But he never lost his determination to return to Uganda and he still talked passionately about his life with the lepers there. And each new anecdote contained more revelations. And each new revelation startled – shocked – stunned poor Aunt Kate. Until finally she hit on a phrase that appeased her: 'his own distinctive spiritual search'. 'Leaping around a fire and offering a little hen to Uka or Ito or whoever is not religion as I was taught it and indeed know it,' she would say with a defiant toss of her head. 'But then Jack must make his own distinctive search.' And when he died suddenly of a heart attack – within a year of his homecoming, on the very eve of the following Lá Lughnasa – my mother and Maggie mourned him sorely. But for months Kate was inconsolable.

My father sailed for Spain that Saturday. The last I saw of him was dancing down the lane in imitation of Fred Astaire, swinging his walking stick, Uncle Jack's ceremonial tricorn at a jaunty angle over his left eye. When he got to the main road he stopped and turned and with both hands blew a dozen theatrical kisses back to Mother and me.

He was wounded in Barcelona – he fell off his motorbike – so that for the rest of his life he walked with a limp. The limp wasn't disabling but it put an end to his dancing days; and that really distressed him. Even the role of maimed veteran, which he loved, could never compensate for that.

He still visited us occasionally, perhaps once a year. Each time he was on the brink of a new career. And each time he proposed to Mother and promised me a new bike.

Then the war came in 1939; his visits became more infrequent; and finally he stopped coming altogether.

Sometime in the mid-fifties I got a letter from a tiny village in the south of Wales; a curt note from a young man of my own age and also called Michael Evans. He had found my name and address among the belongings of his father, Gerry Evans. He introduced himself as my half-brother and he wanted me to know that Gerry Evans, the father we shared, had died peacefully in the family home the previous week. Throughout his final illness he was nursed by his wife and his three grown children who all lived and worked in the village.

My mother never knew of that letter. I decided to tell her – decided not to – vacillated for years as my father would have done; and eventually, rightly or wrongly, kept the information to myself.

Maggie, Chris, Kate and Agnes now resume their tasks.

Chris Well, at least that's good news.

Maggie What's that?

Chris That the young Sweeney boy from the back hills is going to live.

Maggie Good news indeed.

Chris goes to the door and calls:

Chris Michael! Where are you? We need some turf brought in!

She now goes outside and calls up to Gerry. Michael exits.

Are you still up there?

Gerry (*off*) Don't stand there. I might fall on top of you.

Chris Have you any idea what you're doing?

Gerry (*off*) Come on up here to me.

Chris I'm sure I will.

Gerry (*off*) We never made love on top of a sycamore tree.

She looks quickly around: did her sisters hear that?

Chris If you fall and break your neck it'll be too good for you. (*She goes inside.*) Nobody can vanish quicker than that Michael fellow when you need him.

Maggie (*to Agnes*) I had a brilliant idea when I woke up this morning, Aggie. I thought to myself: what is it that Ballybeg badly needs and that Ballybeg hasn't got?

Agnes A riddle. Give up.

Maggie A dressmaker! So why doesn't Agnes Mundy who has such clever hands, why doesn't she dressmake?

Agnes Clever hands!

Maggie looks around for her cigarettes.

Maggie She'd get a pile of work. They'd come to her from far and wide. She'd make a fortune.

Agnes Some fortune in Ballybeg.

Maggie And not only would the work be interesting but she wouldn't be ruining her eyes staring at grey wool eight hours a day. Did you notice how Rosie squints at things now? It's the job for you, Aggie; I'm telling you. Ah, holy God, girls, don't tell me I'm out of fags! How could that have happened?

Chris goes to the mantelpiece and produces a single cigarette.

Chrissie, you are one genius. Look, Kate. (*scowls*) Misery. (*Lights cigarette.*) Happiness! Want a drag?

Kate What's keeping those wonderful Eggs Ballybeg?

Maggie If I had to choose between one Wild Woodbine and a man of – say – fifty-two – widower – plump, what would I do, Kate? I'd take fatso, wouldn't I? God, I really am getting desperate.

Jack enters through the garden.

Maybe I should go to Ryanga with you, Jack.

Jack I know you won't but I know you'd love it.

Maggie Could you guarantee a man for each of us?

Jack I couldn't promise four men but I should be able to get one husband for all of you.

Maggie Would we settle for that?

Chris One between the four of us?

Jack That's our system and it works very well. One of you would be his principal wife and live with him in his largest hut –

Maggie That'd be you, Kate.

Kate Stop that, Maggie!

Jack And the other three of you he'd keep in his enclosure. It would be like living on the same small farm.

Maggie Snug enough, girls, isn't it? (*to Jack*) And what would be – what sort of duties would we have?

Jack Cooking, sewing, helping with the crops, washing – the usual housekeeping tasks.

Maggie Sure that's what we do anyway.

Jack And looking after his children.

Maggie That he'd have by Kate.

Kate Maggie!

Jack By all four of you! And what's so efficient about that system is that the husband and his wives and his children make up a small commune where everybody helps everybody else and cares for them. I'm completely in favour of it.

Kate It may be efficient and you may be in favour of it, Jack, but I don't think it's what Pope Pius XI considers to be the holy sacrament of matrimony. And it might be better for you if you paid just a bit more attention to our Holy Father and a bit less to the Great Goddess . . . Iggie.

Music of 'Anything Goes' very softly on the radio.

Chris Listen.

Maggie And they have hens there, too, Jack?

Jack We're overrun with hens.

Maggie Don't dismiss it, girls. It has its points. Would you be game, Kate?

Kate Would you give my head peace, Maggie.

Chris Gerry has it going!

Maggie Tell me this, Jack: what's the Swahili for 'tchook-tchook-tchook-tchook-tchook'?

Jack You'd love the climate, too, Kate.

Kate I'm not listening to a word you're saying.

Gerry runs on.

Gerry Well? Any good?

Chris Listen.

Gerry Aha. Leave it to the expert.

Jack I have something for you, Gerry.

Gerry What's that?

Jack The plumed hat – the ceremonial hat – remember? We agreed to swap. With you in a second. (*He goes to his bedroom.*)

Maggie Good work, Gerry.

Gerry Thought it might be the aerial. That's the end of your troubles. (*Listens. Sings a line of the song.*) Dance with me, Agnes.

Agnes Have a bit of sense, Gerry Evans.

Gerry Dance with me. Please. Come on.

Maggie Dance with him, Aggie.

Gerry (*sings*)
   'In olden times a glimpse of stocking
   Was looked on as something shocking –'

Give me your hand.

Maggie Go on, Aggie.

Agnes Who wants to dance at this time of –

Gerry pulls her to her feet and takes her in his arms.

Gerry (*sings*)
   '. . . anything goes.
   Good authors, too, who once knew better words
   Now only use four-letter words
   Writing prose,
   Anything goes . . .'

Bring up the sound. With style and with easy elegance they dance once around the kitchen and then out to the garden – Gerry singing the words directly to her face:

'If driving fast cars you like,
If low bars you like,

97

If old hymns you like,
If bare limbs you like,
If Mae West you like,
Or me undressed you like,
Why, nobody will oppose.
When ev'ry night, the set that's smart is in-
truding in nudist parties in
Studios,
Anything goes . . .'

They are now in the far corner of the garden.

You're a great dancer, Aggie.

Agnes No, I'm not.

Gerry You're a superb dancer.

Agnes No, I'm not.

Gerry You should be a professional dancer.

Agnes Too late for that.

Gerry You could teach dancing in Ballybeg.

Agnes That's all they need.

Gerry Maybe it is!

He bends down and kisses her on the forehead. All this is seen – but not heard – by Chris at the kitchen window. Immediately after this kiss Gerry bursts into song again, turns Agnes four or five times very rapidly and dances her back to the kitchen.

There you are. Safe and sound.

Maggie I wish to God I could dance like you, Aggie.

Agnes I haven't a breath.

Gerry Doesn't she dance elegantly?

Maggie Always did, our Aggie.

Gerry Unbelievable. Now, Chrissie – you and I.

Chris (*sharply*) Not now. I wonder where Michael's got to?

Gerry Come on, Chrissie. Once round the floor.

Chris Not now, I said. Are you thick?

Maggie I'll dance with you, Gerry! (*She kicks her wellingtons off.*) Do you want to see real class?

Gerry Certainly do, Maggie.

Maggie Stand back there, girls. Shirley Temple needs a lot of space.

Gerry Wow-wow-wow-wow!

Maggie Hold me close, Gerry. The old legs aren't too reliable.

She and Gerry sing and dance:

'In olden times a glimpse of stocking
Was looked on as something shocking
But now –'

Chris suddenly turns the radio off.

Chris Sick of that damned thing.

Gerry What happened?

Maggie What are you at there, Chrissie?

Chris We're only wasting the battery and we won't get a new one until the weekend.

Maggie It wasn't to be, Gerry. But there'll be another day.

Gerry That's a promise, Maggie. (*He goes to Chris at the radio.*) Not a bad little set, that.

Kate Peace, thanks be to God! D'you know what that thing has done? Killed all Christian conversation in this country.

Chris (*to Agnes, icily*) Vera McLaughlin's calling here tomorrow. She wants to talk to you and Rose.

Agnes What about?

Kate (*quickly*) I didn't tell you, did I? – her daughter's got engaged!

Maggie Which of them?

Kate 'The harvest dance is going to be just supreme this year, Miss Mundy' – that wee brat!

Maggie Sophia. Is she not still at school?

Kate Left last year. She's fifteen. And the lucky man is sixteen.

Maggie Holy God. We may pack it in, girls.

Kate It's indecent, I'm telling you. Fifteen and sixteen! Don't tell me that's not totally improper. It's the poor mother I feel sorry for.

Agnes What does she want to talk to us about?

Chris (*relenting*) Something about wool. Didn't sound important. She probably won't call at all. (*She turns the radio on again. No sound. To Maggie*) Go ahead and dance, you two.

Maggie Artistes like Margaret Mundy can't perform on demand, Chrissie. We need to be in touch with other forces first, don't we, Gerry?

Gerry Absolutely. Why is there no sound?

Kate Maggie, are we never going to eat?

Maggie Indeed we are – outside in the garden! Eggs Ballybeg *al fresco*. Lughnasa's almost over, girls. There aren't going to be many warm evenings left.

Kate Good idea, Maggie.

Agnes I'll get the cups and plates.

Gerry (*with Chris at radio*) Are you all right?

Chris It's not gone again, is it?

Gerry Have I done something wrong?

Chris I switched it on again – that's all I did.

Maggie Take out those chairs, Gerry.

Gerry What about the table?

Maggie We'll just spread a cloth on the ground.

Maggie exits with the cloth which she spreads in the middle of the garden. Gerry kisses Chris lightly on the back of the neck.

Gerry At least we know it's not the aerial.

Chris According to you.

Gerry And if it's not the aerial the next thing to check is the ignition.

Chris Ignition! Listen to that bluffer!

Gerry Bluffer? (*to Agnes as she passes*) Did you hear what she called me? That's unfair, Agnes, isn't it?

Agnes smiles and shrugs.

Let's take the back off and see what's what.

Rose enters the garden from the back of the house. At first nobody notices her. She is dressed as in Act 1. In her right hand she holds the dead rooster by the feet. Its

*feathers are ruffled and it is stained with blood. Rose is
calm, almost matter-of-fact. Agnes sees her first and goes
to her. Chris and Gerry join the others in the garden.*

Agnes Rosie, what is it, Rosie?

Rose My rooster's dead.

Agnes Oh, Rosie . . .

Rose (*holding the dead bird up*) Look at him. He's dead.

Agnes What happened to him?

Rose The fox must have got him.

Agnes Oh, poor Rosie . . .

Rose Maggie warned me the fox was about again. (*to
all*) That's the end of my pet rooster. The fox must have
got him. You were right, Maggie. (*She places it carefully
on the tablecloth in the middle of the garden.*)

Maggie Did he get at the hens?

Rose I don't think so.

Maggie Was the door left open?

Rose They're all right. They're safe.

Maggie That itself.

Agnes We'll get another white rooster for you, Rosie.

Rose Doesn't matter.

Maggie And I'll put manners on him early on.

Rose I don't want another.

Maggie (*quick hug*) Poor old Rosie. (*as she moves away*)
We can hardly expect him to lay for us now . . .

Chris Where's that Michael fellow got to? Michael! He

hears me rightly, you know. I'm sure he's jouking about out there somewhere, watching us. Michael!

Rose sits on the garden seat.

Maggie All right, girls, what's missing? Knives, forks, plates . . . (*She sees Jack coming through the kitchen.*) Jesus, Mary and Joseph!

Jack is wearing a very soiled, very crumpled white uniform – a version of the uniform we saw him in at the very beginning of the play. One of the epaulettes is hanging by a thread and the gold buttons are tarnished. The uniform is so large that it looks as if it were made for a much larger man: his hands are lost in the sleeves and the trousers trail on the ground. On his head he wears a tricorn, ceremonial hat; once white like the uniform but now grubby, the plumage broken and tatty. He carries himself in military style, his army cane under his arm.

Jack Gerry, my friend, where are you?

Gerry Out here, Jack.

Jack There you are. (*to all*) I put on my ceremonial clothes for the formal exchange. There was a time when it fitted me – believe it or not. Wonderful uniform, isn't it?

Gerry Unbelievable. I could do with that for Spain.

Jack It was my uniform when I was chaplain to the British army during the Great War.

Kate We know only too well what it is, Jack.

Jack Isn't it splendid? Well, it was splendid. Needs a bit of a clean up. Okawa's always dressing up in it. I really must give it to him to keep.

Kate It's not at all suitable for this climate, Jack.

Jack You're right, Kate. Just for the ceremony – then I'll change back. Now, if I were at home, what we do when we swap or barter is this. I place my possession on the ground –

He and Gerry enact this ritual.

Go ahead. (*of hat*) Put it on the grass – anywhere – just at your feet. Now take three steps away from it – yes? – a symbolic distancing of yourself from what you once possessed. Good. Now turn round once – like this – yes, a complete circle – and that's the formal rejection of what you once had – you no longer lay claim to it. Now I cross over to where you stand – right? And you come over to the position I have left. So. Excellent. The exchange is now formally and irrevocably complete. This is my straw hat. And that is your tricorn hat. Put it on. Splendid! And it suits you! Doesn't it suit him?

Chris His head's too big.

Gerry (*adjusting hat*) What about that? (*to Agnes*) Is that better, Agnes?

Agnes You're lovely.

Gerry does a Charlie Chaplin walk across the garden, his feet spread, his cane twirling. As he does he sings:

Gerry
'In olden times a glimpse of stocking
Was looked on as something shocking . . .'

Jack (*adjusting his hat*) And what about this? Or like this? Or further back on my head?

Maggie Would you look at them! Strutting about like a pair of peacocks! Now – teatime!

Agnes I'll make the tea.

Maggie You can start again tomorrow. Let me finish off Lughnasa. Chrissie, put on Marconi.

Chris I think it's broken again.

Agnes Gerry fixed it. Didn't you?

Gerry Then Chrissie got at it again.

Chris Possessed that thing, if you ask me.

Kate I wish you wouldn't use words like that, Christina. There's still great heat in that sun.

Maggie Great harvest weather.

Kate I love September.

Maggie (*not moving*) Cooking time, girls.

Kate Wait a while, Maggie. Enjoy the bit of heat that's left.

Agnes moves beside Rose.

Agnes Next Sunday, then. Is that all right?

Rose What's next Sunday?

Agnes We'll get some more bilberries.

Rose Yes. Yes. Whatever you say, Aggie.

Gerry examines the kites.

Gerry Not bad for a kid of seven. Very neatly made.

Kate Look at the artwork.

Gerry Wow-wow-wow-wow! That is unbelievable!

Kate I keep telling his mother – she has a very talented son.

Chris So there, Mr Evans.

Gerry Have you all seen these?

Maggie I hate them.

Gerry I think they're just wonderful. Look, Jack.

For the first time we all see the images. On each kite is painted a crude, cruel, grinning face, primitively drawn, garishly painted.

I'll tell you something: this boy isn't going to end up selling gramophones.

Chris Michael! He always vanishes when there's work to be done.

Maggie I've a riddle for you. Why is a gramophone like a parrot?

Kate Maggie!

Maggie Because it . . . because it always . . . because a parrot . . . God, I've forgotten!

Maggie moves into the kitchen. Michael enters. The characters are now in positions similar to their positions at the beginning of the play – with some changes. Agnes and Gerry are on the garden seat. Jack stands stiffly to attention at Agnes's elbow. One kite, facing boldly out front, stands between Gerry and Agnes; the other between Agnes and Jack. Rose is upstage left. Maggie is at the kitchen window. Kate is downstage right. Chris is at the front door. During Michael's speech Kate cries quietly. As Michael begins to speak the stage is lit in a very soft, golden light so that the tableau we see is almost, but not quite, in a haze.

Michael As I said, Father Jack was dead within twelve months. And with him and Agnes and Rose all gone, the heart seemed to go out of the house.

Maggie took on the tasks Rose and Agnes had done

and pretended to believe that nothing had changed. My mother spent the rest of her life in the knitting factory – and hated every day of it. And after a few years doing nothing Kate got the job of tutoring the young family of Austin Morgan of the Arcade. But much of the spirit and fun had gone out of their lives; and when my time came to go away, in the selfish way of young men I was happy to escape.

> *Now fade in very softly, just audible, the music – 'It is Time to Say Goodnight' (not from the radio speaker).*
> *And as Michael continues, everybody sways very slightly from side to side – even the grinning kites. The movement is so minimal that we cannot be quite certain if it is happening or if we imagine it.*

And so, when I cast my mind back to that summer of 1936, different kinds of memories offer themselves to me.

But there is one memory of that Lughnasa time that visits me most often; and what fascinates me about that memory is that it owes nothing to fact. In that memory atmosphere is more real than incident and everything is simultaneously actual and illusory. In that memory, too, the air is nostalgic with the music of the thirties. It drifts in from somewhere far away – a mirage of sound – a dream music that is both heard and imagined; that seems to be both itself and its own echo; a sound so alluring and so mesmeric that the afternoon is bewitched, maybe haunted, by it. And what is so strange about that memory is that everybody seems to be floating on those sweet sounds, moving rhythmically, languorously, in complete isolation; responding more to the mood of the music than to its beat. When I remember it, I think of it as dancing. Dancing with eyes half closed because to open them would break the spell. Dancing as if language had surrendered to movement – as if this ritual, this wordless ceremony, was now the way to speak, to whisper private and sacred things, to be in touch with some otherness. Dancing as if the very heart of life and all its hopes might be found in those assuaging notes and those hushed rhythms and in those silent and hypnotic movements. Dancing as if language no longer existed because words were no longer necessary . . .

Slowly bring up the music. Slowly bring down the lights.

FATHERS AND SONS

for Tom and Julie

Characters

Arkady Nikolayevich Kirsanov, twenty-two, student
Yevgeny Vassilyich Bazarov, twenty-two, student
Nikolai Petrovich Kirsanov,
forty-four, Arkady's father; estate owner
Pavel Petrovich Kirsanov,
forty-five, Arkady's uncle; retired guardsman
Vassily Ivanyich Bazarov,
sixties, Bazarov's father; retired army doctor
Arina Vlassyevna Bazarov, fifties, Bazarov's mother
Fenichka Fedosya Nikolayevna,
twenty-three, Nikolai's mistress
Anna Sergeyevna Odintsov,
twenty-nine, estate owner; widow
Katya Sergeyevna, eighteen, Anna's sister
Princess Olga, seventies, Anna's aunt
Dunyasha, twenties, servant in Kirsanov home
Prokofyich, sixties, servant in Kirsanov home
Piotr, nineteen, servant in Kirsanov home
Timofeich, sixties, servant in Bazarov home
Fedka, sixteen, servant in Bazarov home

Music:
Act One: Scene One – Beethoven's *Romance* (for violin
and orchestra) in F-major, Op. 50; Scene Two – Piano
duets. In marching, military style.
Act Two: Scene One – Beethoven's *Romance* in G-major,
Op. 40; Scene Two – As in Act One, Scene One; Scene
Three – *Te Deum Laudamus*; Scene Four – 'Drink to me
only' (vocal and piano); 'Drink to me only' (played on
piano-accordion).

Fathers and Sons opened at the Lyttelton Theatre, South Bank, London, on 8 July 1987. The cast was as follows:

Arkady Nikolayevich Kirsanov Ralph Fiennes
Yevgeny Vassilyich Bazarov Robert Glenister
Nikolai Petrovich Kirsanov Alec McCowen
Pavel Petrovich Kirsanov Richard Pasco
Vassily Ivanyich Bazarov Robin Bailey
Arina Vlassyevna Bazarov Barbara Jefford
Fenichka Fedosya Nikolayevna Lesley Sharp
Anna Sergeyevna Odintsov Meg Davies
Katya Sergeyevna Robin McCaffrey
Princess Olga Joyce Grant
Dunyasha Hazel Ellerby
Prokofyich Antony Brown
Piotr Jay Villiers
Timofeich Peter Halliday
Fedka Jim Millea

Directed by Michael Rudman
Designed by Carl Toms
Music Matthew Scott

Act One

SCENE ONE

Before the scene begins bring up the sound of Beethoven's
Romance in F-major, Op. 50, played by Nikolai on the
cello. Early afternoon in May, 1859.
The garden-lawn in front of the Kirsanov home. We can
see into the living-room upstage. A veranda runs across the
front of the house with two steps leading down to the
garden. Some potted plants in front of the veranda. Down-
stage left there is a gazebo/summer-house. Various summer
seats and stools. (Left and right from the point of view of
the audience.) Characters enter from the left – i.e. the yard,
outhouses, servants' quarters off – or from the house.
Nikolai is playing the cello in the living-room.
Fenichka is sitting in the gazebo, knitting a garment for
her baby who is sleeping in a pram at her side. She is an
attractive young woman with innate dignity and
confidence; but because she is no longer a servant and
not yet mistress in the house she is not fully at ease in
her environment. Occasionally she glances into the
pram. She leaves aside her knitting, closes her eyes and
sits listening to the music.
Dunyasha enters left carrying a laundry-basket full of
clothes. She is a plump, open-natured, open-hearted,
practical-minded girl who loves to laugh.

Dunyasha Oh my God, this heat has me destroyed. How
do you stick it?

Fenichka You should have something on your head.

Dunyasha I met the new estate-manager over there at the
clothes-line. Do you know him?

Fenichka Only to see.

Dunyasha He is just so beautiful – isn't he? I could spend my days just gazing at him, with that glossy black moustache and those sleepy brown eyes. Did you notice that beautiful black 'tash?

Fenichka Dunyasha!

Dunyasha flops down beside her. Fenichka begins knitting again.

Dunyasha Honestly. All he'd have to do is raise his little finger and I'd kiss his feet. Anyhow he looked at me and he said, 'Are you going to faint, little one?' All the same that was nice, wasn't it? – 'little one'. And I said, 'What d'you mean – am I going to faint?' 'Oh,' he said, 'your face is all bloated and red.'

Fenichka (*laughing*) He did not. That's another of your stories.

Dunyasha Cross my heart. (*into pram*) Hello, Mitya. How are you today, my little darling? Are you well? (*She spreads out under the sun.*) Beautiful. This must be the hottest May ever. (*eyes closed*) Is that the big fiddle he's playing?

Fenichka You know very well it's called a cello.

Dunyasha Sort of nice, isn't it? Bit lonely – like himself.

Fenichka Is he lonely?

Dunyasha You should know. Not much good for dancing.

Fenichka I heard you were dancing last night.

Dunyasha Five this morning. Oh, that heat's lovely.

Fenichka Any good?

Dunyasha You mean did I click? (*She sits up.*) Tell me this, Fenichka: remember all those young fellows used to be at the dances when you and I went together – all that laughing and all that fun – remember?

Fenichka Yes.

Dunyasha Well, where in God's name have they gone to, those boys? Or haven't they young brothers? All you see now are half-drunk louts that say things like, 'My God, girl, but you're a powerful armful of meat.'

Fenichka laughs.

It's true. That's what a big clodhopper said to me last night. And if it's not the clodhoppers it's the usual old lechers with their eyes half-closed and their hands groping your bum.

She sees Pavel entering left with a book under his arm. She gets quickly to her feet. Pavel is the typical 'Europeanized' Russian of the nineteenth century – wears English clothes, speaks French. His manner is jaded but his emotions function fully and astutely.

Jesus, here comes the Tailor's Dummy! He must have spotted you.

Fenichka Don't go, Dunyasha. Stay with me.

Dunyasha You're well fit to handle that old goat. And Dunyasha's place is in the kitchen.

Fenichka Please.

Dunyasha You're too gentle. Tell him straight out to bugger off.

She rises, makes a curtsy to Pavel and exits quickly left, leaving her basket behind her.
The relationship between Pavel and Fenichka is

uneasy. He looks into the pram and then at Fenichka.

Pavel Am I intruding?

Fenichka No. Not at all.

Pavel Will you be sending into town for groceries today?

Fenichka Yes.

Pavel Would you order something for me?

Fenichka What do you want?

Pavel Tea. Green tea. If you would.

Fenichka Of course.

Pavel Half a pound would suffice.

Fenichka I'll see to that.

Pavel *Merci bien.* (*into pram*) Hello-hello-hello-hello. He has very strong fingers. Maybe he'll be a cellist like his father. How do you like your new bedroom, Fenichka?

Fenichka I love it. It gets the sun in the early morning.

Pavel I see your light on very often in the middle of the night.

She rises and gathers her things.

Fenichka That's his lordship – cutting a new tooth. Aren't you cutting a new tooth, you rascal, and keeping your mother awake at night?

Pavel *Tu es très belle.*

Fenichka Sorry?

Pavel Look – he won't let me go.

Fenichka Let your uncle go, Mitya.

Pavel Fenichka –

Fenichka I think I'll take him inside. This sun's a bit hot for him.

Pavel All I want to say is –

He gets no further because Prokofyich enters left. He is an elderly retainer, excessively dignified and formal in manner; but now he is so excited, indeed so confused, that he almost runs across the stage and proclaims too loudly to nobody in particular:

Prokofyich The carriage has arrived! He's back! Master Arkady is back!

Pavel That's early. They must have made good time.

Prokofyich The carriage is here! He has arrived! He has arrived!

Pavel A bit of life about the place.

Fenichka Yes.

Pavel Fenichka, forgive me if –

Prokofyich Master Arkady is back! The carriage is here! Arkady's home from Petersburg!

Prokofyich is now on the veranda and calling into the living-room. Nikolai emerges with the cello-bow in his hand. He walks with a slight limp. He is a kind, decent, generous-spirited man, vague and bumbling at times but always fully alert to what is happening around him.

The carriage is here! Arkady's home! He's back! He's back!

Pavel All right, Prokofyich, we hear you.

Nikolai Did you hear the news?

Pavel I think so, Nikolai.

Nikolai Arkady has arrived from Petersburg. Wonderful! Where's Piotr? Piotr! Somebody help him with the luggage. Go and meet him, Pavel. (*to Fenichka*) He'll probably want something to eat, won't he? Everything's in such confusion. This is no welcome. Piotr! I'm really going to have to reprimand that young scamp.

General confusion and excitement. Prokofyich rushes off left. Dunyasha rushes on and picks up her basket.

Dunyasha (*privately to Fenichka*) He has a friend with him! Get out your smelling-salts! O sweet Saviour!

Fenichka Take the pram inside, Dunyasha, will you?

Dunyasha Wait till you see *him*! A dark god! Jesus, could this be my lucky day?!

Pavel Who is he bringing with him, Nikolai?

Nikolai Dunyasha, tell Piotr I want him – immediately!

She dashes off with the pram and basket.

Yes, he's bringing a friend with him – a young man called – called – I'm sorry, I've forgotten, Pavel. I'm really going to sack that boy.

Arkady enters.

Ah! There he is! Arkady! Arkady!

Arkady Father! How are you!

Father and son embrace with great warmth. Already Arkady is beginning to resemble his father. Prokofyich, cases in his hands, stands in the background and beams.

Nikolai Welcome home! Welcome home, graduate!

Arkady Thank you.

Nikolai Let me look at you. You're different. Have you lost weight? You're altogether different. Have you eaten? You're pale – that's it – you're very pale –

Arkady All that study and all those exams. What I need is a long rest. Uncle Pavel!

Pavel Welcome back, Arkady.

Arkady It's great to see you.

They embrace warmly.

And . . . Fenichka. It *is* Fenichka, isn't it?

Fenichka It is.

Nikolai Of course it is.

Arkady Indeed. Good to see you, Fenichka.

Fenichka And you, Arkady.

They shake hands and she leaves.

Nikolai Prokofyich usually drives so slowly, we didn't expect you until much later. Had you a good journey?

Arkady It was all right. I've brought a friend with me, Father.

Nikolai You mentioned that in your last letter. Great.

Arkady His name is Bazarov.

Nikolai Wonderful. We'll have a full house again. And wait till you see your bedroom – we've had it all repapered. Pavel chose the colour scheme.

Pavel That was a major row.

Nikolai No, it wasn't – was it?

Pavel A minor row.

Arkady His name is Bazarov – Yevgeny Vassilyich Bazarov. I would like you to make him very welcome.

Nikolai Naturally we'll make him very welcome. Won't we, Pavel?

Arkady Our friendship is very important to me.

Pavel Did he graduate, too?

Arkady Next year. He's doing natural science and medicine. He's probably the most brilliant man I've ever met.

Nikolai Well, the brilliant Bazarov is every bit as welcome as you are . . . well, almost.

Arkady Would you go and meet him, Uncle Pavel?

Pavel (*to Arkady*) See? Still the message-boy. *Plus ça change* . . .

Pavel goes off and Prokofyich is about to follow him.

Nikolai And isn't Prokofyich looking well?

Arkady Prokofyich never changes. Thank you for picking us up.

Prokofyich My pleasure. We'll go out looking for birds' nests tomorrow morning.

Arkady First thing. We'll show Bazarov all the good spots.

Prokofyich Maybe you and I should go by ourselves first and then we –

Pavel (*off*) Prokofyich!

Prokofyich Coming, sir. (*to Arkady*) It's good to have you back, Arkady.

Arkady Thank you.

Prokofyich exits left.

Bird-nesting! He thinks I'm still a schoolboy.

Nikolai In a way so do I.

Arkady And I deliberately mentioned Bazarov because they didn't get on very well on the journey. Prokofyich prefers the old ways, the old formalities. (*He embraces his father again.*) It's great to see you, Father.

Nikolai Thank you.

Arkady And you're looking very fresh.

Nikolai Fresh? At my age?

Arkady And so is Uncle Pavel. What's he doing with himself these days?

Nikolai Oh, you know Pavel – killing time, as he says himself – walking – reading – (*whispering*) going to his English tailor and his French barber – thinking his own very secret thoughts . . . (*after a quick look round*) Arkady, there's one little matter before the others join us – I'm really a bit embarrassed mentioning it –

Arkady It's about Fenichka.

Nikolai Shhh. How did you know?

Arkady Intuition.

Nikolai Yes, it's about Fenichka. You know Fenichka, don't you? What am I talking about – of course you do! Well, as you know, Arkady, I've been very fond of her for a long time now. Her mother was the best housekeeper we ever had here and Fenichka has taken on those responsibilities with great assurance and skill, considering she's only twenty-three, just a year older than yourself; so I'm old enough to be her father, too, amn't I? Ha-ha. Anyhow, as I say, I've been very attached to her for a long time now; and indeed I have asked her – I have insisted – that she move out of that damp flat above the laundry and come into the main house. And I mention this now, Arkady, partly because I – I – because she's afraid you might . . . well, disapprove of her.

Arkady I might disapprove of Fenichka?

Nikolai I hope you don't mind too much, Arkady.

Arkady Mind? Why in God's name should I mind?

Nikolai Well, because . . . well, I just thought that . . . Anyhow, anyhow, the real reason I brought her into the house – and I want you to know that I do, I do care very much for the girl, Arkady – I thought it only proper and correct that she ought to be in the house after – (*Pause.*) – she'd had the baby.

Arkady Baby?

Nikolai Hers and mine.

Arkady You mean –?

Nikolai A boy.

Arkady You and –?

Nikolai Six months old.

Arkady I have a new brother.

Nikolai Half-brother.

Arkady Half-brother.

Nikolai Mitya.

Arkady Mitya.

Nikolai Mitya. Now you know it all. Actually he's the image of me.

Arkady suddenly laughs, throws his arms around his father.

Arkady Father, that is the best news ever!

Nikolai Is it?

Arkady Of course it is! You're a sly old rascal but I think you're great. Congratulations!

Nikolai You're not angry?

Arkady Angry? For God's sake, Father, I'm delighted for you!

Nikolai Thank you, son. Thank you. We'll not talk about it before Pavel. I'm not sure he quite approves of the whole thing. You know Pavel with his silly notions of class and public decorum.

Pavel and Bazarov enter left.

We can talk later.

Bazarov, a student, dark, lean, intense. He senses that he is an outsider politically and socially in this house – hence the arrogance and curt manner.

Arkady There he is! Come on, Bazarov! Come over here. Uncle Pavel you've obviously met – Pavel Petrovich Kirsanov. And this is my father, Nikolai Petrovich Kirsanov. Yevgeny Vassilyich Bazarov.

Bazarov bows formally.

Nikolai You are most welcome to this house, Yevgeny Vassilyich. I hope you can stay with us for most of the summer and I hope you don't find us very dull company.

Pavel Do you remember a Doctor Bazarov in Father's old division? That's his father, he tells me.

Nikolai Really? My goodness, it's a small . . . it's a . . .

Pavel *Extraordinaire, n'est ce pas?*

Nikolai Indeed. And you're going to be a doctor, too? Great. Splendid. Sit down. Sit down. You must be tired after your journey.

Bazarov I'd prefer to stand.

Nikolai Of course. Stand. Naturally. Stretch your legs. By all means – stand . . . Now to organize our lives. Let's have tea out here. Then you young men can have a rest and we'll eat about seven o'clock. All right? Piotr! He deliberately hides on me, you know. It's gone far beyond a joke. Dunyasha! Oh, you've no idea how difficult things are becoming. I'm not exaggerating, Pavel, am I? The old system – of course it had its failings. But now? – now I give all my land to the peasants to farm – *give* it to them. Will they even farm it for themselves? I wish you'd take an interest in it all, Arkady. It's becoming too much for me at my time of – sorry. (*to Dunyasha*) Ah, Dunyasha. Bring the samovar out here.

Pavel Cocoa for me, *s'il vous plaît.*

Nikolai And a bottle of that black sherry in the sideboard. The young men may wish to – to – to dissipate!

    Dunyasha is staring at Bazarov.

Arkady Do you wish to dissipate, Bazarov? We would love to dissipate, Father.

Nikolai Dunyasha!

Dunyasha Sorry, sir?

Nikolai Black sherry. In the sideboard. And glasses.

    She goes into the house.

What's the matter with that girl? And how is your father, Yevgeny Vassilyich?

Bazarov looks blankly at him. Pause.

Your father – is he well?

Bazarov I suppose so. I haven't seen him for three years.

Nikolai He has been away – has he? – travelling?

Bazarov Not that I know of.

Nikolai Ah.

Bazarov I haven't seen him for three years because I haven't been home since I went to the university.

Silence.

Arkady (*quickly*) Let me tell you about this character. He won the gold medal for oratory again this year – the third year in succession.

Nikolai Wonderful!

Arkady And he is also – (*to Bazarov*) – no, don't try to stop me – he is also president of the philosophical society and editor of the magazine. It's an astonishing radical publication – the college authorities banned both issues this year! We were brought before the disciplinary council – remember? 'Revolutionaries! Damned revolutionaries!'

Nikolai Oratory is an excellent discipline; excellent. I approve very strongly of – of – of – of oratory.

Pavel On what do you . . . orate?

Bazarov Politics. Philosophy.

Pavel They have something in common, have they?

Arkady Come on, Uncle Pavel. You know they have.

Pavel (*to Bazarov*) And your philosophy is?

Arkady Nihilism.

Pavel Sorry?

Arkady Nihilism, Uncle Pavel. Bazarov is a Nihilist. So am I.

Nikolai Interesting word that. I imagine it comes from the Latin – *nihil* – nothing. Does it mean somebody who respects nothing? No, it doesn't.

Arkady Someone who looks at everything critically.

Pavel If there's a difference.

Arkady There's a significant difference, Pavel. Don't be so precious.

Pavel Me? – precious? Good Lord.

Arkady Nihilism begins by questioning all received ideas and principles no matter how venerated those ideas and principles are. And that leads to the inevitable conclusion that the world must be made anew. (*to Bazarov*) That's a fairly accurate summary of our stance, isn't it?

Bazarov shrugs indifferently and spreads his hands.

Pavel So you believe only in science?

Arkady We don't *believe* in anything. You can't believe in science any more than you can believe in the weather or farming or swimming.

Nikolai I can tell you farming isn't what it used to be. In the past five years, the advances I've seen in farming techniques –

Arkady I wish you would stop trying to divert me with your juvenile asides, Father.

Nikolai I am sorry.

Pavel A simple question: if you reject all accepted principles and all accepted precepts, what basis of conduct have you?

Arkady I don't understand what the simple question means.

Pavel On what basis do you conduct your life?

Arkady If something is useful – keep it. If it is not useful – out it goes. And the most useful thing we can do is repudiate, renounce, reject.

Pavel Everything?

Arkady Everything without use.

Pavel All accepted conventions, all art, all science?

Arkady What use are they? Out.

Pavel Civilization has just been disposed of, Nikolai.

Nikolai But surely, Arkady, surely rejection means destruction; and surely we must construct, too?

Arkady Our first priority is to make a complete clearance. At this point in our evolution we have no right to indulge in the gratification of our own personal whims.

Nikolai I don't think I had whims in mind, Arkady.

Arkady At times it's difficult to know what you have in mind, Father.

Pavel And when do you begin to preach this gospel publicly?

Arkady We're activists. We aren't preachers, are we, Bazarov? We are not going to –

Pavel Aren't you preaching now? (*to Nikolai*) This is all nonsense; weary old materialistic nonsense I've heard a hundred times.

Arkady We know there is starvation and poverty; we know our politicians take bribes; we know the legal

system is corrupt. We know all that. And we are tired
listening to the 'liberals' and the 'progressives' –

Pavel So you have identified all society's evils –

Nikolai Let him finish, Pavel.

Pavel I would prefer Yevgeny Vassilyich would do his
own talking. (*to Arkady*) But you intend to do nothing
constructive yourselves?

Bazarov We intend to do nothing constructive ourselves.

Pavel Just abuse people who do.

Bazarov Just abuse people who do.

Pavel And that's called Nihilism.

Bazarov And that's called Nihilism. Is this riveting
discussion nearly over?

Pavel *Incroyable*! Let me see have I got it right –

Nikolai I'm sure you've got it right, Pavel. Let's leave it
for now.

Pavel First our saviours will demolish the country and
then they will remake the country. But suppose some
simple person were to suggest that our saviours were just
bletherskites – gold-medal bletherskites?

Bazarov My grandfather was a serf, Pavel Petrovich. I
believe I have some knowledge of the Russian people.

Pavel I'm sure you have a very –

Bazarov Indeed I believe I have at least as accurate and as
sympathetic an understanding of their needs and of their
mute aspirations as those absurd provincial aristocrats
who affect English clothes and English customs; who
believe they are civilized just because they speak cliché
French; who talk endlessly about Mother Russia but who

sit on their backsides and do sweet nothing for the *'bien public'* as they call it.

Pavel I suspect you're deliberately trying to –

Bazarov Words that come so easily to lips like yours – liberalism, progress, principles, civilization – they have no meaning in Russia. They are imported words. Russia doesn't need them. But what Russia does need – and action will provide it, Pavel Petrovich, action, not words – what Russia does need is bread in the mouth. But before you can put bread in the mouth, you have got to plough the land – deep.

Nikolai He's right, you know: ploughing is a very important part of the farming cycle. (*to Arkady*) Sorry. I didn't –

Pavel So the two of you are going to reform Russia.

Bazarov Remake Russia. Yes.

Pavel By force?

Bazarov (*shrugging*) If necessary.

Arkady All that's needed is a few people with total dedication. It was a penny candle that burned Moscow down, Uncle Pavel.

Nikolai That's quite true, you know.

Pavel For God's sake, Nikolai, you know nothing about it!

Nikolai I beg your pardon, Pavel – it *was* a penny candle burned Moscow down. That is an historical fact. Father was able to quote chapter and verse on it.

To Fenichka and Dunyasha, who have entered with a tray and samovar.

Ah! Fenichka! Good! Great! Splendid! And beautifully timed – just when we had all come to a close understanding of one another's position. Have you the sherry? Excellent. (*to Dunyasha*) Just leave the tray there. Thank you. Thank you. You haven't met Arkady's friend, have you, Fenichka? Yevgeny Vassilyich Bazarov.

Bazarov Pleased to meet you.

Fenichka You're welcome.

Bazarov Thank you.

Arkady Dr Bazarov – almost.

Fenichka Welcome, Doctor.

Nikolai (*to Dunyasha who is staring at Bazarov*) Dunyasha, will you put the tray down on the seat, please?

Dunyasha Oh yes – yes, yes, yes.

Nikolai I think this is yours, Pavel (*cocoa*).

Pavel Thanks.

As the cups are being passed round Arkady has a private word with Fenichka.

Arkady Congratulations.

She looks puzzled.

On the baby.

Fenichka Oh. (*She looks quickly towards Nikolai.*)

Arkady He's just told me.

Fenichka He wasn't sure how you'd react.

Arkady I'm pleased for you both.

Fenichka Thank you.

Nikolai is aware of this private conversation.

Nikolai You're sitting with us, Fenichka, aren't you?

Fenichka Not just now. I've got to bath Mitya and put him to bed. I'll join you later.

Nikolai Please do.

Fenichka leaves.

Dunyasha Can I get you anything else?

Nikolai That's everything, I think, Dunyasha.

She is gazing at Bazarov and does not move.

Thank you.

She goes.

There's something the matter with that girl today. Now to organize our lives. Let me tell you what plans we have in store for you. The first formal engagement is on Monday week. It's a rather long and convoluted story that –

Pavel It's quite simple: he's having a welcome-home party for you.

Arkady Great.

Nikolai Some weeks ago quite out of the blue I had a visit from a young lady called Anna Sergeyevna Odintsov. (*to Bazarov*) An unusual name, isn't it? – Odintsov. Are you familiar with it?

Bazarov (*not listening*) No.

Nikolai It was unknown to me, too, I must confess. Anyhow it transpires that the young lady's mother, may she rest in peace, and my good wife, may she rest in peace, were very close friends when they were young girls. But, as so often happens, they lost touch with one another shortly after they got married. But to cut a long story short. Anna Sergeyevna was rummaging in an attic in her home –

Pavel Could I have sugar?

Nikolai – and she came across a bundle of letters written by your good mother, Maria, to her old friend – well, her young friend then. And Anna Sergeyevna had the kind thought that I might like to have these letters since they contain many references to myself. (*to Bazarov*) Arkady's mother and I were, as we say, walking out at the time.

Bazarov (*not listening*) Yes?

Pavel Cream, please.

Nikolai I'd be delighted to have the letters, I said. So the following week Anna Sergeyevna Odintsov called on us again and handed over Maria's epistles and spent a very agreeable couple of hours with us – didn't she, Pavel?

Pavel I found her very . . . measured.

Nikolai Did you think so?

Pavel And emotionally dehydrated.

Arkady Uncle Pavel!

Pavel Oh yes.

Nikolai Well, I liked her very much.

Arkady What age is she?

Nikolai I'm very bad at that sort of thing. I would imagine she might –

Pavel Twenty-nine.

Arkady Interesting.

Nikolai Oh yes, an interesting lady.

Pavel Enormously wealthy. With a huge estate. And a widow.

Arkady *Very* interesting.

Nikolai Very . . .? Oh, I see what you mean now. Very good. Very good. What else do we know about her? She lives with an eccentric old aunt, Princess Something-or-other.

Pavel Olga.

Nikolai Olga. And she has a young sister called – what's the young sister's name?

Pavel Katerina.

Nikolai That's it – Katya. All three are coming on Monday week. (*Pause.*) And we'll have a wonderful party. (*Pause.*) And we'll all have a wonderful time. (*Pause.*) Won't we?

Pavel If you'll excuse me. I get a headache when I sit too long in the sun.

Nikolai We have a meeting with the new estate manager in half an hour, Pavel.

Pavel I'll be in my room.

Nikolai I'll join you in a few minutes.

As he exits Pavel puts his hand on Arkady's shoulder and pats it. Then he leaves.

Nothing Pavel likes better than a vigorous discussion, plenty of thrust and parry. We're inclined to go to seed here in the wilds, Yevgeny.

Bazarov Yes.

Arkady (*quickly*) What were the letters like?

Nikolai Letters?

Arkady The letters Mother wrote to her friend about you.

Nikolai Oh, they were . . . oh-ho, I'm afraid they were a bit naughty in places . . . very naughty in fact . . . in fact a few of them were very naughty indeed . . . You never really know what people are like, do you? We all have our codes. We all have our masks.

Piotr enters left. He is nineteen, exceedingly cocky and self-assured. He knows Nikolai is fond of him and he plays on that. He wears a single ear-ring and his hair is done in various vivid colours.

Piotr You wanted me, sir?

Nikolai Yes, Piotr?

Piotr You sent for me, sir.

Nikolai I did?

Piotr Dunyasha said you wanted me.

Nikolai I'm sure I did, Piotr; and I'm sure you didn't hear me. (*to Bazarov*) Piotr's hearing is erratic.

Piotr (*aggrieved*) My hearing is perfect, sir. I was slaving in the stables. You could scream and I wouldn't hear you there, sir.

Nikolai Never mind now, Piotr. Look who's here.

Piotr I know. I saw the carriage. Welcome home, Arkady.

Arkady Thank you, Piotr.

Nikolai And this is another young graduate – well, almost a graduate – Yevgeny Vassilyich.

Piotr Sir.

Bazarov Hello.

Nikolai Do you like his multicoloured hair?

Arkady It's what all the young dudes in Petersburg are wearing, Piotr.

Piotr I know that. But nobody around this place does.

Nikolai And his single blue ear-ring?

Piotr Pardon me, sir – turquoise.

Nikolai Forgive me, Piotr – turquoise. I beg your pardon. (*waving him away*) No, I don't want you now. Yes, I do. Take this tray away with you. And get the carriage out and bring it round to the back.

Piotr Certainly, sir. No sooner said.

Nikolai 'No sooner said!' He has my heart broken.

Piotr exits.

And I'm very fond of him – he's so cheeky. (*Looks at watch.*) Five thirty. I must run. Show Yevgeny where the guest-room is. Have a wash. Walk around. Take a rest. Do whatever pleases you. We'll eat at seven. And welcome again – both of you. (*He leaves.*)

Arkady is annoyed with his friend: he thinks his exchange with Pavel was too personal. Bazarov is unaware of this. He goes to the samovar.

Bazarov How did your father get that limp?

Arkady Broken leg when he was young. Badly set.

Bazarov I like him. He's a decent man. An astute bird, too. What's the relationship between him and the blonde woman?

Arkady Fenichka. She's his mistress.

Bazarov Ah. I got a whiff of something there.

Arkady I suppose that's one way of putting it.

Bazarov Have they known each other long?

Arkady She has a child by him.

Bazarov Good-looking woman. A nice self-awareness about her. Fenichka.

Arkady He should marry her.

Bazarov Who needs marriage? Your father's a lot more progressive than you, my friend. I suspect – just glancing round the yard – I suspect he's not the most organized landowner in Russia. But his heart's in the right place. Tea?

Arkady I thought you were a bit severe on Uncle Pavel.

Bazarov God, what a freak that is!

Arkady It sounded like a personal attack – cliché French – all that stuff.

Bazarov Have you any idea of the shock it is to walk into a place like this, miles from anywhere, and to be confronted by that – that decaying dandy? And all those archaic theories about 'civilization' and a 'basis of conduct'! He's a bloody absurdity!

Arkady He was considered to be the most handsome officer in the army in his day; and the best gymnast.

Bazarov No, he's not absurd – he's grotesque.

Arkady He was made a captain when he was only twenty-one. Women just threw themselves at him. And he has travelled everywhere and read everything. And he speaks three or four languages. And he dined once with Louis Philippe; and he and the Duke of Wellington corresponded on and off for years.

Bazarov (*imitating Pavel*) Good heavens.

Arkady And then, when he was in his mid-twenties, he fell in love – one of those passions that consumes totally. I remember hearing the story when I was very young. She was a princess; married; with a child.

Dunyasha appears on the veranda and shakes out a table-cloth. Bazarov pretends to think she is waving at him and waves back at her. Dunyasha withdraws coyly.

Bazarov That Dunyasha lady has a sporty eye.

Arkady And she had this radiant golden hair and when she let it down 'it fell to below her knees', like Rapunzel in the fairy story. They lived together for a while. Then she got tired of him. Cleared off to Germany, France, somewhere. Just disappeared. He followed her, of course; pursued her frantically for ten years all over Europe. Then he got word that she had died, apparently in some kind of demented state, in some shabby boarding-house in Paris.

Bazarov Where else.

Arkady Oh yes, there was another detail.

Bazarov (*pretending eagerness*) What was that?

Arkady Early in their affair he gave her a ring with a sphinx engraved on the stone. And the family legend has it that she said to him, 'Why the sphinx?'

Bazarov 'You are that sphinx.'

Arkady That's right! That's what he said! And exactly seven weeks after she died a package was delivered to his club. He opened it up and inside –

Bazarov – was the ring.

Arkady Yes. That was in 1848, the year Mother died. Father was alone here then, lost without his Maria. He asked Uncle Pavel to join him. And he came. And he has lived here, really like a recluse, ever since, in a sort of profound and perpetual melancholy . . . I'm very fond of him. I think he's a good man, Uncle Pavel.

Pause.

Bazarov You astonish me at times, Arkady. I tell myself that you *are* maturing politically, intellectually, emotionally. And then you come out with the greatest load of romantic hogwash that quite honestly alarms me. Rapunzel – radiant golden hair – passions that consume totally –

Arkady If you knew Pavel as well as I –

Bazarov Look at him dispassionately. The shape and character of his entire life was determined by a single, ridiculous passion. And when that ridiculous passion wasn't reciprocated – what happens? He sinks into a 'profound and perpetual melancholy'! For the rest of his life! Because of a crazy woman! That's the behaviour of an imbecile! (*He is beginning to win Arkady over.*) Let me give you Dr Bazarov's Principles Concerning the Proper Ordering of the Relationships between Men and Women.

Arkady I must write these deathless words down.

Bazarov One. Romantic love is a fiction.
   Two. There is nothing at all mysterious between the sexes. The relationship is quite simply physical.
   Three. To believe that the relationship should be dressed up in the trappings of chivalry is crazy. The troubadours were all lunatics.
   Four. If you fancy a woman, any woman, always, always try to make love to her. If you want to dissipate, dissipate.

Arkady Poor old Father – I was a bit sharp with him.

Bazarov And if you can't make love to that particular woman, so what? Believe Dr Bazarov – there are plenty more fish in the sea.

Arkady You're a bastard, Bazarov. You know that?

Bazarov Admit it. Am I not right?

Arkady (*thawing*) A perverse bastard – that's what you are.

Bazarov Draw up a list of all the women you'd like to make love to – no commitment, no responsibilities – just for the sheer pleasure of it.

Arkady Keep your voice down, man.

Bazarov No complications of 'love', romance, none of that rubbish.

Arkady That's a game for undergraduates. I'm a graduate – remember?

Bazarov A quick roll in the hay – great fun – goodbye.

Arkady All gross pigs, you medicals.

Bazarov I'll start you off. Natasha Petrova.

Arkady Natasha who?

Bazarov The inconstancy of the man! Your first year in Petersburg – the landlady's big red-headed daughter – Natasha the Greyhound!

Arkady Come on, Bazarov. There was nothing at all to that.

Bazarov You wrote a sonnet to her.

Arkady I never did!

Bazarov
'Could I outstrip the beauty of that form
That haunts these dark and wretched hours called life –'

Arkady All right – all right! That was just a passing –

Bazarov Exactly. Quick roll – great fun – goodbye. She's number one. Dunyasha?

Arkady Dunyasha? – here?

Bazarov On the list or not?

Arkady I never really thought about her in that –

Bazarov A sporty eye, an open heart, a great armful.

Arkady Now that you mention her, I suppose she –

Bazarov She's elected; number two. Anna Sergeyevna?

Arkady Who's she?

Bazarov The woman who's coming for the party on Monday week.

Arkady We've never seen her.

Bazarov Who cares?

Arkady She's wealthy.

Bazarov Twenty-nine years of age.

Arkady A huge estate.

Bazarov And a widow.

Arkady Is that important?

Bazarov The experience, man.

Arkady Good point. What do you say?

Bazarov If only for the experience – number three. And her young sister – Katya?

Arkady I think so.

Bazarov Vote. Yes or no.

Arkady Katya? I like Katya. I fancy Katya. Yes.

Bazarov Elected. Good. Four so far.

Fenichka appears on the veranda.

Fenichka Yevgeny Vassilyich!

Bazarov Hello.

Fenichka The baby has some kind of a rash on the back of his neck. Would you take a look at it for me?

Bazarov It would be a pleasure. Where is he?

Fenichka He's back here in the kitchen.

Bazarov I'm on my way. (*to Arkady*) My first professional job.

Arkady I'd be sure to get a second opinion, Fenichka.

Bazarov (*softly*) Would you say that Fenichka is a possible number five?

Arkady Bazarov, you –!

Bazarov In jest, my friend, in jest.

He goes towards the veranda where Fenichka is waiting for him.

Arkady (*calls*) Even in jest! Bazarov, for God's sake, man.

Bazarov turns at the steps and smiles back at him. Then he and Fenichka go into the house.

SCENE TWO

Early June. After dinner.
  Nikolai and Katya are playing duets on the piano in the living-room. Katya is eighteen, open, spirited, garrulous. Fenichka is standing beside the piano turning the pages on Nikolai's instructions. Bazarov is outside on the veranda, leaning across the rail, slowly eating a dish of ice-cream. Pavel is sitting alone and remote downstage right; reading. Anna is sitting downstage left, listening to the music. She

*is an elegant, carefully groomed, circumspect woman. She
deliberately lives within certain emotional limits and is
wary of any intrusion inside them or any excursion
outside them. The Princess is sitting upstage right,
beneath an enormous parasol which partly conceals her.
Now and then she emerges from behind it. She is very old,
very eccentric, very energetic. She constantly and
vigorously masticates imaginary food and every so often
brushes imaginary crumbs from her sleeve and skirt.*

   Just before the music comes to an end Nikolai calls:

Nikolai Wonderful, Katya. Terrific. Don't stop. Let's do it
again from the beginning. Splendid. Two-and-three-and –

   *They begin the piece again and keep playing throughout
the early part of the scene.*

    *Arkady rushes through the living-room and out into
the garden, carrying a dish of ice-cream. He is very
elated.*

Arkady (*as he passes behind Bazarov*) Get yourself some
more ice-cream before it all melts. (*He leaps down the
steps.*)

Bazarov (*as Arkady crosses before him*) I think the
dehydrated widow fancies you.

Arkady Doing well, amn't I?

Bazarov Give her a message for me.

Arkady What?

Bazarov Tell her I'd like to do my anatomy practical on her.

Arkady Cut that out, Bazarov.

Bazarov I'm sure she'd agree.

   Arkady crosses over to the Princess.

Arkady Can I get you anything, Princess Olga?

Princess (*emerging*) Cat.

Arkady Sorry?

Princess I smell cat.

Arkady Cat?

Princess Cat-cat-cat. Damn place must be overrun with them. Shoot them all! Shoot them! Shoot them! They'll overrun you if you don't. My father told me that.

She vanishes behind the parasol. He goes to Anna.

Anna It's best to pay no attention to her.

Arkady She sounds so furious.

Anna Ignore her. She lives quite contentedly in her own world.

Arkady There you are. (*He offers her ice-cream.*) I'm afraid it's gone a bit soft.

Anna You have it.

Arkady I've had enough. Go ahead. There's plenty more. Loads of it. We eat it all the time here. In the summer. God, she's really a magnificent pianist, Katya.

Anna She's very competent; no more than that.

Arkady And she can sight-read brilliantly. I love that piece. I remember Father and Mother playing it together when I was very small. I'm sure you play, too?

Anna No.

Arkady Yes, you do. You're being modest.

Anna I don't, Arkady.

Arkady I'm sure you're a brilliant pianist.

Anna No.

Arkady I don't believe you. And I'm told you're a painter.

She shakes her head.

Yes, you are. Katya told me. She says you're terrific with water-colours.

Anna Katerina exaggerates.

Arkady Bazarov and I are going to visit his parents soon, maybe at the end of next week. I was wondering if we could call on you on our way there?

Anna We'd be glad to see you.

Arkady Great! Tomorrow, maybe? Are you sure that's all right?

Anna He looks like a painter. Is he artistic?

Arkady Uncle Pavel?

Anna Your friend – who believes in nothing.

Arkady Bazarov? He's a total philistine! (*He calls.*) We're talking about you!

Bazarov points to his ears, points into the living-room: he cannot hear above the music.

(*shouting*) Anna Sergeyevna wants to know – (*He gives up.*) It doesn't matter.

Anna (*beckoning*) Come and join us.

Arkady Keep him off politics or he'll give you a boring lecture. I'm a Nihilist, too, you know; like Bazarov.

Anna (*watching Bazarov approach*) Really?

Arkady We've a very active cell in Petersburg. There aren't all that many of us but we're absolutely, totally dedicated. Anna wants to know if you're artistic!

146

Anna Arkady says you're a philistine.

Arkady He's the worst kind of philistine – he's a scientist.

Bazarov What is art for?

Arkady (*to Anna*) I told you.

Bazarov Is it necessary?

Anna's attention has switched to Bazarov. In an attempt to hold her Arkady launches into his monologue. While he lectures, Anna and Bazarov conduct a mute dialogue; 'Sit here' – 'No, thanks' – 'There's a stool' – 'I'd prefer to stand' – 'There's a chair' – 'I'm fine' – etc.

Arkady And the answer to that is: what does the word necessary mean in that context? Is that dish necessary? – that tree? – that cloud formation? We're not exactly in unison on this issue, Bazarov and I. He believes that Nihilism and art are seldom compatible. I don't. But I believe that at this point in our history and in our sociological development it would be wrong for us now to channel our depleted energies into artistic endeavour, not because there is anything intrinsically wrong, or indeed right, with artistic endeavour – but I believe that whatever energies we can muster now have got to be poured into the primary and enormous task of remaking an entire society and that imperative is not only a social obligation but perhaps even a moral obligation and indeed it is not improbable that the execution of that task may even have elements of . . . of artistic pursuit . . . or so it seems to me . . .

He tails off in some confusion, unsure that he has made his point, any point, unsure that he has impressed Anna, unsure that she has even listened to him. Pause.

Princess (*suddenly emerging*) My father always said that the quickest and most efficient way to break in a difficult young horse was to hit him over the head with a crowbar. (*She demonstrates.*) Bang between the ears! Ha-ha. He was right, you know. I've done it myself. And it works! It works! It works! (*She vanishes again.*)

Pause.

Bazarov Lively music, isn't it?

Anna So you're not a total philistine.

Bazarov shrugs.

Bazarov Silly word.

Arkady What word?

Bazarov Philistine.

Arkady No, it's not. It's a precise word.

Anna Art can at least help us to know and understand people, can't it?

Bazarov Living does that. (*He lays down the ice-cream dish.*) That was good.

Anna Not to the same extent; not in any depth.

Dunyasha enters and picks up various dishes around the lawn.

Bazarov What is there to understand in depth? All men are similar physically and intellectually. Each has a brain, a spleen, heart, lungs. Intellectually? – darker and lighter shadings, that's all. We're like trees in the forest. Ask any botanist. Know one birch, know them all.

Dunyasha is about to pick up the dish beside Anna.

Anna I'm not finished yet.

Dunyasha Sorry, miss.

148

Bazarov And Dunyasha is the most wholesome and uncomplicated birch-tree in the whole of Russia.

Dunyasha What does that mean?

Bazarov It means that you're beautiful and desirable.

Arkady Don't listen to him, Dunyasha. Uncle Pavel says he's a bletherskite.

Dunyasha loves this. She give a great whoop of laughter.

Dunyasha He did not, did he? A bletherskite! That's great! That's what he is all right! (*She goes off laughing.*)

Bazarov (*calling*) I still think you're beautiful.

Anna So there is no difference between a stupid person and an intelligent person, between a good person and a bad person?

Bazarov Of course there is, just as there is a difference between a sick person and a healthy person. The man with tuberculosis has the same *kind* of lungs as you and I but they are in a different condition; and as medicine advances we know how to correct that condition. Moral disease, moral imbalance has different causes – our educational system, religious superstition, heredity, the polluted moral atmosphere our society breathes. But remake society and you eradicate *all* disease.

Anna Physical and moral?

Bazarov All.

Anna (*to Arkady*) Does he believe that? (*to Bazarov*) That if you reform society –

Bazarov Remake.

Anna Then all illness, all evil, all stupidity disappear?

Bazarov Because in our remade society the words stupid and clever, good and bad, will have lost the meaning you invest them with, will probably come to have no meaning at all. Do they not play polkas in the houses of the gentry?

Anna (*to Arkady*) What do you think?

Arkady I agree with Bazarov. Bazarov's right.

Anna looks keenly at Bazarov.

Anna (*suddenly to Arkady*) Could I have some more of that ice-cream?

Arkady (*jumping to his feet, eager to serve*) Wonderful, isn't it? I made it myself. Ice-cream, Uncle Pavel?

Pavel What's that?

Arkady Ice-cream – do you want some?

Bazarov 'Good heavens, no'.

Pavel Good heavens, no.

Arkady (*coldly to Bazarov*) What about you?

Bazarov Not for me.

Arkady goes to the Princess.

Arkady Princess, would you like –

She emerges momentarily and scowls at him.

Princess Would I like what? What would I like?

Arkady Sorry. (*He flees, tripping on the veranda steps.*)

Anna He's such a nice young man.

Bazarov You have unbalanced him.

Arkady (*calling above the piano music*) Anybody for ice-cream?

Katya Me, Arkady. Please.

Arkady Fenichka?

She signals no. He goes to her and dances her round the room in time to the music. Anna claps.

Anna (*calling*) Very good, Arkady! Lovely!

Bazarov Exquisite.

Anna He's a very good dancer.

Bazarov (*sharply*) Altogether he's such a nice young man.

Anna (*calling*) Beautiful, Arkady. Very elegant.

Arkady Can't hear you.

Bazarov He can't take his eyes off you.

Anna Do you dance?

Bazarov No.

Anna I love dancing.

Bazarov Naturally. All aristocrats love dancing.

Anna I've told you, Yevgeny – I'm not an aristocrat. Tell me more about your Nihilism.

Bazarov It's not mine. I don't possess it like an estate. Tell me what you believe in.

Anna Routine; order; discipline.

Bazarov That's how you conduct your life, not what you believe in.

Anna It's adequate for me.

Bazarov Because you have no beliefs or because your beliefs have no passion?

Anna Passion is a luxury. I make no excursions outside what I know and can handle.

Bazarov These new psychiatrists would say that you avoid belief because belief demands commitment and you're afraid of commitment. And you're afraid of commitment because it would demand everything of you. And because you're not prepared to give everything, you give nothing. And you excuse yourself by calling passion a luxury but you know in your heart that your excuse is a lie.

Anna I'm not a liar, Yevgeny Vassilyich.

Bazarov I haven't met all that many aristocrats like you in my life –

Anna I am not an –

Bazarov – but I've noticed that their brain is divided into two equal parts. One part is totally atrophied – the part that might be capable of generosity, enthusiasm, of a thirst for social change, of the desire for risk, for the big gamble, for that dangerous extreme. So they function, these aristocratic cripples, they function with the portion that is left to them; and like some mutilated organ it becomes unnaturally developed and unnaturally active. Hence your aristocrat's irrational obsession with wheat-yield and good-management and productivity and efficiency –

Anna And routine and order and discipline. Why are you being so difficult?

Bazarov Perhaps I haven't the grace for aristocratic ladies like you.

Anna My father, my handsome, gambling, risking, reckless father died when I was twenty. Katerina was only nine. For two years we lived in penury, the kind of grinding poverty I suspect you have never known, Yevgeny. Then I met a man who was twenty-five years older than me. He was very wealthy, eccentric, a hypochondriac, enormously fat. He had no illusions about himself. He asked me to marry him. I thought about it very carefully and then I said yes. We had six years together. I still miss him. He was a kind man.

Bazarov So?

Anna So that's all. I suppose I'm trying to – Oh I don't know why I told you that.

Bazarov I'm afraid I'm lost here. I mean – am I to applaud your circumspection in netting a rich old eccentric – or commiserate with you on your bereavement? – or congratulate you on your sudden wealth?

Anna Let's not talk about it any more.

Bazarov Or are you just teasing my appetite for the full biography? Because if you are, I'm afraid I find it less than gripping. But it does have the makings of the kind of rags-to-riches novelette that someone like Dunyasha, or indeed the very nice young Arkady, would probably find irresistible.

Anna jumps to her feet and would leave but Bazarov catches her by the arms.

Oh my God, Anna – forgive me – I'm sorry – I'm sorry – please, please forgive me –

The music has stopped. Everybody is aware of the scene, of the raised voices. Everybody is staring at them. Bazarov realizes he is holding her and lets her go.

(*lowering his voice*) I've no idea why I said that – it was unpardonable, unpardonable – I'm sorry – I'm deeply sorry – please forgive me – please.

Silence. Pavel, the only person unaware of the scene, closes his book and walks slowly across the stage towards Anna.

Pavel (*applauding the pianists*) Bravo! Well done! Lovely! Thank you. Your sister is a very talented pianist.

Anna What are you reading, Pavel Petrovich?

Pavel This? *Ne vaut pas la peine d'être lu. The Romance of the Forest* by an English novelist called Mrs Ann Ward Radcliffe. A simple lady. But it kills time. Harmlessly.

As he goes into the living-room, Arkady enters carrying two dishes of ice-cream – one for Katya and one for Anna.

(*with distaste*) Good Lord.

Arkady Good Lord, it's lovely, Uncle Pavel. Here we are! Who ordered what? Katya – there you are – one vanilla ice-cream coated with chocolate dressing and topped with a single glistening cherry.

Katya Thank you, Arkady. Oh, lovely!

Bazarov (*softly to Anna*) Please forgive me. I'm deeply sorry. (*He exits quickly left.*)

Arkady (*to Katya*) My great pleasure. (*He comes outside.*) And one without dressing for Anna Sergeyevna Odintsov.

Katya comes down beside him.

Katya Did you really make it yourself?

Arkady Why the surprise? I'm an expert at all foods, amn't I, Bazarov? Where's Bazarov? In the flat we shared I did all the cooking and he did all the washing and cleaning.

Katya (*to Anna*) You're pale. Are you all right?

Anna I'm fine – fine – we'll soon have to go, Katerina.

Katya No, we're not leaving for some time. I like it here.

Nikolai and Fenichka come down.

Nikolai I really enjoyed that. I haven't played piano duets since Maria and I used to sit in there and – (*recovering*) – oh, not for years and years. Did we go on too long?

Anna Not long enough. We had a lovely evening.

Nikolai I hope it's the first of many. It's beginning to get cold. Do you think the Princess is warm enough?

Anna She's all right. Anyway it's time we got the carriage ready.

Nikolai Piotr! Piotr! He must be somewhere around. Ah, Prokofyich, would you see to Madam Odintsov's carriage?

Prokofyich Certainly, madam.

Anna pushes the parasol aside.

Anna Time to move, Auntie Olga. We have a long journey before us.

Princess Long journeys – short journeys – my father always said they all end up in the same place: nowhere, nowhere, nowhere.

Anna takes her arm and together they go into the living-room. Arkady watches Anna as she goes.

Katya You were to show me the litter of pups, Arkady.

Arkady Sorry?

Katya The litter of pups – you were to show me them.

Arkady So I was. We'll go just now. They're in the stable.

Katya How many are there?

Arkady Four. Would you like one?

Katya What do you mean – would I like one? We talked about this all morning and you said I could have the pick of the litter. Don't you remember?

Arkady Of course I remember. And it's the pick of the litter you'll get, Katerina.

Katya Katya! Katya! Katya! We talked about that, too! I told you I loathe Katerina. Anna's the only one who calls me Katerina.

Arkady Sorry, Katya. The pick of the litter – your choice – whatever one you want. Or take two of them. Or three of them. Or take them all.

Katya 'Take them all'! You're an awful clown, you know.

Arkady Why?

Katya Just the way you go on. If you want my honest opinion, I think you're not a very mature person yet.

Arkady Really?!

Katya But that will come in time.

Arkady Oh, good. Then I'll be like you.

Katya No, no – always a little behind. But close enough. Come on – Anna wants to leave soon.

She leads him off left. Nikolai and Fenichka move downstage. Dunyasha comes into the living-room and tidies around. She is singing.

Nikolai I wouldn't be at all surprised if Arkady has fallen for young Katya. I noticed, when we were playing the piano, she kept watching him.

Fenichka I think it's Anna Sergeyevna he likes.

Nikolai Do you think so? Oh, I would hope not. Anna Sergeyevna is a splendid young woman but much too sophisticated for Arkady. Sit down beside me. You must be tired. You had a busy day.

Fenichka I was tired earlier but I'm fine now. When are the boys leaving?

Nikolai The end of next week, I believe. And I'm glad – no, not that they're leaving – (*whispers*) – but that Bazarov is finally going to his parents. Hasn't seen them for three whole years! Can you imagine – not since he started college!

Fenichka Some people live like that. It doesn't mean he doesn't care for them.

Nikolai That's true. Maybe it's just a matter of being alert to certain sensibilities. He's fond of you – Bazarov.

Fenichka Is he?

Nikolai Oh, yes. He's more relaxed with you than with anybody else in the house.

Fenichka I like him, too. Strange man.

Nikolai And Arkady's also fond of you, thank heaven!

Fenichka I'm very fond of Arkady.

Dunyasha exits. They are alone.

Nikolai And of Mitya. Calls him 'little half-brother'.

Fenichka I've heard him. It's funny to see them playing together.

Nikolai We had a long talk the other day. We were alone in the garden here. It was like old times – just the two of us. And then do you know what he did out of the blue? He scolded me!

Fenichka Arkady?

Nikolai Quite severely. He said I shouldn't have allowed you to live above that laundry for so long.

Fenichka (*becoming embarrassed*) What Arkady doesn't know is that the room above the laundry is the warmest room in the house.

Nikolai It is also damp. Anyhow his point was that you were pregnant and you should have been in the main building; that it was most insensitive of me. And he's right.

Fenichka That's all over, Nikolai. I'm in the main house now. You're right – it is getting cold.

Nikolai He said, too, that we should be married. Yes. He had no doubts whatever. He thinks it's ridiculous we're not married. Remarkable, isn't it?

Fenichka What is?

Nikolai That that is his attitude. And I found it very reassuring. More than reassuring – encouraging, most encouraging. Wouldn't you agree?

Fenichka Oh, yes; most encouraging.

Nikolai And of course Pavel would be in favour. No question about his attitude.

Fenichka Has he said that to you?

Nikolai He doesn't have to say it – I know Pavel. Convention – decorum. Oh, yes, Pavel will want the proprieties observed. So, since I now know what Arkady thinks – and unlike his dithering old father he hadn't a moment's hesitation – and since I've always known that Pavel would be in favour –

Fenichka buries her face in her handkerchief and cries. Nikolai watches her in alarm and bewilderment.

Fenichka? Fenichka, what's the matter with –? My God, what have I done wrong? Did I do anything? – did I say anything? Did somebody hurt you? Who hurt you? Please don't cry, Fenichka. Please. Tell me what's the matter with you. Fenichka? Fenichka?

She continues to cry. He continues to watch her in bewilderment.

SCENE THREE

End of June.
    Arkady and Bazarov are sitting at the dining-room table in Bazarov's home. With them are Bazarov's father, Vassily Ivanyich Bazarov, and his mother, Arina Vlassyevna. Vassily Ivanyich is in his early sixties, a tall, thin, pipe-smoking man dressed in an old military jacket. He is very ill at ease in the presence of his guests and talks too much – and is aware that he is talking too much – to hide his unease.
    Arina Vlassyevna is a small, plump woman in her fifties. The first impression is of a quiet, simple country woman. But she is alert to every nuance in the conversation and watches her son and his friend to gauge their reaction to her husband's compulsive talking. Two servants attend the table – Timofeich, an old retainer, almost decrepit, and Fedka, a very young boy who is employed only because of the visitors. Fedka is barefooted.

Lunch has just finished.

Vassily Very good question, Arkady Nikolayevich: how do I pass the time? Excellent question. And I will tell you the answer to that question. Timofeich, more blackcurrant tea for our guest.

Arkady Just a little. (*to Arina*) That was a very nice lunch. Thank you.

Arina You're welcome.

Bazarov gets to his feet and paces around the room.

Vassily Yevgeny?

Bazarov None for me.

Arina (*privately to Bazarov*) Take another biscuit.

Bazarov (*playfully shaking his head*) Shhh!

Arina I'm going to have to fatten you up over the next two months.

Bazarov responds by puffing out his cheeks and his chest and miming a fat man.

Vassily How do I pass the time? I'm a bit like ancient Gaul: I'm divided into *tres partes*, as our friend Caesar might put it. One part is the reader. Another part is the gardener. And the third part is the practising doctor – even though I'm supposed to have retired years ago. Not a day passes but there's a patient at my door. (*to Arina*) That wouldn't be incorrect, my pet, would it? And interestingly enough all of those three parts add up to one complete integer. My reading is all medical reading. My gardening is all medical gardening – I believe I have the best garden of medicinal herbs in the whole province. That wouldn't be inaccurate, my pet, would it? Nature itself as healer – it's the answer, you know. As our friend

Paracelsus puts it: I trust *in herbis, in verbis et in lapidibus*.

Bazarov (*to Arkady*) Father was a great classical scholar in his day.

Vassily Great? I wouldn't say I –

Bazarov Won a medal for Latin composition. Silver. When he was only twelve.

Vassily I suspect he's mocking me. Are you mocking me?

Bazarov Me?

Arina Finish your story, Vassily.

Vassily Where was I?

Bazarov *In herbis, in verbis et in lapidibus*.

Vassily Tending my garden, attending my patients, and in my spare time looking after my modest farm. (*to Arkady*) I shouldn't say 'my modest farm' – I'm a plebeian, a *homo novus* – Yevgeny's mother is the patrician.

Arina Vassily!

Bazarov bows to his mother and kisses her hand.

Bazarov Her serene highness, Arina Vlassyevna Bazarov.

Arina Behave yourself.

Vassily For God's sake, Fedka, will you put something on your feet. Timofeich, take this little urchin away and dress him correctly. Arkady Nikolayevich will think he's staying with some sort of primitives.

Bazarov Isn't that what we are?

Vassily You're very facetious today, young man. But where was I? Yes, talking of medicine. You'll enjoy this. I hear that a retired major about six miles from here is doing a bit of doctoring. So one day, when we meet at the market, this major and I, I said, 'I hear you're in practice, Major?' 'Yes,' he said. 'Where did you qualify?' 'I never qualified,' he said. 'Never? But where did you study your medicine?' 'I never studied medicine.' 'But you practise medicine, Major?' 'Oh, yes. But not for money – jut for the good of the community.'

Vassily alone laughs at this. Arkady smiles politely.

I love that – 'just for the good of the community' – I really love that. Wonderful man to have around in a typhus epidemic. Incidentally there's a lot of it around . . . typhus . . .

Pause.

Arina (*to Arkady*) How long did you stay with this – this Madam Odintsov?

Arkady A week – (*to Bazarov*) – wasn't it? I've lost track of time.

Bazarov Eight nights.

Arina (*to Arkady*) And you had a nice time there?

Arkady It was sheer luxury. We were a bit overwhelmed at first, weren't we?

Bazarov Were we?

Arkady Well, I was.

Bazarov Yes, you were.

Arkady A butler in black tails, footmen in livery, scores of maids and servants all over the place. It's really a miniature empire she has there.

Arina And she lives with an old aunt and a young sister, this Madam Odintsov?

Arkady The old aunt's as mad as a hatter.

Arina And the young sister?

Arkady Katya is – (*to Bazarov*) – how would you describe Katya?

Bazarov You should have no difficulty. You voted her on your list.

Arina List? What list?

Arkady (*embarrassed*) Oh, we made a list, Yevgeny and I – a sort of silly list of – of – of all the pretty girls we know.

Arina Ah. And Katya is on that list?

Arkady She was on the list – at the beginning. She was on the first list.

Arina I see. She was pretty but she's not pretty now.

Arkady Oh, she's pretty, very pretty, isn't she?

Bazarov You're not alert to Mother's subtleties, Arkady. When she inquires about 'this – this Madam Odintsov', can't you hear the disapproval in her voice? She has already made up her mind that This Madam Odintsov is what novelists call an adventuress.

Arina That's not true.

Bazarov (*hugging her affectionately and laughing*) You're suspicious of her.

Arina Don't be silly, Yevgeny.

Bazarov You dislike her intensely.

Arina I never even heard of the woman until yesterday. He's trying to annoy me.

Bazarov In fact you hate The Woman. I know exactly

what it means when that little nose twitches like that. It always gives you away.

Arina And you? What do you think of her?

Bazarov hugs her again and laughs.

Bazarov Oh no, no, no, no, no, no, no; you're not going to turn the tables like that, Arina Vlassyevna. Isn't she a cunning little squirrel?

Vassily (*to Arkady*) They're well met, the pair of them.

Bazarov The question you really want to ask, Mother – it has tormented you since we arrived yesterday – what you want to ask straight out is: Am I in love with This Madam Odintsov? And the answer is: I don't believe in love, in falling in love, in being in love. Arkady and I spent a pleasant week with Katya and Anna. They're good company. I'm fond of them both. And that's it – *finis fabulae* – (*to Vassily*) – correct?

Vassily Very good, Yevgeny.

Bazarov If there is such a thing as a *maladie d'amour* – as the Tailor's Dummy would put it – I'm immune to it. Why don't you direct your loaded questions to Arkady. You're not immune, are you?

Arina You're too smart for your own good. (*to Timofeich who has entered*) Clear the table, will you.

Timofeich Excuse me, sir. A patient here to see you – a woman.

Vassily Can't you see we're still eating, Timofeich? Tell her to come back tomorrow. (*to Fedka who has entered wearing boots that are much too big for him*) That's more like it. Good boy, Fedka.

Bazarov What's wrong with the woman?

Timofeich She's holding herself as if she was in pain. I think she has the gripes.

Vassily Dysentery – that's what she has. They call it the gripes about here. *Torminum*, Pliny calls it. Cicero uses the plural – *tormina*. (*to Timofeich*) Tell her to come back tomorrow morning.

Bazarov Let me have a look at her, Father.

Vassily No, no; you're on your holidays and –

Bazarov Please. I'd like to.

Vassily If you'd like to. Very well. Certainly. We'll only be a few –

Bazarov I'd prefer to see her by myself.

Vassily Off you go. Give her a good shot of opium – you'll find it in my bag on the desk in the study. She'll be most grateful – probably want to pray over you.

Bazarov has gone. Vassily calls after him.

And she'll offer you four eggs as payment. (*to Arkady*) Do you know how many eggs I was given last week? One hundred and seventy-nine! That's no exaggeration, my pet, is it?

Timofeich is clearing the table. Fedka helps him.

Arina (*sitting again*) Leave the table for the moment, Timofeich. Fedka, put those raspberries out in the pantry.

Both servants leave.

Are you an only child, too, Arkady?

Arkady Yes. No – no – I have a half-brother, Mitya.

Arina Is he at college?

Arkady He's eight months old.

165

Vassily He has a few weeks to wait yet. (*He raises his glass.*) Welcome again, Arkady. It's a great pleasure for us to have you here.

Arkady Thank you.

Vassily A very great pleasure. Isn't that correct, my pet?

Arina You're most welcome.

Now that they have Arkady alone both parents want desperately to ply him with questions about their son. They move physically closer to him.

Vassily And I hope you can stay with us until you go back to college.

Arina You've forgotten, Vassily – Arkady has graduated.

Vassily Forgive me. Of course.

Arina And I'm sure he has hundreds of plans for the rest of the summer.

Arkady I haven't a plan in the world. I'm – at large!

Vassily Then you'll stay. Excellent. It's a delight for us to have Yevgeny's student friends. He usually brings somebody home with him every holiday. Fine young men all of them. And we love the company.

Arina Have you known Yevgeny long?

Arkady For about a year. We met at the philosophical meetings.

Vassily A philosopher, too, is he? Aha! That's a little detail we didn't know, did we?

Arina Has he got a girl in Petersburg?

Arkady Not that I know of.

Vassily I'm sure you have, Arkady; dozens of them.

Arina But nobody special?

Arkady Yevgeny? No; nobody special.

Arina He ate hardly any lunch. Is his appetite always as bad?

Arkady He's not very interested in food – maybe because I do the cooking!

Arina In this flat you share?

Arkady Yes.

Arina How many rooms do you have?

Arkady Three: bedroom, kitchen, washroom.

Arina And how long have you been together?

Arkady Oh, for the past year.

Arina What does he do about his laundry?

Arkady He does it himself. Mine, too. That's the arrangement.

Vassily Does he take any exercise?

Arkady He walks to lectures. And back. That's about it.

Vassily No good. He was always lazy about exercise. Not enough. Not nearly enough.

Arina How do you know when you don't know how far it is from the flat to the university? You just don't know. (*to Arkady*) And that hotel he mentioned – how many hours a week does he work there?

Arkady It varies. Sometimes twenty. Maybe up to thirty.

Arina And does he really make enough to feed and clothe himself?

Arkady Just about.

Arina And pay his fees?

Arkady We all live fairly frugally.

Arina You know he has never accepted any money from us, never since the first day he –

Vassily Arkady Nikolayevich is not interested in our domestic affairs, my pet. Tell me about this revolutionary stuff he was spouting last night, this – this – this –

Arkady Nihilism.

Vassily That's it. He's not really serious about that, is he? All that rubbish about –

Arkady We both are. Deadly serious.

Vassily Well, of course it is always valuable – and important, very important – most important to keep reassessing how we order our society. That's a very serious matter.

Arina I hope he wasn't serious when we were talking about that Madam Odintsov. He said I disliked her – that I hated her for some reason or other! That was very naughty of him.

Arkady He was only joking.

Arina I hope so.

Arkady You know he –

Arina (*rapidly*) Is he in love with her?

Arkady (*deeply confused*) With Anna? . . . Yevgeny? . . . I – I – how would I know? How do you tell? Maybe. I wouldn't know. I really wouldn't know.

Vassily And if he is, that's his own business, Arina. There's just one question I'd like to ask you, Arkady –

Arina You've asked Arkady far too many questions. Let him finish his tea.

Vassily With respect, my pet, it's you who have asked the questions. My one question is this. In Petersburg – in the university – in the circles you move about in – how would he be assessed academically? What I mean is, would he be considered run-of-the-mill, average, perhaps below average –?

Arkady Yevgeny?! Below average?!

Vassily Yes?

Arkady Yevgeny is – well, he's the most brilliant student in the university at present, probably one of the most brilliant students ever there.

Vassily Yevgeny?

Arkady But you must know this yourselves. Yevgeny Vassilyich is unique.

Vassily Unique?

Arkady Yes. Yes – yes – yes; absolutely unique. And whatever he chooses to do, he's going to have a dazzling future.

Vassily Are you listening, Arina?

Arkady Oh yes. You have an extra-ordinary son.

Arina cries quietly. Vassily cries quietly at first but then his emotion gets the better of him. Unable to contain himself, he grabs Arkady's hand and kisses it repeatedly.

Vassily Thank you. (*Kiss.*) Thank you – thank you – thank you. (*Kiss.*) You have made me the happiest man in Russia. (*Kiss.*) And now I'm going to make a confession: I idolize my son. So does his mother. We both do. Worship him. That's not incorrect, my pet, is it? And yet we daren't offer him even the most simple gesture of love, even of affection, because we know he detests any demonstration of emotion whatever. When you arrived here yesterday, I wanted to hold him, to hug him, to kiss him all over. But I daren't. I daren't. And I respect that attitude. It's my own attitude. What we must never forget is that we are talking here about an extra-ordinary man. And an extra-ordinary man cannot be judged by ordinary standards. An extra-ordinary man creates his own standards. Do you understand what I'm trying to say to you, Arkady?

Arkady Yes, I do.

Vassily A dazzling future – did you hear that, Arina?

Arina (*now recovered*) It's a beautiful day now.

Vassily There's no doubt in your mind?

Arkady None at all.

Arina We should all be out in the garden.

Arkady What area he'll move into I can't guess – science, philosophy, medicine, politics – he could be outstanding in any of them. But I do know he's going to be famous.

Vassily 'Going to be famous'. *Non superbus sed humilis sum*. Because some day, Arkady, some day when his biography is written, the following lines will appear: 'He was the son of a simple army doctor who from the beginning recognized his extra-ordinary talents and who despite every discouragement devoted his entire life and every penny he earned to his boy's education.'

> *Bazarov enters. He is instantly aware of the changed atmosphere and notices Vassily putting away his handkerchief. Arina gets quickly to her feet.*

Arkady Ah, Dr Bazarov on call!

Arina It didn't take you long.

Arkady Where are the eggs? Did you not deserve a fee?

Bazarov The woman had a sprained wrist. All I had to do was strap it.

Arina Timofeich!

Bazarov What's been happening here?

Arina You boys are about to go out and get a bit of colour in your faces. (*to Bazarov*) Take Arkady round by the acacia plantation and down to the old mill.

Vassily I want to show them my herb garden first.

Arina I need you to help me put up new curtains in the study, Vassily.

Bazarov There's something going on here.

Vassily (*unable to contain his excitement any longer*) There certainly is something going on here. *Primo:* Arkady Nikolayevich has just decided to spend the rest of the summer here with us. *Secundo:* I have just decided to invite Anna and Katya Odintsov to come and have dinner here with us next Sunday.

Arina None of this has been –

Vassily Please. Allow me. And *tertio:* I have had a bottle of champagne in my study for the past three years – and now is the time to open it.

Arina We'll celebrate later, Vassily. We'll have your champagne at dinner tonight. Can you come into the study now?

Vassily Your curtains are much less important –

Arina Now. (*to Bazarov and Arkady*) We'll eat at seven. Have a nice walk.

She catches Vassily by the elbow and leads him quickly and firmly out.

Bazarov What's this all about?

Arkady What's what all about?

Bazarov You know damn well what I mean.

Arkady Just a moment, Bazarov. Just calm down. Your mother asked me what plans I had. I said none. Your father then said – excellent, spend the summer here.

Bazarov Fine – fine – fine. Spend the summer here. But you'll spend it here alone. And what's this about inviting Anna over here next Sunday?

Arkady You're shouting, Bazarov.

Bazarov How did that come up? Whose brilliant idea was that?

Arkady Your father's.

Bazarov Who else! The moment you used the words miniature empire I could see the peasant eyes dilate. Well, that is not going to happen.

Vassily puts his head around the door.

Vassily A patient outside. Sorry – am I intruding? Suffering from icterus. I have him on a diet of centaurion minus, carrots and St John's wort. Now I know you don't believe in medicine, Yevgeny, but I'd welcome your opinion on this. Not now, of course. Later. Later. Sorry. (*He withdraws.*)

Bazarov A whole summer of that? Icterus – do you hear him! – icterus! He couldn't say bloody jaundice, simple bloody jaundice like anybody else. And he's prescribing bloody cabbage water and bloody carrots! For jaundice! The man's a fool! That's what he is – a fool, a fool, a fool! And he's killing that poor bugger out there!

Arkady I like him.

Bazarov You like him.

Arkady He's a nice man.

Bazarov My mother's nice. My father's nice. The lunch was nice. Your Uncle Pavel is nice. I've no idea what the word means. Let's look at my father's life and see can we not find a more exact word. What does he do all day? Fusses about his garden. Dabbles in medicine. Bores my mother to death with his endless and pointless prattle. And he'll go on fussing and dabbling and boring until the whole insignificant little episode that was his trivial life is over. We can hardly call that nice, can we? What about futile? – fatuous? – would you risk ridiculous?

Arkady And your life is so meaningful, Bazarov, so significant?

Bazarov When we were out walking this morning we passed the new cottage that Father has just built for his bailiff and you said, 'Only when every peasant has a decent place like that to live in, only then will Russia be close to perfection. And it's our responsibility to bring that about.' And your face positively glowed with . . . niceness. And I thought to myself, I thought: there really is an unbridgeable chasm between Arkady and me. He thinks he loves those damned peasants. I know I hate them. But I know, too, that when the time comes I will risk everything, everything for them, and I'm not at all sure if Brother Arkady is prepared to risk anything. But of course the ironic thing is that those same damned peasants won't thank me – won't ever know of my existence. So there they'll be, all nice and cosy and smiling in their comfortable cottages and sending eggs up to

Arkady in his big house; and Bazarov will be feeding the worms in some unmarked grave in the wilderness.

Arkady I don't know what your point is.

Bazarov That life is ridiculous and he doesn't know that it is.

Arkady And your life?

Bazarov Equally ridiculous. Maybe more ridiculous. But I'm aware that it is.

Arkady I'm going out for a walk.

Bazarov To be in good shape for the revolution or for Anna Sergeyevna?

Arkady If I stay we'll fight, Bazarov.

Bazarov Then by all means stay. Let's have a fight, Arkady. A fight between us is long overdue.

Arkady (*flushed with anger*) I'm fond of you, Bazarov. But there are times when I find your arrogance very hard to take. Only Bazarov has the capacity for real sacrifice. Only Bazarov is a fully authentic revolutionary. Only Bazarov has the courage and the clarity of purpose to live outside ordinary society, without attachments, beyond the consolation of the emotions.

Bazarov Yes, I have that courage. Have you?

Arkady I'm not as cleansed as you, Bazarov. I like being with people I'm fond of. I even love some people – if you know what that means.

Bazarov What what means?

Arkady Love – loving – do you know what loving means?

Pause.

174

Bazarov Yes, I know what loving means, Arkady. I love my mother. I love her very much. And I love my father very much. I don't think there are two better people in the whole of Russia.

Arkady You don't behave like that.

Bazarov How do you expect me to behave? Kiss them? Hug them? Paw over them? You're talking like an idiot. Uncle Pavel would be proud of you.

Arkady What did you call Uncle Pavel?

Bazarov An idiot. The Tailor's Dummy is an idiot.

Arkady Bazarov, I'm warning you . . .

Bazarov It's interesting, you know, how deep-seated domestic attachments can be. Six weeks ago – a month ago you were preaching the dismantling of the whole apparatus of state, the social order, family life. But the moment I say your Uncle Pavel is an idiot, you revert to the old cultural stereotype. We're witnessing the death of a Nihilist and the birth – no, the rebirth of a very nice liberal gentleman.

> *Arkady goes rapidly and in sudden fury towards Bazarov. He is almost certainly going to strike him when the door opens and Vassily puts his head in. He speaks softly and is very embarrassed.*

Vassily There's something I – may I come in? – there's something I want to talk about to both of you. (*He comes in and closes the door behind him.*) You're sure I'm not intruding?

Arkady No, not at all.

Vassily Well. Before we eat this evening, a local priest, Father Alexei, is going to call on us. At your mother's request. She's a very devout woman, as you know,

Yevgeny. Unlike myself, as you know, too. And the purpose of his visit is to – to – to gather the family around – your mother, myself in all probability, Yevgeny if he chooses, Arkady if he chooses – you'd be most welcome – to gather us all around in one large domestic circle and – and – well, really to offer up some prayers of thanksgiving for your arrival home. A *Te Deum, Laudamus*. 'We praise Thee, Lord'. The little informal service will be held in my study – hence the new curtains. If you'd like to attend, please do. I can't tell you how grateful your mother would be if you did. But if you don't – and that's an attitude I'd respect, I certainly would – then – then – then don't. And we'll all meet for our celebratory dinner at seven. With champagne. And that's it. All right.

Bazarov Yes. I'll be at the service, Father.

Vassily (*delighted and relieved*) You will?!

Bazarov Why not. You and Mother would like me to be there.

Vassily Like you to?! We would –

Bazarov So I'll be there.

Vassily This is – this is just – just magnificent! Thank you, Yevgeny. Thank you from the bottom of my heart. You have no idea how much I appreciate that – how thrilled your mother will be!

Bazarov Not at all. (*to Arkady*) You'll join us, won't you? But if you'd prefer not to –

Arkady I'll join you of course. And sorry for losing my temper just now, Bazarov. I mean that.

Bazarov catches his hand.

Bazarov We were both a bit hasty. But I don't withdraw anything I said.

Arina enters.

Arina Vassily, are you going to help me or are you not?

Vassily Arina! Good news! Great news!

Bazarov I'm just telling Father I'd be happy to attend the *Te Deum* service, Mother.

Arina Vassily?

Vassily Yes.

Bazarov It's this evening, isn't it?

Vassily Before we eat.

Bazarov Fine. As long as it's today some time. You see I'm leaving first thing in the morning.

Arina Leaving?

Bazarov Yes. I've exams in September and I've a lot of work to catch up with.

Arina But, son, you've only just arrived.

Vassily And you can study here, can't you? Amn't I right, my pet? My study is –

Bazarov My books are all at Arkady's home. I'll work there – if they will allow me. If they don't, I'll go back to Petersburg. But I'll come and see you for a night or two before next term begins. That's a solemn promise. Well. What time do you expect Father Alexei to arrive? When do we all sing the *Te Deum* together?

Quick black.

Act Two

SCENE ONE

Late August. Just before noon. Scene as in Act One.

Anna Sergeyevna and Nikolai have spent the morning looking at accounts and touring the Kirsanov estate. They have just returned. She is alone on stage, sitting at a table, examining estate maps and accounts with a quick and efficient eye. Bazarov enters. He is looking for Anna but when he sees her he pretends to be surprised. He is very tense.

Bazarov Ah. So you're back.

Anna Yes.

Bazarov The grand tour's over?

Anna Yes.

Bazarov It didn't take you long.

Anna A few hours.

Bazarov Nice day for it.

Anna Lovely.

Bazarov Beautiful. (*Pause.*) I think I left a book out here somewhere . . . (*He looks around.*) Probably in the living-room.

Anna (*just as he is about to exit*) How are the studies going?

Bazarov Well. No, not well.

Anna When do the exams begin?

Bazarov Early September. I didn't hear you come back.

Anna Oh, we're back about half an hour.

Bazarov Really?

Anna Yes. Maybe an hour.

Bazarov I didn't hear you. Well, you couldn't have chosen a better day.

Anna Lovely.

Bazarov Beautiful. (*Pause. Then he moves beside her and speaks softly and with intensity.*) We've got to have a talk before you leave, Anna. Last Wednesday in your house you said something I've thought a lot about –

> *He breaks off because Nikolai enters with another bundle of estate maps.*

Nikolai Leave a thing out of your hand for five minutes in this house and somebody's sure to lift it. D'you know where they were? In the pantry! Maps in the pantry! Bats in the belfry! Ha-ha! (*seeing Bazarov*) Do you know where Arkady is, Yevgeny?

Bazarov Yes; he's gone for a swim with Katya.

Nikolai I'm glad Master Arkady's enjoying himself. He ought to have been with Anna and me all morning. This is all going to be his one day and the sooner he masters the very complicated business of running an estate – (*He drops one of the maps. Picks it up quickly.*) – firmly and efficiently, the better. Now let's organize our lives.

> *He sits at the table beside Anna. Bazarov goes off. Anna watches him go.*

We had got the length of (*map*) number four. Where's five? – five? – five? – here we are. (*He spreads the fifth map across the table.*) Now. That's where we crossed the river. And somewhere about here – yes, there it is – that's the old well. Remember? – I pointed it out to you. (*aware that Anna is not listening*) Are you sure you're not exhausted?

Anna Not a bit.

Nikolai Some tea? Coffee? Perhaps a glass of –?

Anna I'm quite fresh. (*concentrating fully*) Let's carry on.

Nikolai This is a tremendous help to me, Anna. I can't tell you how grateful I am. Now. We drove along that road there and that's the area that is under wheat. The estate manager's cottage would be about here; Adam's house.

Anna And that's where the new threshing machine is sunk in the quagmire.

Nikolai Yes.

Anna But that's clearly marked as a swamp ground.

Nikolai Yes, it is, isn't it?

Anna Why didn't Adam take all the heavy machinery in from the far side?

Nikolai I suppose he just – just took the short-cut.

Anna But he must have known he couldn't get across that swamp.

Nikolai Do you think I should abandon it – the thresher?

Anna When your tenants have finished stripping it there won't be much of a thresher left.

Nikolai That means I've lost the entire wheat crop.

Anna Where's the map of the land east of the river?

Nikolai Here we are. These buildings are my new cheese and yogurt plant. I'm afraid I spent a great deal of money on those buildings. It hasn't been exactly an unqualified success, that plant.

Anna Did you sell any cheese at all last year?

Nikolai Not a lot. Very little. None.

Anna Yogurt?

Nikolai A few cases. But the cheese didn't go to loss. The poorer peasants were very grateful for it when –

Anna What map is that?

Nikolai The stables – paddock – the area behind the house here –

Anna No, don't open it. I know that area.

She checks some detail in an account book. He waits. Pause.

Nikolai The Kirsanov estate; all five thousand acres of it. A bit of a mess, isn't it? What do you advise?

Anna Right. We're now in the last week of August. What I'll do is this. My crops are ready for harvesting. With a bit of organization I may be able to begin next Monday. That means that in two weeks' time all my machinery will be available. It will take – say – two days to transport it over here. So you must be ready to start the moment it arrives otherwise your wheat and corn and oats will have become too heavy and the thresher won't lift them.

Nikolai But I can't possibly –

Anna I want to have another look at your cheese and yogurt accounts for the past year.

Nikolai Of course. Piotr! Piotr!

Anna No, no; not now. Later. But from the quick look I had this morning it seems to me that the best thing you can do at this stage is cut your losses and close the dairy plant down.

Nikolai My new plant? But it's only –

Anna I know you've spent a lot of money on the buildings but I think you can use them more profitably to store your wheat and oats and hay. You need more storage space anyway.

Nikolai You're right.

Anna And finally you've got to sack that estate manager – what's his name? – Adam.

Nikolai Sack my Adam?! Oh Anna, I'm afraid that's something I just couldn't –

Anna At best he's incompetent. And I suspect he may be corrupt. According to these records fifty foals were born last year and yet I counted only twelve yearlings this morning in the paddock.

Nikolai There's an explanation for that. Apparently last winter wolves got into the enclosure and –

Anna That's his story. I've talked to Prokofyich. He says there have been no wolves around here for almost twenty years. You cannot run an estate this size unless you have a manager who is both competent and trustworthy.

Piotr enters, as usual breathless with haste and a bogus eagerness to serve.

Piotr You wanted me, sir?

Nikolai Yes, Piotr?

Piotr You called me, sir.

Nikolai I did?

Piotr No question about it, sir. I heard you myself.

Nikolai I'm sure I did, Piotr. And I'm sure you pretended you didn't. (*to Anna*) Piotr's hearing is erratic.

Piotr That's unfair, sir. With the deepest respect, sir, that's a bit unfair.

Nikolai I apologize, Piotr. Your hearing is perfect.

Piotr I was carrying logs into the kitchen, sir. The moment I heard you I dropped everything.

Nikolai Very well, Piotr. I'm sure you did. Anyhow, I don't want you now. Here – take all this stuff with you. You know where to leave it.

Piotr I certainly do, sir. Leave it to Piotr, the man in the gap. (*He takes the maps and account books and exits.*)

Nikolai The man in the gap! I don't know where he gets these expressions. Well. That's a splendid morning's work. Thank you again.

Anna I hope it's some help.

Nikolai I really feel ashamed of – of – of my stewardship. I'm not trying to make excuses for myself but the whole place fell into my lap the year I graduated. I was the same age as Arkady is now. I knew nothing at all about the land . . . Anyhow. Invaluable. I do mean that. (*to Bazarov who has entered as before*) Ah, Yevgeny, taking a break from the books, eh? (*to Anna*) I keep telling him – he studies too much. Excellent. Splendid. I must tell Pavel about my plans. (*to Bazarov*) Anna Sergeyevna has clarified my thinking wonderfully. I'm going to close down the cheese and yogurt plant and I'm going to get rid of Adam, the estate manager. He is neither competent nor trustworthy. I'll be back shortly.

He goes off. Bazarov is as awkward and ill at ease as before. Pause.

Anna I don't think I clarified his thinking at all. (*Pause.*)
He sounds full of purpose now but I wouldn't be
surprised if some of the resolution is gone before he talks
to Pavel. (*Pause.*) He thinks that his responsibilities ended
when he gave the estate to the peasants to farm.

Bazarov I want to talk to you about a conversation you
and I had last Wednesday at your house.

Anna Last Wednesday?

Bazarov It was just before dinner. We were sitting
together in the conservatory. Somebody was playing a
guitar in the distance. Katya's pup was lying between us
and there was a circle of moisture where his nose rested
on the tiled floor. You said I should offer him my handkerchief and I laughed very heartily because it sounded
very, very funny . . . at that moment.

> *Dunyasha appears briefly to do some housekeeping and
> exits immediately.*

Anna For no reason at all that maid annoys me intensely.

Bazarov You were wearing a pale blue dress with a white
collar and white lace cuffs. Anyhow Katya and Arkady
joined us at that point when I was just about to explain
what I had meant a short time before when I had said that
it seemed to me that we both appeared to act on the
assumption that we talked to one another across some
very wide chasm that seemed to separate us even though
neither of us knew why that chasm was there, if indeed it
was there; but because it seemed to both of us that it was,
we behaved towards one another with a certain kind of
formality that was more appropriate to people who had
only just met . . . Probably none of this makes much sense
to you. You probably don't remember any of it – do you?

Anna Yes, I do.

Bazarov Do you?

Anna Bits . . . fragments . . . more your intensity than
what you said . . .

Bazarov It was a conversation of some importance to me
and I'd just like to summarize it briefly – very briefly – if I
may, and to say what I intended to say then if Katya and
Arkady hadn't joined us and interrupted us . . . me . . .

Anna Katya and Arkady are having a long swim, aren't
they?

Bazarov We were talking about relationships. We were
talking about happiness. You said that for you happiness
always seemed to be just that one step beyond your
reach but that you still believed that some day you
would grasp it.

You said we had a lot in common; that you had been
poor, too, and that you had been ambitious.

You asked me what would become of me. I said I
would probably end up a country doctor somewhere in
the back of beyond and you said I didn't believe that for
a minute but that I wasn't prepared to tell you what I
really thought.

You said you believed you could talk truthfully and
openly about how you felt about things. I said I couldn't
do that. You asked me why not. I said I always found it
difficult to express exactly how I felt but that when I was
with you I found it – found it even more difficult.

And that's how the issue of a chasm between us came
up. And how that chasm inhibited us – well, inhibited me.
Because at the point when Katya and Arkady joined us, I
was about to say that that chasm had prevented me from
saying to you what I have wanted to say to you for weeks,
what I have wanted to say to you ever since that very first
day when we met here away back last May just after I
had come from Petersburg – that I'm mad about you,

Anna Sergeyevna, hopelessly, insanely, passionately, extravagantly, madly in love with you.

Anna Oh Yevgeny, Yevgeny –

Bazarov Yes, I am, I am. You know I am. I can't eat. I can't sleep. I can't study. I'm obsessed with you. I'm besotted by you. Let me kiss you, Anna. Please. Please let me kiss you.

He takes her in his arms and kisses her. She does not free herself immediately. Then suddenly she pushes him away roughly.

Anna Yevgeny! Please! Oh, my God! You shouldn't have done that.

Bazarov Yes-yes-yes.

Anna No, you shouldn't. You've misunderstood the whole situation. You've misread the whole thing.

Bazarov No, I haven't, Anna. And you wanted me to kiss you. Admit that.

Anna Yes, you have, Yevgeny. Oh, yes, you have. Misread it totally. Oh, my God . . . (*She rushes into the house.*)

Bazarov Anna –! Anna, please –!

But she is gone. He is distraught. He does not know whether to run after her or to run away. Then he hears Katya and Arkady approach – they are laughing and calling to one another. He cannot escape that way. The only other hiding place is the gazebo. He rushes to it, sits down, pulls a book from his pocket, opens it at random and pretends to be immersed in it.

Arkady (*off*) Give that shoe back to me!

Katya (*off*) I will not!

186

Arkady (*off*) Katya, I'm warning you.

Katya (*off*) Come and get it yourself. (*She runs on laughing; her hair wet, her towel flying, his shoe in her hand.*) Oh, my God! (*She looks round frantically for somewhere to hide the shoe. She sees Bazarov in the gazebo.*) I've got his shoe! He's going mad! Can I hide it here?

Arkady (*off*) Katya! Katya?

She approaches Bazarov and realizes at once that something is amiss. Pause.

Katya (*quietly, seriously*) Yevgeny? Are you all right, Yevgeny?

Arkady (*off*) Katya! Where are you?

She gazes at him, hunched, tense, behind his book. She reaches out to touch him.

Katya Yevgeny?

Arkady You're for it, madam – I'm telling you!

Arkady is just outside. She withdraws her hand and runs out of the gazebo.

Katya I've hidden it in the gazebo, Arkady!

She runs into the living-room and hides behind a door. Arkady enters, limping; a limp similar to his father's.

Arkady I'm warning you, girl! You've crippled me – that's what you've done! (*to himself*) The gazebo . . . (*He goes to the gazebo and searches it. As he does:*) Was Katya here, Bazarov? Where did she hide my shoe? I'm going to kill that girl!

Katya (*appearing on the veranda*) Cold, Arkady. Very cold. Getting colder, much colder.

Arkady Come on, Katya! Where is it? Where is it? My feet are wrecked with bloody thorns!

Katya (*holding up a shoe*) This isn't yours, is it?

She laughs and disappears into the living-room. He runs/hops after her. As he does:

Arkady You told me lies! You misled me! Just you wait there, madam! I'm going to twist your neck! Katya! Katya! Wait there! Wait!

He disappears into the living-room. Their laughter dies away. Bazarov closes his book. He sits with his eyes shut tight, his shoulders tensed and hunched, his whole body rigid and anguished. Fenichka enters carrying a large bunch of roses she has just cut. Just before she enters the house she glances over at the gazebo, thinks she sees somebody, looks again and recognizes Bazarov. She approaches slowly and studies him for a few seconds before she speaks to him. She speaks softly.

Fenichka Yevgeny, is there something wrong?

He opens his eyes suddenly. He is startled.

Bazarov Hello? – yes? – yes?

Fenichka Are you all right, Yevgeny? Is something the matter?

He flashes a smile at her and speaks with excessive enthusiasm, almost in panic.

Bazarov Fenichka! It's you! How are you? I'm glad to see you – I'm delighted to see you! Yes, yes, I'm fine, I'm fine, I'm really fine, Fenichka. I mean that – I really do – honestly. It's all over and I'm still alive. In fact I'm perfectly well. But how are you? I haven't seen you for days and days and I've missed you. Where have you been hiding?

Fenichka You're the one who has been hiding – upstairs reading those books of yours.

Bazarov Sit down beside me. Talk to me.

She sits beside him.

Fenichka What about?

Bazarov It doesn't matter. About chasms and relationships and happiness – about your healing presence in this disturbed house – about those tranquil roses. They're beautiful roses.

Sound of Nikolai playing the cello in the distance: Beethoven's Romance *for violin and orchestra in G-major, Op. 40.*

Fenichka They're past their best. But Nikolai likes to have flowers on the dining-room table.

Bazarov Nikolai is blessed. That's a strange word for me to use – blessed. Six months ago I would have said the word had no meaning. But it has – it describes the condition of someone, anyone, to whom the beautiful Fenichka turns her open face and on whom she smiles. Yes, I have missed you. It's not that we ever talk – this is probably the first time we've ever been alone together – but I'm always aware of your presence in the house, even when you're not there. I think it's because you generate goodness. That's another strange word for me. And suddenly it has meaning, too. You're equipping me with a new vocabulary, Fenichka!

Fenichka Will you stop talking like that, Yevgeny! I don't understand a word you're saying!

Bazarov Are you happy, Fenichka? I hope you are. Are you?

He takes her hand in his. Pavel enters from the living-

*room. He is engrossed in a book. He pauses on the
veranda and then moves slowly downstage.*

Fenichka I don't think about things like that.

Bazarov Then you are.

Fenichka I'm young. I have my health. I have Mitya.

Bazarov And you have Nikolai.

She withdraws her hand.

Fenichka Nikolai is a kind man.

Bazarov Yes, he is. Do you love him?

Fenichka Do you remember those drops you gave me
for Mitya? Three days ago – remember? – he was
vomiting – you thought he had eaten something. Well,
they worked miracles. He was as right as rain in a
couple of hours.

Bazarov I'm glad of that. So now you must pay me.

Fenichka is unsure and embarrassed.

Fenichka I –?

Bazarov Doctors have to be paid, don't they? Doctors are
notoriously greedy people, aren't they?

Fenichka You're right, Yevgeny. I'm sorry. I'll speak to
Nikolai today and he'll –

Bazarov No, no, no, no, no, no, Fenichka. I don't want
money. It's not mere money I want. I want something
personal – from you.

Fenichka What is that?

Bazarov Guess.

Fenichka I'm no good at guessing, Yevgeny.

Bazarov All right. I'll tell you what I want from you. I want . . . one of those roses.

The cello music stops.
She laughs with relief. He laughs with her.

Fenichka What colour would you like, sir?

Bazarov A red one. A small red one, Fenichka Fedosya.

Fenichka There you are, Yevgeny Vassilyich – one small red rose.

Between them they drop it. Together they stoop down to pick it up. Their hands meet on the ground. They laugh briefly and then stop. They look at one another. He kisses her on the lips. Pavel is now downstage and happens to look across at them at the moment they kiss. Fenichka looks over Bazarov's shoulder and sees Pavel watching.

Pavel So this is how Nihilists betray hospitality.

Fenichka (*jumping to her feet and moving towards Pavel*) There is nothing, Pavel Petrovich – I swear before God – there is nothing at all – (*She rushes off.*)

Bazarov Fenichka, your flowers – (*He begins to pick them up.*)

Pavel What are your views on duelling, Monsieur Bazarov?

Bazarov Sorry?

Pavel I said what are your views on duelling?

Bazarov I have no 'views' on duelling.

Pavel Would you accept that it is a method by which gentlemen can settle their differences?

Bazarov I think it's just another method of killing – or being killed.

Pavel But if you were insulted you would demand satisfaction?

Bazarov I don't know. Maybe. I suppose so.

Pavel Excellent.

Bazarov has now gathered the scattered flowers and for the first time faces Pavel.

Bazarov What's all this about?

Pavel I wish to fight you.

Bazarov now realizes that Pavel is deadly serious.

Bazarov A duel? You want to fight a duel with me?!

Pavel Tomorrow morning at six.

Bazarov You're not serious!

Pavel Behind the birch plantation.

Bazarov But – but – but why would you want to fight with me?

Pavel It is sufficient for you to know that I despise you – indeed, I detest you.

Bazarov But that's no reason to *fight*, Pavel Petrovich!

Pavel raises his walking-stick as if to strike Bazarov.

Pavel If you wish I'll give you a more immediate reason.

Bazarov You're serious! Good God, the man's serious!

Pavel We will use pistols at a distance of ten paces.

Bazarov I can't shoot.

Pavel Every gentleman can shoot.

Bazarov I haven't got a pistol.

Pavel We will use my pistols.

Bazarov I'm not taking part in this, Pavel.

Pavel We will dispense with seconds. I'll get Piotr to act as witness.

Bazarov Why are you doing this? What is this all –?

Pavel Nobody else need be involved. Tomorrow morning at six, then.

Bazarov Good God Almighty! What in Christ's name is the – (*He stops suddenly because he suddenly knows the reason for the challenge.*) You're jealous, Pavel Petrovich! You saw me kissing Fenichka and you thought –

Pavel Behind the birch plantation. Be there. (*He moves away.*)

Nikolai appears on the veranda. Neither Pavel nor Bazarov sees him nor hears him.

Nikolai Ah, Pavel. We should both go and have a word with –

Bazarov That's it! Of course! You're jealous, Pavel Petrovich! You're jealous because you're in love with Fenichka! Oh, my God! (*remembering his duel*) Oh, my God . . .

Nikolai retreats into the living-room. Bazarov drops into a seat.

SCENE TWO

The following morning.
Dunyasha is gathering up dishes that are on a table downstage left close to the gazebo. She has only recently stopped crying – her face is red and she is snivelling.

Prokofyich enters from the living-room. He is carrying a case which he leaves upstage left. When Dunyasha sees the case she sobs again.

Prokofyich Get a move on, Dunyasha. Don't spend all morning picking up a few dishes.

Dunyasha (*sotto voce*) Shut up, you old get.

Prokofyich I'm talking to you, miss.

Dunyasha (*sotto voce*) Bugger off.

Prokofyich The guest room is empty – at last. Change the sheets and the pillowcases and sweep the place out thoroughly.

Dunyasha Have I your permission to finish this job first, Prokofyich, sir?

Prokofyich We'll do without your lip, missy. Then take the mattress and the floor mats and leave them out in the sun for the rest of the day. Maybe they should be fumigated. (*to Piotr who has entered with another case*) Come on, boy! Move! Move! Move! The sooner this house gets back to normal the better.

Prokofyich goes back into the house. Piotr leaves his case beside the first and goes downstage to join Dunyasha. All the assurance, all the perkiness is gone. He is thoroughly wretched. He has to tell his story to somebody. Dunyasha does not want to listen – she has her own grief. He holds out his hands. They are trembling.

Piotr Look, Dunyasha – look – look – I can't stop them – look. And my whole body feels as if it's trembling, too. Give me your hand – put it there (*his heart*) – it's galloping like a bloody horse; and about every ten minutes or so it stops – dead.

She ignores him and continues working and snivelling.

194

Dunyasha Get out of my road, will you!

Piotr What – what – what's that?

Dunyasha You're in my way, Piotr!

Piotr (*almost in tears*) I don't hear a word you're saying, Dunyasha. As true as God's above. I'm as deaf as a post.

Dunyasha So you've told me.

Piotr What happened was this –

Dunyasha I don't want to hear about it.

Piotr Yevgeny was about there and I was about here and the Tailor's Dummy was about there – (*His hands tremble.*) – look! – didn't I tell you – there! – there! – there! God, the sight of this is going to break my mammy's heart. Anyway, Yevgeny and the Tailor's Dummy had their backs to one another; and just when they were about to turn to face each other, Yevgeny called me to him and he whispered, 'How do you cock a gun, Piotr?' and the sweat's standing out on his forehead and he's holding the gun like this and his eyes are half-shut and he's facing the other way. 'How do you cock a gun?' – for Christ's sake! And I'm standing as close to him as I am to you now and I reach over to pull the hammer back and he sort of turns towards me and whatever messing we're both at, suddenly, suddenly there's this huge explosion right beside my cheek –

Prokofyich (*on the veranda*) Piotr!

Piotr – and I thought, my God, I thought, he's blown my head off –

Dunyasha You're wanted, Piotr.

Piotr – because I fell to the ground and I could hear nothing and see nothing and feel nothing. And then the smoke cleared and there, lying across a fallen birch tree, there's –

Prokofyich has come up behind Piotr and now grips him by the arm.

Prokofyich Are you a guest here, boy?

Piotr What's that, Prokofyich? I think my drums are ruptured.

Prokofyich (*very loudly into his face*) Can you hear me now, Piotr?

Piotr Shouting's no help, Prokofyich.

Prokofyich If you don't get back to work at once – at once! – I'll rupture your head, Piotr. Harness the carriage. Bring it round to the back. Now!

He pushes Piotr roughly. Piotr goes off left. Prokofyich now turns to Dunyasha. She is wiping the surface of the table.

That's all right. Leave it now. No need to make a meal of it. Get upstairs and clean out that guest-room.

As he is about to go off left:

Dunyasha I'm thinking of leaving, Prokofyich.

Prokofyich (*without hesitation*) Don't think about it, miss. Just leave.

Dunyasha Well, if I do, I won't do it just because you would want me to do it. If I do it, I'll do it because I want to . . .

But he has already gone. She wipes her nose, lifts her tray and goes towards the house.

Just as she approaches the veranda steps, Arkady and Pavel and Nikolai come out of the living-room. Pavel is very pale and his arm is in a sling.

Arkady comes first, walking backwards. Nikolai holds Pavel's 'good' arm even though Pavel has a walking-stick. Arkady and Nikolai fuss over him as if he were very ill. He is barely able to keep his temper.

Arkady Careful, Uncle Pavel, careful.

Nikolai Watch that step.

Arkady Take it slowly. There's no rush.

Nikolai (*to Dunyasha*) Watch, girl. Out of the way.

Arkady Get a cushion, Dunyasha. Two cushions.

She goes into the house.

Nikolai Let me take that stick, Pavel, and you can hold on to my arm.

Arkady (*preparing a seat*) Here we are, Uncle Pavel.

Nikolai Turn it round. He doesn't like the direct sun. Splendid. Now get something for his feet.

Pavel (*groaning*) Oh, my God . . .

Nikolai (*misunderstanding the groan*) I know you're in pain. Hang on for another second. That's it now, Pavel – here we are. Sink back into that – gently – gently – that's it – lovely. Can you lean forward a little? (*He slips a cushion behind Pavel.*) Excellent.

At the same time Arkady puts the second cushion, which Dunyasha has brought, on a stool and slips the stool under Pavel's feet.

Thank you, Arkady. Now we're more comfortable, aren't we?

Dunyasha leaves.

Arkady Should I get a lower stool?

Nikolai I think that's about right. (*to Pavel*) That bandage isn't too tight, is it?

Arkady He lost a lot of blood, you know.

Nikolai As long as the fingers are free to –

Pavel (*almost a shout*) Please! (*now softly and controlled*) S'il vous plaît. I got a superficial cut. I lost a few drops of blood. I am properly bandaged. I am in no pain.

Nikolai Pavel, you have been through a shocking –

Pavel I am perfectly well and perfectly comfortable, thank you very much, and I would be very grateful if both of you would leave me alone now. There's a green-backed book sitting on the couch in the conservatory, Arkady. Would you bring it to me?

    Arkady goes into the house. Pause.

I owe you an apology, Nikolai. I am sorry to have caused all this . . . upset. I apologize. I won't mention it again. (*Pause. He puts perfume on his hands.*) If anybody's going into town today, I'd be grateful if they'd get me some eau-de-Cologne. (*Pause.*) I overhead young Katya talking to her sister yesterday afternoon. She referred to me as 'beau-de-Cologne'. Not bad, I thought. I like that little lady. Spirited. (*Pause.*) And I understand Bazarov is leaving us.

Nikolai Why did you have the duel with him, Pavel?

Pavel It was my fault entirely.

Nikolai What did you fight about?

Pavel We had a political disagreement.

Nikolai What about?

Pavel I don't wish to discuss it further, Nikolai.

Nikolai I would like you to tell me exactly what the disagreement was about, Pavel.

Arkady returns with the book.

Arkady *The Castles of Athlin and Dunbayne* – is this it?

Pavel Set in Scotland. The wonderful Mrs Ann Ward Radcliffe. She's charming – she understands nothing.

Arkady There's something I'd like to say, Uncle Pavel. Formally. In my father's presence.

Pavel Oh dear – a manifesto.

Arkady Because I brought Bazarov to this house, I feel at least partly responsible for whatever happened this morning – I know now I shouldn't have brought him here in the first place but –

Nikolai Nonsense, Arkady. This is your home.

Arkady I'm trying to be rational and fair, Father. Our friendship was very important to me. It still is. So I want to be fair to that friendship and at the same time I don't want to judge anybody quickly or rashly. So I'm afraid I must ask you, Uncle Pavel, to tell me exactly, if you would, please, exactly what –

Pavel Exactly – exactly – exactly! Why this sudden passion for exactitude? Very well. Let's get the damned thing said once and for all. But first I want a promise from you both that what I am going to tell you will not be repeated by either of you to anybody. Do I have that assurance?

They both nod.

Arkady Of course you do.

Pavel Well. Monsieur Bazarov and I were talking about English politicians. About Sir Robert Peel, to be exact, and his family background. I said Peel's father was a wealthy land-owner. Bazarov said he was a cotton manufacturer. I've looked it up since. I was wrong. Bazarov was in the right. Not that that matters – the issue itself was trivial. But one word, as they say, borrowed another. Tempers, as they say, too, flared. In a moment of irrationality I challenged him to a duel. He was astonished – naturally. And he met me this morning merely to flatter my pathetic pride. All in all he behaved admirably. His gun went off accidentally. I fired into the air. I have acquired some respect for Monsieur Bazarov. Some modest respect. (*Pause.*) I will never mention that episode ever again. (*Pause.*) Now will somebody please tell my why Prokofyich is stumping about the house like an enraged beast?

Arkady He disliked Bazarov from the beginning. Now he believes he has a reason to hate him.

Pavel Isn't he a loyal soul? Life must be very simple for him.

Piotr enters from the left, exactly as we saw him at the beginning of the scene.

Piotr The carriage is waiting in the yard, sir.

Immediately after he makes his announcement Piotr turns and goes off left.

Nikolai Thank you, Piotr. Oh, Piotr – my straw hat's in the hall. Would you bring it to – Piotr! Piotr! My God, did you see that! He ignored me! The insolent pup ignored me! Oh-ho, Master Piotr is certainly going to go. There are going to be changes about here. I'm not going to be insulted in my own house by a servant or by anybody else.

Pavel I don't think he heard you, Nikolai.

Nikolai (*violently*) That's a damned lie! And you know

that's a damned lie! The bastard never hears me! Never! Never! I'm sick of him never hearing me! Sick to death of it! (*quickly recovering*) Forgive me . . . I'm sorry . . . That was unpardonable . . . Forgive me . . . I think I'll play the cello for a while . . . The cello, I find, is very . . . healing . . .

He goes into the house. Arkady is astonished at the outburst. Pavel has some idea why it happened.

Pavel Good Lord. What was that all about?

Arkady He never really warmed to Bazarov either.

Pavel Perhaps.

Arkady I know Bazarov likes him very much but he can't show affection easily.

Pavel What are his plans?

Arkady He intended going to Petersburg to study. But when he was packing this morning he got a message that there's a typhus epidemic in his home province; so he's going there first to help his father out.

Pavel Ah. Very worthy. I'm thinking of moving out myself.

Arkady What do you mean?

Pavel Just going away. Leaving.

Arkady Where to?

Pavel Germany. France. England. Maybe Scotland! Perhaps I should buy the castle of Dunbayne?

Arkady You don't mean leaving for good, Uncle Pavel, do you?!

Pavel We'll see. But certainly not until after the harvest is saved. They couldn't save the hay without my muscle, could they? Ah, Monsieur Bazarov. I hear you're going home?

Bazarov enters left with a book in his hand. He is dressed for travelling. He leaves his jacket beside his cases and comes down to Arkady and Pavel.

This is now a fully mature young man – neither in his clothes nor in his demeanour is there any trace of the student. His manner is brisk, efficient, almost icy.

Bazarov How is the arm?

Pavel Fine, thank you. You dressed it well.

Bazarov Take the bandage off after three days and let the fresh air at the wound.

The sound of Nikolai playing the cello: Romance *in F-Major, Op. 50.*

Pavel *Le malade n'est pas à plaindre qui a la guérison en sa manche.*

Bazarov I don't speak French.

Pavel Montaigne. It means: don't pity the sick man who –

Bazarov turns abruptly away from him.

Bazarov (*to Arkady*) I must say goodbye to your father.

He goes towards his cases. Arkady follows him, takes his arm and speaks to him quietly, privately, in an attempt to restore the old intimacy. Pavel goes off to the far side of the garden and reads.

Arkady I have a plan, Bazarov. I'll go to Petersburg at Christmas; back to the old flat; and we'll –

Bazarov No, you won't do that, Arkady. By Christmas you and Katya will probably be married.

They continue this conversation as Bazarov opens a case and puts his book into it.

Arkady Married?! Me?! For God's sake, man, we Nihilists don't believe in –

Bazarov And I'm pleased for you. She'll take you in hand and you want to be taken in hand. You're naturally complementary. And natural elements that complement one another tend to create a balanced and stable unit.

Arkady Cut that out, Bazarov! Stop addressing me, man! This is your old matey, Arkady, your old cook and bottle washer. And what I'm going to do is fix a date for a big reunion. Immediately after you finish your exam! – Mid-September! I'll go to Petersburg. We'll get a keg of beer. We'll get all the boys from the old cell together and –

Bazarov We won't be getting together again, Arkady. We both know that. We are saying goodbye now. From your point of view you're making all the sensible choices because instinctively you know you're not equipped for our harsh and bitter and lonely life.

Arkady Who the hell do you mean by 'our', Bazarov? I'm a Nihilist, too, remember?

Bazarov When you were a student. But your heart never really forsook the gentry and the public decencies and the acceptable decorum. Of course you have courage and of course you have your honest passion. But it's a gentleman's courage and a gentleman's passion. You are concerned about 'difficult issues' but you believe they are settled by rational, gentlemanly debate and if that doesn't work, by gentlemanly duels. But that's not how real change, radical change is brought about, Arkady. The world won't be remade by discussion and mock battles at dawn. As you told your uncle a long, long time ago we're long past the stage of social analysis. We are now into the era of hostilities – of scratching, hurting, biting, mauling, cutting, bruising, spitting. You're not equipped for those indecencies. When it would come to the bit you would retreat into well-bred indignation and well-bred resignation. Your upbringing has provided you with that let-out. Mine didn't. I am committed to the last, mean, savage, glorious, shaming extreme.

Arkady I see.

Bazarov To be blunt with you, Arkady: you are not good enough for us.

Arkady Was it that savage, shaming side of you that frightened Anna Sergeyevna off? I shouldn't have said that. Forgive me, Bazarov.

Bazarov responds as calmly and as coldly as before.

Bazarov No need to apologize. I may very well have frightened Anna Sergeyevna. But if that is what happened, I have no regrets. Miniature empires have no appeal to me. My sights are trained on a much, much larger territory. We had a good year together, Arkady. Thank you for that.

Arkady Bazarov, I still think we should –

He stops because Fenichka has come from the living-room and joins them. She has a package of sandwiches for Bazarov.

Fenichka So you're all set.

Bazarov Yes.

Fenichka Did someone say something about a typhus epidemic?

Bazarov My father. He like dramatic language. It's all probably a ruse to get me home.

Fenichka Well, don't take any unnecessary risks, Doctor. I made a few sandwiches for the journey. I know you like cold lamb.

Bazarov Thank you very much.

The conversation is punctuated by the awkward silences that farewells create.

Arkady Who's driving you?

Bazarov Prokofyich. He volunteered.

Fenichka You're honoured. He doesn't drive me.

Bazarov He's just making sure he's getting rid of me. (*Brief laughter. Silence.*) I must say goodbye to your father.

Arkady Yes.

Fenichka He told me he prefers playing piano duets with Katya to playing the cello by himself.

Arkady Yes, I think he enjoys the duets.

Fenichka He says Katya is as good as your mother.

Arkady Did he say that?

Dunyasha appears at the living-room door.

Dunyasha (*calling*) Fenichka.

Fenichka Yes?

Dunyasha beckons.

What is it? (*She goes to Dunyasha.*)

Arkady Dunyasha's suddenly very coy.

Dunyasha gives the bottle of milk to Fenichka. They exchange a few words. Dunyasha keeps her face averted.

Bazarov (*calling*) Goodbye, Dunyasha.

Dunyasha disappears. Fenichka returns.

Fenichka She has a very bad head-cold. This is a bottle of milk for the journey. She says to say goodbye.

Bazarov Thank her for me, will you?

Fenichka I will.

Bazarov I think she thought I wasn't sticking at the books enough: she kept bringing cups of tea up to my room.

Silence.

Arkady He's talking about going away, too. Uncle Pavel. France. Germany. Scotland, maybe!

Fenichka For a holiday?

Arkady For good, he says.

Bazarov You'll have an empty house.

Fenichka He's not serious, is he?

Arkady I think he is.

Fenichka When is he leaving?

Arkady After the harvest is in. He wants to do his share of the scything.

Fenichka Pavel?!

Arkady Yes!

Fenichka You're joking!

Arkady No, I'm not. Yes, of course I am.

Fenichka Pavel scything! Can you imagine? Shh . . .

Again the brief laughter. The cello stops. Silence. Pavel moves towards them.

Pavel Are the beautiful Katya and Anna joining us for dinner tonight?

Arkady Great! (*recovering*) Are they? That's news to me.

Pavel Am I wrong?

Fenichka It's tomorrow night.

Arkady I thought it was Sunday.

Pavel (*looking straight at Fenichka*) Ah. Then I was wrong. Yet again.

Fenichka They're coming straight here after church. That was the arrangement.

Pavel (*still looking straight at Fenichka*) My mistake. I get things wrong, Fenichka. Sorry.

Fenichka Tomorrow night.

Pavel I see. *Bon. Bon.*

Bazarov I think I should call Prokofyich.

Arkady (*holding on*) Katya has finally chosen a name for her pup, Pavel.

Pavel Pup? What pup?

Arkady The borzoi pup she got from us at the beginning of the summer! She's going to call it Pavel!

Brief laughter. Nikolai joins them.

Pavel I suppose it's one way to be remembered?

Nikolai We're all ready for departure, are we, Yevgeny? Good. Great. And Piotr's driving you, is he? Good. Excellent. (*He calls.*) Piotr!

Arkady Prokofyich's taking him, Father.

Nikolai Prokofyich? (*softly*) Much better. Much more

reliable. You should be in Petersburg well before night.

Bazarov I'm not going to Petersburg. I'm going home.

Nikolai Good. Good. Excellent in fact. I'm sure your parents will be delighted to have you. Indeed. Just as we were.

Bazarov Thank you for all your hospitality, Nikolai Petrovich.

Nikolai It was my pleasure. It was our pleasure. We'll all miss you – won't we? I'll miss all those early morning walks we had – occasionally. And Pavel will miss those – those – those stirring political discussions. And Arkady will miss the student banter. And Fenichka – Fenichka – Fenichka will miss your excellent medical advice – won't you? And –

Prokofyich appears left. Absurdly stiff-backed and formal. He stares at a point above everybody's head.

Prokofyich (*loudly*) I beg your pardon.

Nikolai What is it, Prokofyich?

Prokofyich The carriage is about to depart.

Nikolai Yes, we know, Prokofyich. Thank you.

Prokofyich I merely mention the fact in case any person wishes to travel in it. (*He lifts the cases and exits stiffly.*)

They stare after him in astonishment and amusement. A quick, stifled giggle from Fenichka. One from Arkady. Then Fenichka explodes. Then they all laugh, excessively, in relief. Bazarov only smiles. He observes the happy family group from the outside.

Nikolai Shhh! He'll hear you.

Arkady He couldn't – he couldn't even look at us!

Nikolai I know – I know –

Arkady In case any person – any person wishes to travel in it!

Fenichka It's going to be a – a – a – (*She breaks down again.*)

Pavel A what?

Fenichka Can't say it.

Nikolai Shhh!

Arkady I know what she's trying to – (*He breaks down.*)

Pavel A what?

Fenichka It's going to be a very chatty journey!

Again they explode. Then as suddenly the laughter dies. Silence.

Nikolai Oh dear – oh dear – oh dear.

Arkady It was that eye fixed on the sky.

Fenichka I know. And the shoulders back.

Nikolai Poor old Prokofyich. But we mean no harm, do we? No, no; we mean no harm at all.

Arkady About to depart. Oh, I'm sore. Very sore.

Silence. Bazarov goes to Nikolai.

Bazarov Again, thank you for everything.

Nikolai You'll come and stay with us again – perhaps.

They shake hands. Bazarov now goes to Pavel.

Bazarov (*bowing*) Pavel Petrovich.

They shake hands.

Pavel Thank you. *Adieu.*

Bazarov goes to Fenichka. He takes her hand.

Bazarov I wish you every happiness, Fenichka. Take care of yourself.

Fenichka You, too, Yevgeny.

He goes to Arkady and holds out his hand.

Bazarov Arkady.

Arkady hesitates and then impulsively embraces him.

Arkady I don't give a damn what you say! Mid-September! After the exams! That's settled! And make it two kegs. (*He releases Bazarov. He is crying.*) Come on, you twisted, perverse bastard! Clear out to hell! Move! Move!

He pushes Bazarov in front of him. They exit. Nikolai follows them, then Pavel.

He's coming, Prokofyich! Here's your passenger!

Fenichka is alone on stage. She listens to the voices off. The lines overlap.

Nikolai (*off*) Put the bags at your feet.

Arkady (*off*) Where's your jacket?

Pavel (*off*) Good luck, Yevgeny.

Bazarov (*off*) Thank you very much.

Arkady (*off*) All set?

Bazarov (*off*) I left a book somewhere.

Arkady (*off*) It's in your hand. Fool.

Bazarov (*off*) Thank you again.

Nikolai (*off*) Good luck with the exams.

Arkady (*off*) Mid-September. That's settled.

Pavel (*off*) Have a good journey.

Arkady (*off*) Give my love to your father and mother.

Bazarov (*off*) Goodbye.

Arkady (*off*) Write me, Bazarov.

Bazarov (*off*) I will.

Nikolai (*off*) Goodbye.

Pavel (*off*) Goodbye.

> *A chorus of goodbyes. Fenichka waves tentatively and says 'goodbye' quietly.*
> *Dunyasha, who has been watching from the living-room, now comes down and stands behind Fenichka. Fenichka turns and sees her. She is sobbing helplessly.*

Dunyasha All he had to do, Fenichka – all he had to do was raise his little finger and I'd have kissed his feet.

Fenichka Oh, Dunyasha –

Dunyasha Oh God, I would have, Fenichka. Just raise his little finger.

> *She throws her arms around Fenichka and sobs. Fenichka holds her.*

Fenichka Shhh. I know, Dunyasha. I know. I know.

SCENE THREE

Early September. Afternoon. The dining-room in the Bazarov home. Vassily is standing at the head of the table, always on the point of lighting his pipe. Arkady is sitting at the bottom of the table, immobile, staring at the ground. (This is not where he sat in Act One, Scene Three). He is scarcely aware that Vassily is speaking.

Vassily is smiling as fixedly as in Act One and is even more breezy and energetic. But the energy is spurious and it is soon apparent that occasionally he forgets what he is saying – hence the repetitions in his speech – and that he is on the point of breakdown.

Vassily Yes, yes, that was a memorable lunch. I recall every detail of that lunch with total clarity. Oh yes, that was one of the happiest occasions ever in this house. We'd been expecting you for so long, you see – for years, for heaven's sake! And now here you were, in this very room, around this very table. And all I can say now – and I was aware of it then, too – was that your presence alone quickened these ancient bones again. *Omnia animat, format, alit*, as Cicero says ... *omnia animat* ... That doesn't sound like Cicero, does it? ... Oh yes, that was a lunch to remember. That's the event that furnished us with the richest and warmest memories – that's not inaccurate, my pet, is it? ... (*He looks around and realizes she is not there.*) Where had she placed us? I was here. And she was there. And you were sitting where you're sitting now. And Yevgeny was over there. And I have one particularly vivid recollection. I had just told you that story of the retired major who practises medicine 'just for the good of the community'; and the two of you gazed at me for a second and then suddenly collapsed with laughter; and there you both are, spread across the table, convulsed, unable to speak! Oh, that's a particularly vivid memory. 'Just for the good of the community'. Couldn't move. Couldn't speak.

Timofeich shuffles in. He seems even more decrepit than before. He begins pottering aimlessly with the dishes on the table.

And Timofeich was looking after us as usual, weren't you, Timofeich?

Timofeich She's awake.

Vassily, suddenly alert, leads Timofeich to the side so that Arkady will not hear the conversation. Arkady is scarcely aware that Timofeich is there.

Vassily Well?

Timofeich No change.

Vassily Did she speak?

Timofeich Not a word.

Vassily Is she still in bed?

Timofeich She's in the study.

Vassily What's she doing there?

Timofeich Sitting.

Vassily On the couch?

Timofeich On the swivel chair. You should comb her hair for her. (*Timofeich returns to the table.*)

Vassily Leave that stuff, Timofeich. And stay with her, will you?

Timofeich She can't go on without food in her. You should get her to eat.

Vassily (*suddenly fearful*) Where's my medicine bag, Timofeich?

Timofeich points to a high shelf where the bag is almost hidden.

Ah! Good man. Thank you. Thank you.

Timofeich What are you thanking me for? You hid it there yourself.

Timofeich exits. Vassily assumes the smile again and the breezy manner.

Vassily He's been a tower of strength to me, old Timofeich. I don't know what I'd have done without him.

Arkady How is Arina Vlassyevna?

Vassily She'll be with us in a while. Arina Vlassyevna is – what's the cliché? – she is as comfortable as can be expected – everything considered – considering everything. But we were discussing that lunch, weren't we? Oh, that was a memorable occasion. Do you happen to remember a boy who helped at table that day? – a very young boy? – in his bare feet? – Fedka? I have a confession to make about Fedka: Fedka wasn't a servant of ours at all. We hired Fedka for that occasion. To impress you, my friend. To give Yevgeny's background that tiny bit of extra weight. *Vanitas vanitatum et omnia vanitas.* Ecclesiastes, I think. But don't trust me on that. I can still quote with some accuracy but the attribution . . . the attribution seems to . . . That lunch, yes. And Fedka. I had asked Father Alexei could he recommend somebody. And what did he present us with? – the butcher's second son with the running nose and not a shoe to his name – in a manner of speaking. Serving at the table, barefoot! Good Lord. I can laugh at it now. I remember I said, 'Arkady Nikolayevich will think he's staying with some sort of primitives.' And Yevgeny lifted his head – you know how he lifts his face and turns it slightly sideways – and gave me that sharp, quick eye of his – and he said – he said – and nobody's wittier than Yevgeny as you well know – he lifted his head and he gave me – gave me – (*He breaks down: sudden, uncontrollable sobbing. He recovers almost immediately.*) I should pray to God, they say. How can I go on? – that's what I say to God. How do you expect me to go on? – I say. What do you think we're made of? – I say.

Pause.

Arkady It was very late when I got back from Petersburg. My father was waiting up for me. 'I've got very bad news for you, son. I can't tell you how bad the news is.' 'It's Bazarov,' I said. 'Yes,' he said. 'It's Bazarov.'

Pause.

Vassily At the end of that first week there were so many people sick and dying that we decided to split up: he took the whole town and the region to the north and west. I had the south and east. Some nights he didn't get home at all. And when the epidemic spread to the neighbouring province we didn't see him for days on end. 'All for the bloody peasants,' he said to me. 'Everything for the bloody peasants, damn them!' And then I came in this night – it was Friday – amn't I correct, my pet? There was a light under his bedroom door. And I was tiptoeing past when he called me. He was sitting up in the bed, propped up against the pillow; and even though the candle was behind his head the first thing I noticed was how bright, how bright his eyes shone. And he said in that ironic tone of his, 'Father,' he said, 'I'm going to make you a present of a much larger practice. I'm going to present you with the town and the region to the north and west.' 'What does that mean?' I said. (*His voice begins to waver.*) 'It means,' he said – 'It means,' he said – 'It means that I'm considering retiring. What's your opinion of this, Dr Bazarov? Does it look like typhus?' And he pulled up the sleeve of his night-shirt and held his bare arm over to the candle and there were the purple blotches.

Arkady is now crying quietly.

Arkady I'm sorry for behaving like this . . .

Vassily There was nothing we could do. His mother made him lime-flower tea and she tried to feed him spoonfuls of beetroot and cabbage soup. But he was too weak to

swallow anything. And the next morning – that was
Sunday – amn't I right, my pet? – yes, I am – that was
Sunday – he opened his eyes and said, 'Do something for
me, Father. Send a messenger to Anna Sergeyevna Odintsov
and tell her that Yevgeny Vassilyich Bazarov is dying.'

Arkady All Katya knew was that a messenger came to the
house and that within five minutes Anna was gone.

Vassily And late that same evening a grey carriage with
red wheels and drawn by four horses drew up at our door
and a footman in dark green livery opened the carriage
door and this lady in a black veil and a black mantle got
out. She told me she was Anna Sergeyevna Odintsov and
asked to see my son. I argued with her. I said it was too
dangerous. But she was determined. So I brought her to
him. I left them together. She stayed with him for half an
hour. He was too weak to talk. She just sat with him and
held his hand.

Arkady Nobody has seen her since. She didn't go home
when she left here. She sent the carriage home and she
went on to Moscow. She probably wants to be by herself
for a while.

Vassily He passed away that same evening. His mother
sent for Father Alexei. He was dead by then but Father
Alexei gave him the last rites anyway.

Arkady My father didn't know what to do. I was
somewhere in the Petersburg area buying a new thresher –
that's all he knew. But where I was staying – how to get in
touch with me – he was at his wits' end. Finally he sent
Piotr to look for me – just to walk the streets of
Petersburg and look for me. And all the time I was in our
old flat. That never occurred to them.

Vassily We tried to get word to some friends. Timofeich
did the best he could. I thought it best to have a short

wake because of the nature of the illness and because his
mother was a little . . . *perturbata*. So we buried him on
Monday morning, early. A quiet funeral; his mother,
Father Alexei, Timofeich, myself. And Fedka, the worthy
Fedka, properly shod. It was nice of him to come. And
brave. A few prayers. Flowers. The usual. I'll take you
there if you wish. It's only a ten-minute walk. But if you
prefer not . . . some people find cemeteries . . . difficult.
There's something not right about a father burying his
son, isn't there? Some disorder in the proper ordering of
things, isn't it? It's not the way things should be, is it?

Arkady He was the best friend I ever had, Vassily Ivanyich.

Pause.

Vassily (*almost in a whisper but with a sudden and
astonishing passion*) Damn you, Almighty Father! I will
not stand for it! I certainly will not stand for it!

Arkady He was the only real friend I ever had.

Vassily What's that?

Arkady (*suddenly resolute*) I'm going to carry on his
work, Vassily Ivanyich! I'm going to dedicate myself to his
memory and to the work he was so involved in! I have
none of his brains and none of his talent. But whatever
talent I have and whatever energy I have I will give to the
revolution, to Bazarov's revolution.

Vassily (*dreamily*) Oh, yes. Politics are very important.

Arkady He never thought I was capable of much. But I
am! I am! And I am now more than ever because I'm
doing it for him!

Vassily pats him on the shoulder.

Vassily Every so often he would regain consciousness.
One time he opened his eyes and he said, 'I am no loss to

Russia. A cobbler would be a loss to Russia. A butcher would be a loss. A tailor would be a loss. I am no loss.' It never occurred to him the loss he'd be to his mother and me.

Arkady If you would take me to the cemetery, I'd like to make my solemn promise to him there.

Arina enters, her hair dishevelled, wearing slippers and an odd assortment of clothes. When she enters her face is vacant. Then she sees Vassily and she smiles. Vassily greets her with great warmth and enthusiasm. Arkady gets to his feet.

Vassily Ah – Arina! Now that's an improvement! Now you're looking really well, my pet! Do you know that you slept for almost three hours? And who's going to do the housework if my wife lies in bed and spends the day sleeping? Tell me that, my sweet and beautiful wife? And look who's here! Look who's come to see us!

She looks blankly at Arkady.

Yes! It's Arkady, my pet! It is, indeed! Arkady Nikolayevich! The very moment he heard he came straight over. He was afraid he'd have to leave without seeing you.

Arkady All I can say, Arina Vlassyevna – (*He begins to cry again.*) – all I can say is that – that – that – that I'm shattered, just shattered.

Vassily We've looked after ourselves as you can see. But what we've got to do now is get you something to eat. What can I offer you? What would tempt you? I have it! Arina Vlassyevna is partial to a cup of blackcurrant tea! The very thing!

Arkady I'll never forgive myself that I wasn't here. I was away in Petersburg. I didn't hear a thing until late last night.

218

Vassily (*breezy, busy*) One small cup of blackcurrant tea and two very tiny but very appetizing home-made biscuits – that's what this aristocratic lady requires and that is what she is going to eat. What does Cicero say? *Tantum cibi et potionis* – we should drink and eat just enough to restore our strength – no more, no less.

Arkady I can't tell you how devastated I am. I know I'll never get over it.

Arina now sits. Pause. She looks at Arkady as if she were trying to remember him, as if she were going to speak to him. Her face is placid, child-like, almost smiling. And when she sings it is the gentle, high-pitched voice of a very young girl.

Arina (*singing*) *Te Deum laudamus: te Dominum confitemur. Te aeternum Patrem omnis terra veneratur.*

As soon as she begins singing Arkady looks in alarm at Vassily. Vassily responds by putting his finger to his lips and shaking his head as if to say – Say nothing; don't interrupt. Then he sits beside his wife, puts both arms round her, and sings with her and directly to her:

Vassily and Arina *Tibi omnes Angeli, tibi Caeli et universae Potestates. Tibi Cherubim et Seraphim incessabili voce proclament: Sanctus, Sanctus, Sanctus, Dominus Deus Sabaoth.*

Slowly bring down the lights as they sing together.

SCENE FOUR

After dinner. Early October. The lawn-garden in front of the Kirsanov home.

Arkady is standing at the piano and singing 'Drink to me only'. He sight-reads the words. Katya accompanies

*him. Anna sits by herself in the living-room, listening to
the music.*

> *Pavel stands on the veranda.*

Pavel (*singing very softly*)
'But might I of Jove's nectar sup,
I would not change for thine.'

Fenichka Very nice, Pavel.

> *Pavel realizing that he has been overheard wags his
> finger in admonition. He then lapses into his own
> private thoughts. Two or three times we hear the faint
> sound of dance music played on the piano-accordion
> some distance away. These brief coincidences of the two
> sounds – the piano and the piano-accordion – produce
> an almost eerie noise.*
>
> *The Princess is sitting alone downstage right, partly
> concealed behind her unnecessary parasol, vigorously
> masticating and every so often brushing her sleeve and
> skirt.*
>
> *Prokofyich and Piotr have assembled a large trestle-
> table in the centre of the lawn. They now cover it with
> a white cloth and arrange chairs around it.*
>
> *Fenichka oversees this work with a proprietorial eye.
> She is now very much mistress of the house and fully at
> ease in Pavel's presence. Piotr, slightly intoxicated, is
> completely restored to health and cockiness and jaunty
> self-assurance. He nips down behind the gazebo on the
> pretext of getting a chair and tosses back a quick, secret
> drink from a hip-flask. He is about to pour a second
> drink when the Princess calls him.*

Princess You, boy! Come here! Come here! Come here!

> *He quickly hides his flask and does a little dance as he
> goes to her.*

Piotr Princess, can I help you?

Princess What's that noise?

Piotr That noise, Princess, is Arkady singing and Miss Katya playing the piano for –

Princess The noise! The damn noise! There – d'you hear that?

Piotr My apologies. That is the musician getting ready for tonight – the annual harvest dance. We hold it in the granary.

Princess Musician? What musician?

Piotr A piano-accordion player, Princess. He comes from the town of Orel.

Princess My brother, Josef, had the first accordion ever brought into Russia. My father lit a bonfire in the yard and burned the damn thing before the whole household. Then he whipped Josef with his own hunting crop until he apologized publicly to everybody – family and servants. Ha-ha. That ended damn accordions in our house!

Piotr I'm sure it did.

Princess Josef was black and blue for a month. Tell your friend from Orel that story. Ha-ha. Whipped him! Whipped him! Whipped him!

Piotr I'll tell him, Princess.

She withdraws. Piotr returns to his work. Pavel comes down and joins Fenichka.

Pavel I bought that song-book in London – oh, it must be twenty-five years ago. (*suddenly remembering*) I know exactly when I bought it – the day they made Arthur Wellesley foreign secretary. We were out on the town, celebrating!

Fenichka Who was that, Pavel?

Pavel Arthur? The first Duke of Wellington. Good man. Good fun. We had a lot of laughs together . . . Nice time of the day, this.

Fenichka Lovely.

Pavel Nice time of the year. Do you like October, Olga?

Princess I detest every month – for different reasons.

Pavel It's my favourite season, the autumn. I tell myself it's the one time of the year when the environment and my nature are perfectly attuned.

Princess It seems to me you tell yourself a lot of rubbish. And you'd need to be careful – the way you carry yourself – you could be mistaken for an accordion player.

Pavel I beg your pardon?

Princess You look very like one to me, with your shoulders so far back.

Pavel (to Fenichka) I didn't catch what she said. I could be a –?

Fenichka An accordion player.

Pavel Me?!

Princess They all carry their shoulders back. That's because the weight is all down the front here. Ha-ha, you could end up being whipped by mistake!

Pavel Good heavens, could I? (to Fenichka) Why do they whip accordion players?

Fenichka I don't know. Do they?

Pavel So it seems.

Fenichka (to Piotr) There's a vase of dahlias and a vase of chrysanthemums outside the pantry door. Put the dahlias here and the chrysanthemums there.

Piotr Anything the lady wishes.

Pavel Arkady has a pleasing voice. From the mother's side of the house. Maria had a sweet voice.

Fenichka (*to Piotr as he dances off*) And napkins from the linen-press. On the top shelf. (*to Pavel*) What is that song?

Pavel 'Drink to me only'.

Fenichka I never heard him singing that before.

Pavel (*speaking*)
'I sent thee late a rosy wreath,
Not so much honouring thee
As giving it a hope that there
It could not withered be . . .'

Fenichka has been counting the chairs.

Fenichka Sorry, Pavel – what was that?

Pavel Nothing. Just mumbling to myself.

Dunyasha enters left.

Fenichka I've noticed you doing that a lot recently. You're not beginning to dote, are you? There are only wine glasses here, Dunyasha. Bring out the champagne glasses, will you?

Pavel, wounded, moves away. Dunyasha is so excited she can scarcely keep her voice down. Fenichka continues moving around the table, adjusting the settings. Dunyasha follows her. Fenichka listens with interest but her manner hints that the days of confidences are over.

223

Dunyasha Brilliant news, Fenichka! Absolutely brilliant! The aunt died at half past three this morning! Can you believe it!

Fenichka Who?

Dunyasha The aunt – the old aunt – the old bitch that reared Adam!

Fenichka Oh, I'm sorry to hear –

Dunyasha He'll be able to sell her cottage. And she has left him about two hundred roubles. And he wants to get married, Fenichka.

Fenichka To you?

Dunyasha Jesus, you don't think he fancies the Tailor's Dummy, do you?!

Fenichka Dunyasha, I –

Dunyasha Of course it's to me! At five this morning – the old cow couldn't have been right stiff – he was up banging on my bedroom door: 'Little one, will you make me the happiest man in Russia?' That's what he said! Can a duck swim, says I to myself. He didn't go back to the corphouse till well after nine. Jesus, you should have seen that glossy black 'tash of his twitching! D'you know what we should do, Fenichka? – you hang on for another couple of months and we'll get married together! Wouldn't that be a howl! A double wedding! Drive the poor old Tailor's Dummy astray in the head altogether!

Fenichka I don't want you to call Pavel Petrovich by that name again, Dunyasha.

Dunyasha The Tailor's Dummy? Between ourselves, for God's sake; it's only to you and Piotr and –

Fenichka I never want to hear it again.

Dunyasha Are you –?

Fenichka Is that clearly understood? Good. I'm sorry about the old aunt. But Adam should have no regrets: he was more than attentive to her. I'll take those napkins from you, Piotr; thank you. You arranged those flowers beautifully, Dunyasha. I'm glad you're thinking of marrying him. He'll make a very reliable husband. Now – what's missing? The champagne glasses. (*to Dunyasha*) Would you get them for me?

Dunyasha stumps off.

No, the other way round, Piotr – the dahlias on this side. Don't you think so?

Piotr I'm sure you're right. The dahlias are left-handed. (*While he was out Piotr has had a few more drinks.*) What else can I do for you, Fenichka? You just tell Piotr.

Fenichka That's all for now.

Piotr Have you enough chairs?

Fenichka I think so.

Piotr What about some stools?

Fenichka They won't be needed.

Piotr Stools are a very efficient means of seating large numbers of guests in an outdoor environment, Fenichka.

Fenichka We haven't got large numbers, Piotr.

Piotr Once again you are right. Another few bottles of wine, perhaps?

Fenichka (*dismissing him*) Thank you, Piotr.

Piotr I know a poem. Would you like me to recite it?

Fenichka Not now, Piotr.

Piotr Later perhaps. I could spell chrysanthemum for you.

Fenichka That is all for the time being, Piotr.

Piotr Well, as soon as the time being is up, Piotr will be at your elbow and at your command. (*He bows formally and goes off left.*)

Fenichka The harvest party has begun early. (*She holds up an empty bottle.*) Since lunch time. (*to Anna who comes out*) Come and join us, Anna.

Anna The days are shortening already, aren't they? (*She pauses beside the Princess.*) Are you all right, Auntie?

Princess Why do you always ask that absurd question when you know the answer. No, I am not all right. There's a constant buzzing in my head. I can scarcely walk with arthritis. That meal they gave us was inedible. And I am about to be sick with the smell of cat in this damn place. (*She rises and leaves left.*) When you're ready to leave you'll find me in the paddock. There's a black filly there that needs to be broken.

Anna She gets great comfort from her misery.

Pavel I'm studying her carefully. We could have a lot in common.

Fenichka You don't have her vigour, Pavel.

Pavel I could simulate that, too, couldn't I?

Fenichka Nikolai tells me you had a good harvest.

Anna I was away for most of it. Yes, it was a good harvest. (*She gestures her indifference.*) The best I've ever had . . . It's good to hear Arkady singing.

Fenichka Yes.

Anna And Katerina tells me he's out and about again.

Fenichka He hadn't much choice. The estate's his now. He was needed on the land.

Anna They're a handsome couple.

Pavel Aren't they.

Anna A pity you'll miss the wedding, Pavel.

Fenichka The weddings, Anna.

Anna Of course.

Pavel Yes, I'm sorry about that. I'm due to arrive in Zurich that day.

Fenichka waters the plants in front of the veranda.

Any news of the epidemic? – the typhus epidemic?

Anna I'm told it's almost died out.

Pavel Has it?

Anna So I've heard.

Pavel Ah. Good.

Anna Yes.

Pavel So it's over now?

Anna Almost. Not quite.

Pavel Good. They cause great devastation, those things. But they pass – they pass.

Anna That's true.

Pavel And the world carries on.

Anna I suppose so. Yes, of course it does.

Pause.

Pavel I got to know him slightly just before he left here. I hadn't understood him at all before that. In my stupidity. He was a fine man.

Anna He was also a . . . difficult man.

Pavel He was that, too.

Anna He wanted to marry me.

Pavel I gathered that.

Anna (*crying quietly*) I should have married him, Pavel . . .

Pavel Perhaps – perhaps.

Anna Oh, yes, I should. Oh, yes. It would have been a difficult marriage but I should have married him, It's very hard to carry on when you know you've made so enormous a mistake, Pavel. How do you carry on?

Pavel I wish I could help you, Anna. I very much wish I could help you. I have no answers to anything. We all want to believe at least in the possibility of one great love. And when we cannot achieve it – because it isn't achievable – we waste our lives pursuing surrogates; at least those of us who are very foolish do.

Fenichka Soon be time to bring them inside.

Pavel And that's no life, no life at all. (*He puts his hands on Anna's shoulders.*) A kind of contentment is available, Anna: in routine, acceptance, duty.

Anna I had that life.

Pavel It has its consolations. Is that a terrible thing to say?

Anna He thought so.

Pavel I know. But it's the only threadbare wisdom I have for you. I don't believe a word of it myself.

Dunyasha enters with the glasses. She barely conceals her fury.

Dunyasha Miss, the champagne glasses, miss.

Fenichka (*very calm*) Thank you, Dunyasha. Put them on the table.

Dunyasha Is there anything else I can get you, miss?

Fenichka That will be all for now, Dunyasha.

Dunyasha Sir, what about you, sir?

Pavel Sorry?

Dunyasha Sir, can I get you anything, sir?

Pavel (*alarmed at this attention*) Me? No . . . nothing . . . nothing, thank you.

Dunyasha stumps off into the house.
     Nikolai enters from the left. He is wearing a very brightly coloured jacket – a jacket for a much younger man. Now and again bring up the sound of distant piano-accordion music.

Nikolai I've held you all up, have I?

Fenichka I thought you'd gone dancing by yourself.

Nikolai Ha-ha. Just saying a word of formal thanks and encouragement to the workers for their sterling efforts over the past weeks. (*A quick kiss and embrace for Fenichka.*) This looks splendid! Excellent! I love those dahlias.

Fenichka These are the dahlias.

Nikolai Are they? I never get them right. They're beautiful anyhow. (*to all*) Incidentally some time later on it would be greatly appreciated if we all put in a brief appearance at the dance; just to – you know – just to – to pass ourselves.

No obligation whatever to – to participate – not that some of us could . . . (*indicating his lameness*) . . . even if we wished to. I'll ask Arkady to dance with you on my behalf – just once!

Pavel You'll have to let me have one dance, too, Nikolai.

Nikolai Yes?

Pavel Of course. The brother-in-law to be. I was an excellent dancer once upon a time. (*to Fenichka*) That's agreed, then.

Nikolai Good. Good. Yes. Fine. Anyhow. Now to organize our lives. Is everybody here? (*He looks into the living-room where Katya and Arkady are talking heatedly.*) Look at those two love-birds.

Katya bangs the piano-lid shut.

Fenichka Squabbling love-birds.

Nikolai Arkady! Katya! Come out here at once! Where's the Princess?

Anna She's walking around somewhere.

Nikolai I'll go and get her.

Anna No. Leave her. She's happier by herself.

Katya and Arkady join the others.

Arkady Well – well – well – well!

Ironic clapping.

Feast your eyes on that wonderful sight!

Nikolai What's the matter?

Arkady Just look at that astonishing jacket! Where did that come from?

230

Nikolai I agree with you, Arkady. I think myself it's much too young for a man of –

Fenichka I chose it, Arkady.

Arkady Did you now?

Fenichka And I think he's very handsome in it.

Katya So he is. And it's a wonderful jacket. (*to Arkady*) We all agree.

Arkady I'm sure you do. I still think it's remarkable.

Nikolai does a mock pirouette.

Nikolai What do you think, Anna?

Anna (*in a reverie*) Sorry – sorry?

Nikolai Do you approve of it?

Anna Approve of –?

Pavel (*quickly*) We all think you're gorgeous, Nikolai. And I'm madly jealous. One Tailor's Dummy in the house is sufficient.

Nikolai Who is the Tailor's Dummy?

Pavel Didn't you know? That's what the servants call me.

Nikolai I never heard that, Pavel.

Pavel I don't mind in the least. It's not without affection, is it?

Fenichka Show them the lining, Nikolai.

Nikolai I certainly will not!

Fenichka Go on! For my sake.

With mock coyness Nikolai unbuttons the jacket and opens it to reveal an even more brilliant lining.

Applause and laughter.

Nikolai And this, of course, is the real Nikolai Petrovich.

Fenichka Feast your eyes on that!

Katya Yes – yes – yes – yes!

Arkady Ridiculous.

Fenichka And when he's tired of it, I'm going to wear it – inside out.

Nikolai Enough of this. I'm not sure you're all not taking a hand at me. Let's all gather round the table and get a glass. There's going to be no formality. And no speeches. Just an exchange of congratulations and good wishes between friends. Come over here beside me, Fenichka. Has everybody got something in his glass?

Katya (*filling her glass*) Just a second, Nikolai.

Nikolai Give me your hand, Katya. Good. Splendid. Well. The harvest is saved. It has been a good, an especially good, year. And first of all we want to thank you most warmly, Anna – don't we, Arkady? – most warmly indeed for all the tremendous help you have been to us not only in your advice and wisdom over the past months but more particularly, indeed most particularly, for your spontaneous and generous offer of your machinery – an offer, may I say –

Arkady You said no speeches.

Nikolai And there'll be none.

Arkady Good. Thank you, Anna.

Nikolai Thank you most sincerely, Anna. And if the situation is ever –

Arkady Father!

Nikolai Sorry – sorry. Thank you. We all thank Anna – don't we?

Clapping. Raising of glasses.

Fenichka Incidentally did you hear that Adam's old aunt has died?

Nikolai Somebody did mention that. When did it happen?

Fenichka Early this morning. Are you still thinking of sacking him?

Nikolai Yes. No. He worked like a Trojan this past month. But this is a matter for you, Arkady. You're master of the estate now.

Arkady I'll think about it. I'll watch him. He knows he's on probation.

Nikolai Why do you ask?

Fenichka No reason. Just wondering. Who's for more wine?

Katya Me, please. We're all going to miss you very much, Uncle Pavel.

Pavel For all of two minutes.

Arkady I think you've had enough wine, Katya.

Katya (*dismissively*) I'll make that decision. (*to Pavel*) Yes, we will. A whole lot.

Pavel (*to Katya*) Did I hear you playing 'Drink to me only'?

Katya And Arkady was singing. Weren't you?

Arkady ignores her.

Nikolai That used to be my song . . . long ago . . . Shakespeare wrote the words – did you know that?

Pavel No.

Nikolai Yes, he did.

Pavel Jonson.

Nikolai What's that, Pavel?

Pavel A contemporary of Shakespeare.

Nikolai Yes?

Pavel Ben Jonson.

Nikolai What about him?

Pavel He wrote the words.

Nikolai What words?

Pavel Ben Jonson.

Nikolai Who is this Ben Jonson, Pavel?

Pavel Nothing – nothing – just that you said that Shakespeare wrote the words of –

Arkady (*shouting*) Who cares! (*controlled*) Who cares who wrote the bloody words! Who gives a damn! Exactly four weeks ago today Bazarov died – and who cares about that? – who even remembers? Not even one of you! All you care about is stupid jackets and big harvests and stupid bloody songs! Well, I care. And I remember. And I will always remember. And in the coming years I'm going to devote my life to his beliefs and his philosophy – to our philosophy – to carrying out his revolution. That's what I'm going to do for the rest of my life. And nothing in the world – absolutely nothing – is going to stop me! (*He breaks down and cries.*)

> *There is a long, embarrassed silence. Katya pours another drink. Nikolai, unable to endure the silence, begins to hum but tails off quickly. Silence again.*

Then Fenichka goes to Nikolai and whispers in his ear.

Nikolai Sorry? What's that?

Fenichka The books.

Nikolai Books? What books? Oh the books! Of course! Piotr'll get them for me. P –

He is about to shout 'Piotr!' – and miraculously there is Piotr, now very drunk, at his elbow.

Ah. There you are, Piotr. Isn't that remarkable?

Piotr Sir.

Nikolai I didn't call you, did I?

Piotr Yes, sir, you did.

Nikolai Did I?

Piotr With great clarity. Twice. And here I am.

Nikolai Well, if you say so, Piotr. Splendid. Run up to my bedroom and on the table beside my bed you'll find two books. Bring them here to me, will you?

Pause.

Piotr C-h-r-y-s-

Nikolai Sorry? What's that?

Piotr C-h-r-y-s-a-n-t-

Nikolai What's he saying?

Piotr -r-y-s-a-n-t-m-t-m-r-s-y-

The others laugh. Prokofyich, stiff and stern, enters.

Nikolai You're not intoxicated, Piotr, are you?

Piotr I know it. I'm telling you I know it. Let me try again. C-h-r-s-y-

Prokofyich leads Piotr off left.

Prokofyich Come on, boy. You're for bed. (*to all*) Sorry about this. It won't happen again. Come on. Move, boy. (*to all*) You know you are all cordially invited to the dance later on.

Nikolai Thank you, Prokofyich. We'll go for a short time.

Prokofyich Very good. I'm sorry about this.

They exit; Piotr still trying to spell.

Katya I'll get those books, Nikolai.

Nikolai Poor old Piotr. Poor boy must be suffering terribly.

Fenichka He's been at it since lunch-time.

Pavel And it's time I went and got some packing done. I hope the wedding – no, weddings – will be a great success. I'm sure they will. (*He produces a tiny box.*) I have ordered a proper present – it's due to arrive at the end of the week. In the meantime – it's only a token. (*He hands the box to Fenichka.*)

Fenichka Thank you very much, Pavel.

Nikolai What is this?

Fenichka It's a ring. It's beautiful, Pavel, really beautiful. Thank you.

Nikolai Let me see.

Fenichka kisses Pavel on the cheek.

Pavel Make it two dances.

Nikolai Lovely, Pavel. Thank you very much. What's engraved on the stone? Is it a sphinx?

Pavel Is it? It's only a token. No value whatever.

Fenichka I don't believe that.

Nikolai Put it on.

Fenichka I love it. I'll think of you every time I wear it.

Nikolai It's a beautiful memento, Pavel.

Pavel *Magnifique!* That's two occasions I'll be recalled: whenever you wear that ring; and every time borzoi fanciers get together and Katya's damned pup is discussed. (*to Arkady*) I've ordered something for you and Katya, too. I hope you'll like it.

Arkady Thank you – from both of us.

Katya returns with two books.

Katya Here you are.

Nikolai Thank you, Katya. And these are for you, Pavel. Something to read on your journeyings.

Pavel What's this?

Nikolai Fenichka chose them. We hope you like them.

Pavel Mrs Ann Ward Radcliffe! Never! *The Romance of the Forest* and *The Mysteries of Udolpho*. Wonderful! Where did you get them? They've been out of print for years!

Fenichka Piotr hunted them out when he was in Petersburg last month.

Pavel Absolutely wonderful! You couldn't have given me greater pleasure! Darling, innocent Mrs Ann Ward Radcliffe. And the two I'm missing. Can I bear so much intellectual stimulation?

General laughter. He kisses Fenichka and then Nikolai.

Nikolai Brother – brother Pavel.

Pavel I'll carry them with me wherever I go. *Merci. Merci beaucoup.*

Nikolai (*wiping away his tears*) Now. One final toast. Yes, I'm sorry, Arkady. I'm going to make a short speech – a very short speech.

Katya I would like to hear a very long speech.

Nikolai What I just want to say is that this house, this home, is about to suffer a permanent and irreparable loss. Pavel is leaving. We will miss him terribly. And I want him to know that wherever he goes, our love will accompany him always, everywhere. But there is a silver lining to – to – to every – We do have a compensation, indeed a very substantial compensation. Fenichka Fedosya has consented to be my wife and for that – that – that benediction I am profoundly grateful. And on the same day – this day two weeks, amn't I correct? – and on this very lawn another marriage will be celebrated between Katya Sergeyevna and my son, Arkady. And by that union, too, I am profoundly gratified. Some people might think that there is something inappropriate about a father and a son getting married on the same day, some disorder in the proper ordering of things. But I know that for both of us it will be an occasion of great joy and great fulfilment. And who is to determine what is the proper ordering of things?

Bring up the accordion playing 'Drink to me only'.

Fenichka Listen, Nikolai.

Nikolai (*to Katya*) That clever musician – he picked it up from you.

They all listen for a few seconds.

That was our song, long ago. Maria and I. I sang the melody and she sang the seconds. Our party piece. Her

eyelids fluttered when she sang. Shakespeare wrote the
words – did you know that?

> *He begins to sing. Fenichka watches him with a strained
> smile. He puts his arm around her and hugs her.*

Sing!

> *She gives him an uncertain smile but does not sing.*
> *Katya moves beside Arkady. She catches his hand.*
> *She begins to sing and sings the words directly into his
> face. He does not sing.*
> *Pavel moves across to Anna who is sitting away from
> the others. He catches her hand.*

Pavel Do you sing?

Anna Occasionally. When I'm alone.

Pavel Yes. *Je comprends . . .*

Nikolai and Katya
  Drink to me only with thine eyes,
  And I will pledge with mine;
  Or leave a kiss but in the cup
  And I'll not look for wine.
  The thirst that from the soul doth rise
  Doth ask a drink divine;
  But might I of Jove's nectar sup,
  I would not change for thine.

MAKING HISTORY

for Basil and Helen

Characters

Hugh O'Neill, Earl of Tyrone
Harry Hoveden, O'Neill's private secretary
Hugh O'Donnell, Earl of Tyrconnell
Peter Lombard, Titular Bishop of Armagh and
Primate of All Ireland
Mabel, Countess, O'Neill's wife
Mary Bagenal, Mabel's sister

Act One: Before Kinsale
Scene One: O'Neill's house in Dungannon
Scene Two: The same

Act Two: After Kinsale
Scene One: The Sperrin mountains
Scene Two: Penitenzieri Palace, Rome

Making History was first performed by Field Day Theatre Company in the Guildhall, Derry, on 20 September 1988. The cast was as follows:

Hugh O'Neill Stephen Rea
Harry Hoveden Niall O'Brien
Archbishop Lombard Niall Tiobin
Hugh O'Donnell Peter Gowan
Mabel (Bagenal) O'Neill Clare Holman
Mary Bagenal Emma Dewhurst

Directed by Simon Curtis
Set design by Julian McGowan
Lighting by Rory Dempster

Act One

SCENE ONE

A large living-room in O'Neill's home in Dungannon,
County Tyrone, Ireland. Late August in 1591. The room
is spacious and scantily furnished: a large, refectory-type
table; some chairs and stools; a sideboard. No attempt at
decoration.

O'Neill moves around this comfortless room quickly
and energetically, inexpertly cutting the stems off flowers,
thrusting the flowers into various vases and then adding
water. He is not listening to Harry Hoveden who consults
and reads from various papers on the table.

O'Neill is forty-one. A private, sharp-minded man, at
this moment uncharacteristically outgoing and talkative.
He always speaks in an upper-class English accent except
on those occasions specifically scripted. Harry Hoveden,
his personal secretary, is about the same age as O'Neill.
O'Neill describes him as a man 'who has a comforting
and a soothing effect'.

Harry That takes care of Friday. Saturday you're free all
day – so far. Then on Sunday – that'll be the fourteenth –
O'Hagan's place at Tullyhogue. A big christening party.
The invitation came the day you left. I've said you'll be
there. All right? (*Pause.*) It's young Brian's first child – you
were at his wedding last year. It'll be a good day. (*Pause.*)
Hugh?

O'Neill Yes?

Harry O'Hagan's – where you were fostered.

O'Neill Tell me the name of these again.

Harry Broom.

O'Neill Broom. That's it.

Harry The Latin name is *genista*. Virgil mentions it somewhere.

O'Neill Does he really?

Harry Actually that *genista* comes from Spain.

O'Neill looks at the flowers in amazement.

O'Neill Good Lord – does it? Spanish broom – magnificent name, isn't it?

Harry Give them plenty of water.

O'Neill Magnificent colour, isn't it?

Harry A letter from the Lord Deputy –

O'Neill They really transform the room. Splendid idea of yours, Harry. Thank you.

O'Neill silently mouths the word Genista *again and then continues distributing the flowers.*

Harry A letter from the Lord Deputy 'vigorously urging you to have your eldest son attend the newly established College of the Holy and Undivided Trinity in Dublin founded by the Most Serene Queen Elizabeth'. That 'vigorously urging' sounds ominous, doesn't it?

O'Neill Sorry?

Harry Sir William Fitzwilliam wants you to send young Hugh to the new Trinity College. I'm told he's trying to get all the big Gaelic families to send their children there. He would like an early response.

O'Neill This jacket – what do you think, Harry? It's not a bit . . . excessive, is it?

Harry Excessive?

O'Neill You know . . . a little too – too strident?

Harry Strident?

O'Neill All right, damn it, too bloody young?

Harry (*looking at his papers*) It's very becoming, Hugh.

O'Neill Do you think so? Maybe I should have got it in maroon. (*He goes off to get more flowers.*)

Harry A reminder that the Annual Festival of Harpers takes place next month in Roscommon. They've changed the venue to Roosky. You're Patron of the Festival and they would be very honoured if you would open the event with a short –

> *He now sees that he is alone. He looks through his papers. Pause. O'Neill enters again with an armful of flowers.*

O'Neill *Genista*.

Harry Yes.

O'Neill Spanish broom.

Harry Really?

O'Neill They need plenty of water.

Harry A bit of trouble. O'Kane of Limavady says he can't pay his tribute until the harvest is saved but in the meantime he's sending ten firkins of butter and twenty casks of beer. As usual he's lying. It might be an idea to billet fifty extra gallowglass on him for the next quarter. That'll keep him in line. Sir Garret Moore invites you down to Mellifont Abbey for a few days' fishing on the Boyne. He says it's the best salmon season he's ever had. The Lord Chancellor'll be there. And Sir Robert

Gardener. You knew him when you were in England, didn't you?

O'Neill Who's that?

Harry Sir Robert Gardener, the Lord Chief Justice.

O'Neill Oh, that was twenty-five years ago. Haven't seen him since.

Harry Might be worth renewing that friendship now.

O'Neill (*Tyrone accent*) Just to show him I haven't reverted completely to type – would that be it?

Harry For political reasons.

O'Neill We'll see. Have the musicians arrived?

Harry Yes.

O'Neill And the rhymers and the acrobats?

Harry I've told you – everything's ready.

O'Neill And you're sure nobody has heard a whisper?

Harry I've said you were in Dublin at a meeting of the Council. Everything's in hand.

O'Neill Good. (*He continues with his flowers.*)

Harry And more trouble: the Devlins and the Quinns are at each other's throats again. The Quinns raided the Devlins' land three times last week; killed five women and two children; stole cattle and horses and burned every hayfield in sight. The Devlins remind you – once more they say – that they have the right to expect protection from their chieftain and that if Hugh O'Neill cannot offer them safety and justice under the Brehon Law, they'll have to look for protection under the new English Law. And they will, too.

O'Neill I know what I'll do, Harry.

Harry That's a squabble needs to be sorted out quickly.

O'Neill I'll make the room upstairs into our bedroom!
And I'll shift that consignment of Spanish saddles down
to the back room. They should be closer to the stables
anyway. The room upstairs faces south and there's a good
view down to the river. Yes – that's a good decision. Don't
you agree?

Harry Why not?

O'Neill Excellent. (*He returns to his flowers.*)

Harry Bad news from London. Young Essex's been
arrested and thrown in the Tower.

O'Neill stops working.

O'Neill What for?

Harry There's a list of charges. One of them is treason.

O'Neill Damn it.

Harry 'For conferring secretly with the basest and vilest
traitor that ever lived, Hugh O'Neill, in a manner most
disloyal to Her Majesty, Queen Elizabeth.'

O'Neill Damn it.

Harry He was fond of you.

O'Neill I was fond of him – despite everything.

Harry I know.

O'Neill Crazy man.

Short pause.

Harry What else is there? Hugh O'Donnell and Peter
Lombard want to see you.

O'Neill All right. Some day next week.

Harry They're here, Hugh.

O'Neill Now?!

Harry Waiting outside.

O'Neill Oh, come on, Harry! I'm scarcely in the door –

Harry O'Donnell knows you're home. And the Archbishop's been waiting here four days for you. And he has done an enormous amount of work. (*He points to a large pile of papers.*) That's only half of his file.

O'Neill Oh, my God. All right – I'll give them ten minutes and that's all.

Harry Did you know that he's begun writing a book on you?

O'Neill (*suddenly alert*) Lombard?

Harry So he told me.

O'Neill We have our own annalist.

Harry He knows that.

O'Neill What sort of book?

Harry He said something about a history – I don't know – *The Life and Times of Hugh O'Neill*, I imagine.

O'Neill He might have hold me about that.

Harry He spent all Tuesday checking dates with me.

O'Neill I don't think I like this idea at all.

Harry Maybe I got it all wrong. Ask him yourself. And this (*letter*) – you'll want to read this yourself. It arrived a few hours ago.

O'Neill What's that?

Harry From Newry.

He reaches the letter towards O'Neill. O'Neill stretches out to take it – and then withdraws his hand.

O'Neill Bagenal?

Harry Bagenal.

O'Neill Her father or her brother?

Harry Brother.

O'Neill Give me that! No, no, read it to me.

Harry 'From Sir Henry Bagenal, Queen's Marshal, Newry, to Sir Hugh O'Neill, Earl of Tyrone, Dungannon –'

O'Neill clicks his fingers impatiently.

(*reluctantly*) It's a – it's just a catalogue of accusation and personal abuse. Your first marriage was never properly dissolved. So your second marriage was ambiguous. And of course this third.

O'Neill Bastard.

Harry He's threatening to bring a charge of abduction against you.

O'Neill What's he talking about?

Harry Because she's under twenty-one.

O'Neill 'Abduction'!

Harry He's threatening to come and take her back by force.

O'Neill She's not exactly Helen of Troy, for Christ's sake! (*He regrets this instantly.*) And what's that?

Harry We got our hands on a copy of a letter he's written to the Queen: 'I am deeply humiliated and ashamed that my blood, which my father and I have often shed in repressing this rebellious race, should now be mingled with so traitorous a stock.'

O'Neill 'My blood'! Staffordshire mongrel!

Harry He's going to be troublesome, Hugh.

O'Neill No wonder our poets call them Upstarts. That's all he is – a bloody Upstart! Ignore him. He'll bluster for a few days. I'm going to see about that bedroom.

As he is about to exit, O'Donnell and Lombard enter.
O'Donnell is a very young man in his early twenties. He is impulsive, enthusiastic and generous. He has a deep affection for O'Neill. Archbishop Lombard is a contemporary of O'Neill. By profession he is a church diplomat and his manner is careful and exact. But he is also a man of humour and perception and by no means diminished by his profession. He now carries a large candelabra and an elegant birdcage.

O'Donnell I knew I heard the voice!

O'Neill Young O'Donnell!

O'Donnell How are you, man?

O'Neill Good to see you, Hugh. You're welcome.

O'Donnell Good to see you, too.

They embrace with great affection.

I haven't seen you since the horse-swimming at Lough Owel, the day you rode the –! (*He breaks off.*) Jesus, lads, what about that – eh? Is that not a sight for sore eyes!

O'Neill Do you like it?

O'Donnell I bet you that's a London job – eh?

O'Neill Of course.

O'Donnell And the smell of perfume off him!

O'Neill Peter.

Lombard How are you, Hugh?

O'Neill Welcome back to Dungannon.

Lombard Thank you.

O'Donnell My poor sister's not seven months dead and I bet you the bugger's on the prowl again! (*to Harry*) Am I right?

Harry spreads his hands.

Lombard Gifts for you, Hugh. From the Pope.

O'Neill What's all this?

Lombard A silver birdcage and a gold and silver candelabra.

O'Donnell Look at that for craftsmanship.

O'Neill Lovely. Indeed. Beautiful.

O'Donnell He sent me a present, too. Guess what I got – a papal blessing!

Lombard (*to O'Neill*) With his warmest good wishes.

O'Neill I'm not being paid off, am I?

Lombard He's solidly behind you in principle.

O'Neill He always is. But no money?

Lombard These things take time, Hugh. I've a letter from him for you too.

O'Neill (*aside to Harry*) See about that room now. (*to Lombard*) So you're just back from Rome?

Lombard Home a week last Sunday. Came via Spain. I've a lot to report.

O'Neill Good. Will you sit here, Peter?

*Harry exits. O'Donnell goes to the sideboard where
there are bottles, wine and glasses.*

Lombard (*sitting*) Thank you.

O'Donnell Can we help ourselves, Hugh?

O'Neill Of course. Sorry. Peter?

Lombard Not for me, thanks. I have copies here for
everybody.

O'Donnell Do you know that the floor in the hall out
there is going to cave in with dry rot?

Lombard This is all the recent correspondence with Spain
– our case to Philip II and his responses, including his last
reply which you haven't seen yet.

O'Donnell We had dry rot in the house at Ballyshannon
and my mother had to tear out every piece of timber in
the place.

Lombard And this is a résumé of my *Commentarius* – a
thesis I'm doing on the Irish situation. Briefly my case is
this. Because of her mismanagement England has forfeited
her right to domination over this country. The Irish
chieftains have been forced to take up arms in defence of
their religion. And because of your birth, education and
personal attributes, you are the natural leader of that
revolt. I'll go into it in detail later on.

O'Donnell Do you know what my mother did? She got
oak off those Armada wrecks lying about the coast and
replaced every floor and window in the house. It's a
terrific job. You could gallop a horse across those floors
now. You should do the same here, Hugh.

O'Neill And I hear you're writing our history, Peter?

Lombard Ah. Harry has been talking.

O'Neill Have you begun?

Lombard No, no; only checking some events and dates.

O'Neill And when your checking is done?

Lombard Then I suppose I'll try to arrange the material into a shape – eventually.

O'Neill And interpret what you've gathered?

Lombard Not interpret, Hugh. Just describe.

O'Neill Without comment?

Lombard I'll just try to tell the story of what I saw and took part in as accurately as I can.

O'Neill But you'll tell the truth?

Lombard I'm no historian, Hugh. I'm not even sure I know what the historian's function is – not to talk of his method.

O'Neill But you'll tell the truth?

Lombard If you're asking me will my story be as accurate as possible – of course it will. But are truth and falsity the proper criteria? I don't know. Maybe when the time comes my first responsibility will be to tell the best possible narrative. Isn't that what history is, a kind of story-telling?

O'Neill Is it?

Lombard Imposing a pattern on events that were mostly casual and haphazard and shaping them into a narrative that is logical and interesting. Oh, yes, I think so.

O'Neill And where does the truth come into all this?

Lombard I'm not sure that 'truth' is a primary ingredient – is that a shocking thing to say? Maybe when the time comes, imagination will be as important as information.

But one thing I will promise you: nothing will be put down on paper for years and years. History has to be made – before it's remade.

Harry returns.

Harry That's being looked after.

O'Neill Good. Now, let's make this short and brisk, shall we? What's on the agenda?

Harry Hugh has got information that the English are planning new fortifications along the –

O'Donnell Do you know what the hoors are at? They're going to build a line of forts right across the country from Dundalk over to Sligo. That'll cut us off from the south. (*He illustrates this by tearing a sheet of paper in two.*) The second stage is to build a huge fort at Derry so that you and I will be cut off from each other. (*He illustrates this by cutting the half-page into quarters.*) Then, when Donegal and Tyrone are isolated, then they plan to move in against each of us.

Harry And the Archbishop has news about help from Spain.

Lombard I have letters from both the King and –

O'Donnell But their first move is to strengthen the forts they already have: Bagenal's place at Newry; Armagh; and the Blackwater.

Lombard (*as he passes papers around*) I've spent a lot of time in Madrid recently, Hugh, and I can tell you that Europe is looking more and more to us as the ideal springboard for the Counter-Reformation.

O'Donnell And another thing I want to talk about: the shit O'Doherty up in Inishowen. Do you know what the wee get's at, Hugh? Nipping down as far as Killybegs,

stealing our sheep and shipping them off to France!
Running a bloody big export business – with my sheep!

Lombard The initial shock of the Reformation is over.
Catholic Europe is now gathering itself together for a
Counter-Reformation. And the feeling is that culturally,
geographically and with some military assistance we
could be the spearhead of that counter-attack.

O'Donnell Now I can go in today and snatch the bastard
and chop his head off. But if I do that all Inishowen's up
in arms and already I have O'Rourke of West Breffny
threatening to quarter me. (*He now joins the others at the
table.*) Did you hear what we did to O'Rourke last week?
Jesus, you'll love this, Hugh. We got word that he was
away down in Clare at a funeral. So we slipped down to
Lough Allen and took away every horse and foal he
owns! Six hundred prime animals! Jesus, he's going mad!
Because he can't come after us! Because he has no
transport! Good one, Hugh – eh?

Harry Let's begin with the Archbishop, shall we?

O'Donnell You'll help me against the shit O'Doherty,
won't you? Because if I do nothing, the bugger'll think he
has me bet.

Harry You sit there, Hugh.

O'Donnell Damn it, maybe I could poison him! The very
job! Send him a peace offering – a cask of Bordeaux
Special!

Lombard Has everybody got a copy?

O'Donnell Or better still you (*O'Neill*) send him the
Bordeaux. He'd never suspect you. I got a jar of this
deadly stuff from Genoa last week – just one drop in your
glass and – plunk!

Harry Go ahead, Peter.

Lombard Thank you. Three months –

O'Donnell All the same that jacket takes years off him.

Lombard If I may, Hugh (*O'Donnell*) –

O'Donnell You would never think he was forty-one, would you? Almost forty-two. (*offering Lombard the floor*) Peter.

Lombard Three months ago you (*O'Neill*) wrote again to Philip asking for Spanish arms and money. You have a copy – dated May 14 last.

O'Donnell I have no copy.

Harry points to a paper in front of O'Donnell.

Ah. Sorry.

Lombard The final sentence reads: 'With such aid we hope to restore the faith of the Church and to secure you a kingdom.'

O'Donnell I never agreed with that stuff about offering him a kingdom.

Lombard I have brought his reply back – the document dated August 3. 'I have been informed you are defending the Catholic cause against the English. That this is acceptable to God is proved by the signal victories you have gained –'

O'Donnell Not against the shit O'Doherty.

Lombard 'I hope you will continue to prosper and you need not doubt but I will render you any assistance you may require.' Now after all these years I think I have a very good idea how the Spanish court thinks. They have a natural sympathy and understanding of us because we share the one true faith. And they genuinely abhor England's attempt to impose the new heretical religion on us. But don't assume that that sympathy is unqualified – because it is not. Their interest in us is practical and political. I have had a series of meetings with the Duke of Lerma –

O'Donnell Whoever he is.

Lombard He determines their foreign policy. And every time he says the same thing to me. Spain will help you only if you are useful to us. And when I look at you what do I see? A small island located strategically to the west of our enemy, England. A tiny portion of that island, the area around Dublin, under English rule. A few New English families living in isolation round the country. But by far the greater portion of your island is a Gaelic domain, ruled by Gaelic chieftains. And how do they behave? Constantly at war – occasionally with the English – but always, always among themselves. And how can fragmented and warring tribes be any use to us?

O'Donnell Constantly at war? Jesus, I haven't an enemy in the world!

Lombard But what Lerma is really saying is that if we can forge ourselves into a cohesive unit, then, then we can go back to him and say: we are not fragmented; we are not warring; we are a united people; now help us. Now to return to my *Commentarius* – it's the document with the blue cover. The full title is *De Regno Hiberniae Sanctorum Insula Commentarius* –

O'Donnell I have no –

Harry points to the document in front of him.

Ah, sorry.

Lombard My thesis is this. If we are to understand the Irish situation fully we must go back more than four hundred years – to that famous October 17 when Henry II of England landed here. He had in his hand a copy of Pope Adrian the Fourth's Bull, *Laudabiliter*, making him *Dominus Hiberniae* –

O'Donnell Whatever that means.

Lombard King of Ireland. And that Bull had two consequences –

O'Neill I got married last night.

There is a long, shocked silence.

O'Donnell What?

O'Neill I got married last night.

O'Donnell You're a liar! (*to Harry*) He's a liar! (*to O'Neill*) You bugger, you never did!

O'Neill Yes.

O'Donnell God Almighty! (*to Harry*) You said he was in Dublin at a meeting of the Council.

Harry He was in Dublin.

O'Donnell Jesus God Almighty! The bloody jacket – didn't I tell you the tail was high!

Lombard You kept that very quiet, Hugh.

O'Donnell Who to, you bugger, you? I have it! – the big redhead you had here all last month – that Scotch woman – Annie McDonald!

O'Neill No.

Lombard Congratulations.

O'Neill Thank you.

O'Donnell I've got it! – Brian McSwiney's daughter – the

Fanad Whippet – what's her real name? – Cecelia! Jesus, not Cecelia!

O'Neill shakes his head.

Who then? Come on, man! Tell us!

Lombard Did you say last night?

O'Neill In fact at two o'clock this morning. We eloped . . .

O'Donnell 'We el–'! Sweet Jesus God Almighty! We eloped! (*He drums the table in his excitement.*) Lay me down and bury me decent! The hoor eloped! Yipeeeeee! (*He embraces O'Neill.*) Terrific, man! Congratulations!

Lombard Who's the new Countess, Hugh?

O'Donnell Jesus, I hope I have the same appetite for it when I'm your age!

O'Neill Neither of you knows her. She's from Newry.

O'Donnell Magennis! Siobhan Magennis!

O'Neill No. She's –

O'Donnell The other sister then – the one with the teeth – Maeve!

O'Neill I met her first only a few months ago. On her twentieth birthday.

O'Donnell She's only –?!

O'Neill Her name is Mabel.

O'Donnell (*very grand*) Mabel.

O'Neill She's one of the New English. Her grandfather came over here from Newcastle-under-Lyme in Staffordshire. He was given the Cistercian monastery and lands around Newry and Carlingford – that's what brought them over.

Pause.

O'Donnell Come on, Hugh. Quit the aul fooling. Tell us her real –

O'Neill She is Mabel Bagenal. She is the daughter of the retired Queen's Marshal. She is the sister of Sir Henry Bagenal, the present Queen's Marshal.

Silence.

Harry Anybody for more wine?

Silence.

Lombard Where did you get married?

O'Neill The Bishop of Meath married us in Drumcondra – on the outskirts of Dublin.

Lombard Which Bishop of Meath?

O'Neill Tom Jones, the Protestant Bishop. Mabel is a Protestant.

O'Donnell Hold on, Hugh – wait now – wait – wait. You can't marry into the Upstarts! And a sister of the Butcher Bagenal! Jesus, man –

O'Neill I'm going to ask her to come and meet you.

O'Donnell Keep her for a month, Hugh – like that McDonald woman – that's the very job – keep her for a month and then kick her out. Amn't I right, Harry? (*to O'Neill*) She won't mind, Hugh, honest to God. That's what she'll expect. Those New English are all half tramps. Give her some clothes and a few shillings and kick her back home to Staffordshire.

O'Neill Her home is Newry.

O'Donnell Wherever she's from. (*to Harry*) That's all she'll expect. I'm telling you.

O'Neill I'm going to ask her to join us.

O'Donnell Amn't I right, Peter?

Lombard We have all got to assess the religious and political implications of this association, Hugh.

O'Neill Marriage, Archbishop.

Lombard Will Spain think so? Will Rome?

O'Neill (*very angry, in Tyrone accent*) I think so. And this is *my* country. (*quietly, in his usual accent*) I have married a very talented, a very spirited, a very beautiful young woman. She has left her people to join me here. They will never forgive her for that. She is under this roof now, among a people she has been reared to believe are wild and barbarous. I am having a celebration tonight when I will introduce her to my people. I particularly ask you two to welcome her here. But if that is beyond you, I demand at least civility.

> *He leaves. Silence. Lombard begins gathering up his papers. Harry helps him. After a very long pause:*

O'Donnell The bugger's off his aul head! – that's all there is to it! She's turned the bugger's aul head.

Harry (*to Lombard*) Stay overnight. We can meet again tomorrow morning.

O'Donnell And he let me blather on about the English building new forts – and him jouking about the Newry fort all the time! That's a class of treachery, Harry – that's what that is!

Harry You're talking rubbish, Hugh.

O'Donnell Do you know where the Butcher Bagenal was last week? In the Finn valley. Raiding and plundering with a new troop of soldiers over from Chester – the way you'd blood young greyhounds! Slaughtered and beheaded fifteen families that were out saving hay along the river bank, men, women and children. With the result that at this moment there are over a hundred refugees in my mother's place in Donegal Town.

Harry (*to Lombard*) I'll have copies made of these.

O'Donnell I'll tell you something, Harry Hoveden: as long as he has that Upstart bitch with him, there'll be no welcome for him in Tyrconnell!

Lombard is about to leave with his papers.

Harry At least wait and meet her, Peter. For his sake.

O'Neill enters, leading Mabel by the elbow.
   Mabel is twenty, forthright, determined. Now she is very nervous. Her accent has traces of Staffordshire.

O'Neill Here we are. I want you to meet two of my friends, Mabel. Hugh O'Donnell – Sir Hugh O'Donnell – Earl of Tyrconnell. My wife, Mabel.

Mabel I'm pleased to meet you.

She holds out her hand. O'Donnell has to take it. He does not speak. Pause.

O'Neill And Dr Peter Lombard, Titular Bishop of Armagh and Primate of All Ireland.

Mabel I'm pleased to meet you.

Again she holds out her hand. After a pause Lombard takes it. He does not speak. Pause.

O'Neill We've got to keep on the right side of Peter: he's writing our history.

Lombard That seems to make you uneasy for some reason.

O'Neill Not as long as you tell the truth.

Lombard You keep insisting on this 'truth', Hugh.

O'Neill Don't you believe in the truth, Archbishop?

Lombard I don't believe that a period of history – a given space of time – my life – your life – that it contains within it one 'true' interpretation just waiting to be mined. But I do believe that it may contain within it several possible narratives: the life of Hugh O'Neill can be told in many different ways. And those ways are determined by the needs and the demands and the expectations of different people and different eras. What do they want to hear? How do they want it told? So that in a sense I'm not altogether my own man, Hugh. To an extent I simply fulfil the needs, satisfy the expectations – don't I? (*He turns away.*)

Harry You're looking rested now.

O'Neill And Harry Hoveden you know.

Mabel Oh yes. I know Harry.

Harry Do you like the flowers?

Mabel Yes, they're lovely.

O'Neill Broom.

Mabel Yes.

O'Neill Spanish broom.

Mabel Yes.

O'Neill Member of the *genista* family.

Mabel Ah. I wouldn't know that.

O'Neill Actually that's Spanish broom . . . comes from Spain. They need plenty of water.

Mabel Broom? No, they don't. They need hardly any water at all.

O'Neill looks accusingly at Harry.

O'Donnell I'll have another slug of that wine – if that's all right with you, Hugh.

O'Neill Of course. Anybody else?

Silence.

Harry Did you have a rest?

Mabel I lay down but I didn't sleep any – I was too excited. Everything's so . . . And the noise of those cows! I mean, I looked out the window and all I could see was millions of them stretching away to the hills. I mean, I never saw so many cows in one place in all my life. There must be millions of them. Cows and horses.

Harry We're moving you into the bedroom just above us. It's quieter there.

Lombard If you'll pardon me. I've some letters to write.

O'Neill The celebration begins at nine, Peter.

Lombard exits.

Harry (*taking O'Donnell's elbow*) And Hugh hasn't eaten since this morning.

O'Donnell What are you talking about? I ate only –

Harry We'll join you later.

He steers O'Donnell out in front of him. The moment they are alone O'Neill grabs Mabel from behind and buries his face in her neck and hair.

Mabel Oh, my God.

O'Neill Put your arms around me.

Mabel I'm trembling all over.

O'Neill I want you now.

Mabel 'Come and meet two friends,' you said.

O'Neill Now! – now! – now!

Mabel You should have warned me, Hugh.

O'Neill Let's go upstairs.

Mabel I'm in pieces, I am! Hugh O'Donnell and a popish priest all in a couple of minutes! Did you not see my hand? – it was shaking!

O'Neill I want to devour you.

Mabel Our Henry calls him the Butcher O'Donnell. He says he strangles young lambs with his bare hands.

O'Neill That's true.

Mabel Oh God! Are you serious?

O'Neill And eats them raw.

Mabel Oh God! – you're not serious?

O'Neill We all do that here.

Mabel Stop it, Hugh. And he speaks so funny! Why doesn't he speak like you?

O'Neill How do I speak?

Mabel 'How do I speak?' – like those Old English nobs in Dublin.

O'Neill (*Tyrone accent*) That's why you're fair dying about me.

Mabel And I met a popish priest, Hugh! That's the first

time in my life I ever even *saw* one of them! And I said,
'I'm pleased to meet you'! Oh, my God, wait till my sister
Mary hears this!

O'Neill And your brother Henry.

Mabel Our Henry would shoot me, Hugh!

O'Neill Would he?

Mabel You know he would! I shook the hand of a popish
priest!

O'Neill An archbishop.

Mabel Is that worse?

O'Neill Much worse. And look at it.

Mabel At what?

O'Neill Your hand.

She looks at her hand.

It's turning black.

Mabel It's –?! (*She suddenly realizes she has been fooled.
She gives a great whoop of laughter and punches him.*)
Oh, my God, I actually looked! You're a bastard, Hugh
O'Neill – that's what you are – a real bastard! (*She laughs
again, this time on the point of tears.*) Oh, my God, it's a
bit too much, Hugh . . . I think maybe – I think maybe
I'm going to cry – and the stupid thing is that I never ever
cry . . . All that secrecy – running away – the wedding
ceremony – all the excitement – being here – meeting
those people . . . (*now crying*) They weren't very
welcoming, Hugh – were they? I mean they couldn't even
speak to me – could they?

O'Neill Give them time.

Mabel Just when I was riding away from home I turned

round and there was my father looking out the landing window. And he smiled and waved – he had no idea I was running away. And he'll never understand why I did. He's a good man and a fair-minded man and he'll try; but it will never make sense to him. And he's going to be puzzled and hurt for the rest of his life.

O'Neill Shhhh.

Mabel I'm all right. Just a little bit confused, Hugh. Just a little bit nervous. Everything's so different here. I knew it would be strange – I knew that. But I didn't think it would be so . . . foreign. I'm only fifty miles from home but I feel very far away from everything I know.

O'Neill Give me your hand.

Mabel It's not black. I'll be all right, Hugh. Just give me time. We're a tough breed, the Upstarts.

O'Neill I have a present for you.

Mabel Yes?

O'Neill It's a new invention – a time-piece you carry around with you. It's called a watch.

Mabel A what?

O'Neill A watch. You wear it on your finger just like a ring.

Mabel Where did you get that thing?

O'Neill I had it made for you in London; specially.

Mabel Oh, Hugh –

O'Neill The only other person I know who has one is Queen Elizabeth.

Mabel It's a beautiful thing, Hugh, really beautiful.

O'Neill Elizabeth wears it on this finger.

Mabel The Queen has one! And I have the only other one! Queen Elizabeth and Countess Mabel – why not?

O'Neill Why not indeed?

Mabel It really is beautiful. Thank you. Thank you very much. (*She kisses him.*) I'm sorry, Hugh. I'll never cry like that again. That's a promise. Never again. Ever. We're a tough breed, the O'Neills.

Quick black.

SCENE TWO

Almost a year has passed. The same rooms as in Scene One, but Mabel has added to the furnishings and the room is now more comfortable and more colourful.

Mabel is sitting alone doing delicate and complicated lacework. She works in silence for some time. Then from offstage the sudden and terrifying sound of a young girl shrieking. This is followed immediately by boisterous laughter, shouting, horseplay and a rapid exchange in Irish between a young girl and a young man.

Mabel is terrified by the shriek. She drops her lacework. Her eyes are shut tight. She sits frozen in terror for a few seconds – even when it is obvious that the screaming is horseplay. Then in sudden fury she jumps to her feet and goes to the exit left. As she goes – and unseen by her – her sister Mary enters right. Mary Bagenal is slightly older than Mabel. Like Mabel there is a hint of Staffordshire in her accent. And like Mabel she is a determined young woman.

Mabel (*at exit*) Shut up out there! D'you hear me? Just shut up! If you want to behave like savages, go on back to the bogs! (*She is suddenly aware – and embarrassed – that Mary has overheard her outburst.*) Just horseplay. You would think they were killing each other, wouldn't you? And I'm wasting my breath because they don't understand a word of English. (*There is an awkward silence. Mabel picks up her lacework.*)

Mary They're getting my carriage ready. It's a long way back to Newry.

Mabel It's only fifty miles.

Mary I suppose that's all.

Mabel (*impulsively*) Stay the night, Mary.

Mary I can't.

Mabel Please. For my sake. Please.

Mary I'd like to, Mabel; you know I would but –

Mabel Just one night.

Mary If I'm not home before dark – you know our Henry – he'd be worried sick.

Mabel Let him worry about you for a change.

Mary I really can't, Mabel. Not this time. Anyhow you and I always fight after a few hours.

Mabel Do we?

Mary Well . . . sometimes.

Mabel In that case.

Mary Next time . . . maybe.

Mabel Next time.

Mary That's a promise.

Another brief burst of shrieking and horseplay off. The sisters smile uneasily at each other. Pause.

I left a box of nectarine and quince in your pantry. And a few jars of honey. Last year's, I'm afraid. If it crystallizes just dip it in warm water.

Mabel Thank you.

Pause.

Mary They have no bees here, have they?

Mabel No, we haven't.

Mary I've finally persuaded our Henry to move his hives away from the house, thank heavens. Do you remember – just beyond the vegetable garden? – where Father built the fishpond? – that's where they are now. In a semicircle round the pond.

Mabel Yes.

Mary He has over a hundred hives now.

Mabel Has he?

Mary Maybe more.

Mabel Really?

Mary We sold about four thousand pounds of honey last year. To the army mostly. They would buy all he can produce but they don't always pay him. (*Pause.*) And do you remember that bog land away to the left of the pond? Well, you wouldn't recognize that area now. We drained it and ploughed it and fenced it; and then planted a thousand trees there in four separate areas: apple and plum and damson and pear. Henry had them sent over from Kent. They're doing beautifully.

Mabel Good.

Mary They have no orchards here, have they?

Mabel No, we haven't.

Mary Mostly vegetable growing, is it?

Mabel We go in for pastoral farming – not husbandry; cattle, sheep, horses. We have two hundred thousand head of cattle here at the moment – as you have heard. Did you say something about a herb garden?

Mary Oh, that's a great success. That little square where we used to have the see-saw – do you remember that patch outside the kitchen window?

Mabel I'm not gone a year, Mary.

Mary Sorry. I've brought you some seeds. (*She produces envelopes from her bag.*) I've labelled them for you. (*She reads:*) Fennel. Lovage. Tarragon. Dill. Coriander. Borage. I had tansy, too, but I'm afraid it died on me. Do you remember every Easter we used to make tansy pudding and leave it – sorry. Don't plant the fennel near the dill or the two will cross-fertilize.

Mabel Is that bad?

Mary You'll end up with a seed that's neither one thing or the other. Borage likes the sun but it will survive wherever you plant it – it's very tough. I should have some valerian seeds later in the year. I'll send you some. Are you still a bad sleeper?

Mabel Was father conscious at the end?

Mary Father? Conscious? You should have heard him! Leaving personal messages for everybody –

Mabel Messages?

Mary And detailed instructions about everything. The west door of the fort needs new hinges. The last

275

consignment of muskets has defective hammers. Never
depend totally on London because they don't really
understand the difficult job we're doing over here.

Mabel Personal messages?

Mary He forgot nobody. I'm to take up book-binding if
you don't mind! Henry spends too much time at
paperwork and not enough at soldiering. Old Tom, the
gardener, should rub beeswax into his arthritic joints.
Give a new Bible to the two maids from Tandragee. Half
an hour before he died he asked what price we were
getting for our eggs! Wonderful, wasn't it?

Mabel Yes.

Mary I miss him terribly, Mabel. I know he had a hard
life but it was a very full life. You forget that almost
single-handed he tamed the whole of County Down and
County Armagh and brought order and prosperity to
them. And God blessed his great endeavours; and Dad
knew that, too. And that was a great consolation to him
at the end. (*Pause.*) To all of us. (*Pause.*) So. (*Pause.*) I miss
you so much, Mabel.

Mabel I miss you, too.

Mary I locked your bedroom door the day you left and it
hasn't been opened since. But the house seems to be
getting even bigger and emptier.

Mabel You enjoy the garden, don't you?

Mary Henry says I should get out more – meet more
people. Where am I supposed to go out to? We're
surrounded by the Irish. And every day more and more of
their hovels spring up all along the perimeter of our lands.

Mabel You visit the Freathys, don't you?

Mary They left. Months ago. Back to Cornwall.

Mabel Why?

Mary Couldn't take any more, I suppose. The nearest neighbour we have now is Patrick Barnewall of Rathfriland and that's fifteen miles away.

Mabel But think of the welcome you always get from Young Patrick! Remember the day he said to you: (*lisping*) 'Mith Mary, come down to the old millhouse with me.' God, we laughed at that for weeks. Do you remember?

Mary Yes.

Mabel It became a kind of catchphrase with us – 'Mith Mary' – do you remember?

Mary cries quietly.

Here. Come on. We'll have none of that.

Mary He was sixty-five last week, Young Patrick Barnewall.

Mabel Are you all right, Mary?

Mary He wants to marry me, Mabel. I told him I'd think about it.

Mabel Oh, Mary, you –!

Mary And I *am* thinking seriously about it.

Mabel Mary, he's an old –!

Mary I promised him I'd give him my answer next month. Our Henry thinks very highly of him.

Mabel Mary, you can't marry Patrick Barnewall.

Mary We'll see. I'm not sure yet. I think I will.

Mabel The man's an old fool, Mary! He was always a fool! He has been a joke to us all our years!

Mary He's still one of us, Mabel. And whatever about his age, he's a man of great honour. (*now formal and distant*) Once more – it's time I was going. I've left nothing behind me, have I? Did you see my new horses? Of course you did. Aren't they handsome? Henry got them from Wales for my birthday. They're very sure-footed and they have tremendous stamina. You'll give my regards to Hugh?

Mabel I don't know where he's got to. He'll be sorry to have missed you.

Mary No, he won't. The twice we met we fought bitterly. I'll try to come again, Mabel – if I get a chance. But you know how angry Henry is.

Mabel Is he still?

Mary He still talks about taking you home by force.

Mabel This is my home, Mary.

The sudden shrieking as before. Mary moves beside her and speaks with concern and passion.

Mary No, it's not. This can never be your home. Come away with me now, Mabel.

Mabel Please, Mary –

Mary Yes, I know they have their colourful rituals and their interesting customs and their own kind of law. But they are not civilized, Mabel. And you can never trust them – you must know that now – how treacherous and treasonable they are – and steeped in religious superstition.

Mabel That's enough, Mary.

Mary You talk about 'pastoral farming' – what you really mean is no farming – what you really mean is neglect of the land. And a savage people who refuse to

278

cultivate the land God gave us have no right to that land.

Mabel Stop that at once, Mary!

Mary I'm sure some of them are kind and decent and trustworthy. Of course they are. And yes – I know – Hugh is different – Hugh was educated in England. But his people are doomed in spite of their foreign friends and their popish plotting because their way of life is doomed. And they are doomed because civility is God's way, Mabel, and because superstition must yield before reason. You know in your heart what I'm saying is true.

Mabel I became a Roman Catholic six months ago.

Mary Oh God, Mabel, how could –?!

Mabel Out of loyalty to Hugh and to his people. As for civility I believe that there is a mode of life here that is at least as honourable and as cultivated as the life I've left behind. And I imagine the Cistercian monks in Newry didn't think our grandfather an agent of civilization when he routed them out of their monastery and took it over as our home.

Mary Hugh has two mistresses! – here! – now! Under this roof! Is that part of his religion?

Mabel That is part of his culture.

Mary For God's sake! Is it part of his culture that he bows and scrapes before the Lord Deputy in Dublin and promises obedience and loyalty for life – and the very next day he's plotting treason with Spain?

Mabel That is politics.

Mary 'Politics'! Listen to yourself. You're becoming slippery like them! You're beginning to talk like them, to think like them! Hugh is a traitor, Mabel – to the Queen, to her Deputy, to everything you and I were brought up to believe in. Do you know what our people call him? The Northern Lucifer – the Great Devil – Beelzebub! Hugh O'Neill is evil incarnate, Mabel! You tell me he has twenty gold and velvet suits – but I have seen him eating with his bare hands! You tell me that he speaks three or four languages and that every leader in Europe respects him – but I can tell you that –

She breaks off because O'Neill enters with Harry.

Harry The consignment of lead has arrived from England.

O'Neill Have you got the import licence?

Harry Here.

O'Neill Check the order forms against the customs papers and see that – Mary!

Mary Hello, Hugh.

O'Neill When did you arrive?

Mary A few hours ago.

O'Neill Well, this is a surprise.

Mary I'm just about to leave.

They shake hands.

O'Neill What's the hurry?

Mabel She wants to get home before dark.

Mary Hello, Harry.

Harry You're a stranger, Mary. How are you?

They shake hands.

Mary I'm well, Harry. How are you?

Harry Fine, thank you, fine.

O'Neill Well, this is unexpected.

Mabel Isn't she looking well?

O'Neill Indeed. And have the sisters had a good long gossip?

Mabel We're about talked out – aren't we?

O'Neill And how's the Queen's Marshal?

Mary Henry's well, thank you.

O'Neill Henry's well.

Mary Yes.

O'Neill Good.

Mary Yes. (*Pause.*) He's very well.

O'Neill Splendid. But disquieted, I imagine, by that little difficulty with Maguire down in Fermanagh?

Mary I don't know anything about that, Hugh.

O'Neill Of course not; naturally; affairs of state. But he does have a problem there – or at least so we've heard, Harry, haven't we?

Mary Henry doesn't discuss those things with me.

O'Neill The difficulty – as we understand it – is that London has asked Maguire to make a public profession of his loyalty and obedience – to 'come in' as they coyly phrase it, as in to come in out of the wilderness, the Gaelic wilderness, of course. Nothing more than a token gesture is asked for – the English, unlike us, never drive principles to embarrassing conclusions. For heaven's sake, I've made the gesture myself, haven't I, Harry? And I've brought young Hugh O'Donnell 'in'. And I assure you, Mary, it means nothing, nothing. And in return for that symbolic . . . courtesy London offers you formal acknowledgement and recognition of what you already are – leader of your own people! Politically quaint, isn't it?

Mary So taking a solemn oath of loyalty to Her Majesty is neither solemn nor binding to you, Hugh?

O'Neill Good heavens, no! I'm loyal today – disloyal tomorrow – you know how capricious we Gaels are. Anyhow, where was I? Yes, our friend Maguire. Maguire is having difficulty making that little courtesy. And so London gets peevish. And heated messages are exchanged. And terrible threats are made. And who gets hauled in to clean up the mess? Of course – poor old Henry! It's always the Henrys, the menials in the middle, who get the kicks, isn't it?

Mary Our Henry's well able to handle rebels like Maguire.

O'Neill 'Our Henry'? Nobody better. London couldn't have a more dutiful servant than Our Henry. As you and I know well – but as London keeps forgetting – it's the plodding Henrys of this world who are the real empire-makers. But the point I'm getting to – (*to Harry*) I'm not being indiscreet, Harry, am I? – the reason I mention the problem at all is that Maguire has thrown the head up and proclaims he'll fight to the death before a syllable of loyalty to a foreign queen will ever issue from his pure lips! I know. I know. Trapped in the old Gaelic paradigms of thought. It's so familiar – and so tedious. But then what does he do? Comes to me who has already made the token gesture, me, the 'compromised' O'Neill in his eyes, comes to me and begs me to fight beside him! Now! Look at the dilemma that places me in, Mary. You do appreciate my dilemma, don't you?

Mary I don't want to hear anything about this, Hugh.

O'Neill I try to live at peace with my fellow chieftains, with your people, with the Old English, with Dublin, with London, because I believe – I know – that the slow, sure tide of history is with me, Mary. All I have to do is . . . just sit – and – wait. And then a situation like this arises and how am I to conduct myself?

Mabel It's time Mary set off.

O'Neill Do I keep faith with my oldest friend and ally, Maguire, and indeed with the Gaelic civilization that he personifies? Or do I march alongside the forces of Her Majesty? And I've marched with them before, Mary. You didn't know that? Oh yes, I've trotted behind the Tudors on several expeditions against the native rebels. I've even fought alongside Our Henry in one little skirmish – oh, years and years ago, when you and Mabel were still playing with your dolls. Oh, yes, that's a detail our annalists in their wisdom choose to overlook, perhaps because they believe, like Peter Lombard, that art has precedence over accuracy. I'm beginning to wonder should we trust historians at all! Anyhow back to Maguire – and my dilemma. It really is a nicely balanced equation. The old dispensation – the new dispensation. My reckless, charming, laughing friend, Maguire – or Our Henry. Impulse, instinct, capricious genius, brilliant improvisation – or calculation, good order, common sense, the cold pragmatism of the Renaissance mind. Or to use a homely image that might engage you: pasture – husbandry. But of course I'm now writing a cliché history myself, amn't I? Because we both know that the conflict isn't between caricatured national types but between two deeply opposed civilizations, isn't it? We're really talking about a life-and-death conflict, aren't we? Only one will survive. You wouldn't disagree with that, would you?

Mabel Mary wants to leave, Hugh.

O'Neill No, no, it's a nice point and I would welcome
Mary's wholesome wisdom. I'll be very direct. Do I grasp
the Queen's Marshal's hand? – using Our Henry as a
symbol of the new order which every aristocratic instinct
in my body disdains but which my intelligence
comprehends and indeed grudgingly respects – because as
a boy I spent nine years in England where I was nursed at
the very wellspring of that new order – think of all those
formative years in the splendid homes of Leicester and
Sidney and indeed at the Court itself – hence the grand
accent, Mary –

Mabel Hugh, I think –

O'Neill No – allow me – or – or do I grip the hand of the
Fermanagh rebel and thereby bear public and imprudent
witness to a way of life that my blood comprehends and
indeed loves and that is as old as the Book of Ruth? My
dilemma. Help me, Mary. Which hand do I grasp?
Because either way I make an enemy. Either way I
interfere with that slow sure tide of history. No, that's
unfair. I mustn't embarrass you. Let's put it another way.
Which choice would history approve? Or to use the
Archbishop's language: if the future historian had a choice
of my two alternatives, which would he prefer for his
acceptable narrative? Tell me.

Mary I don't know anything about history, Hugh.

O'Neill All right; then which hand do I grasp?

Mary Queen Elizabeth made you an Earl. And you
accepted that title. And you know that that title carries
with it certain duties and responsibilities.

O'Neill Those duties I have honoured faithfully.

Mary Then as long as you continue to do that, Hugh,

and if you are at peace with your conscience, you have no dilemma.

O'Neill (*to Harry*) She's right, you know. (*to Mary*) A wise answer that, Mary. You have an admirably tidy little mind. That's what I'll do. And hope that history's approval and the guidance of my conscience are in accord.

Mary gathers her belongings together. She embraces Mabel.

Mary I'm glad to see you looking so well.

Mabel Write to me.

They kiss.

Thank you for all you brought.

Mary I'll not forget the valerian. Goodbye, Harry.

Harry Safe journey, Mary.

They shake hands.

Mary Goodbye, Hugh.

Hugh is examining the seed packets with excessive interest.

O'Neill Sorry?

Mary Goodbye.

O'Neill Oh – goodbye – goodbye – remember me to Our Henry.

Both women exit. Long pause.

Harry All that will go straight back to the Marshal.

O'Neill What's that, Harry?

Harry Everything you said will be reported to Bagenal – and to London.

O'Neill That's why I told her.

Harry You want it known that you've promised Maguire you'd help him?

O'Neill I don't think I told her that, did I? (*He reads:*) 'The coriander seed. Watch this seed carefully as it ripens suddenly and will fall without warning.' Sounds like Maguire, doesn't it? – Coriander Maguire.

Harry Because if you renege on that promise he certainly will fall.

O'Neill What herb are you, Harry? What about dill? 'Has a comforting and soothing effect.' Close enough. And who is borage? 'Inclined to induce excessive courage, even recklessness.' That's O'Donnell, isn't it? Borage O'Donnell.

Harry Or are you saying that you're going to take the English side against Maguire, Hugh?

O'Neill gathers the envelopes of seeds together.

In fact are you going to betray your old friend, Maguire?

O'Neill (*roaring*) 'Betray my old –'! For Christ's sake don't you start using language like that to me, Harry! (*softly*) Maguire is a fool. He's determined to rise up and nobody can stop him and he'll be hacked to pieces and his people routed and his country planted with Upstarts and safe men. It happened to Fitzmaurice. And McDermott. And Nugent. And O'Reilly. And O'Connor. And O'Kelly. Their noble souls couldn't breathe another second under 'tyranny'. And where are they now? Wiped out. And what did they accomplish? Nothing. But because of their nobility, survival – basic, crude, day-to-day survival – is made infinitely more difficult for the rest of us.

Harry You are unfair to Maguire, Hugh. He's impetuous but he's no fool.

O'Neill I know – I know – of course I know Maguire's no fool. Maguire has no choice. Maguire has to rise. History, instinct, his decent passion, the composition of his blood – he has no alternative. So he will fulfil his fate. It's not a tragic fate and it's not a heroic fate. But his open embrace of it has elements of both, I suppose. Of course I know all that, for Christ's sake . . .

O'Donnell bursts in. He is breathless with excitement.

O'Donnell News, boys! News! News! News! Wait till you hear the news, Hugh! Big news – huge news – enormous news! Sorry for bursting in on you like this, Harry. Peter Lombard's with me. We've been riding since dawn. God, I'm wild dry – give us a swig of that wine, Harry. This is it, Hugh boy! I'm telling you – this is it!

O'Neill This is what?

O'Donnell Don't ask me. I can't tell you. Wait for Peter – I can't spoil it on him. But I'll say this much, Hugh O'Neill: I never thought I'd live to see the day! (*He accepts a glass.*) Decent man, Harry. (*He toasts.*) To the future – to a great, great future – to the three of us –

Enter Lombard.

– to the four of us! (*to Lombard*) I haven't opened my mouth – have I?

Lombard is equally excited but controlled. He shakes hands with O'Neill and then Harry.

Lombard Hugh. Good to see you.

O'Neill Welcome, Peter.

Lombard Harry. (*to O'Neill*) I was going to send a

messenger but I thought it was much too important.

O'Donnell Spout it out, Peter!

Lombard It really is astonishing news, Hugh.

O'Neill It's Spain, isn't it?

O'Donnell The aul wizard. I never said a word.

Lombard It's Spain, Hugh. After all these years. God be praised a thousand times. It is indeed Spain.

O'Donnell Can you believe it?

Lombard Years of begging, cajoling, arguing – years of hoping – years of despairing.

O'Donnell Years of praying, Peter.

Lombard Years of praying indeed. But he has kept his promises, Hugh. Don Francisco Gómez de Sandoval y Rojas, fifth Marquis of Denia, Duke of Lerma, my friend, Ireland's friend, he has kept his promise.

O'Donnell Lerma determines their foreign policy.

O'Neill moves away and stands alone downstage.

Harry This isn't the first time Lerma has made promises.

Lombard Passed by the Council of State last Thursday week. Signed by King Philip himself the following morning. This isn't a promise. This is guaranteed. And solid. And substantial.

O'Donnell Yipeeeeee!

Lombard At this moment they are mustering an army and assembling a fleet.

O'Donnell Do you see those wee Spanish soldiers in the field, Harry? Bloody ferrets! Jesus, they'd go down a rabbit hole to get you!

Harry How solid? How substantial?

Lombard At least thirty-five ships – galleons, men-of-war and some hundred-ton vessels.

Harry Where are they going to land?

Lombard I don't know. That's a military matter.

Harry But it's crucial. It has got to be somewhere along the north coast.

Lombard I think I heard some mention of Kinsale.

O'Donnell Wherever that is. Never heard of it.

Harry Kinsale's out of the question. We'd have to march an army through the full length of the country to join forces with them. (*to O'Neill*) It can't be Kinsale, Hugh.

Lombard Then tell them it can't be Kinsale.

Harry Who's the commander-in-chief?

Lombard Don Juan del Aguila.

O'Donnell Whoever he is. Don Hugho del Ballyshannon's for more wine, boys!

Harry Tell me about Aguila.

Lombard He's from the Barraco in the province of Avila. Not brilliant but very competent, very experienced.

Harry How many men?

Lombard At least six thousand.

Harry Not enough.

Lombard They'll be fully trained and equipped; and it's up to us to match that number. (*to O'Neill*) You and Hugh here have got to tour the whole country and whip every Gaelic chieftain into shape.

Harry Where are they mustering their men?

Lombard Most of them are Spanish but they hope to levy a few companies of Italians.

O'Donnell Do you see those Italians? Bloody savages! The only time they ever smile is when they're sinking a sword in you! Jesus, Hugh, we'll go through the English quicker than a physic!

Mabel enters. O'Donnell embraces her warmly.

We're up, Mabel darling! We're up and the Spanish are beside us!

She looks at O'Neill.

Lombard Forgive us, Mabel. We're a bit elated.

Mabel The Spanish are coming?

O'Donnell Lift up your heart, Dark Rosie!

Lombard The Spanish are coming. At long last. And there's more, Hugh (*O'Neill*). There's still more.

O'Donnell Belt it out, Archbishop Lombard.

Lombard A Bull of Indulgence from His Holiness Pope Clement VIII.

O'Donnell Quiet! Quiet! Let the dog see the rabbit!

Lombard (*reading*) 'To the archbishops, bishops, prelates, chiefs, earls, barons and people of Ireland. Encouraged by the exhortations of our predecessors and ourself you have long struggled to recover and preserve your liberty and to throw off the yoke of slavery imposed on you by the English, deserters from the Holy Roman Church. Now, to all of you who follow and assist our beloved son, Hugh O'Neill, and the Catholic army, if you truly repent and confess and if possible receive the Holy Communion, we grant plenary pardon and remission of all sins, as usually granted to those setting out to the war against the Turks for the recovery of the Holy Land. Rome. The Ninth Year of Our Pontificate.'

O'Donnell Jesus, great word that – 'pontificate'.

Lombard Which means, Hugh, that now you aren't fighting a mere war – you are fighting a holy crusade.

O'Donnell Goddamn bloody right, Peter!

Lombard Which means, too, that we are no longer a casual grouping of tribes but a nation state united under the Papal colours.

O'Donnell Is that big enough news for you, man – eh?

Everybody looks at O'Neill. Silence. He walks slowly across the room.

Hi! Hugh!

Silence.

(*to others*) What's wrong with the bugger? (*to O'Neill*) O'Neill! Sir Hugh! Tyrone! Did you hear what the man's just said?

O'Neill Yes; yes, I heard.

O'Donnell 'Yes, I heard'! What the hell's wrong with the bugger?

Silence. Then when O'Neill finally speaks, he speaks very softly, almost as if he were talking to himself.

O'Neill I'm remembering Sir Henry Sidney and Lady Mary, may they rest in peace. We spent the winters in the great castle at Ludlow in Shropshire. I've few memories of the winters. It's the summers I remember and the autumns, in Kent, in the family seat at Penshurst. And the orchards; and the deerpark; and those enormous fields of wheat and barley. A golden and beneficent land. Days without blemish. Every young man's memories. And every evening after dinner Sir Henry would propose a topic for discussion: Travel – Seditions and Troubles – Gardens – Friendship and Loyalty – Good Manners – The Planting of Foreign Countries. And everyone round the table had to contribute – the family, guests, even myself, even his son Philip who was younger than I. And Sir Henry would tease out the ideas and guide the conversation almost imperceptibly but very skilfully so that by the time we rose from the table he had moulded the discourse into a well-rounded and formal essay on whatever the theme was. I was only a raw boy at the time but I was conscious not only that new ideas and concepts were being explored and fashioned but that I was being explored and fashioned at the same time. And that knowledge wasn't unflattering. Drake was there once, I remember. And Frobisher and his officers on the eve of their first South American voyage. Gross men; vain men. But Sir Henry's grace and tact seemed to transform all that naked brutality and imperial greed into boyish excitement and manly adventure. He was the only father I ever knew. I was closer to him and to Lady Mary than I was to O'Hagan who fostered me. I loved them both very much.

Anyhow, time came to come home. I was almost seventeen then. And the night before I left Lady Mary had an enormous farewell dinner for me – there must have been a hundred guests. And at the end of the meal Sir Henry got to his feet – I knew he was slightly drunk, maybe he was more drunk than I knew – and he said: 'Our disquisition tonight will explore a matter of some interest to England and of particular interest to Master O'Neill who goes home tomorrow to become a leader of his people. And the matter is this, and I quote from a letter I have just received from my friend, Andrew

Trollope. "Those Irishmen who live like subjects play but as the fox which when you have him on a chain will seem tame; but if he ever gets loose, he will be wild again." So. Speak to that, Fox O'Neill.'

And then he laughed. And everybody joined in. And then a hundred people were laughing at me . . .

I left the next morning before the household was awake. And ever since – up until this minute – ever since, that trivial little hurt, that single failure in years of courtesy has pulsed relentlessly in a corner of my heart. Until now. And now for no reason that pulse is quiet and all my affection for Sir Henry returns without qualification. (*Pause.*) But all that is of no interest to anybody but myself.

O'Donnell Damned right it isn't. Bloody pulse? – what's he blathering about?

O'Neill claps his hands, dismissing the entire episode. He is now suddenly very brisk and very efficient.

O'Neill The present. (*to Lombard*) You're right. Hugh and I will tour the country to gather support. We'll set out next Monday. (*to O'Donnell*) No cap-in-hand. We go with authority and assurance.

O'Donnell Damned right we do!

O'Neill (*to Harry*) Get a letter off to Lerma today. Kinsale is out of the question. If they insist on landing in the south – anywhere in the south – tell them to cancel the expedition. (*to Lombard*) What equipment are they bringing?

Lombard Six battery pieces and six hundred hundredweight of powder.

O'Neill (*to Harry*) We'll need at least five hundred small guns. Tell Lerma we're expert in guerrilla warfare but inexperienced in open battle.

Lombard And see that Archbishop Oviedo gets a copy – he's very influential.

Harry Right.

Lombard (*to O'Neill*) The Pope has ordered him to sail in the *San Andrea* – that's the flagship.

O'Donnell Flagship! (*He salutes.*) Jesus, that word flagship's like music to me!

O'Neill They're bringing their own saddles?

Lombard Yes; but they expect you to supply the horses.

O'Neill (*to Harry*) A levy of five horses on every family. And oatmeal. And butter. (*to Lombard*) A Bull of Indulgence isn't enough. Everybody who opposes us must be publicly identified. I need a Bull of Excommunication.

Lombard You won't get that, Hugh.

O'Neill We got one before.

Lombard Twenty years ago.

O'Neill I want a Bull of Excommunication, Peter.

Lombard I've tried. I'll try again. Oviedo's our only hope.

O'Neill (*to Harry*) Messages to all the Ulster leaders: a meeting here the day after tomorrow – at noon.

Harry Noon.

O'Neill Send Brian O'Hagan across to the Earl of Argyle for mercenaries.

Harry How many?

O'Neill As many as he can get. And pay in advance.

Harry How much money will he need?

O'Neill Whatever Argyle asks. (*to O'Donnell*) You're the expert on horses.

O'Donnell Bloody right.

O'Neill (*to Harry*) Take him up to the upper meadows and show him the new stock. (*to O'Donnell*) Pick only the horses that are strong enough for a long campaign.

O'Donnell How many are up there?

O'Neill Something over three thousand.

O'Donnell I'll have a look.

Harry and O'Donnell go to the door. O'Donnell stops there.

With all the excitement I forgot to tell you the rumour that's going round Dublin: the Lord Deputy's about to proclaim you a traitor.

O'Neill That'll do no harm at all. Good. Excellent.

O'Donnell And do you know what they're offering as a reward for you? Go on – guess – guess.

O'Neill All right. Tell me.

O'Donnell £2000 alive, £1000 dead. The same as they were offering five years ago – for the shit O'Doherty! (*He gives a great whoop and exits.*)

O'Neill (*to Lombard*) Your network of priests could be useful. How many are you in touch with?

Lombard Twenty, twenty-five.

O'Neill Every week? Every month?

Lombard It varies. They have a price on their head, too.

O'Neill Get in touch with them as soon as possible. Tell them I'll need them as messengers all over Europe.

Lombard I'll do what I can. (*He goes to the door.*)

O'Neill And put Oviedo to work on that Excommunication Bull.

Lombard Oviedo can't demand it, Hugh. The decision is the Pope's. Excommunication is a spiritual matter.

O'Neill Don't play those games with me, Peter. The situation is as 'spiritual' now as it was twenty years ago. I need Excommunication for solidarity here, for solidarity with Europe. I expect you to deliver it.

Lombard As I said, I've tried. I'll try again.

He leaves. O'Neill goes to the desk and busies himself with papers. Silence. Mabel watches him for a while and then goes to him.

Mabel Stop it, Hugh.

O'Neill Stop what?

Mabel This Spanish business. Don't let it happen.

O'Neill Why should I do that?

Mabel Because you know this isn't what you really want to happen.

O'Neill I've spent twenty years trying to bring it about, haven't I?

Mabel This isn't your way.

O'Neill But you know what my way is.

Mabel Calculation – deliberation – caution. You inch forward – you withdraw. You challenge – you retreat. You defy – you submit. Every important move you have ever made has been pondered for months.

O'Neill I have –

Mabel That's why you're the most powerful man in
Ireland: you're the only Irish chieftain who understands
the political method. O'Donnell doesn't. Maguire doesn't.
McMahon doesn't. That's why the Queen is never *quite*
sure how to deal with you – you're the antithesis of what
she expects a Gaelic chieftain to be. That's your strength.
And that's why your instinct now is not to gamble
everything on one big throw that is more than risky.

O'Neill This time Spain is with us.

Mabel Spain is using you.

O'Neill We're using each other. We've courted each other
for years.

Mabel And that has given you some small negotiating
power with England. But the manoeuvrings are over now.
And I promise you, Hugh, England will throw everything
she has into this war.

O'Neill So will Spain.

Mabel No, she won't. It's not Spain's war. It's your war.
And you're taking on a nation state that is united and
determined and powerful and led by a very resolute
woman.

O'Neill Is there an echo of pride in that?

Mabel Please, Hugh.

O'Neill Are we so inconsiderable? We aren't without
determination. We aren't disunited.

Mabel Just look calmly at what you are.

O'Neill I know exactly what we are.

Mabel You are not united. You have no single leader.
You have no common determination. At best you are an
impromptu alliance of squabbling tribesmen –

O'Neill Careful!

Mabel – grabbing at religion as a coagulant only because they have no other idea to inform them or give them cohesion.

Pause.

O'Neill Is that a considered abstract of the whole Gaelic history and civilization, Mabel? Or is it nothing more than an honest-to-goodness, instant wisdom of the Upstart? (*He is instantly sorry and grabs her and holds her in his arms.*) I'm sorry, Mabel. Forgive me. I'm very sorry. I'm a bit on edge. (*He kisses the top of her head.*) Of course you're right. We have no real cohesion. And of course I'm worried. Even O'Donnell's enthusiasm worries me: for him it's all a huge adventure – cattle-raiding on an international scale.

Mabel moves away.

And I never quite know what the Archbishop is thinking.

Mabel He talks about a Catholic Confederation, a Catholic Army, about you leading Europe in a glorious Catholic Counter-Reformation. But I always have the feeling that when he's talking about you and about Ireland, he's really talking in code about Rome and Roman power. Is that unfair to him?

O'Neill I don't know.

Mabel Just as Spain's only interest is in Spain and in Spanish power. But my only real concern is you, Hugh. This is not going to be just another skirmish at the edge of a forest. This is a war that England must win because her very survival is at stake. And all I know for sure is that, when the war is over, whatever the outcome, the Lombards and the Oviedos won't be here – they'll have moved on to more promising territories. (*Pause.*) I shouldn't have spoken. (*Pause.*) I didn't mean to intrude. (*Pause.*) I'm sure I don't really understand the overall thing.

O'Neill The overall thing.

Mabel That's what matters in the end, isn't it?

O'Neill The overall thing – we don't even begin to know what it means.

Silence. She gathers her pieces of lace and goes to the door.

Mabel Something Mary told me: a new Lord Deputy is about to be appointed, somebody called Lord Mountjoy. Henry says he's meticulous, and a ruthless fighter. Blount – that's his real name; Charles Blount. That's all she knows. Oh yes – he smokes a lot. It's all very secret. She made me swear not to tell you.

She is about to leave when she is arrested by the controlled passion of O'Neill's voice.

O'Neill I have spent my life attempting to do two things. I have attempted to hold together a harassed and a confused people by trying to keep them in touch with the life they knew before they were overrun. It wasn't a life of material ease but it had its assurances and it had its dignity. And I have done that by acknowledging and indeed honouring the rituals and ceremonies and beliefs these people have practised since before history, long before the God of Christianity was ever heard of. And at the same time I have tried to open these people to the strange new ways of Europe, to ease them into the new assessment of things, to nudge them towards changing evaluations and beliefs. Two pursuits that can scarcely be followed simultaneously. Two tasks that are almost self-cancelling. But they have got to be attempted because the formation of nations and civilizations is a willed act, not a product of fate or accident. And for you to suggest that religion is the only coagulant that holds us together is to grossly and ignorantly overlook an age-old civilization. In one detail you are right: it is not my nature to gamble everything on one big throw –

Mabel So have your war.

O'Neill But if I don't move now that civilization is certainly doomed.

Mabel So go and fight. That's what you've spent your life doing. That's what you're best at. Fighting to preserve a fighting society. I don't care any more.

O'Neill Because you're not quite sure which side you're on?

Mabel Why do you keep rejecting me, Hugh?

O'Neill I can see it wouldn't break your heart to see the Gaelic order wiped out. But let's look at what the alternative is: the buccaneering, vulgar, material code of the new colonials –

Mabel (*leaving*) Excuse me.

O'Neill The new 'civility' approved, we're told, by God Himself. Isn't that your coagulant – God? No, better still, God and trade. Now there's a combination.

She swings back and glares at him in hatred. He ignores her and pretends to busy himself at the desk.

Mabel I want your mistresses out of this house immediately.

O'Neill (*Tyrone accent*) Aw, now sorry, ma'am.

Mabel What does sorry mean?

O'Neill That my mistresses stay.

Mabel I will not live in the same house as those – those harlots! Get those tramps out of here!

O'Neill No.

Mabel Then I go.

O'Neill That's your choice.

Pause. She tries not to cry.

Mabel I'm pregnant, Hugh.

O'Neill goes to the exit.

O'Neill (*calling*) Harry! Have you a moment?

Mabel Did you hear what I said?

He returns to the desk.

O'Neill That you're pregnant? Yes, I heard. So if all goes well – isn't that the expression? – if all goes well that will be ten legitimate children I'll have sired and about – what? – maybe thirty bastards.

Mabel Oh, Hugh –

O'Neill Or so my people boast. An affectionate attribute every nation bestows on its heroes.

Again he has instant remorse. As she runs to the door he runs after her.

Mabel! Mabel, I'm –

O'Donnell dashes on.

O'Donnell A messenger from Spain outside, Hugh! (*to Mabel*) It gets better by the minute! (*to O'Neill*) The Spanish fleets sails on September 3! (*to Mabel*) Maybe you speak Spanish? You should hear your man out there: 'Beeg fleet – beeg ships'!

O'Neill Where do they sail from?

O'Donnell Lisbon. On the first tide.

O'Neill And where do they land?

Harry enters.

Harry Did you call me?

O'Neill Where do they land?

O'Donnell 'Keen-sall.'

O'Neill Where – where?

O'Donnell 'Keen-sall' – Kinsale, I suppose.

O'Neill Oh, God, no.

O'Donnell Wherever Kinsale is. This is it, Mabel darling! This is it! Yipeeeeee!

Quick black.

Act Two

SCENE ONE

About eight months later. The edge of a thicket some-
where near the Sperrin mountains.
   O'Neill is on his knees. He is using a wooden box as a
table and he is writing – scoring out – writing rapidly,
with total concentration, almost frantically. Various loose
pages on the ground beside him. He looks tired and
anxious and harassed. He is so concentrated on his
writing that he is unaware of O'Donnell's entrance. Then,
when he is aware, he reaches perfunctorily for the dagger
at his side. O'Donnell, too, looks tired and anxious. He is
also spattered with mud and his boots are sodden.

O'Donnell It's only me. I suppose you thought something
had happened to me.

O'Neill You were longer than you thought.

O'Donnell I had to make detours going and coming back
– the countryside's crawling with troops. And then there
were a lot of things to see to at home – disputes –
documents – the usual. Look at my feet. These Sperrins
aren't mountains – they're bloody bogs! I suppose you
wouldn't have a spare pair of boots?

O'Neill What you see is all I have.

O'Donnell I was afraid you might have had to move on
to some new place.

O'Neill It's been very quiet here.

O'Donnell God, I'm exhausted.

   He throws himself on the ground and spreads out in

303

exhaustion. His eyes closed. O'Neill continues writing.
Silence.

O'Neill Have you any food?

O'Donnell opens his leather bag and produces a scone
of bread. O'Neill goes to him, takes the bread and eats
it hungrily.

O'Donnell My mother made me half-a-dozen of them but
I met a family begging on the roadside near Raphoe.
Everywhere you go there are people scavenging in the
fields, hoking up bits of roots, eating fistfuls of watercress.
They look like skeletons. Where's Mabel?

O'Neill Harry took her to relatives of Ruadhaire Dall O
Cathain's near Dungiven. She wasn't able to keep moving
about any more.

O'Donnell Proper order, too. When is she due?

O'Neill Next week probably.

O'Donnell She's been terrific, Hugh. Not a whimper out
of her all these months – and us skulking about like
tramps.

O'Neill I know.

O'Donnell Next week. Great. At least that'll be
something to celebrate. I'm wild dry. Have you any
water?

O'Neill hands him a bottle.

O'Neill Well?

O'Donnell I hate this aul brown Tyrone water – with all
respects. How do you drink it?

O'Neill What did you learn?

O'Donnell I never made Ballyshannon. Dowcra's troops

304

were waiting for me there. I got no further than Donegal Town. My mother says to tell you she was asking for you.

O'Neill Well?

O'Donnell Well, it's a complete collapse, she says. The countryside's in chaos, she says: slaughter, famine, disease. There must be eight thousand people crowded into Donegal Town looking for food.

O'Neill Where's Mountjoy?

O'Donnell Mountjoy's riding up and down the country and beheading everything that stirs. And every week somebody new caves in; and those that are holding out are being picked off one after the other. But do you know what I heard? Jesus, wait till you hear this, Hugh. We were betrayed at Kinsale! They knew we were going to attack that morning. They were sitting waiting for us. And do you know how they knew? Brian Og McMahon slipped them the word! Time, place, number of men, everything. And do you know how they bought him? With a bottle of whiskey! Jesus, wouldn't it break your heart? That's what they're all saying at home. There could have been 10 million Spanish soldiers and we still wouldn't have won. Because one of our own captains bloody well betrayed us.

O'Neill Rubbish.

O'Donnell What d'you mean – rubbish?

O'Neill All lies.

O'Donnell You don't believe me?

O'Neill You don't believe it yourself.

O'Donnell It's what everybody at home's saying . . . I don't know . . . maybe . . . but you'll agree those McMahons were always shifty buggers.

O'Neill How big is the collapse?

O'Donnell It's all over. It's all finished, Hugh.

O'Neill Who has submitted? Names.

O'Donnell My mother says they're crawling in on their hands and knees and offering hostages and money and whatnot. It would be easier to count the handful that are still holding out.

O'Neill Names.

O'Donnell Names . . . where do you begin? . . . all right, names . . . Jesus, I just hate saying them . . . Turlough McHenry of the Fews. The two Antrim O'Neills. O'Malley of Mayo. O'Flaherty of Annaly. Maguire of Fermanagh –

O'Neill Cuchonnacht?

O'Donnell God, no! The wee get, Connor Roe. Christ, man, aul Cuchonnacht's still dodging about the Lisnaskea area with fifteen picked men and hammering away every chance he gets! The McDevitts of Ballybeg, all of them, every branch of the family. The McSwineys of Fanad. Wouldn't it sicken you? – the bloody McSwineys that our family has kept and protected for generations and then when you're down in your luck. (*suddenly brightening*) But do you know who's holding out? You'd never guess! Still the same wee maggot he always was but at least he hasn't caved in yet. The sheep-stealer! – the shit O'Doherty from Inishowen! Jesus, isn't it well we didn't slip him the Bordeaux Special that time?

O'Neill Go on.

O'Donnell O'Kelly of Kilconnell. Brave enough; he held out until last Sunday and then do you know what he did? The aul eejit, Jesus, pompous as ever; he had this blond wig that an aul aunt had brought home from Paris. Anyhow he sticks the blond wig on his head, puts on a scarlet jacket, marches into Galway town and offers his surrender – in French! Poor aul bugger – trying to make a bit of a gesture out of it . . . Anyhow, one swing of an axe and the aul blond head was rolling about the street . . .

O'Neill Go on.

O'Donnell Who else? . . . O'Reilly of East Breffni. McWilliam Burke of Connaught. O'Kane –

O'Neill Which O'Kane?

O'Donnell Your daughter Rose's husband. Sure you always knew he was a bloody weed. Fitzmaurice of Kerry. Donnell McCarthy of Bandon. I can go on forever. O'Dowd. O'Dwyer of Kilnamanagh. God, Hugh, I'm telling you – it's endless.

    O'Neill picks up his papers and puts them in order. Silence.

O'Neill Where's Chichester?

O'Donnell He's taken over your place at Dungannon.

O'Neill Hah!

O'Donnell He controls the whole of East Ulster. Dowcra controls the whole of West Ulster. Carew controls the whole of Munster. And Mountjoy controls the whole country. (*Pause.*) He did a kind of a dirty thing last week, Mountjoy.

    O'Neill stops and looks at him.

He smashed the O'Neill crowning stone at Tullyhogue. There was no call for that, was there? (*Pause.*) What else is there? The King of France has written to Elizabeth to come to terms with us. Wasting his bloody time. All your

Derry lands have been given to Bishop Montgomery and
your Armagh lands to the new Protestant bishop there . . .
I don't think I heard anything else . . . they've taken over
your fishing rights on the Bann and the Foyle . . . And I've
resigned, Hugh.

O'Neill What do you mean?

O'Donnell Handed over to the brother, Rory.

O'Neill Oh, Hugh.

O'Donnell And I'm leaving at the end of the week.

O'Neill Where for?

O'Donnell I don't know. Wherever the ship takes me.
Maybe Spain. (*Pause. He smiles resolutely and
uncertainly.*) No, it's not a sudden decision. I've been
thinking about it for months, ever since Kinsale. And
Rory'll be a fine chieftain – he's a solid man, very calm,
very balanced. He hasn't my style or flair, of course; but
then I have a fault or two, as you know. The blood gets
up too easy and I was always useless at dealing with civil
servants and Lord Deputies and people like that. Not like
you. Even with my own people, for God's sake: the
bloody McSwineys of Fanad couldn't wait to get a thump
at me. Anyhow the chieftain isn't all that important – isn't
that what our bards tell us? The land is the goddess that
every ruler in turn is married to. We come and we go but
she stays the same. And the Tyrconnell goddess is getting
a new man. Trouble is, no matter who she's married to,
I'll always be in love with her . . . (*He takes a drink of
water.*) Jesus, that stuff would physic an elephant!

O'Neill When are you leaving?

O'Donnell Next Friday.

O'Neill Where from?

O'Donnell I'm getting a ship at a place called Castle-haven – wherever that is.

O'Neill Near Skibbereen.

O'Donnell Wherever Skibbereen is.

O'Neill You'll be back, Hugh.

O'Donnell Aye. In a blond wig and a scarlet jacket and leading a hundred thousand Spaniards! And next time we'll land in Derry – better still Rathmullan and my mother'll get landing fees from the buggers – right? (*He laughs.*) No, it's all over, Hugh. Finished for all time. Poor aul Peter Lombard, terrible bleak ending for his history, isn't it? I mean, Jesus, how can the poor man make an interesting story out of a defeat like this – eh? If he'd any sense he'd scrap the whole thing. Yes, there is one thing that might bring me home sometime – to get my sheep back from the shit O'Doherty. Oh, man . . .

> *Impulsively, about to break down, he flings his arms around O'Neill. They embrace for several seconds. Then O'Donnell goes to his bag for a handkerchief.*

What about you? What are you going to do?

O'Neill I don't have many choices. And I'm not as young as you.

O'Donnell Damned right – twenty years older at least.

O'Neill My instinct is to leave like you.

O'Donnell What does Mabel think?

O'Neill She's urging me to hang on, pick up the pieces, start all over again. They're very tenacious, the New English.

O'Donnell Maybe she's right. She's a very loyal wee girl.

O'Neill Her reasoning is that since the country is in such anarchy Mountjoy has neither the energy nor the resources to impose order; but if I were to make a public declaration of loyalty to the Queen and if she were to reinstate me –

O'Donnell Are you out of your –?!

O'Neill With only nominal authority, without political or military power whatever, then Mabel says I should accept almost any conditions, no matter how humiliating, as long as I'd be restored to my base again and to my own people.

O'Donnell And why in God's name would Elizabeth restore you?

O'Neill Because she knows that the only way she can rule Ireland at this point is by *using* someone like me. She hates me – but she can rule through me provided she has control over me. At least that's Mabel's argument. I think I could get enough of my people behind me and she thinks some of the New English would back it – those that are sick of England.

O'Donnell So you're writing your submission?

O'Neill What's the alternative? The life of a soured émigré whingeing and scheming round the capitals of Europe.

O'Donnell Like me.

O'Neill I didn't mean that, Hugh.

O'Donnell Show me that. You know, you're a tenacious bugger, too. You and Mabel are well met.

At first O'Donnell reads his portions of the submission in mocking and exaggerated tones. He is unaware that O'Neill is deadly serious. But as they proceed through

*the document – O'Donnell reading his sections, O'Neill
speaking his by heart – O'Donnell's good humour
drains away and he ends up as formal and as grave as
O'Neill.*

(*reading*) I, Hugh O'Neill, by the Queen of England,
France and Ireland her most gracious favour created Earl
of Tyrone, do with all true and humble penitency
prostrate myself at her royal feet – (*He drops on his
knees.*) – absolutely submit myself to her mercy. (*not
reading*) Mercy, Queen, Mercy!

O'Neill Most sorrowfully imploring her gracious
commiseration and appealing only to her princely
clemency, without presuming to justify my unloyal
proceedings against her sacred majesty.

O'Donnell (*reading*) May it please Her Majesty to
mitigate her just indignation against me for my unnatural
rebellion which deserves no forgiveness and for which I
can make no satisfaction, even with my life. (*not reading*)
Jesus, you are one great fraud, O'Neill!

O'Neill I do most humbly beg Her Majesty to restore me
to my former living and dignity where as an obedient
subject I vow to continue hereafter loyal to her royal
person, to her crown, to her prerogatives, and to her
English laws.

O'Donnell Her English –?! Hey, steady on, man, steady –!

O'Neill I do renounce and abjure all foreign power
whatever and all kind of dependency upon any other
potentate but Her Majesty, the Queen of England, France
and Ireland –

O'Donnell (*reading*) And do vow to serve her faithfully
against any foreign power invading her kingdom; and
especially do I abjure and renounce all manner of

dependency upon the King of Spain and shall be ready with the uttermost of my ability to serve Her Majesty against him or any of his forces or confederates.

O'Neill I do resign all claim and title to any lands but such as shall now be granted to me; and lastly I offer to the Queen and to her magistrates here my full assistance in anything that may tend to the advancement of her service and the peaceable government of this kingdom.

O'Donnell (*reading*) Particularly will I help in the abolishing of all barbarous Gaelic customs which are the seeds of all incivility.

O'Neill And for the clearing of all difficult passages and places –

O'Donnell (*reading*) Which are the nurseries –

O'Neill Which are the nurseries of rebellion. And I will endeavour to erect habitations –

O'Donnell (*reading*) Civil habitations.

O'Neill Civil habitations for myself and for the people of my country to preserve us against any force but the power of the state –

O'Donnell (*reading*) By which power –

O'Neill By which power we must rest assured to be preserved as long as we continue in our loyal and faithful duties to Her Majesty –

O'Donnell (*reading*) To her most clement –

O'Neill To her most clement, most gracious, most noble and most forgiving majesty.

O'Donnell (*reading*) To whom I now most abjectly and most obediently offer my service and indeed . . . my life . . .

Silence. Then O'Neill moves away as if to distance himself from what he has just said. O'Donnell is still on his knees.

This is the end of it all, Hugh, isn't it? (*Pause.*) Jesus. (*He gets to his feet, brightening.*) All the same they say she's a peculiar woman, the Queen..Damn it, wouldn't it be a good one if she believed you – eh?

O'Neill She won't believe me.

O'Donnell But if she did! Damn it, I'd make a submission to her myself!

O'Neill Belief has nothing to do with it. As Mabel says, she'll use me if it suits her.

O'Donnell And your people?

O'Neill They're much more pure, 'my people'. Oh, no, they won't believe me either. But they'll pretend they believe me and then with ruthless Gaelic logic they'll crucify me for betraying them.

Harry enters. He looks quickly first at O'Neill and then at O'Donnell – they have not noticed his arrival. He then greets them with deliberate heartiness.

Harry It wouldn't be hard to surprise you two.

O'Donnell Harry! How are you, man?

Harry When did you get back?

O'Donnell Just arrived.

Harry We thought we had lost you – (*to O'Neill*) didn't we?

O'Donnell I tried to surrender to Dowcra but he wouldn't take me.

O'Neill How was the journey?

Harry The journey was fine. We had a fine journey.

O'Neill And the O Cathains were expecting her?

Harry A big welcoming party. Everything quiet here?

O'Neill She was in good form when you left her?

Harry That's a great place they have there. (*to O'Donnell*) Ethna O Cathain and your mother are cousins, aren't they?

O'Donnell Second cousins.

Harry Yes, she mentioned that. (*rummaging in his bag*) And she sent you both some food: some oatmeal bread and milk and what's this – biscuits – strange-looking biscuits –

O'Neill They know exactly where I am?

Harry Of course they know; raisins, flour –

O'Neill And they'll send me word immediately?

Harry Yes. And she sent this specially to you, Hugh. (*He hands over a bottle to O'Donnell.*)

O'Donnell Is it whiskey?

Harry Ten year old.

O'Donnell Decent woman, Ethna. And thank God I don't put water in it.

Harry Anybody else hungry?

O'Neill No, thanks.

O'Donnell (*drinking*) Good luck. Hugh?

O'Neill Not for me.

O'Donnell What's the news about Dungiven, Harry?

Harry (*eating*) Let me see. Nothing very much. Archbishop Lombard's gone to Rome.

O'Donnell For good?

Harry They've invented some sort of job for him there.

O'Donnell You may be sure aul Peter'll always land on his feet.

Harry And Archbishop Oviedo's gone to England. The morning after Kinsale he headed straight for London to sweeten the authorities there – in case there'd be a backlash against the Catholics in England.

O'Donnell They don't miss a beat, those boys, do they? Beautiful stuff this. Sure you don't want some, Hugh?

Harry Leave some for the rest of us.

O'Neill They have their own physicians, the O Cathains, haven't they?

Harry Sean O Coinne. I met him there. Seemed very competent. What else is new? Oh, yes, Sir Garret Moore wants to get in touch with you – I imagine at Mountjoy's prompting. He wants to explore what areas of common interest might still exist between you and the crown. The pretext for getting you down to the Boyne is the first run of sea trout. If you were to go, I'm sure he'd have some civil servants there.

O'Donnell So they do want to talk to you, Hugh. Mabel was right.

Harry What else? . . . There's a rumour that Mountjoy himself may be in trouble because of some woman in England – Lady Penelope Rich? – is that the name? Anyhow if the scandal becomes public they say Mountjoy may be recalled. What else was there . . .? Sean na bPunta is still going calmly round the country with his brown leather bag, collecting your rents as if the place weren't in chaos! . . . Tadhg O Cianain is writing a book on the past ten years –

O'Donnell Another history! Jesus, if we had as many scones of bread as we have historians!

Harry It will be a very exact piece of work that Tadhg will produce . . . And portions of another book are being circulated and it seems the English government is paying a lot of attention to it. Written by an Englishman called Spenser who used to have a place down near the Ballyhouras mountains – wherever they are – I'm getting like you, Hugh – they're in County Cork, aren't they? – anyhow this Spenser was burned out in the troubles after the battle of the Yellow Ford . . . (*He suddenly breaks down but continues speaking without stopping.*) Oh, my God, Hugh, I don't know how to say it to you – I don't know how to tell you – we had only just arrived at O Cathain's place –

O'Donnell Harry –?

Harry And the journey *had* been fine – she was in wonderful form – we sang songs most of the way – I taught her 'Tabhair Dom Do Lamh', Ruadhaire Dall's song, because the O Cathains are relatives of his and she could show off before them and we laughed until we were sore at the way she pronounced the Irish words – and she taught me a Staffordshire ballad called 'Lord Brand, He was a Gentleman' and I tried to sing it in a Staffordshire accent – and she couldn't have been better looked after – they were all waiting for her – Ethna, the doctor O Coinne, two midwives, half-a-dozen servants. And everything seemed perfectly normal – everything *was* fine. She said if the baby was a boy she was going to call it Nicholas after her father and if it was a girl she was going to call it Joan after your mother – and when Ethna asked her were you thinking of going into exile she got very agitated and she said, 'Hugh?' She said, 'Hugh would never betray his people' – and just then, quite normally, quite naturally, she went into labour – and whatever happened – I still don't really know – whatever happened, something just wasn't right, Hugh. The baby lived for about an hour – it was a boy – but she never knew it had died – and shortly afterwards Ethna was sitting on a stool right beside her bed, closer than I am to you – and she was sleeping very peacefully – and then she gave a long sigh as if she were very tired and when Ethna put her hand on her cheek . . . It wasn't possible to get word to you – it all happened so quickly – herself and the baby within two hours – the doctor said something about poisoning of the blood – Oh, God, I'm so sorry for you – I'm so sorry for all of us. I loved her, too – you know that – from the very first day we met her – remember that day in May? – her twentieth birthday? – she was wearing a blue dress with a white lace collar and white lace cuffs . . . If you had seen her laid out she looked like a girl of fourteen, she was just so beautiful . . . God have mercy on her. God have mercy on all of us.

Long silence.

O'Neill (*almost in a whisper*) Yes, I think I'll take some of that whiskey now, Hugh. Just a thimbleful, if you please. And no water. Oh, dear God . . .

Quick black.

SCENE TWO

O'Neill's apartment in Rome many years later.
  When the scene opens the only light on the stage is a candle on a large desk. This is Lombard's desk; littered

317

with papers; and in the centre is a large book – the
history. The room is scantily furnished – a small table,
some chairs, a stool, a couch.

O'Neill is now in his early sixties. His eyesight is
beginning to trouble him – he carries a walking stick. And
he drinks too much. We first hear his raucous shouting
off. When he enters we see that he is slightly drunk. His
temper is volatile and bitter and dangerous. He is carrying
a lighted taper.

O'Neill (*off*) Anybody at home? Harry? Why are there
no damned lights out here? (*now on*) Catriona? Your
slightly inebriated husband is back! I really shouldn't have
had that last bottle of – (*He bumps into a stool and*
knocks it over. As he straightens it:) Forgive me, I do beg
your pardon. Perhaps you could assist me, signor. Am I in
the right building? You see, I'm a foreigner in your city,
an émigré from Ireland in fact – yes, yes, *Irlanda*. Ah!
You've been there? *Bella*, indeed: indeed *bellissima*; you
are very kind. What's that? Oh, yes, that is perfectly true
– everybody does love us. And I'll tell you why, my friend:
because we are a most attractive and a most loyal people.
Now, if you'd be so kind, I'm trying to make my way to
the Palazzo dei Penitenzieri which is between the Via della
Conciliazione and the Borgo Santo Spirito where I live
with – (*He breaks off suddenly because, holding his taper*
up high, he finds himself standing at the desk and looking
down at the book. He stares at it for a few seconds. Very
softly) The right building indeed. Home. Everything is in
order . . . (*He takes a few steps away from the desk and*
calls:) Archbishop? Harry? (*No answer. He returns to the*
book and turns it round so that he can read it. He leans
over the page, his face close to it and reads:) 'In the name
of God. Herewith I set my hand to chronicle the life of
Hugh O'Neill, Earl of Tyrone, son of Feardorcha, son of
Conn Bacagh, son of Conn Mor, noblest son of noble

lineage who was fostered and brought up by the high-
born nobles of his tribe, the O'Hagans and the O'Quinns,
and who continued to grow and increase in comeliness
and urbanity, tact and eloquence, wisdom and knowledge,
goodly size and noble deeds, so that his name and fame
spread throughout the five provinces of Ireland and
beyond –' (*Suddenly, violently, angrily he swings away
from the desk. He bellows:*) Where the hell is everybody?
Catriona? Your devoted earl is home! (*He listens. There is
no sound.*) At vespers, no doubt. Or in the arms of some
sweaty Roman with a thick neck and bushy stomach. (*He
goes to the small table and lights the candles there. Then
he empties the dregs from two empty bottles into a wine
glass. As he does these things:*) Enormously popular in
this city, my Countess. Of course she is still attractive –
indeed all the more attractive since she has gone ever so
slightly, almost judiciously, to seed; no doubt an intuitive
response to the Roman preference for over-ripeness.
Curious people, these Romans: they even find her vulgar
Scottish accent charming. Happily for them they don't
understand a word she . . . (*With the glass in his hand he
has drifted back to – cannot resist the pull of – the open
book. Again myopically he leans over it and reads:*) 'And
people reflected in their minds that when he would reach
manhood there would not be one like him of the Irish to
avenge their wrongs and punish the plunderings of his
race. For it was foretold by prophets and by predictors of
futurity that there would come one like him –

A man, glorious, pure, faithful above all
Who will cause mournful weeping in every territory.
He will be a God-like prince
And he will be king for the span of –'

He shuts the book in fury.

Damn you, Archbishop! But this is one battle I am not
going to lose! (*Wheeling away from the table, he bellows:*)

Where the hell is everybody?! Catriona, you bitch, where are you? Haaaa-reeee!

He turns round. Harry is at his elbow. He is embarrassed.

Ah, there you are. Why do you keep hiding on me? Where the hell is everybody?

Harry Catriona has gone out. She says –

O'Neill (*furious again*) Out! Out! Tell me when the hell my accommodating wife is ever in! (*softly*) Sorry.

Harry And the Archbishop is upstairs. You were to have spent the afternoon with him.

O'Neill Why would I have done that?

Harry He wanted confirmation of some details.

O'Neill What are you talking about?

Harry For his history.

O'Neill 'His history'! Damn his history. I haven't eaten all day, Harry. I suppose I ought to be hungry.

Harry Let me get you –

O'Neill No, I don't want food. What's happened here since morning?

Harry A reply from the King of Spain.

O'Neill Wonderful!

Harry Eventually. Thanking you for your last three letters –

O'Neill But –

Harry But reminding you again that England and Spain have signed a peace treaty. It's fragile but it's holding.

O'Neill The King of Spain has betrayed us, Harry.

320

Harry He believes that the interests of Ireland and Spain are best served by '*inacción*'.

O'Neill *Inacción*.

Harry And he urges you to remain in Rome for the time being.

O'Neill I have remained in Rome for the time being at his insistence for the past eight years!

Harry He says he values your Christian patience.

O'Neill (*shouting*) He values my Christian –! (*softly*) I'm going to die in this damned town, Harry. You do know that, don't you? And be buried here, beside my son, in the church of San Pietro. (*He laughs.*) The drink makes God-like princes maudlin.

Harry Not a good day?

O'Neill Oh, wonderful! Animating! The usual feverish political activity and intellectual excitement. First I walked to the top of the Janiculum hill. Then I walked down again. Then I stood in line at the office of the Papal Secretary and picked up my paltry papal pension and bowed and said, '*Grazie. Grazie molto.*' Then I stood in line at the office of the Spanish Embassy and picked up my paltry Spanish pension and bowed and said, '*Gracias. Muchas gracias*'. And then I – (*He breaks off, points to the ceiling.*) The Archbishop?

Harry nods yes.

(*whispering*) Then I spent a most agreeable hour with Maria the Neapolitan.

Harry That's a new name.

O'Neill Yes. Wonderful girl, Maria. Steeped in Greek mythology and speaks half-a-dozen languages. Anyhow I left some of my money with her; Spanish money, of course. And when I was leaving, d'you know what she said to me, Harry? '*Grazie, signor. Grazie molto.*'

Harry laughs.

She did. And I believe she meant it. I'm an old man – I was flattered momentarily.

Harry And then you met Neachtain O Domhnaill and Christopher Plunkett.

O'Neill Have you been spying on me?

Harry They were here this morning looking for you.

O'Neill And we spent the afternoon together – as you can see.

Harry O Domhnaill was drunk when he was here.

O'Neill And once more we went over the master plan to raise an army and retake Ireland. Spain will provide the men, France will supply the artillery and the Pope will pay for the transportation. Naturally O'Neill of Tyrone will lead the liberating host. But because my eyesight is less than perfect, Plunkett will ride a few paces ahead of me. And because Plunkett's hearing is less than perfet, O Domhnaill will ride a few paces ahead of him. O Domhnaill's delirium tremens has got to be overlooked because he refuses to acknowledge it himself. Our estimate is that it may take the best part of a day to rout the English – perhaps two if they put up a fight. The date of embarkation – May 19: you see, the eighteenth is pension day.

Harry What drinking house were you in?

O'Neill Pedro Blanco's. Full as usual. Plunkett insisted the customers were all Englishmen, disguised as Romans, spying on us. And so for security reasons our master plan has been code-named – this was O Domhnaill's only inspiration – Operation Turf Mould . . . I can't stand it much longer, Harry. I think my mind is beginning to . . . Maybe I should eat something.

Harry Good. I'll get you –

O'Neill Not now. Later. If you would be so kind – (*He holds out his glass for Harry to fill.*)

Harry Sorry, Hugh. We're out of wine. There's no wine in the house.

O'Neill Why?

Harry (*reluctantly*) The supplier turned me away this afternoon. I'm afraid we've run out of credit.

O'Neill Who is this supplier?

Harry His name is Carlo something. We've always dealt with him. His place is at the back of –

O'Neill And he refused you?

Harry We already owe him eight hundred ducats.

O'Neill He refused you?

Harry He's a decent man but he has six young children.

O'Neill (*shouting*) Don't be so damned elusive, Harry. (*softly*) Did this fellow refuse you?

Harry He refused me.

O'Neill And he knew who the wine was for?

Harry I'm sure he did.

O'Neill Did you tell him the wine was for Hugh O'Neill?

Harry I've been going to him ever since we –

O'Neill Did you specifically tell him the wine was for Hugh O'Neill?

Harry Yes, of course he knew the wine was for Hugh O'Neill and what he said was that Hugh O'Neill's credit was finished – no payment, no wine. And you might as well know, too, that we owe money to Catriona's tailor and to the baker and that the rent in this place is six months overdue.

O'Neill (*icily*) You're shouting at me, Harry.

Harry Sorry. I can't stand it much longer either, Hugh.

O'Neill And perhaps this is as good a time as any to take a look at how you're squandering the money I entrust to you to manage my affairs, or perhaps more importantly *why* you're squandering that money. Because my suspicion is that this isn't just your customary ineptitude in money matters –

Harry goes to the door.

Harry We'll talk tomorrow, Hugh.

O'Neill What I suspect is that the pride you once professed in being a servant of the O'Neill is long gone – and I suppose that's understandable: I can't be of much use to you any more, can I?

Harry You suspect everybody and –

O'Neill And because that pride is gone, what I suspect is that some perverse element in your nature isn't at all displeased to see Hugh O'Neill humiliated by this anonymous back-street wine-vendor.

Harry Hugh –

O'Neill But it does distress me to see you so soured that it actually pleases you to have the bailiffs fling O'Neill out on the street. What's gnawing at you, Harry? Some bitterness? Some deep disappointment? Some corroding sense of betrayal?

Harry Soured? You talk to me about being soured, about betrayal? (*He controls himself.*) Leave the door open for the Countess.

O'Neill What was it I called you once, Harry? Was it borage? No, that was O'Donnell, may he rest in peace; loyal, faithful Hugh. No, you were . . . dill! The man with the comforting and soothing effect! And the interesting thing is that I chose Harry Hoveden to be my private secretary precisely because he wasn't a Gael. You see, I thought a Gael might be vulnerable to small, tribal pressures – to little domestic loyalties – an almost attractive human weakness when you come to think of it. So instead I chose one of the Old English because he would be above that kind of petty venality. So I chose Harry Hoveden because he claimed to admire Hugh O'Neill and everything Hugh O'Neill was attempting to do for his people and because when he left the Old English and joined us he protested such fealty and faithfulness not only to Hugh O'Neill but to the whole Gaelic nation.

Harry If you weren't so drunk, Hugh –

He breaks off because Lombard enters.

O'Neill The fault, of course, is mine. I suppose that easy rejection of his old loyalties and the almost excessive display of loyalty to us ought to have alerted me. Certainly Mabel was never taken in by it.

Harry I'm sorry for you, Hugh. You have become a pitiable, bitter bastard.

O'Neill Don't you believe in loyalty any more, Harry? In keeping faith? In fealty?

Lombard assesses the situation instantly and accurately and in response he assumes a breezy, energetic manner which he sustains right through the scene. As he enters he holds up a bottle. O'Neill immediately regrets his outburst but is unable to apologize and slumps sulkily in a chair.

Lombard I've come at a bad moment, have I? No? Good. And look what I have here. You'd never guess what this is, Harry.

Harry A bottle.

Lombard Brilliant. D'you see, Hugh?

O'Neill Yes.

Lombard Arrived this very day. From home. But it's a very special bottle, Harry. Poitín. Waterford poitín. I was never much help to their spiritual welfare but they certainly don't neglect the state of my spirit! (*He laughs.*) Have you some glasses there? (*to O'Neill*) Catriona says she'll be late, not to wait up for her. Something about a tailor and a dress fitting. (*to Harry*) Good man. This, I assure you, is ambrosia.

Harry Not for me, Peter. But he needs some very badly.

As Harry leaves Lombard calls after him.

Lombard I'll leave this aside for you and if you feel like joining us later . . . And for the Earl himself, just a drop. It's pure nectar, Hugh. (*He takes a sip and relishes it.*) Tell me this: are the very special delights of this world foretastes of eternity or just lures to perdition? It's from my own parish; a very remote place called Affane, about ten miles from Dungarvan. And it has been made there for decades by an old man who claims he's one of Ormond's bastards. If he is, God bless bastards – God forgive me. (*He takes another sip.*) Exquisite, isn't it? Affane must be an annex of heaven – or Hades.

O'Neill puts his untouched drink to the side.

O'Neill I'll try it later, Peter.

Lombard Of course. Now. (*going to his desk*) You're not too tired to help me check a few details, are you? Splendid. (*He sees the book has been closed.*) You know, Hugh, you were very naughty today.

O'Neill Was I?

Lombard You and I were to have spent the afternoon on this.

O'Neill What's that?

Lombard My history. (*He laughs.*) 'My history'! You would think I was Thucydides, wouldn't you? And if the truth were told, I'm so disorganized I'm barely able to get all this stuff into chronological order, not to talk of making sense of it. But if I'm to write about the life and times of Hugh O'Neill, the co-operation of the man himself would be a help, wouldn't it?

O'Neill Sorry, Peter.

Lombard No harm done. Here we are – let me tell you the broad outline.

O'Neill I had a bad day.

Lombard I know. Pension day. That's understandable.

O'Neill A stupid, drunken day with Plunkett and O Domhnaill.

Lombard I saw them this morning. A sorry sight. They were two great men once.

O'Neill And I was cruel to Harry just now.

Lombard I sensed something was amiss.

O'Neill I told him Mabel didn't trust him. That was a damned lie. Mabel loved Harry.

Lombard I know she did. And Harry understands. We all understand. It's been a difficult time for you, Hugh. That's why this history is important – is vitally important. These last years have been especially frustrating. But what we must remember – what I must record and celebrate – is the *whole* life, from the very beginning right through those glorious years when aspiration and achievement came together and O'Neill was a household name right across Europe. Because they were glorious, Hugh. And they are a cause for celebration not only by us but by the generations that follow us. Now. (*He finds his outline.*) I think this is it – is it? Yes, it is.

O'Neill Mabel will be in the history, Peter?

Lombard Mabel? What sort of a question is that? Of course Mabel will be in the history.

O'Neill Central to it, Peter.

Lombard And so will your first wife, Brian MacFelim's daughter. And so will your second, the wonderful Siobhan. And so will Mabel. And so will our beautiful Catriona – she says not to wait up for her. They'll all be mentioned. What a strange question! (*confidentially*) But I've got to confess a secret unease, Hugh. The fact that the great Hugh O'Neill had four wives – and there were rumours of a fifth years and years ago, weren't there? – long before you and I first met – but the fact that O'Neill had four, shall we say acknowledged, wives, do you think that may strike future readers as perhaps . . . a surfeit? I'm sure not. I'm sure I'm being too sensitive. Anyhow we can't deliberately suppress what we know did happen, can we? So. Back to my overall framework.

O'Neill This is my last battle, Peter.

Lombard Battle? What battle?

O'Neill That (*book*).

Lombard What are you talking about?

O'Neill That thing there.

Lombard Your history?

O'Neill *Your* history. I'm an old man. I have no position, no power, no money. No, I'm not whingeing – I'm not pleading. But I'm telling you that I'm going to fight you on that and I'm going to win.

Lombard Fight –? What in the name of God is the man talking about?

O'Neill I don't trust you. I don't trust you to tell the truth.

Lombard To tell the truth in –? Do you really think I would –?

O'Neill I think you are not trustworthy. And that (*book*) is all that is left to me.

Lombard You *are* serious! Hugh, for heaven's sake –! (*He bursts out laughing.*)

O'Neill Go ahead. Laugh. But I'm going to win this battle, Peter.

Lombard Hold on now – wait – wait – wait – wait. Just tell me one thing. Is this book some sort of a malign scheme? Am I doing something reprehensible?

O'Neill You are going to embalm me in – in – in a florid lie.

Lombard Will I lie, Hugh?

O'Neill I need the truth, Peter. That's all that's left. The schemer, the leader, the liar, the statesman, the lecher, the

329

patriot, the drunk, the soured, bitter émigré – put it *all* in, Peter. Record the *whole* life – that's what you said yourself.

Lombard Listen to me, Hugh –

O'Neill I'm asking you, man. Yes, damn it, I am pleading. Don't embalm me in pieties.

Lombard Let me tell you what I'm doing.

O'Neill You said Mabel will have her place. That place is central to me.

Lombard Will you listen to me?

O'Neill Can I trust you to make Mabel central?

Lombard Let me explain what my outline is. May I? Please? And if you object to it – or to any detail in it – I'll rewrite the whole thing in any way you want. That is a solemn promise. Can I be fairer than that? Now. I start with your birth and your noble genealogy and I look briefly at those formative years when you were fostered with the O'Quinns and the O'Hagans and received your early education from the bards and the poets. I then move –

O'Neill England.

Lombard What's that?

O'Neill I spent nine years in England with Leicester and Sidney.

Lombard You did indeed. I have all that material here. We then look at the years when you consolidated your position as the pre-eminent Gaelic ruler in the country, and that leads on to these early intimations you must have had of an emerging nation state. And now we come to the first of the key events: that September when all the people

330

of Ulster came together at the crowning stone at
Tullyhogue outside Dungannon, and the golden slipper is
thrown over your head and fastened to your foot, and the
white staff is placed in your right hand, and the True Bell
of St Patrick peals out across the land, and you are
proclaimed . . . The O'Neill.

O'Neill That was a political ploy.

Lombard It may have been that, too.

O'Neill The very next month I begged Elizabeth for
pardon.

Lombard But an occasion of enormous symbolic
importance for your people – six hundred and thirty
continuous years of O'Neill hegemony. Right, I then move
on to that special relationship between yourself and Hugh
O'Donnell; the patient forging of the links with Spain and
Rome; the uniting of the whole of Ulster into one great
dynasty that finally inspired all the Gaelic chieftains to
come together under your leadership. And suddenly the
nation state was becoming a reality. And talking of Hugh
O'Donnell – (*He searches through a pile of papers.*) This
will interest you. Yes, maybe this will put your mind at
ease. Ludhaidh O'Cleary has written a life of Hugh and
this is how he describes him. Listen to this. 'He was a
dove in meekness and gentleness and a lion in strength
and force. He was a sweet-sounding trumpet –'

O'Neill 'Sweet-sounding'!

Lombard Listen! '– with power of speech and eloquence,
sense and counsel, with a look of amiability in his face
which struck everyone at first sight.'

O'Neill laughs.

O'Neill 'A dove in meekness'!

Lombard But you'll have to admit it has a ring about it. Maybe you and I remember a different Hugh. But maybe that's not the point.

O'Neill What is the point? That's certainly a bloody lie.

Lombard Not a lie, Hugh. Merely a convention. And I'll come to the point later. Now, the second key event: the Nine Years War between yourself and England, culminating in the legendary battle of Kinsale and the crushing of the most magnificent Gaelic army ever assembled.

O'Neill They routed us in less than an hour, Peter. Isn't that the point of Kinsale?

Lombard You lost a battle – that has to be said. But the telling of it can still be a triumph.

O'Neill Kinsale was a disgrace. Mountjoy routed us. We ran away like rats.

Lombard And again that's not the point.

O'Neill You're not listening to *me* now. We disgraced ourselves at Kinsale.

Lombard And then I come to my third and final key point; and I'm calling this section – I'm rather proud of the title – I've named it 'The Flight of the Earls'. That has a ring to it, too, hasn't it? That tragic but magnificent exodus of the Gaelic aristocracy –

O'Neill Peter –

Lombard When the leaders of the ancient civilization took boat from Rathmullan that September evening and set sail for Europe.

O'Neill As we pulled out from Rathmullan the McSwineys stoned us from the shore!

Lombard Then their journey across Europe when every crowned head welcomed and fêted them. And then the final coming to rest. Here. In Rome.

O'Neill And the six years after Kinsale – before the Flight of the Earls – aren't they going to be recorded? When I lived like a criminal, skulking round the countryside – my countryside! – hiding from the English, from the Upstarts, from the Old English, but most assiduously hiding from my brother Gaels who couldn't wait to strip me of every blade of grass I ever owned. And then when I could endure that humiliation no longer, I ran away! If these were 'my people' then to hell with my people! The Flight of the Earls – you make it sound like a lap of honour. We ran away just as we ran away at Kinsale. We were going to look after our own skins! That's why we 'took boat' from Rathmullan! That's why the great O'Neill is here – at rest – here – in Rome. Because we ran away.

Lombard That is my outline. I'll rewrite it in any way you want.

O'Neill That is the truth. That is what happened.

Lombard How should it be rewritten?

O'Neill Those are the facts. There is no way you can make unpalatable facts palatable. And your point – just what is your point, Peter?

Lombard I'm no historian but –

O'Neill Then don't write my history. Or maybe you could trust me to write it myself: one of the advantages of fading eyesight is that it gives the imagination the edge over reality.

Lombard May I try to explain something to you, Hugh? May I tell you what my point is?

O'Neill I'm weary of all this.

Lombard People want to know about the past. They have a genuine curiosity about it.

O'Neill Then tell them the whole truth.

Lombard That's exactly what my point is. People think they just want to know the 'facts'; they think they believe in some sort of empirical truth, but what they really want is a story. And that's what this will be: the events of your life categorized and classified and then structured as you would structure any story. No, no, I'm not talking about falsifying, about lying, for heaven's sake. I'm simply talking about making a pattern. That's what I'm doing with all this stuff – offering a cohesion to that random catalogue of deliberate achievement and sheer accident that constitutes your life. And that cohesion will be a narrative that people will read and be satisfied by. And that narrative will be as true and as objective as I can make it – with the help of the Holy Spirit. Would it be profane to suggest that that was the method the Four Evangelists used? – took the haphazard events in Christ's life and shaped them into a story, into four complementary stories. And those stories are true stories. And we believe them. We call them gospel, Hugh, don't we? (*He laughs suddenly and heartily.*) Would you look at that man? What are you so miserable about? Think of this (*book*) as an act of *pietas*. Ireland is reduced as it has never been reduced before – we are talking about a colonized people on the brink of extinction. This isn't the time for a critical assessment of your 'ploys' and your 'disgraces' and your 'betrayal' – that's the stuff of another history for another time. Now is the time for a hero. Now is the time for a heroic literature. So I am offering Gaelic Ireland two things. I'm offering them this narrative that has the elements of myth. And I'm offering them Hugh

O'Neill as a national hero. A hero and the story of a hero. (*Pause.*) It's a very worldly nostrum for a clergyman to propose – isn't it? I suppose, if I were a holy man, not some kind of a half priest, half schemer, I suppose I would offer them God and prayer and suffering. But there are times when a hero can be as important to a people as a God. And isn't God – or so I excuse my perfidy – isn't God the perfect hero?

A very long silence. Lombard gathers up his papers and closes the book. O'Neill assimilates what he has heard.

O'Neill How do you write about Harry?

Lombard What is the 'truth' about Harry? Well, we know, for example, that his Old English family threw him out, that he was destitute and that when you offered him a job, any job, he grabbed at it. We know, for example, that he was once passionately loyal to the Queen but that, when he joined you, he seemed to have no problem in betraying that loyalty. Or simply – very simply – we know for example that Harry Hoveden was a man who admired and loved you without reservation and who has dedicated his whole life to you. For all I know there may be other 'truths' about Harry.

O'Neill Which are you recording?

Lombard I know which one history prefers. As I keep telling you, histories are stories, Hugh, and stories prefer faithful friends, don't they? And isn't that the absolute truth about Harry? – is Harry Hoveden not a most faithful friend?

Another long silence.

O'Neill And Mabel?

Lombard Yes?

335

O'Neill (*shouting*) Don't play bloody games with me, Archbishop! You know damned well what I'm asking you!

Lombard You're asking me how Mabel will be portrayed.

O'Neill (*softly*) Yes, I'm asking you how Mabel will be portrayed.

Lombard I've tried to explain that at this time the country needs a –

O'Neill How-will-Mabel-be-portrayed?

Pause.

Lombard The story of your life has a broad but very specific sweep, Hugh –

O'Neill Peter, just –!

Lombard And all those ladies you chose as your wives – splendid and beautiful and loyal though they undoubtedly were – well, they didn't contribute significantly to – what was it Mabel herself used to call it? – to the overall thing – wasn't that it? I mean they didn't reroute the course of history, did they? So I have got to be as fair as I can to *all* those ladies without diminishing them, without inflating them into something they were not, without lying about them. I mean our Catriona, our beautiful Catriona, would be the last to claim some historical eminence, wouldn't she? But they all did have their own scales; and they recognized what those dimensions were; and in fairness to them we should acknowledge those dimensions accurately.

O'Neill So Mabel . . .?

Lombard (*pretending irritation*) You're incorrigible, Hugh O'Neill! You know that, don't you? You never give up. All I've got down on paper is a general outline and a

336

couple of opening pages and the man keeps badgering me about minor details!

O'Neill So Mabel . . .?

Lombard Let me ask you a question. In the big canvas of national events – in your exchanges with popes and kings and queens – is that where Mabel herself thought her value and her importance resided? Is that how she saw herself? But she had her own value, her own importance. And at some future time and in a mode we can't imagine now I have no doubt that story will be told fully and sympathetically. It will be a domestic story, Hugh; a love story; and a very beautiful love story it will be. But in the overall thing, Hugh . . . How many heroes can one history accommodate? And how will I emerge myself for heaven's sake? At best a character in a subplot. And isn't that adequate for minor people like us? Now, Hugh, tell me, how do you want to rewrite my outline?

O'Neill The overall thing – yes, that was her expression.

Lombard I made you a solemn promise. I'll rewrite it in any way you want. What changes do you want me to make? (*Pause.*) Not necessarily anything major. (*Pause.*) Even small adjustments. (*Pause.*) Just say the word. (*Pause.*) Now I'm badgering you – amn't I? Forgive me. And if any idea or suggestion does occur to you over the next weeks or months, sure I'll be here, won't I? Neither of us is going anywhere – unless Plunkett and O Domhnaill recruit us for their next expedition. Now. It's time for a drink. We've earned it. My poor mouth's dry from blathering. Affane – where are you?

O'Neill A lure to perdition – is that what you called it?

Lombard A foretaste of immortality. It really is wonderful. Easy – easy – don't gulp it down. Sip it slowly. Savour it.

Harry enters, carrying a bottle.

Ah, Harry! We're just about to kill this bottle of poitin. But, as the man says, it's not going to die without the priest. Will somebody please hit me every time I make one of those hoary clerical jokes? What's that you have?

Harry A bottle of wine.

Lombard Where did that come from?

Harry I got it ten minutes ago.

O'Neill I thought we had no money?

Harry It's only cheap chianti.

O'Neill Where did the money come from?

Harry I had an old pair of shoes I didn't want. The porter had some bottles to spare. Who wants a glass?

Lombard Do you know what you are, Harry? A loyal and faithful man. Now that is a truth! (*He pauses beside Hugh as he goes to the desk. Privately*) Trust it, Hugh. Trust it. (*aloud*) To all of us. May we live for ever – in one form or another. And now I'm going to give the first public recital of *The History of Hugh O'Neill*. In the name of God – I know the opening by heart! In the name of God. Herewith I set my hand to chronicle the life of Hugh O'Neill –

> *When O'Neill speaks he speaks almost in a whisper in counterpoint to Lombard's public recitation. His English accent gradually fades until at the end his accent is pure Tyrone.*

O'Neill By the Queen of England, France and Ireland her most gracious favour created Earl of Tyrone –

Lombard Son of Feardorcha, son of Conn Bacagh, son of Conn Mor, noblest son of noble lineage, who was fostered

338

and brought up by the high-born nobles of his tribe –

O'Neill I do with all true and humble penitency prostrate myself at your feet and absolutely submit myself to your mercy, most sorrowfully imploring your commiseration and appealing only to your clemency –

Lombard He continued to grow and increase in comeliness and urbanity, tact and eloquence, wisdom and knowledge, goodly size and noble deeds so that his name and fame spread throughout the five provinces of Ireland and beyond –

O'Neill May it please you to mitigate your just indignation against me for my betrayal of you which deserves no forgiveness and for which I can make no satisfaction, even with my life –

Lombard And people reflected in their minds that when he would reach manhood there would not be one like him of the Irish to avenge their wrongs and punish the plunderings of his race –

O'Neill Mabel, I am sorry . . . please forgive me, Mabel . . .

Lombard For it was foretold by prophets and by predictors of futurity that there would come one like him –
A man, glorious, pure, faithful above all
Who will cause mournful weeping in every territory.
He will be a God-like prince
And he will be king for the span of his life.

O'Neill is now crying. Bring down the lights slowly.

WONDERFUL TENNESSEE

for D. E. S. Maxwell

Characters

Three married couples
all in their late thirties/early forties:

Terry
Berna

George
Trish

Frank
Angela

Terry is Trish's brother.
Angela and Berna are sisters.

Set

The action takes place in the present day on a remote pier in north-west Donegal.

A stone pier at the end of a headland on the remote coast of north-west Donegal. The stonework is grained with yellow and grey lichen. The pier was built in 1905 but has not been used since the hinterland became depopulated many decades ago. The pier extends across the full width of the stage. It begins stage left (the mainland) and juts out into the sea so that it is surrounded by water on three sides – the auditorium, the area stage right, and the back wall (left and right from the point of view of the audience).

From the floor of the pier stone steps lead down to the sea/auditorium. Steps also lead up to the catwalk, eighteen inches wide and about five feet above the floor of the pier. From the catwalk one can see over the back wall of the pier (about ten feet high) and right across the surrounding countryside and sea.

There are some weather-bleached furnishings lying around the pier floor: fragments of fishing nets, pieces of lobster pots, broken fish-boxes. Some rusty bollards and rings. A drift of sand in the top right-hand corner. Stones once used as weights inside lobster pots. A listing and rotting wooden stand, cruciform in shape, on which hangs the remnant of a life-belt.

People can enter and exit only stage left.

Wonderful Tennessee was first performed at the Abbey Theatre, Dublin, on 30 June 1993. The cast was as follows:

Terry Donal McCann
Berna Ingrid Craigie
George Robert Black
Trish Marion O'Dwyer
Frank John Kavanagh
Angela Catherine Byrne

Directed by Patrick Mason
Designed by Joe Vanek
Lighting by Mick Hughes

Act One

SCENE ONE

A very warm day in August. Early afternoon. Silence and complete stillness. Then after a time we become aware that there are natural sounds: the gentle heave of the sea; a passing seagull; the slap and sigh of water against the stone steps. This lasts until we have established both a place and an environment of deep tranquillity and peace.

Now we hear another sound from a long distance away – an approaching minibus, and almost as soon as we identify the sound, discrepant and abusive in this idyllic setting, fade in the sound of people singing 'Happy Days are Here Again'. Boisterous singing, raucous singing, slightly tiddly, day-excursion singing that is accompanied on the piano accordion. Trish sings a solo line and this is greeted with laughter, mockery, cheers, encouragement. Then everybody joins in again.

Now the minibus has arrived and stops at the end of the pier (i.e. stage left off) and the idyllic atmosphere is completely shattered: doors banging; shouting; laughter; a sense of excitement and anticipation; animated, overlapping chatter:

Trish Help! We're lost!

Berna Where are we?

Terry This is it.

Trish You're lost, Terry; admit it; we're lost.

Frank It – is – wonderful!

Angela This can't be it, is it?

Terry Believe me – this is it.

Trish Help!

Frank (off) sings the title line of the song, 'Happy Days are Here Again'.

Angela Where's this wonderful island? I see no island.

Trish We're lost – we're lost – we're lost! Help!

Terry This is where we get the boat, Trish.

Trish Oh my God – lost!

Frank Anybody see my camera?

Trish Lost – lost!

Terry Isn't it wonderful?

Frank Sober up, everybody, please.

Angela You're joking, Terry, aren't you?

Trish Lost, I'm telling you. This is the back of nowhere.

Terry This is it – believe me.

George plays 'O Mother, I could weep for mirth / Joy fills my heart so fast'. Trish sings, '– weep for mirth –' and says:

Trish So could I, George.

And Frank simultaneously sings the line, 'Joy fills my heart so fast' to George's accompaniment.

Berna Mind the step.

Angela Admit it, Terry: you're lost.

Berna Here's your camera, Frank.

Trish Let me out of here. Help!

Frank Thanks, Berna.

Trish I'm going straight back with you, Charlie.

Angela What in God's name are we doing here?

Terry Admit it – isn't it wonderful?

Trish Wonderful, he says! Help!

Terry Yes, I think it's wonderful.

Frank There's not a house within a hundred miles.

Berna Let's all go back with Charlie.

Trish Heeeeeeeeelp!

Now George begins to play 'I Want to be Happy'. Cheers and mocking laughter at the choice. Through his playing:

Angela Right, George! So do I!

Trish Happy – here?

Angela Yeah-yeah-yeah-yeah! Why not?

Berna Happy, happy, happy, happy.

Frank Yes, George, yes.

And they join in the song and continue talking through it.

Berna Whose sleeping-bag is this?

Trish Mine, Berna. Thank you.

Angela At least we'll get a bit of sun.

Trish Hand me that blanket, Berna.

Frank We're the first people ever to set foot here.

Berna Here's your sun hat, Angela.

Frank Careful. I'm closing this door.

Trish Help!

Terry enters, animated, laughing, excited. Like all the others he is dressed in colourful summer clothes. He has a sleeping-bag slung over his shoulder and carries two large expensive hampers filled with food and drink.
    As Terry enters, calling, off:

Is this your idea of a joke, Terry?

George stops playing.

Terry (*on*) What's that?

Trish (*off*) Is this some kind of practical joke?

Terry Believe me – it's everything you ever dreamed of.

Frank (*off*) Wonderful!

Terry Believe me.

And immediately George strikes up 'I Want to be Happy' again.

Quite right, George! (*sings:*)
'. . . But I won't be happy
Till I make you happy, too'.

George continues with the song; and some of the people off join in the singing. But Terry's laughter suddenly stops. Eagerly, with a hint of anxiety, he searches out the island (at the back of the auditorium, right) and at the same time in a low, barely audible voice, he mumbles/speaks the words of the song the others are singing off. Now he has found the island. He drops the hampers. He slips the straw hat off his head, holds it against his chest and gazes out to sea. After a few seconds Frank enters. Like Terry he is dressed in bright summer clothes.

Frank The minibus is about to –

Terry is so intent on the island that he does not hear him.

Terry, your minibus is about to head home and Charlie wants to know – (*He calls, impatiently:*) Please, Angela!

Terry Look, Frank.

Frank Turn it down, Angela, would you?

Terry There it is.

Frank That's a crowd of lunatics you have there. So what time tomorrow is Charlie to come back for us?

Terry Whenever it's bright.

Frank It'll be sort of bright all night, I hope. Let's say – what? – seven? – seven thirty?

Terry That's fine.

Frank Seven thirty OK with you?

Terry (*indifferently*) Fine – fine.

Burst of laughter off.

Frank Surely to God they can't keep that pace up all night!

As he turns to leave, Berna enters. Dressed for the outing and carrying a hold-all, various bags, a sleeping-bag, etc.

Berna (*singing earnestly*) 'When skies are grey and you say you are blue –'

Frank Certainly am, Berna.

He swings her round in a dance and sings along with her.

Frank and Berna 'I'll send the sun smiling through –'

Frank Wowo-wow-wow-wow! Hey, Terry; some mover that lady of yours! (*exiting*) Right, Charlie. All settled. Seven thirty tomorrow morning.

The moment Frank exits, Berna's brittle-bright face is transformed with anxiety. She goes quickly to Terry's side and speaks in a low, urgent voice. George suddenly stops playing 'I Want to be Happy' in mid-phrase and plays 'Jesu, Joy of Man's Desiring'.

Trish Lovely, George. (*She sings with George.*)

Berna I want to go home.

Terry There it is, Berna. Look.

Berna Take me home, Terry – please.

Terry Wonderful, isn't it?

Berna Please, Terry.

Terry Just for tonight, Berna – just one night. Believe me – you'll love it.

Berna Have you any idea how desperately unhappy I am?

Terry Berna, I –

Berna I don't think I can carry on, Terry.

Terry Of course you can carry on. The doctor says you're a lot better. (*He reaches out to touch her.*) Did you remember to take your pills this morning?

The music stops.

Berna (*quietly, almost with pity*) For God's sake . . .

She moves quickly away from him and busies herself with her belongings. The moment she says 'For God's sake' the engine starts up. Again the overlapping voices off:

Trish He's going.

Angela See you tomorrow morning.

Trish Help!

Frank Don't go, Charlie! Don't abandon us!

Angela Thank you, Charlie.

Trish Stop him! Don't let him go!

George begins to play 'Aloha' and this is greeted with laughter and groans and singing.

Frank Perfect, George! (*He sings a phrase of the song.*)

Trish Come back, Charlie! Help! Come back!

Angela 'Bye, lovely world!

Frank continues singing.

Trish 'Bye, civilization.

Angela 'Bye, Charlie.

Trish Don't forget us, Charlie.

All 'Bye . . . 'bye . . . 'bye . . .

Terry and Berna stand in silence, motionless, watching the departing bus.

Berna (*softly*) 'Bye, Charlie . . . 'bye . . .

The music, the singing, the shouting all stop. The sound of the departing bus fades away. Silence. Once again the landscape is still and totally silent. Then Angela, unaccompanied and at half the song's usual tempo, belts out the defiant line –

Angela (*sings*) 'I want to be happy –'

Trish Damn right, Angela!

Angela (*sings*) 'But I won't be happy –'

Trish Why not?

Angela (*sings*) 'Till I make you happy, too.'

And at this point she is joined first by George on the accordion, then by Trish, and then, very privately, almost inaudibly, by Berna. After Angela's first line, 'I want to be happy', slowly accelerate the tempo to normal.

Now enter – immediately after the line 'Till I make you happy too' – George, Angela, Frank and Trish (in that order); each holding on to the waist of the person in front; all (except George) singing lustily; all doing a clownish, parodic conga dance, heads rolling, arms flying – a hint of the maenadic. All are dressed in bright summer clothes and each carries some gaudy summer equipment – straw bags, sun hats, sleeping-bags, sun umbrellas, cameras, binoculars, etc., etc. Suddenly the pier becomes a fairground. George is the accordionist. His neck is swathed in a white bandage. On those rare occasions when he speaks his voice is husky and barely audible. Trish has a plastic cup (wine) in one hand. Angela swings an empty wine bottle by the neck. The moment they come on stage Terry's face lights up and happily, extravagantly, he joins in the singing and the dance.

All 'Life's really worth living –'

Trish Come on, Berna! Party time!

And after a moment's hesitation Berna joins in the parade and the singing with earnest, deliberate enthusiasm.

All
'When we are mirth-giving –
Why can't I give some to you?'

Frank now stands aside and takes a series of rapid photographs. Now only Terry and Angela sing to

George's accompaniment.

Terry and Angela 'When skies are grey –'

Trish Terrific, Angela!

Terry and Angela '– and you say you are blue –'

Terry Your wife's a star, Frank.

Frank Blessed, amn't I?

Angela (*solo*) 'I'll send the sun smiling through –'
Give me your hand, Berna! So –

> *Now back to the very slow tempo and the exaggerated steps. Angela and Berna, hand in hand, dance/promenade across the pier.*

Angela and Berna 'I want to be happy –'

Frank The wonderful sisters!

Angela and Berna
'But I won't be happy
Till I make you happy too.'

> *Angela suddenly stops and holds her head.*

Angela Oh God!

> *The music stops.*

The head's beginning to reel!

Frank (*sings*) 'In the good old summer time –'

> *George drowns Frank's singing with a very formal 'Amen' cadence.*

Terry Thank you, George.

> *General laughter. Terry holds his hands up.*

And now, my children – please.

Trish Quiet, everybody!

Terry Your attention, please.

Frank Please!

Terry I bid you all welcome.

Frank Thank you, Terence.

Trish Where are we, Terry?

Frank Arcadia.

Terry Ballybeg pier – where the boat picks us up.

Trish County what?

Terry County Donegal.

Trish God. Bloody Indian territory.

Frank Where does the boatman live?

Terry Back there. At the end of the sand dunes.

Trish (*to George*) Ballybeg, George. In County Donegal.

  George nods and smiles.

Terry Right. So – stage one complete. Welcome again.

Angela Sounds proprietorial, doesn't he?

Terry I'm only the sherpa.

Trish Only what? (*to Berna*) What's a sherpa?

Frank (*up on catwalk*) Next parish Boston, folks!

Terry (*privately*) Are you all right?

Angela A little too much wine.

Terry And you've changed your hair.

Angela For the big occasion! Of course!

Terry Lovely.

She touches his shoulder quickly, lightly, and moves away. They deposit their belongings at various places along the pier – that place becomes that person's 'territory' for the rest of the night. Now they all move around slowly, silently, assessing the pier itself and its furnishings and the surrounding sea and countryside. Terry watches them. He is anxious to have their approval.

Well?

Frank (*in approval*) Well–well–well–well.

Terry So far so good?

Frank So far wonderful, Terry.

Terry (*to all*) Isn't it?

Frank Wonderful. (*He comes down from the catwalk.*)

Terry Some place, George?

George Yes. Yes.

Trish Sorry, Terry – where is this again?

Frank (*to Terry*) Permanently lost, that sister of yours.

Terry Ballybeg pier.

Trish In County –?

Frank Wasting your time, Terry.

Terry Donegal. This is where the boat picks us up.

Trish You've told me that three times. (*to George*) The boat picks us up here.

George nods and smiles. Pause. Again they gaze around, touching the furnishings, sitting on the

*bollards. As they move around George plays 'Jesu, Joy
of Man's Desiring'. Angela busies herself with her
belongings, deliberately ignoring the surroundings.*

A long time since this has been used.

Terry Not for fifty years.

Frank More. I'd say.

Terry Well?

Frank Listen! Not a sound.

Terry Trish?

Trish Very . . . remote, isn't it?

Terry But worth four hours in that minibus?

Trish (*not quite certain*) Oh yes . . .

Frank The bus was fine. It's Charlie's terrible jokes I can't
take. If he were my driver, Terry, I'd muzzle him.

Terry (*to Angela*) Some place, isn't it?

Trish Wonderful, Terry. Isn't it, Berna?

Berna Yes.

Frank These (*rings*) were made to last.

Terry And that stone – all cut by hand. (*He again
attempts to include Angela.*) What do you call that mossy
stuff – lichen?

Trish And that view! Look!

Frank What were these stones for?

Terry Weights for lobster pots.

Frank Amazing. Another world altogether.

Trish Heavenly.

Terry Yes.

Trish You'd think you could see *beyond* the horizon. It really is wonderful. Oh, my goodness . . . (*to George*) Ballybeg pier. In County Donegal.

George I know, Trish!

Terry (*to Angela*) What do you think of it?

Angela 'Wonderful' . . . I know another happy song, George.

She sings the first line of the refrain of 'I Don't Know Why I'm Happy'. George picks it up immediately.

Yes! He's a genius!

She sings the second line of the refrain.

Terry Your wonderful wife – off again.

Frank (*spreading his hands*) Your wonderful sister-in-law.

Terry sings the third and fourth line with Angela.

Terry Once more!

And accompanied by George and with Trish clapping in time they sing the whole refrain again.

Remember Father singing that every Christmas?

Trish Don't remember that. Did he?

Angela Your George is a genius, Trish.

Trish I know.

Angela Give me a kiss, George. (*She kisses him.*) You should be wearing a toga and playing a lyre and gorging yourself with black grapes. (*She picks up a wreath of dried seaweed and places it on his head.*) There! Dionysus!

Trish I have a suggestion, Terry: let's have the party here.

359

Frank (*holding up a fragment of the lifebelt*) Anybody drowning?

Terry We have a boat coming for us, Trish.

Trish We don't have to take it, do we?

Terry Yes, we do.

Trish Why?

Frank Because it's all arranged.

Trish Berna, what do you say?

Berna I don't care. Here's fine. Here's wonderful.

Trish Angela?

Angela I know another happy song!

Frank (*icily*) Angela, we're all trying to –

Terry (*sings*) 'Here we are again –'

Angela That's it!

   George picks up the melody.

(*sings*) 'Happy as can be –'

Trish I know that!

Trish, Terry and Angela (*sing together*) 'All good pals and jolly good company.'

   Angela now continues alone. She hoists up her skirts and does a parodic dance up and down the pier as she sings.
    Terry and Trish clap hands. Angela's performance is full and exuberant but at the same time there is a hint of underlying panic.

Angela (*singing and dancing*)
'A kiss for Bernadette,

My darling sister, B.
I think I need a very strong cup of tea.'

Frank (*icily*) Not at all! You're wonderful!

Angela
'I may be slightly drunk
As teachers oughtn't be.
But Frank, my husband,
Tra-la-la-la-la-la-lee –'

Oh God . . . (*She flops on to a bollard.*)

Frank Thank you very much. Now – what about this boat, Terry?

Trish I vote we stay here. Berna?

Frank Terry's day, Trish.

Trish Aren't we all happy enough here?

Angela (*sings to same air*) 'Today is Terry's day –'

Frank (*to Terry*) What do you say?

Terry You think this is great? Believe me, my children, you ain't seen nuthin' yet.

Angela One final happy song –

Frank For Christ's sake!

Angela And despite my husband's encouragement the last happy song I'll sing.

Trish Yes, Angela, sing! Let's have a song!

Angela And this last happy song is for our host, Terry Martin –

Trish My wonderful brother.

Frank Mister Terence Martin!

Terry Terence Mary Martin.

Angela Concert promoter.

Terry She means showman.

Angela Turf accountant.

Frank Yeah!

Terry She means bookie.

Angela Gambler.

Terry She means eejit.

Angela And a man of infinite generosity and kindness.

   Overlapping voices:

George Yes!

Frank Hear, hear!

Angela Yeah–yeah–yeah!

Trish Perfectly true!

Frank Yes!

Terry (*embarrassed*) That sho' is me, folks.

Angela (*raising a bottle*) To Terence Mary.

Trish To Terry and Berna.

Angela Friend, brother-in-law, most generous of –

   George plays another 'Amen' chord that drowns out the rest of her speech.

Behave yourself, you!

Terry Wait–wait–wait–wait–wait. Give me a hand here, Frank.

   Terry throws open a hamper and produces bottles.

362

Frank We're not having the party here, are we?

Angela I want to sing another cheap song.

Terry There are more cups in that bag.

Angela You sing, Berna!

Berna Later, maybe.

Trish It's not champagne, is it?

Terry That's what the man sold me.

Angela George! A cheap song!

George We'll drink first.

Trish Oh God, Terry!

Frank Anybody need a cup?

Trish A bit mad this, isn't it? What time of day is it? (*to Berna*) Maybe we're all mad, are we?

Berna Maybe.

Frank May concerts and gambling and bookmaking always prosper.

Trish Oh, God, Terry, something wrong with this, isn't there?

Terry Why?

Angela (*sings*) 'Oh, Terry Martin, what can I do?'

Terry (*sings*) 'I took a bus to Ballybeg and I found myself with you.' Berna? (*Drink.*)

Berna Up to the top, please.

Terry (*softly*) You OK?

Berna (*loudly*) That's not the top.

Terry Shouldn't you go easy on –?

Berna That's sufficient, thank you.

Angela (*to Frank*) Both up to the brim, please. (*Cups.*)

Frank You'll get your share.

Angela Jesus, how I love a prodigal man! To cheap songs!

Terry George? (*Drink.*)

George Please.

Trish Just a little, Terry.

> *But George tilts the bottle and fills his cup to*
> *overflowing.*

George Lovely. Thanks.

Terry Good idea this, isn't it?

Trish We're blessed in the weather. He's (*George*) looking
well, isn't he?

Terry Great. To the old band, George.

George The Dude Ranchers.

Terry The Dude Ranchers. The best band ever to tour
Ireland. How many years were we on the road?

Trish Twenty-one.

Terry Were we?

George A lifetime.

Trish A lifetime, he says.

George And we'll do it again.

Trish You were told not to speak.

Terry Yes, we'll do it again! And this time we'll tour the
world!

George smiles, spreads his hands and moves away.

Berna I'll have some more champagne, Frank.

Frank On the way.

Angela (*to Berna*) Shouldn't you go easy on that, love?

Frank Don't spare it. Loads more in that hamper.

Berna Thank you, Frank.

Trish and Terry are alone.

Terry How is he? (*George*)

Trish He plays all day long. As if he were afraid to stop.

Terry He's looking great.

Trish You've got to stop sending that huge cheque every week, Terry.

Terry Nothing. It's –

Trish We can manage fine.

Terry It's only –

Trish We don't need it. Honestly.

Terry How was the check-up last week?

Trish Three months at most.

Terry Oh Christ. Does he know?

Trish He's very brave about it.

Terry Is there anything –?

Trish (*aloud*) Quiet, please! The brother is going to make a speech!

Terry The brother is –!

Frank Speech! Silence! Speech!

Terry The brother is going to do nothing –

Frank Glasses all full?

Overlapping talk:

Any more champagne?

Trish Listen to the brother.

Angela Good man, Terry.

Trish Go ahead.

Frank Please! Quiet!

Trish And make it short, Terry.

Angela Terence Mary Martin!

Frank But first – first – may I say something? To Terry, for whom we all have the utmost respect and affection; and to his lovely Berna; both of whom have made all our lives –

Angela (*quickly, lightly*) Happy birthday.

Frank A very happy –

And the rest is drowned by George playing 'Happy Birthday to You'. And everybody joins in the singing. Terry covers his face in exaggerated but genuine embarrassment and pretends to hide behind the lifebelt stand while they sing to him. When the chorus ends he sings the first two lines of the refrain of 'I'm Twenty-one Today'. General laughter.

Trish All right, Terry. One very short speech.

Terry No–no–no–no–no. No speeches. May I have your attention, please? Berna? George?

Frank Attention, please.

Terry OK?

They all fall silent. Terry points out to sea. They line up around him – Frank, Trish, Berna, George. Angela moves off and stands alone.

Straight out there. That island. That's where we're going.

Frank Yes . . .

Trish I'm lost – where? – is it –?

Frank Wonderful . . .

Terry (*to Trish*) Directly in front of you.

Frank Further left, Trish.

Terry (*to Berna*) Straight out there.

Berna I see it, Terry.

Frank (*to Trish*) Got it?

Trish Think so . . .

Terry George?

George See it.

Terry See it, Angela?

She does not answer.

Frank That's no distance out, Terry.

Terry I suppose not.

Trish It's shaped like a ukulele, is it?

Frank That's a perfect circle for God's sake.

Terry So. There we are. See it, Angela? Our destination.

Angela (*softly, toasting*) Our 'destination'.

Trish I do see it. Yes.

Terry Wonderful, isn't it?

Berna It's not circular, Frank. That's a rectangle.

Trish God, that's miles away, Terry.

Terry Is it?

Trish Miles. And that's in County Sligo too, is it?

Frank Jesus.

Terry Donegal.

Trish Ah.

Terry Wonderful, isn't it?

Angela (*softly, toasting*) A destination of wonder.

Frank (*coldly*) Aren't you going to join us, Angela?

Trish (*to George*) Not Sligo, George. Still Donegal.

Angela stands beside the lifebelt stand, leans against it and sings in Marlene Dietrich style the first line of 'Falling in Love Again'.

Frank Angela, please –

George accompanies her now. She sings the next two lines and breaks off suddenly. George finishes the verse and then stops. Silence again as they all – except Angela – gaze out at the island, each with his/her thoughts. Angela takes off her sun hat and hangs it on the arm of the lifebelt stand.

Trish You never said it was a big island, Terry.

Terry It's not big, is it?

Trish That's a huge island.

Terry Is it?

Frank Hard to know what size it is – it keeps shimmering.

368

Now for the first time Angela joins them and looks out to sea.

Angela Has it a name, our destination?

Terry Oileán Draíochta. What does that mean, all you educated people?

Trish That rules me out. Where's our barrister? (*Berna*)

Berna Island of Otherness; Island of Mystery.

Trish God, it's not spooky, Terry, is it?

Berna Not that kind of mystery. The wonderful – the sacred – the mysterious – that kind of mystery.

Frank Good girl, Berna!

Trish All the same it's beautiful. (*to George*) Isn't it?

George Yes.

Trish Dammit, I've lost it again. (*to Terry*) You're sure it's not a mirage?

Frank catches her head and turns it.

Frank You're looking away beyond it.

Trish Am I?

Terry There is a legend that it was once a spectral, floating island that appeared out of the fog every seven years and that fishermen who sighted it saw a beautiful country of hills and valleys, with sheep browsing on the slopes, and cattle in green pastures, and clothes drying on the hedges.

And they say they saw leaves of apple and oak, and heard a bell and the song of coloured birds. Then, as they watched it, the fog devoured it and nothing was seen but the foam swirling on the billow and the tumbling of the dolphins.

Trish Will we see dolphins? God, I love dolphins.

Angela You know that by heart.

Terry (*embarrassed*) Do I?

Berna When did it stop being spectral?

Terry On one of its seven-year appearances fishermen landed on it and lit a fire.

Frank What was wrong with that?

Terry Fire dispels the enchantment – according to the legend. (*to Angela*) You're right. From a pamphlet about the place my father had.

Frank Maybe it is a bit like a ukulele.

Terry Nearly forgot – shoes off, everybody!

Frank What?

Terry We're supposed to be barefoot.

Frank You're joking, Terry!

Trish Why barefoot?

Terry Don't ask me. That's the custom. That's what people used to do long ago.

> *They slip out of their shoes. And again they gaze out to sea.*

Berna There are bushes on it.

Frank Come on, Berna! And clothes drying on the hedges?

Berna Whins, I think. Yes; they're whins. And a small hill away to the left.

Trish God, you've all powerful eyes.

Frank Looks more like clouds to me.

Berna A low hill. At the end of that side.

Angela (*to Terry*) You're our expert. Is there a hill there?

Terry Expert! I was there just once with my father. I was only seven at the time.

Trish I never heard that story.

Terry We fasted from the night before, I remember. And for the night you were on the island you were given only bread and water. (*to George*) Like some of our digs when we were on the road!

> *George nods and smiles. Frank now takes a series of photographs – of the others, of the island, of the furnishings of the pier.*

Trish And what did you do out there?

Terry I don't remember a lot. There were three beds – you know, mounds of stone – and every time you went round a bed you said certain prayers and then picked up a stone from the bottom of the mound and placed it on the top.

Frank Trish! (*Photograph.*)

Trish Oh, Frank!

Terry And I remember a holy well, and my father filling a bottle with holy water and stuffing the neck with grass – you know, to cork it. And I remember a whin bush beside the well –

Trish There! Good for you, Berna!

Terry And there were crutches and walking sticks hanging on the bush; and bits of cloth – *bratóga*, my father called them – a handkerchief, a piece of shawl –

371

bleached and turning green from exposure. Votive offerings – isn't that the English word? And there's the ruins of a Middle Age church dedicated to Saint Conall. (*to Frank*) Isn't that the period you're writing your book about?

Frank Something like that. Close enough.

Trish But it's not a pilgrimage island now?

Terry No, no; that all ended years and years ago.

Trish Why?

Frank People stopped believing, didn't they?

Terry Nobody does that sort of thing nowadays, do they? And when the countryside around here was populated apparently they made poitín out there – that wouldn't have helped the pilgrimage business. There were even stories of drunken orgies.

Angela (*salute*) Saint Dionysus!

Trish But years ago people went there to be cured?

Berna To remember again – to be reminded.

Trish To remember what?

Frank George! (*Photograph.*)

Berna To be in touch again – to attest.

Frank Angela! (*Photograph.*)

Terry People went there just to make a pilgrimage, Trish.

Frank And to see apparitions. Patricia! (*Photograph.*)

Trish But you saw crutches on that bush. So people must have been cured there.

Frank Apparitions were commonplace in the Middle

Ages. Saint Conall must have seen hundreds of apparitions in his day. Terry! (*Photograph*.)

Trish Don't be so cheap, Frank.

Frank Thousands maybe.

Trish (*to Terry*) Do you believe people were cured there?

Terry All I know is that at seven years of age just to get sitting up all night was adventure enough for me. The first time I ever saw the dawn. I remember my head was giddy from want of sleep.

Trish And father?

Frank Berna! (*Photograph*.)

Trish Why did Father go out there? He believed in nothing.

Frank You're beautiful.

Trish Why did Father go out there?

Terry For God's sake, Trish! That was another age. To pray – to do penance –

Berna To acknowledge – to make acknowledgement.

Terry You had another word, Berna – to attest!

George makes a sound.

What's that, George?

Trish To attest to the mystery, he says.

Terry And why not! (*He laughs*.) I'm a bookie for God's sake. All I know is: that's where we'll have our party tonight. OK?

Angela Once when the Greek god Dionysus was going to the island of Naxos he was captured by pirates who took him to be a wealthy prince –

Frank You'd never guess. My wife teaches Classics.

Angela But suddenly his chains fell away, and vines and ivy sprouted all over the pirate ship, and the sailors were so frightened they jumped into the sea and turned into dolphins.

Trish Will we really see dolphins? God, I love dolphins.

Frank is now up on the catwalk.

Frank Where does our boat come from?

Terry A house just across there. (*to Angela*) You know *that* by heart.

Frank No house. No boat. Nothing from here to Boston except a derelict church – without a roof.

Trish I'm sure it's very beautiful out there. But I'd be happy to settle for this. But if you all . . .

Silence as they gaze out again. Then suddenly Angela leaps on top of a bollard, flings her hands above her head and proclaims in the style of an American evangelist:

Angela There it is, friends – Oileán Draíochta, our destination! Wonderful – other – mysterious! Alleluia! So I ask you to join with me in that most beautiful song, 'Heavenly Sunshine'. Brother George?

As George plays a brief introduction:

Now – open your minds, your lungs, your arms, your hearts. All together, brothers and sisters – (*sings*) 'Heavenly sunshine, heavenly sunshine –' Can't hear you, friends. 'Flooding my soul with glory divine –'

Terry now joins her.

Angela and Terry
'Heavenly sunshine, heavenly sunshine,
Alleluia, Jesus is mine.'

Angela And one more time! Sister Tricia, Sister Berna –?

Terry, Trish, Berna and Angela (*sing together*)
'Heavenly sunshine, heavenly sunshine,
Flooding my soul with glory divine,
Heavenly sunshine, heavenly sunshine,
Alleluia, Jesus is mine –'

Angela And one more time, Brother George –

But instead of a reprise – and without a break in his playing – George goes straight into 'Knees-up, Mother Brown'. This is greeted with laughter, cheers, derision – voices overlapping:

George!

Frank Wonderful!

Trish Good man, George!

Terry Sing it, Angela!

Berna I know that one!

And they all – except George – dance around the pier and sing the chorus at the top of their voices. When they get to the end of the chorus:

Terry One more time!

And again they sing the chorus. Just before it ends Frank shouts:

Frank Quiet, please! Shut up, will you?

They fall silent.

We have a problem, good brethren. I'm telling you – there is no boat.

Angela Who's for a quick drink?

Trish nods yes.

375

Frank And not only is there no boat, there isn't a house within a hundred miles of us.

Angela (*to Trish*) Champagne?

Trish nods yes.

Trish (*to Frank*) Use these (*binoculars*).

Terry Yes, there is, Frank. Just beyond the sand dunes.

Angela (*sings to the air of 'Abide with Me'*)
'Beyond the sand dunes
You will find our boat –'

Frank Nothing but bogland from here to the mountains. And not a boat from here to the horizon.

Terry A thatched cottage – further to your left.

Frank Sorry.

Trish You're the one with the eyes, Berna.

Terry As far as I remember it's down at the very edge of the water.

Frank Hold on . . . yes . . . is that not a byre?

Terry They're the people who do the ferrying.

Frank Deserted, Terry. And there's grass growing out of the thatch.

Terry Carlin's the name. Been there for generations.

Angela (*holding up a bottle*) Berna?

Berna signals no.

Frank Hold on . . . wait . . . Yes, you're right! There's smoke coming out of the chimney! God, that's a hovel. (*He comes down.*) Right, I'll go and get Carlin. Are we all set to leave?

Terry Think so. Aren't we?

Frank And he picks us up on the island tomorrow morning – when? – about seven?

Terry That's the plan.

Frank Right.

Angela (*sings to the air of 'Abide with Me'*)
'That is the place!
That shapes our destiny –'

Frank (*as he passes behind Angela, privately*) You're making a nuisance of yourself.

Angela sings the title of the song 'I Don't Know Why I'm Happy'.)

What if Carlin isn't at home?

Trish Or refuses to ferry bowsies.

Angela Or is dead.

Frank Seriously. What if –?

Terry Someone from the house will take us, Frank. They've been ferrying people for thousands of years.

Frank I'm sure they have. All I'm asking is: supposing there is nobody free now to –

Terry (*sharply, impatiently*) Tell him the new owner of the island sent you for him! (*He stops short; tries to laugh.*) I didn't mean to . . . (*'let that out' is unsaid*)

Pause.

Trish Well, aren't you a close one, Terry Martin!

Terry I'm sorry. I –

Trish You kept that a big secret.

Frank You've actually bought Oileán Draíochta?

Terry Four months ago. Sight unseen. Ridiculous, isn't it?

Angela So it's your island we're going to?

Terry Stupid, I know. Heard by accident it was on the market. (*to Angela*) Miles from anywhere – good for nothing, isn't it?

Angela spreads her hands.

Angela Challenge for a sherpa.

Terry I know it's ridiculous. I know it sounds –

Frank This is no mystery tour he's taking us on – he's taking us home! Wonderful, Terry!

Trish And I wish you luck with it. Congratulations. (*to Berna*) So you own your own island, Mrs Martin. Very posh.

Berna It's news to me.

Terry I was going to tell you all out there tonight – tomorrow morning – whenever. Anyhow . . . (*to Frank*) Will you get Carlin for us?

Frank I'm away. Well done. Terrific!

Frank goes off. Terry feels that some further explanation is necessary.

Terry Haven't seen it for over forty years . . . and I was always curious to have another look at it . . . obsessed in a kind of way . . . and the fact that it came on the market . . .

Trish Good. Great.

They drift apart and attend to their belongings. Terry goes to Trish.

All I can say is – you have money to burn.

378

Terry Not true at all, I'm afraid.

Trish Berna seems in better form.

Terry Do you think so?

Trish Plenty of chat out of her in the minibus.

Terry She's really most content when she's in the nursing home.

Trish (*very softly*) Mother was right, you know: if you didn't spoil her so much.

Terry Trish! (*to George*) Met an old friend of yours in London last week – Michael Robinson.

Trish You never did! (*to George*) He met Michael Robinson in London, George. (*to Terry*) And how was he?

Terry Great . . . fine . . . well, not so good. Bumped into him in a pub. Didn't recognize him – not that I ever knew him well. Actually I thought he was a down-and-out touching me.

Trish Michael?

Terry I know – awful. Asking very warmly for you (*George*). Talked for over an hour about you and him at college together . . . doing your degree . . . and the duets you used to play –

Trish Sonatas.

Terry That's it – sonatas.

Trish Beethoven sonatas.

Terry Talked for over an hour. Couldn't shut him up. Eventually I gave him some money and just . . . walked away.

George moves away and sits on a bollard.

Trish That's all they did for three whole years at college –
play piano and violin sonatas – day and night. The
Aeolians – that's what they called themselves.

Terry He said you talked about going professional.

George Maybe . . .

Trish They were the stars of the college. Oh such stars
they were. Michael was going to be Ireland's first great
concert violinist. He could have been, too. And there was
absolutely no doubt that George was the new
Rachmaninov – no doubt at all about that. And together
they were so brilliant, especially in the Beethoven sonatas.
Oh, I can't tell you how brilliant they were . . . Michael
Robinson . . . oh my goodness . . .

> *Pause. Berna hums the line 'O Mother, I could weep for
> mirth' and stops suddenly.*

Terry (*to Angela*) I know you think it's crass.

Angela What's that?

Terry Bookie Buys Island Sight Unseen.

Angela But an island remembered, however vaguely.

Terry I did it on impulse. In memory of my father, maybe.

Angela A new venue for rock concerts, wrestling
matches?

Terry Why not? Bullfights, revivalist meetings. I was
afraid you mightn't come this morning.

Angela Terry Martin Productions! Dionysian Nights On
Oileán Draíochta!

Terry If you hadn't come I'd have called it off.

Angela Celebrate The Passions That Refuse To Be Domesticated!

Terry I would have –

Angela Nature Over Culture! Instinct Over Management!

Terry Angela –

Angela A Hymn To The Forces That Defy Civilization!

Terry Oh God, Angela –

Angela (*passionately, urgently*) Please, Terry – for Christ's sake – please, not now – not now!

Berna stands on a fish-box and proclaims:

Berna Lord, it is good for us to be here!

Angela Amen to that, sister!

Terry Careful, Berna. That box is rotten.

Berna I want to sing a hymn.

Angela Yes! Sing your hymn, Berna!

Berna now sings, her face frozen in a fixed and desperate smile.

Berna (*sings*) 'O, Mother, I could weep for mirth –'

Terry Berna –

Berna 'Joy fills my heart so fast –' Help me, George!

Angela Help her, George.

Berna I'll start again. Give me a note.

George gives her a chord.

Thank you.
'O, Mother, I could weep for mirth
Joy fills my heart so fast –'

Angela now sings with her.

Berna and Angela
'My soul today is heaven on earth
O could the transport last.'

Trish Good girl, Berna!

Now Trish joins them.

Berna, Angela and Trish 'I think of thee and what thou
art –'

Now Terry joins them.

Berna, Angela, Trish and Terry
'Thy majesty, thy state.
And I keep singing in my heart
Immaculate! Immaculate!'

SCENE TWO

*Before the lights come up we hear George playing the
entire first verse of 'Oft in the Stilly Night'.*

*About twelve hours later – the early hours of the
following morning. The pier is lit by a midsummer-night
glow that illuminates with an icy, surreal clarity.*

*The boisterous, day-excursion spirit has long ago
evaporated. Waiting for the boat has made them weary
and a bit irritable. Each has retreated into his/her own
privacy and does not wish to be intruded on.*

*Angela is sitting on a bollard, gazing without interest
through the binoculars in the general direction of the
island. Trish is sitting with her back to the pier wall, her
arms round her legs, her face on her knees. Frank is on
the catwalk and looking towards Carlin's house. Berna is
sitting on the edge of the pier (stage right), her legs
hanging over the edge of the pier floor. George is sitting*

on a fish-box, head back, eyes closed, body erect and tense, playing the last bars of the song. Terry looks casually through the hampers, examining the contents, tidying up, killing time.

The music ends.

Terry Anybody for a slice of melting birthday cake?

No answer. He continues tidying. Pause.

Glass of flat champagne?

No answer. He continues tidying. Pause.

Venison and apricot compote? Honey gâteau? Ever hear of honey gâteau?

Trish Give our heads peace, Terry, would you?

Terry Maybe I should bring this cake over to Carlin. Might soften his bark.

Frank Hey-hey-hey-hey-hey! Look at that! There's smoke coming from the chimney again!

Trish (*wearily*) Wonderful.

Frank He lets the fire die at midnight and then three hours later he lights it up again. What the hell is Mr Carlin up to?

Trish We could do with a fire. It's got chilly.

Frank What sort of a game is he playing with us?

Terry Time has no meaning for a man like that. (*He holds up a small box.*) Cherry and mandarin chartreuse –? (*to Trish*) Sorry.

Pause. George now plays the full chorus of 'Down by the Cane-brake'. He plays very softly and more slowly than the song is scored. His arrangement with its harmonium-style chords endows the song with the tone

and dignity of a hymn. It sounds almost sacred.
Immediately after he plays 'Down by the cane-brake,
close by the mill' Angela looks at him.

Angela 'Down by the Cane-brake.'

George Know it?

Angela Haven't heard it in years.

Terry What's a cane-brake?

Angela Shelter-belt of canes, I suppose. Protection against the elements.

Terry Ah.

Frank If he's not playing some sort of bizarre game with us, then explain why he lights his fire at three in the morning.

Angela He just loves tormenting us.

Trish The poor man's cold, Frank.

Frank Not that man. That man has no human feelings.

Angela Maybe he wants to dispel the enchantment.

Terry Marrons glacés – whatever they are. George?

George No, thanks.

Frank He has betrayed us, the bastard.

Terry He'll come, Frank. Believe me.

Trish We could do with a cane-brake here.

Frank If he never had any intention of ferrying us across – fine! – say that straight out! 'Sorry, bowsies, no ferrying today.'

Terry He'll come.

Trish Couldn't we rent his boat from him and row ourselves out?

Frank Where's the boat? Has he got a boat?

Terry (*to Trish*) He'd never allow that.

Trish Why not?

Terry That's his job.

Trish Too late to go out now anyway.

Terry It's only ten to three. We'll still make it – believe me.

Trish Of course, when I proposed we spend the night here, I was shouted down. Perverse – that's what you are.

Frank 'Give me a while at the turf, sir. That's all I need.' And four hours later, 'A mouthful of tea and I'll be over behind you.'

Trish Maybe he's past ferrying people. Is he very old?

Frank Ancient; and filthy; and toothless. And bloody smiling all the time.

Angela Forget Mr Carlin, my darlings. Put Mr Carlin out of your thoughts.

Frank God, I always hated peasants.

Trish And bloody Sligo peasants are the worst, I'm sure.

Terry He'll come. Believe me. He'll come.

Angela 'Believe me – believe me' – I suppose it's enviable in a way, isn't it?

Terry What is?

Angela does not answer. She goes to Berna at the end of the pier.

Angela What's the water like?

Berna Warm. Warmish.

385

Angela Wouldn't mind a swim. Brighten us all up. (*She hugs Berna quickly.*) And how's the baby sister?

Berna shrugs.

You're looking much stronger.

Berna Am I?

Angela Terry says you'll be back in the practice in a month.

Berna That's not true. Who's looking after the children tonight?

Angela The McGuires next door.

Berna The whole brood?

Angela I know. Hearts of gold.

Berna I have a birthday present for young Frankie. I'll drop it in at the weekend.

Angela You have that godson of yours spoiled.

Berna No, I'll get Terry to leave it in. The godson has got very . . . tentative with me recently.

Angela You couldn't make that –

Berna I make him uneasy. You know how intuitive children are. I think maybe I frighten him.

Angela Frankie's dying about you, Berna.

Berna Frighten is too strong. When I reach out to touch him he shrinks away from me. I . . . disquiet him. Anyhow. Do you really think I look stronger?

Angela I know you are.

Berna Terry thinks the reason for my trouble is that we couldn't have a child. That's what he tells the doctors.

386

And that never worried me all that much. But it's an obsession with him. He's even more neurotic than Trish about not having children. A Martin neurosis, I tell him.

Angela Shhh.

Berna And he would have been so good with children. Married the wrong sister, didn't he?

Angela Berna –

Berna Oh, yes; oh, yes. When you married Frank a little portion of him atrophied. Then he turned to me. I'm the surrogate.

Angela You've got to –

Berna Are you happy, Angela?

Angels hums 'Happy Days Are Here Again'.

There are times when I feel I'm . . . about to be happy. That's not bad, is it? Are you laughing at me?

Angela Of course I'm not laughing at you.

Berna Maybe that's how most people manage to carry on – 'about to be happy'; the real thing *almost* within grasp, just a step away. Maybe that's the norm. But then there are periods – occasions – when just being alive is . . . unbearable.

Terry Marinated quail and quince jelly. God!

Trish The delights of the world – you have them all there.

Angela There are times when all of us –

Berna He has no happiness with me – Terry. Not even 'about-to-be' happiness. He should leave me. I wouldn't mind if he did. I don't think I'd mind at all. Because in a way I feel I've moved beyond all that. (*She stands up.*) But then what would he do, where would he go? (*She moves away.*)

Angela picks up the binoculars.

Terry Six months ago there was a horse called Quince Fruit running at Cheltenham. Worst mistake of my whole life. Practically cleaned me out – Quince Fruit almost ruined me.

Pause. Now Berna begins singing the verse of 'Down by the Cane-brake'. Immediately George accompanies her. She sings in the mood George established earlier, softly, quietly, but not quite as slowly as George played the chorus. She tells the story of the song with intimacy and precision, as do the others when they sing or join in, each singing in the same quiet, internal personal way.

Berna (*sings*)
'Down by the cane-brake, close by the mill
There lived a blue-eyed girl by the name of Nancy Dill –'

Terry (*to Trish*) Mother's song.

Trish nods.

Berna (*sings*)
'I told her that I loved her, I loved her very long,
I'm going to serenade her and this will be my song –'

Trish now sings the chorus with Berna.

Berna and Trish
'Come, my love, come, my boat lies low,
She lies high and dry on the O-hi-o.
Come, my love, come, and come along with me
And I'll take you back to Tennessee.'

A very brief bridging passage by George. Then Terry sings alone.

Terry (*sings*)
  'Down by the cane-brake some happy day
  You'll hear a wedding bell a-ringing mighty gay.
  I'm going to build a cabin and in a trundle bed
  There'll be a blue-eyed baby and all because you said –'

*Chorus sung by Frank, Berna, Trish and Terry. Then
Trish alone:*

Trish
  'Down by the cane-brake that's where I'll stay
  Longside of Nancy Dill till we are laid away.
  And when we get to heaven and Peter lets us in
  I'll start my wings a-flappin' and sing to her again –'

*Chorus sung by Frank, Berna, Trish, Terry and Angela.
Then a final cadence from George. Brief pause.*

What time is it?

Terry Just after three.

Trish Night, everybody. See you in the morning. 'Bye.

*Again they all retreat into their privacies. Angela looks
through the binoculars.*

Terry (*passing behind Angela*) Tennessee still there?

Angela Lost it again?

Terry Still there. 'Believe me.'

*She shrugs and smiles. Terry looks around at them all.
Then he addresses them.*

I know – I'm sorry – it's a mess. And when we were
planning it, it seemed a wonderful idea. It still is a
wonderful idea. And there's still a good chance we'll make
it – a very good chance. Carlin *will* come. I honestly . . .
Anyhow . . . sorry, sorry . . .

Pause.

Trish (*sits up*) I know when I was in Sligo before! Seventeen years ago – at a bridge congress.

Terry Donegal, Trish.

Trish No, Sligo. At the old Great Southern Hotel. My partner was a man –

Frank Here he comes! There he is! Look! Look!

Trish What? – who? –

Frank The boatman! Carlin! With his boat! He's here! He's bloody here!

Suddenly everybody is excited, agitated. They all talk at the same time:

Trish Who's here?

Terry Carlin.

Berna Oh God!

Terry Where is he?

Trish Who's Carlin?

Angela I don't believe it.

Terry Great – terrific! Are you sure, Frank?

Berna (*anxious, agitated*) Oh God! – Oh my God! –

Angela The bastard – where is he?

Trish Where, Frank? Where?

Angela I don't believe it.

Berna Oh my God!

Terry Is he alone? Quiet, please!

Berna Oh my God, Angela –

Terry Where is he, Frank?

Trish Can you see him?

Angela I don't believe it.

Terry Where is he, Frank?

Frank 'Wolf!' cried the naughty boy. 'Wolf.'

Trish What? Where is he?

Frank 'Wolf – wolf.'

Berna He's not there at all?

Frank 'Fraid not. Woke you up all the same, didn't it?

Terry (*quiet fury*) That is not funny, for Christ's sake.

Trish Oh, Frank, how could you?

Frank Joke.

Angela (*calmly*) Damn you, Frank.

Frank A joke – that's all.

Terry Not funny at all, Frank.

Frank Sorry.

Trish Oh, Frank, that was cruel.

Frank Sorry – sorry – sorry. For God's sake, what's eating you all?

> Again they retreat into themselves. And as they do
> George plays 'Regina caeli, laetare, alleluia; quia quem
> meruisti portare . . .' He breaks off mid-phrase. Silence.

Angela (*suddenly, with great energy*) All right,
everybody! Story time! So we're stuck here! We're going
nowhere! We'll pass the night with stories.

Trish Good for you, Angela. Yeah–yeah–yeah–yeah!

Angela 'Once upon a time' – who goes first? Terry!

Terry I don't know any stories.

Trish Yes, you do. He's a wonderful story-teller.

Angela We'll get him later. You start off, Trish.

Trish Let someone else start. I'll go second. Berna, tell us one of your law stories.

Berna All right. Let me think of one.

Trish A clean law story! We'll come back to you. Frank – 'Once upon a time –'

Frank Pass.

Terry Get it over with, Frank.

Trish Come on, Frank. Be a sport. It's only a bit of fun.

Frank Later. After Berna.

Angela I think George wants to go first.

Frank What about yourself, Terry?

Terry Couldn't tell a story to save my life.

Angela Have you a story to tell, George?

Trish What's wrong with you all? You go first, Angela. Then a clean law story. Then Frank. Then –

Angela George?

George Yes?

Trish Then me. Then Terry –

Angela George will go first. Tell us your story, George.

Trish Right – I'll kick off.

Angela (*to George*) 'Once upon a time –'

Frank Stop bullying, Angela.

George moves into the centre of the group.

Trish This woman had ten children, one after the other, and –

Angela Right, George?

Terry Angela –

Angela (*to George*) Ready?

Trish And the ten children all had red hair like the –

Angela (*to Trish*) Please. (*to George*) 'Once upon a time –'

Silence. George looks at each of them in turn. Then he plays the first fifteen seconds of the third movement ('Presto') of Beethoven's Sonata No. 14 ('Moonlight'). He plays with astonishing virtuosity, very rapidly, much faster than the piece is scored, and with an internal fury; so that his performance, as well as being dazzlingly dextrous and skilful and fast – because of its dazzling dexterity and skill and speed – seems close to parody. And then in the middle of a phrase, he suddenly stops. He bows to them all very formally, as if he had given a recital in a concert hall.

George Thank you. Thank you very much.

He now removes the accordion and puts it in the case. Pause.

Trish (*almost shouting, very emotional, close to tears*) Are you satisfied now? Happy now, are you? Do you see, you all? – not one of you is fit to clean his boots!

George now spreads out a sleeping-bag and lies on top

393

of it. Trish spreads a rug over him. Pause.

Berna I'm going for a swim. Anybody coming?

Terry Please, Berna; not now.

Berna Angela?

Terry That water could be dangerous, Berna.

Angela Wait until daybreak. I'll go with you then. I'd love a swim, too. As soon as it's daylight.

Frank comes down from the catwalk. He goes to Terry.

Frank Waiting – just waiting – waiting for anything makes you a bit edgy, doesn't it? Sorry about that wolf thing.

Terry makes a gesture of dismissal and continues looking through the hampers.

It wasn't meant cruelly. Just stupid.

Terry Brandied peaches and Romanian truffles. Christ. I order two hampers of good food and they fill them with stuff nobody can eat. (*He holds up a bottle.*) Drop of brandy?

Frank If you had some whiskey.

Terry Should have.

Frank Can't take it neat though.

Terry (*searching hamper*) Of course – everything except water. (*He points to a shallow hollow on the floor of the pier where water has gathered.*) Is that rain water or salt water?

Frank dips a finger and tastes it.

Frank We're in business. (*He scoops some water into a paper cup and makes a drink. Toasts:*) Happy birthday, Terry.

Terry That was yesterday.

Frank Was it? All the same.

Terry How's the book coming on?

Frank The finishing post is in sight . . . at last. Time for it, says you, after three-and-a-half years.

Terry Great.

Frank I know I shouldn't say this but I hope – God damn it, I pray – this is going to be the breakthrough for me. And some instinct tells me it will. Well . . . maybe . . . touch wood.

Terry You've told me a dozen times – I'm sorry – clock-making through the ages – is that it?

Frank Terence!

Terry Sorry.

Frank *The Measurement of Time and its Effect on European Civilization.*

Terry Ah.

Frank I know. But they assure me there is a market for it – not large but worldwide. It *is* fascinating stuff. I never seem to thank you for all your help, Terry.

Terry Nothing – nothing. Another splash? (*He pours more whiskey into the cup.*)

Frank How can I thank you adequately? Only for you I'd still be sitting in that estate agent's office. Instead of which – ta-ra! – the thrilling life of a journeyman writer, scrounging commissions. Angela going back to lecturing after all these years – that was a huge help, too, of course. And the poor girl hates it, hates it. But your support, Terry, every bloody week – magnanimous! I hope some day I'll –

Terry Don't talk about it. Please.

Frank A new Medici.

Terry Is that a horse?

Frank You know very well –

Terry I'd put money on that myself!

Frank Thanks. That's all I can say. Thank you. (*He finishes his drink rapidly and makes another.*)

Trish puts a pillow under George's head.

Trish Lift your head. Good. Are you warm enough? That's better.

Frank I annoyed Trish a while ago. She said I was cheap, joking about apparitions out there.

Terry She has her hands full.

Frank Tough life. Courageous lady.

Terry Yes. So – the clock book – when is it going to appear?

Frank Another apparition. This time next year, we hope. Actually I was thinking of doing a chapter on apparitions – well, visions, hallucinations, whatever.

Terry In a book about clocks?

Frank Time measurement, Terry! Did you know that the accurate measurement of time changed monastic practices in the Middle Ages, when Saint Conall and company flourished out there? See? You never knew that! Before that monks prayed a few times during the day – a casual discipline that depended on nature – maybe at cock-crow, at high noon, when it got too dark to work in the fields. But Saint Benedict wanted more than that from his monks: he wanted continuous prayer. And with the invention of clocks that became possible.

Terry But there weren't clocks then, were there?

Frank No, no; crude time-pieces; sophisticated egg-timers. But with these new instruments you could break the twenty-four hours into exact sections. And once you could do that, once you could waken your monks up at *fixed* hours two or three times a night, suddenly – (*He claps his hands.*) – continuous prayer!

Terry What has that to do with apparitions?

Frank Think about it. At the stroke of midnight – at 2.00 a.m. – at 4.00 a.m. – at 6.00 a.m. – you chase your monks out of their warm beds. Into a freezing chapel. Fasting. Deprived of sleep. Repeating the same chant over and over again. And because they're hungry and disoriented and giddy for want of sleep and repeating the same droning chant over and over again, of course they hallucinate – see apparitions – whatever. Wouldn't you?

Terry (*laughing*) Frank!

Frank Honestly! Medieval monks were always seeing apparitions. Read their books. And all because of the invention of time-pieces. A word of warning, Terry. Be careful at matins – that's just before dawn. That's when you're most susceptible.

Terry Is that going to be in your book?!

Frank Maybe. Why not? Anything to explain away the wonderful, the mystery.

Terry But you don't believe a word of that, do you?

Frank How would I know? But there must be some explanation, mustn't there? The mystery offends – so the mystery has to be extracted. (*He points to the island.*) They had their own way of dealing with it: they embraced it all – everything. Yes, yes, yes, they said; why bloody not? A rage for the absolute, Terry – that's what they had. And because their acceptance was so comprehensive, so open, so generous, maybe they *were* put in touch – what do you think? – so intimately in touch that maybe, maybe they actually *did* see.

Terry In touch with what? See what?

Frank Whatever it is we desire but can't express. What is beyond language. The inexpressible. The ineffable.

Terry To spend their lives out there in the Atlantic, I suppose they must have been on to something.

Frank And even if they were in touch, even if they actually did see, they couldn't have told us, could they, unless they had the speech of angels? Because there is no vocabulary for the experience. Because language stands baffled before all that and says of what it has attempted to say, 'No, no! That's not it at all! No, not at all!' (*He drinks rapidly.*) Or maybe they did write it all down – without benefit of words! That's the only way it could be written, isn't it? A book without words!

Terry You've lost me, Frank.

Frank And if they accomplished that, they'd have written the last book ever written – and the most wonderful! And then, Terry, then maybe life would cease! (*He laughs. Brief pause.*) Or maybe we've got it all wrong as usual, Terry. Maybe Saint Conall stood on the shores of the island there and gazed across here at Ballybeg and said to his monks, 'Oh, lads, lads, *there* is the end of desire. Whoever lives there lives at the still core of it all. Happy, happy, lucky people.' What do you think?

Frank is now very animated. He laughs again. He drinks again.

Terry That's us – happy people.

Frank (*calling*) Come and join us, Conall! It's all in place here! (*to Terry*) Well – why not?

Terry Indeed.

Frank (*laughs*) Despite appearances.

Terry Why not? (*He fills the outstretched cup again.*)

Frank Can't drink it without water.

Terry Any left in the holy well?

Frank Enough. (*Again he scoops up water and makes a drink.*) Aren't you joining me?

Terry Pass this time. To the book.

Frank No, no, not to the book. The book's nothing, nothing at all; a silly game of blind man's buff. No, to the other, to the mystery itself, Terry. To the goddamn wonderful, maddening, necessary mystery. (*He shudders as if with cold.*)

Terry You're cold in that shirt. Here. Put this on. (*He takes off his jacket and puts it round Frank's shoulders.*) That's definitely your colour.

Frank And to my goddamn wonderful wife. Is it profane to talk about her in the same breath as the sacred?

Terry Is it?

Frank Look at her. Now there's an apparition. She's . . . miraculous in that light, isn't she? Fourteen years married and the blood still thunders in my head when I look at her . . . Have you any idea, Terry, have you any idea at all of the turmoil, the panic people like me live in – the journeymen, the clerks of the world? No, no, the goddamn failures for Christ's sake.

Terry Frank, you –

Frank Of course I am. Husband – father – provider – worthless.

Terry Your book will –

Frank The great book! (*He makes a huge gesture of dismissal.*) She pretends to believe in it, too. But she's such a bright woman – she knows, she knows. You both know. Oh, Jesus, Terry, if only you knew, have you any idea at all just how fragile it all is . . .? (*He calls:*) Maybe you should stay where you are, lads. It's not quite all in place here yet . . . Damn good whiskey. What is it? Coleraine 1922! That's very special. May I help myself? (*He proclaims:*) Lord, it *is* good for us to be here! Isn't it . . .? (*He moves away.*)

   Pause.

Angela (*softly, tentatively*) Oh my God . . .

Terry What is it?

Angela Oh God, is it . . .?

Trish What's the matter, Angela?

Angela I think – oh God – I think –

Trish Angela, are you sick?

Angela There's our boat.

Berna Where?

Trish Stop that, Angela.

Frank Where? Where is it?

   George sits up.

Berna I see no boat.

Terry Where is it, Angela?

Frank Are you sure?

Trish Where? – show me – where? (*to George*) The boat's here, she says.

Angela (*pointing*) There. It is, Terry, isn't it?

Trish Is it, Terry?

Berna There is no boat.

Angela Oh God, Terry, that's our boat – isn't it?

Trish Point to it.

Angela Maybe it's only – can you see nothing? – that patch of light on the water – just beyond that I thought I saw –

Frank Nothing. There's nothing.

Trish Where's the patch of light?

Berna There's no patch of light.

Terry Is it anywhere near that mist?

Frank Nothing. All in her head.

Angela He's right . . . sorry . . . nothing . . . for a minute I was certain . . . sorry . . .

Berna You shouldn't do that, Angela.

Angela Sorry.

Berna You really shouldn't do that.

Angela I'm very sorry. I really am.

Terry There *is* a patch of light there; and if you stare at it long enough it seems to make shapes . . . Anyhow, no harm done. (*Pause. Privately to Angela*) I ordered your

401

favourite chocolate mints. Somebody must have eaten them. I suspect Charlie.

Angela The boatman?

Terry My driver. Minibus Charlie. How could you forget Charlie? And the boatman's name is Carlin.

Angela Give me a drink, Terry, would you?

Terry Wine? Gin? Vodka?

Angela Anything at all. Just a drop.

Berna (*suddenly standing up and proclaiming*) All right! I'll tell my story now!

Trish Good girl, Berna.

Berna I had a different psychiatrist in the clinic last week, a very intense young Englishman called Walsingham. He told me this story.

Angela (*accepting drink from Terry*) Thanks.

Terry Anybody else?

Frank Quiet.

Trish Attention, please. (*to Berna*) 'Once upon a time . . .'

Berna Not once upon a time, Trish. I can give you the exact date: 1294. And in the year 1294, in the village of Nazareth, in the land that is now called Israel, a very wonderful thing happened. There was in the village a small, white-washed house built of rough stone, just like these; and for over a thousand years the villagers looked on that house as their most wonderful possession; because that house had been the home of Mary and Joseph and their baby, Jesus.

And then in the year 1294, on the seventh day of March, an amazing thing happened. That small, white-washed house rose straight up into the air, right away up into the sky. It hung there for a few seconds as if it were a bird finding its bearings. Then it floated – flew – over the Mediterranean Sea, high up over the island of Crete, across the Aegean Sea, until it came to the coast of Italy. It crossed that coast and came to a stop directly above a small town called Loreto in the centre of Italy. Then it began to descend, slowly down and down and down, until it came to rest in the centre of the town. And there it sits to this day. And it is known as the Holy House of Loreto – a place of pilgrimage, revered and attested to by hundreds of thousands of pilgrims every year. The Holy House of Loreto.

Nobody knows how to respond. Pause.

Trish A flying house? . . . And it's there now? . . . Well, heavens above, isn't that a –

Berna And because it took off and flew across the sea and landed safely again, all over the world Our Lady of Loreto is known as the Patron Saint of Aviation.

Another brief pause.

Frank There you are . . .

Trish (*breezily*) Good girl, Berna.

Frank Never knew that . . .

Trish Live and learn.

Frank Indeed . . . live and learn . . .

Terry Wonderful story, Berna. Well done.

Frank Terry says this is my colour. What do you think?

Berna In our second year we had a lecturer in Equity, a Scotsman called – I've forgotten his name. We called him Offence to Reason because he used that phrase in every single lecture. We used to wait for it to come. 'Does that constitute an offence to reason?' (*She laughs.*) He was in awe of reason. He really believed reason was the key to 'truth', the 'big verities'.

Terry The sun's trying to come up, is it?

Berna No, it's not a wonderful story, Trish. It's a stupid story. And crude. And pig-headed. A flying house is an offence to reason, isn't it? It marches up to reason and belts it across the gob and says to it, 'Fuck you, reason. I'm as good as you any day. You haven't all the fucking answers – not by any means.' That's what Dr Walsingham's story says. And that's why I like it.

She begins to cry quietly. Terry moves towards her. But Trish holds up her hand and he stops. Then Trish goes to Berna and holds her.

Trish Shhh, love, shhh . . .

Berna (*into Trish's face*) It's defiance, Trish – that's what I like about it.

Trish I know . . . I know . . .

Berna It's stupid, futile defiance.

Trish Shh . . .

She moves away from Trish and goes to the end of the pier. Her narrative has charged the atmosphere with unease, with anxiety.

Frank (*breezily*) You're right, Terry; the sun is trying to come up.

Terry Yes?

Frank (*sings*) 'Dear one, the world . . .' You and I could do a neat dance to that, Berna. Anybody know it?

Terry (*sings*) '. . . is waiting for the sunrise –'

Frank and Terry sing together.

Terry and Frank 'Every rose is heavy with dew . . .'

Frank George?

Trish George is tired. He (*Frank*) knows the words of everything. What sort of a head have you got?

Frank (*brightly*) Full of rubbish. And panic. (*He sings.*) 'The thrush on high his sleepy mate is calling . . .' (*He fades out.*)

Angela Did you bring a swimsuit, Berna?

    No answer. *Berna now moves up to the catwalk.*

Trish (*to Berna*) I brought mine. You can have mine.

Frank Or better still, Berna – I say, I say, I say – you may have mine!

Angela We're all too tired, Frank.

Frank Are we? (*He sings the first two lines of the refrain of 'Lazy River'. Brief pause.*) Right, Trish – all set?

Trish What?

Frank You're next!

Trish What's he talking about?

Frank For a story!

Terry Yes, Trish!

Trish I don't know any –

Terry You're a wonderful story-teller. Isn't she, Berna?

Trish Ah, come on, Terry. You know very well –

Angela Go on, Trish!

Frank Any kind of fiction will do us.

Angela Myth – fantasy –

405

Terry A funny story –

Angela A good lie –

Frank Even a bad lie. Look at us for God's sake – we'll accept anything! Right, Berna?

Now Trish understands that their purpose is to engage Berna again.

Trish You want a story? Right! (*She jumps to her feet and launches into her performance with great theatricality and brio.*) So I'm on then? All right–all right–all right!

Frank Certainly are.

Trish (*stalling, improvising*) You want a story?

Angela We need a story.

Terry Come down and hear this, Berna.

Berna looks over the wall.

Trish A story. Absolutely. Yes. Once upon a time and a very long time ago –

Terry She's bluffing.

Angela Terry!

Terry Look at her eyes.

Frank What do her eyes say, George?

Angela (*to Trish*) Pay no attention to him (*Terry*). Once upon a time . . .?

Trish May I proceed?

Frank Let the lady speak.

Terry That's no lady – that's-a ma sista.

Angela Terry!

Trish Once upon a time and a very long time ago –

Frank sings the first line of 'Just a Song at Twilight'.

Angela Please, Frank.

Suddenly Trish knows what her story is.

Trish The morning we got married, George! OK?

George OK.

Frank Good one. Yeah.

Angela What story's that?

Trish May I, George?

George Go ahead.

Angela I've forgotten that story.

Terry That's a boring story, Trish.

Frank Is it? Boring is soothing.

Angela Do I know the story?

Frank Boring reassures.

Terry 'Course you do.

Frank I'm all for boring. Sedate us, Trish.

Trish If I may continue . . .?

Frank And it came to pass –

Trish Twenty-two years ago. Saint Theresa's Church.

Frank Parish of Drumragh.

Trish Ten o'clock Mass.

Terry Best man. (*He bows.*)

Trish And little Patricia, all a quiver in gold tiara, cream chiffon dress and pale-blue shoes with three-quarter heels, has left her home for the last time and –

Frank (*sings*) 'There was I –' George?

George picks up his accordion.

Terry You were bridesmaid, Berna. Remember?

Angela (*remembering*) It's the story of the missing –!

Frank Don't! (*i.e., interrupt*)

Trish May I? She arrives at the door of Saint Theresa's. And now her little heart starts to flutter because just as she enters the church on her Daddy's arm, Miss Quirk begins to play the harmonium –

She is suddenly drowned out by George playing the first line of 'There was I' – which is immediately picked up by Frank.

Frank (*sings*) '. . . waiting at the church –' That's it! 'Waiting at the church –' Terry!

Terry and Frank do a dance/march routine and sing together:

Frank and Terry
'Waiting at the church
When I found –'

Frank What?

Terry '– he'd left me in the lurch –' Angela!

Angela (*sings*) 'Oh, how it did upset me –'

Terry and Frank (*sing*) 'Tra-la-la-la-la.'

Angela Sorry, Trish.

Trish (*pretending anger*) Fine – fine –

Angela Behave yourselves, you two!

Trish Have your own fun.

Frank Please, Trish –

Trish No point, is there?

Frank Go on, Patricia: 'The flutter bride was all a-chiffon –'

Trish See?

Terry Anyhow we all know how the story ends, don't we?

Frank So what? All we want of a story is to hear it again and again and again and again and again.

Angela Are you going to let the girl finish?

Frank And so it came to pass . . .

George now plays Wagner's 'Wedding March' very softly, with a reverence close to mockery.

Trish Thank you, George. (*She blows him a kiss.*) The church is full to overflowing. My modest eyes are still on the ground. Daddy's gaze is manfully direct. We walk up that aisle together with quiet dignity until we come to the altar –

Frank She's a natural!

Trish And then for the first time I raise those modest eyes so that I can feast on my handsome groom-to-be, my beloved George.

Frank Yes?

Trish But lo –

Frank Go on!

Trish Who steps out to receive me –?

409

Frank But –

Terry The anxious bookie – the groomsman!

Frank Groomsman? Where's the groom?

Trish No groom. No George.

Howls of dismay.

Angela Shame, George, shame!

Frank Where can he be?

Terry (*calls*) George!

Frank (*calls*) We need you, George!

Terry (*calls*) Where are you, George?

Frank (*calls*) Heeelp!

Frank and Terry (*call*) Heeelp!

Angela Will you let the girl finish her story?

Trish Haven't seen him for over a week. Last heard from him two days ago from Limerick –

Terry Cork.

Trish – where the Aeolians – Michael Robinson and himself – they've been giving Beethoven recitals in schools and colleges there.

Terry Knew she'd get it wrong.

Frank (*to Terry*) Please.

Trish But these concerts, I know, are finished. Why isn't he here?

Terry Playing with the Dude Ranchers.

Trish Why isn't he here for his wedding?

Terry Finishing a tour in County Cork.

Trish Terry, the Aeolians were in Limerick doing a series of –

Terry The Aeolians had broken up three months before you got married.

Trish Don't you think I might –?

Terry George was working full-time with the Ranchers when you and he got married.

Trish Terry –

Frank Those details don't –

Terry That's why George packed in the Aeolians – to make some money – so that you and he could get married. Right, George?

Angela So what? The point of Trish's story is –

Terry (*to Trish*) You asked me to take George on. Don't you remember?

Trish So that when we –?

Terry And that's when the Ranchers really took off. When he packed in the Aeolians and joined the Ranchers. He made the Ranchers. We would never have come to anything without George.

Trish (*totally bewildered*) But how could I? . . . God . . . And when did –?

Terry You've forgotten – that's all. (*He hugs her quickly.*) I'd signed George up three months before your wedding.

Angela And all this has nothing to do with the story. The point is that he did turn up at Saint Theresa's – and only ten minutes late. Well done, George.

Terry (*to Trish*) I didn't mean to –

Trish But how could I have –?

Frank Certainly did turn up. On a motorbike – right? Soaked through and purple with cold.

Angela With the wedding-suit in a rucksack on his back.

Frank Changed in the organ-loft – remember?

Trish Oh my God, how could that have happened?

Angela That was a good day.

Frank Great day.

Terry (*to Trish*) Sorry.

Frank A wonderful day . . . God . . . what a day that was . . .

Angela Well done, Trish. A great story. The best story yet. Very well done.

> *Silence. Again they withdraw into themselves. Berna now climbs from the catwalk up to the top wall. As she does she sings, without words, 'O Mother, I Could Weep'. She walks along the top of the wall. Terry now sees her.*

Terry Berna, please come down from there.

Frank Berna.

Terry That is dangerous, Berna.

Trish (*to Terry*) For God's sake bring her down!

Angela Berna, love –

Terry (*commanding*) Come down, Berna! At once!

> *Berna, still singing, is now at the end of the wall. Without looking at anybody she jumps into the sea.*

Frank Berna!

Terry Jesus!

Angela Berna!

Terry Oh Jesus Christ . . .!

Act Two

Before the lights go up we hear George playing:
> *'All things bright and beautiful, all creatures great and*
>   *small*
> *All things wise and wonderful, the Good Lord made*
>   *them all.'*

At that point lights up.

A new day has opened. A high sky. A pristine and brilliant morning sunlight that enfolds the pier like an aureole and renovates everything it touches.

Berna, a cardigan round her shoulders, is in different clothes – her Act One clothes are drying across a bollard. Trish is brushing and combing Berna's hair. Terry is up on the catwalk, looking casually across the landscape, occasionally using binoculars. Angela is playing a game she has invented. From a distance of about five feet she pitches stones (lobster-pot weights) at an empty bottle placed close to the lifebelt stand. (When the game ends there is a small mound of stones.) On the lifebelt stand now hangs – as well as Angela's sun hat from Act One – the silk scarf Berna wore in Act One. George continues playing:
> *'Each little flower that opens, each little bird that sings,*
> *He made their glowing colours, he made their tiny*
>   *wings.*
> *All things bright and beautiful, all creatures great and*
>   *small –'*

Now Angela sings to the music:

Angela (*sings*)
> 'All things wise and wonderful,
> the Good Lord made them all.'

You are 'wise and wonderful', George: you're the only one of us that slept all night.

George Did I?

Angela For an hour. And you snore.

George Sorry. (*He beckons her to him.*) If I ever decide to go, I want your children to have this (*accordion*).

Angela You are going –

George One of them might take it up.

Angela George, that's –

George Bit battered but it's working all right.

Angela That's a lovely thought. (*She kisses him.*) Thank you.

George *If* I ever decide to go.

Terry Where did Frank say he was going?

Angela To take photographs, he said. Probably to beat the head off poor old Carlin.

Pause.

Terry Listen to those birds.

Angela Larks, are they?

Terry 'And they heard the song of coloured birds.' You wouldn't believe me.

Angela They're larks, Terry. Ordinary larks.

George begins to play 'Skylark' very softly.

Exactly, George.

Terry Has it a name, that game?

Angela It's called: how close can you get without

415

touching it? Anybody got the time?

Terry Just after seven.

Berna (*looking at her watch*) Stopped. Salt water finished it.

Angela When does the minibus come for us?

Terry Half an hour or so.

Berna takes off her watch, shakes it and holds it to her ear.

Berna That's that.

She casually tosses it into the sea. Only Trish sees this.

Terry There must be hundreds of them (*birds*). And they *are* coloured.

Trish (*quietly*) You put the heart across us, Berna, jumping into the sea like that.

Berna Are you nearly finished? (*Hair-dressing.*)

Trish You shouldn't have done that.

Berna I wanted a swim.

Trish It was a naughty thing to do. It was a cruel thing to do.

Berna I told you – I wanted a swim.

Trish Particularly cruel to Terry.

Berna Oh, poor Terry. (*She stands up abruptly.*) That's fine, Trish. Thank you. (*to Angela*) May I play?

Angela Of course.

Terry Well, would you look at that! Carlin has lit his fire again! (*He laughs.*) What a strange man.

Angela (*to Berna*) There are stones over there.

Terry Maybe he'll come for us after he's had his breakfast. What do you think?

Trish (*wearily*) Terry.

Angela (*to Trish*) Going to play?

Trish Yes.

Terry We still have time for a quick dart out and straight back. We'd do it in less than an hour.

Trish D'you know what I would love? A cup of strong tea!

Terry There's still a chance. Why not? I'm offering five to one against. Three to one. Any takers?

> *George has come to the last line of 'Skylark'. Trish sings the line.*

Trish Now. Tell me what to do.

> *The music stops.*

Angela The aim is to get as close as possible to that bottle. But every time you touch it you lose a point.

Trish You *lose* a point? What sort of a makey-up game is that!

Terry Looks wonderful in this light (*the island*). I'm not giving up. Two to one against. Even money.

Trish We should all be exhausted, shouldn't we? But I feel . . . exhilarated. Play something exhilarating, George.

> *He plays 'Regina Caeli' right through.*

(*immediately he begins*) That's not exhilarating, is it?

Angela (*to Trish*) Your throw.

Berna Is there a chill in the air?

Trish (*preparing to throw*) Right.

Berna reaches out to take her scarf from the lifebelt stand.

Angela (*quickly*) No; take mine. It's warmer. Like a hall stand, isn't it? Good one, Trish. You have the hang of it.

Berna drapes Angela's scarf around her shoulders. Frank enters.

Frank Well–well–well! What Eden is this? And what happy people have we here, besporting themselves in the sunlight?

Terry (*coming down*) We thought we had lost you.

Frank For you, George. Found it in the sand dunes back there.

The music stops.

George Yes?

Frank Interesting, isn't it? Polished flint-stone. The head of an axe, I think.

George Thank you.

Frank That's the hole for the handle. Beautifully shaped, isn't it?

George Lovely.

Terry Where did you find it?

Frank Just behind the pier. Probably buried in the sand at one time. Then the sand shifted.

Terry May I see it?

George Thank you, Frank.

Frank Some weapon. That's a lethal edge there.

Terry And the weight of it.

Frank We'll make a handle for it; and on your next tour, if audiences aren't appreciative enough – (*He mimes striking with the axe.*)

Terry That *is* sharp.

Frank Meant for business, that weapon.

Terry Did you get some good pictures?

Frank Don't talk to me about pictures! Tell you all in a moment.

He goes to Berna and presents her with a bunch of wild flowers.

For you, my lady. (*He kisses her.*)

Berna Oh, Frank.

Angela Aren't they pretty? Look at that blue.

Trish You got them around here?

Frank Just over the sand dunes.

Trish (*to George*) He's a *real* gentleman.

Frank (*to Berna*) And d'you know what? – I could eat you in that dress.

Berna They're beautiful, Frank. Thank you.

Frank Welcome.

Angela Now – Berna (*the game*).

Trish You want to know how it's really done, girls? Just watch this.

They continue playing.

419

Terry Lovely flowers. Thank you.

Frank The place is full of them.

Terry We thought maybe you'd gone to chastise Mr Carlin.

Frank Just before daybreak there was a white mist suspended above the island; like a white silk canopy. And as the sun got up you could see the mist dissolve and vanish. So of course I thought: Oileán Draíochta emerging from behind its veil – capture this for posterity!

Terry Did you get it?

Frank Two bloody spools of it. Wasted all my film.

Angela (*to Trish*) Not bad. Not bad.

Trish Not bad? Wonderful!

Berna Very close, Trish. Good one.

Trish I think this could well be my game. Want to play, Frank?

Frank (*to all*) Listen to this. You won't believe what I saw out there, Trish.

Trish What?

Brief pause.

Berna What did you see, Frank?

Frank looks at them. He is not sure if he will tell his story.

Frank Just as the last wisp of the veil was melting away, suddenly – as if it had been waiting for a sign – suddenly a dolphin rose up out of the sea. And for thirty seconds, maybe a minute, it danced for me. Like a faun, a satyr; with its manic, leering face. Danced with a deliberate, controlled, exquisite abandon. Leaping, twisting, tumbling, gyrating in wild and intricate contortions. And for that thirty seconds, maybe a minute, I could swear it never once touched the water – was free of it – had nothing to do with water. A performance – that's what it was. A performance so considered, so aware, that you knew it knew it was being witnessed; wanted to be witnessed. Thrilling; and wonderful; and at the same time – I don't know why – at the same time . . . with that manic, leering face . . . somehow very disturbing.

Berna Did you get pictures of it?

Frank Nothing. You'd almost think it waited until my last shot was used up before it appeared. Thirty seconds, maybe a minute . . . Unbelievable. (*embarrassed laugh*) Another apparition, Terry.

Terry Maybe.

Pause. Frank is now embarrassed at his own intensity and because the others are all staring at him. He laughs again.

Frank So I saw a porpoise or a dolphin or something leap out of the water and dance about a bit. Wonderful!

Trish I love dolphins. I think they are terrific. (*briskly*) Right. Who's next?

Angela, Trish and Berna play their game.

Frank Left them speechless, didn't it? – my Ballybeg epiphany.

Terry Sorry I missed that.

Frank (*to George*) Upset me, that damn thing, for some reason.

Berna nods and smiles.

Terry Drink?

Frank (*gesturing no*) Could have done with one back there. It really was a ceremonial dance, Terry – honest to God. And they look so damned knowing – don't they? – with those almost human faces . . . I'm getting to like this (*jacket*).

Terry Well, what are our chances?

Frank Chances?

Terry indicates Carlin's house.

Forget him. Next time we'll bring our own boat.

Terry Sorry. Not allowed.

Frank Maybe you're right. Maybe he still will come. Who's to say?

Terry moves to the end of the pier where he sits by himself.

Angela That hit the bottle. Point lost, Trish.

Trish Didn't hit it, did it?

Angela Sorry. Point down. Berna?

Berna, her flowers still in her hand, picks up a stone close to Frank. At the same time she puts one of her flowers in her hair and blows a kiss to him. As she does this George plays 'Bring Flowers of the Rarest':
'Bring flowers of the rarest, bring blossoms the fairest
From garden and woodland and hillside and dale
Our full hearts are swelling, our glad voices telling
The praise of the loveliest flower of the vale.'

Trish (*immediately after George plays the first line and as he continues playing*) I know that song, don't I?

Frank So do I.

Berna It's a hymn – is it?

George Guess.

Frank It *is* a hymn – isn't it?

Berna Play the chorus, George.

Trish I do know it, whatever it is.

Frank I do, too.

> *George now begins the chorus: 'O Mary, we crown thee with blossoms today –'*

Trish Yes! (*sings*) '– Queen of the angels and queen of the May –'

Frank Haven't heard that since I was a child.

Trish and Berna (*sing*)
'O Mary, we crown thee with blossoms today,
Queen of the angels and queen of the May.'

(*to George*) Thank you.

Frank Not since I was a child.

> *Brief pause. And immediately Angela plunges into 'O Dem Golden Slippers'. And as she sings, George accompanies her. She picks up Frank's shoes, and singing loudly, raucously, defiantly, and waving the shoes above her head she parades/dances around the pier. She sings the entire chorus. She stops suddenly. The performance is over. Pause. Now she sings very softly the first two lines of the chorus of 'I Don't Know Why I'm Happy'. She tails off listlessly. She looks at the shoes and tosses them over to where Frank is sitting. She looks at them all.*

Angela What a goddamn, useless, endless, unhappy outing this has been! (*Pause.*) I'm sorry, Terry . . .

Pause.

Frank (*to Terry*) May I (*drink*)? (*He pours a drink and scoops up water.*) Should do a rain dance. Well's almost dry.

Terry now rises and joins them.

Terry I just remembered – I do have a story.

Trish Too late, Terry. Story time's over.

Frank No, it's not. It's always story time. Right, Berna?

Berna Is it?

Frank Certainly is.

Trish All right. But make it short, Terry. Short and funny. I need a laugh.

Frank Terence . . .?

Terry Yes. Well. The solicitor who is handling the sale of Oileán Draíochta – he told me this story. We were having lunch together. No; we had finished eating. He was having coffee and I was having tea and we both –

Trish The story, Terry.

Terry (*almost reluctantly*) Yes – yes – the story. Well, the story he told me was this. Many years ago a young man was killed out there.

Berna Killed how?

Terry I suppose . . . murdered.

Frank God.

Terry His name was Sean O'Boyle. He was seventeen years of age. If you were to believe my solicitor friend he was . . . ritually killed.

424

Trish What do you mean?

Terry A group of young people – he was one of them –
seven young men and seven young women. It wasn't a
disagreement, a fight; nothing like that. They were all
close friends.

Angela And what happened?

Terry The evidence suggests some sort of ritual, during
which young O'Boyle was . . . (*He shrugs.*)

Trish Oh, my God.

Berna What evidence?

Terry Burned-out fires – empty wine bottles – clothes left
behind – blood smeared on rocks. It's thought there was
some sort of orgy. Anyhow, at some point they
dismembered him. That's accurate enough – from the
pieces they found.

Frank Jesus Christ, Terry . . . oh, Jesus Christ . . .

Angela When did this happen?

Terry 1932. On the night of June 26.

Angela These young people – they were from here?

Terry Part of a group from this parish who had just
returned from Dublin from the Eucharistic Congress. The
older people went straight to their homes. The young
group – our fourteen – apparently they had been drinking
all the way home from Dublin – they stole a half-decker –
from this pier actually – and headed out for Oileán
Draíochta. Some people say they had poitín stashed out
there and that one of the girls was a great fiddler and that
they just went out to have a dance. My friend has his own
theory. These people were peasants, from a very remote
part of the country. And he believes they were still in a

state of intoxication after the Congress – it was the most spectacular, the most incredible thing they had ever witnessed. And that ferment and the wine and the music and the dancing . . .

Trish I don't know what you're saying, Terry.

Terry That young O'Boyle was . . . sacrificed.

Frank Jesus Christ.

Berna The other thirteen – they were charged?

Terry No charges were ever brought.

Trish Why not?

Angela The police weren't brought in?

Terry Oh, yes. But by then the situation was away beyond their control. The parish was in uproar. Passions were at boiling point. Families were physically attacking one another. The police were helpless. The only person who could control the situation was the bishop of the time. He had led the group that had just made the pilgrimage to the Eucharistic Congress. And every year on August 15 he organized a pilgrimage out to the island.

Trish So?

Terry So the thirteen were summoned to the bishop's palace. All that is known is that they made a solemn pledge never to divulge what happened that night on the island; that they had to leave the country immediately and for ever, and that before the end of the week they had all left for Australia.

Trish Oh, my God.

Berna So nobody was ever charged?

Terry Nobody. O'Boyle was an only child. Both his

parents were dead within the year.

Angela Oileán Draíochta – wonderful.

Terry Then the war came. Times were bad. People moved away. Within ten years the area was depopulated – that's your derelict church back there, Frank. The local belief was that the whole affair brought a curse on the parish and that nothing would ever prosper here again.

Frank Jesus Christ, what a story! Jesus Christ, we don't know half of what goes on in the world!

Terry (*to Trish*) I'm sure that's the real reason why the pilgrimage out there really petered out. Couldn't have survived that.

Trish Damn you, Terry Martin, how could you have brought us out to a place like that?

Terry Trish, it is just an –

Trish And how could you have bought an evil place like that?

Terry The place is not evil, Trish.

Trish I hate that story. That's a hateful story. You shouldn't have told us that story. (*She moves quickly away and busies herself with her belongings.*)

Silence.

Berna (*to Frank*) These grew (*her flowers*).

Frank What's that?

Berna He said nothing ever grew again. These did.

Frank True . . . that's true . . . Going to be another warm day.

Terry Think so?

Frank Yes. Very warm. Wonderful.

They all drift apart.

Trish Shouldn't we tidy the place up a bit? Carlin could arrive any time.

Berna You mean Charlie, don't you?

Trish Do I? Whatever.

They begin tidying up, each attending to his/her own belongings. First they put on their shoes. Then Terry puts bottles, flasks, etc. back into the hampers. Trish folds up sleeping-bags and packs her other belongings. Berna folds her now dry clothes and puts them away. Frank looks after his cameras, binoculars, etc. Angela makes a pile of the paper napkins, plastic cups, etc., scattered around the pier. George watches the others at their tasks. While all this tidying up is taking place, the following episodes happen:
  Berna takes her scarf off the lifebelt stand and puts it round her neck. Then she sees Angela's hat.

Berna Isn't this your hat, Angela?

Angela Thanks.

Berna Do you want it?

Angela My good hat for God's sake! Why wouldn't I want it? Thank you. The only sun hat I have.

Berna hands the hat to Angela. A moment's hesitation. Then she removes the scarf from her neck and knots it on one of the arms of the stand. Frank witnesses this episode.

Trish (*to George*) I'll take that (*accordion*).

George Why?

428

Trish What d'you mean 'why'? I'll put it in the case for you.

George Why?

Trish Because we're about to – Fine – fine! Suit yourself!

George Yes.

Trish moves away from him. Frank goes to the stand, takes off his belt and buckles it round the upright. Now he sees Terry watching him.

Frank (*breezily*) Maybe that's a bit reckless, is it? D'you think they'll stay up by themselves?

Terry I'm all for a gamble.

Frank Pot belly. Safe enough.

Trish witnesses this episode. Trish looks at the mound of stones.

Trish Should we put these back where we found them?

Berna I wouldn't bother. They were scattered all over the place when we got here.

Trish goes to the stand. She takes off her bracelet and hangs it on one of the arms, balancing Berna's scarf. Then she goes back to George, who is standing immobile beside their belongings.

Trish Give me your handkerchief.

George does not move. Trish takes the handkerchief out of his breast pocket, returns to the stand and knots the handkerchief beside her bracelet.

Angela (*to Terry*) Did you say you had honey cake?

Terry Yes. Are you hungry? (*He produces the cake from the hamper. A sealed tin.*) How do you open this thing?

Angela No, no; don't open it. I'll leave it here, I think. (*She places the tin on top of a bollard.*)

Terry What are you doing?

Angela For Carlin. You don't mind, do you? He's sure to come snooping around after we've gone. A present.

Terry Will you ever come back here?

Angela Just to keep him sweet.

Berna Is this yours, Frank (*camera case*)?

Frank Just looking for that. Thank you.

Angela (*to Terry*) Sorry for that outburst a while ago.

Terry Please . . .

Angela It was a lovely birthday.

Terry We'll not talk about that. Interesting place, though.

Angela Pretty.

Terry Wonderful, isn't it?

Angela (*gesturing to the island*) I can live without all that stuff, Terry. Honestly. Housework – the kids – teaching – bills – Frank – doctors – more bills – just getting through every day is about as much as I can handle; more than I can handle at times. (*remembering that the island is his*) I really wish you luck with it. Yes–yes–yes, of course it's wonderful – beautiful and wonderful.

Terry When will I see you?

Angela Terry –

Terry Next Sunday?

Angela No. Please.

She spreads her hands as if to say, 'What's the point?

Can't you see there's no point?' Then, very quickly, she takes his hands in hers, squeezes them, and then swiftly moves away from him. Frank has found a small bottle. He holds it up.

Frank Anybody mind if I pour this out? (*He reads:*) Cherry Brandy. (*He empties it out.*) God, that's a sin, isn't it?

Now he picks up a plastic cup, scoops whatever water is left in the 'well' and pours it into the brandy bottle. Now he is aware that Terry and Angela are watching him. He laughs.

For a quick shot on the way home. In case Charlie's jokes get too bad. Hardly any (*water*) left . . .

He corks the bottle with paper tissues. Trish goes to the small pile of rubbish (paper tissues, plastic cups, etc.) that Angela gathered. She strikes a match. Just as she is about to set fire to the refuse, Angela rushes to her and stamps the fire out with her foot.

Angela For God's sake, woman!

Trish What have I –?

Angela You can't light a fire here! (*calm again*) We can take this away with us, can't we? That would be simpler, wouldn't it? (*She begins piling the rubbish into a plastic bag.*)

Trish (*excessive astonishment*) Oh good Lord, we're suddenly very house-proud, aren't we?

Angela puts her hand on Trish's elbow.

Angela Sorry, Trish. Could do with some sleep.

She moves away to the end of the pier and looks around. The various tasks have been completed.

Frank Now, Terry. Yourself.

Terry What's that?

Frank You're going to leave a visiting card, aren't you?

Terry A visiting –?

Frank On the stand. 'Terry Martin Was Here.'

Terry (*laughing*) Nothing to leave. (*He produces coins.*) Is money any good?

Trish Useless, Terry.

Terry What else can I give you?

Frank What else can he give us? What about that shirt?

   Suddenly everybody is listening, watching.

Berna Yes, Terry. The shirt.

Frank Is the shirt what we want?

Trish The shirt will do.

Berna We want the shirt!

Trish Hand it over, Terry.

Terry Ah, come on now –

Frank We all want the shirt, don't we?

George Yes–yes–yes!

   Now Trish sings rapidly – and keeps singing again and again: 'I want the shirt – I want the shirt'; to the air of 'Here Comes the Bride'.

Frank We'll take it now, Terry.

Berna We want it now, Terry, now.

Terry Here – I'll give you a pen-knife – matches –

Frank No good. The shirt, Terry. Hand it over.

Terry tries to back away from them. They encircle him. They sing with Trish:

All 'We want the shirt – we want the shirt – (*etc.*)'

Terry My shoes! My shoes and socks –

Berna The shirt, Terry.

Trish The shirt – the shirt!

Frank The shirt – the shirt – the shirt!

All sing again, 'We want the shirt – we want the shirt –' George starts playing 'Here Comes the Bride'.

Terry For God's sake, this is the only shirt I have here!

Frank Grab him!

Terry Frank –!

And suddenly they all grab him (all except Angela who is by herself at the end of the pier – but watching). Terry falls to the ground. They pull at his shirt. As they do, overlapping:

Berna We have him!

Frank Hold his feet!

Terry For God's sake!

Trish Give it to us!

Frank Hold him – hold him!

Trish We want it – we want it!

Terry Help!

Berna Want it – want it – want it!

Frank Want it, Terry – want it!

Berna Pull – pull – pull!

Trish I've got it!

Berna Rip it off!

Terry Angela, help –!

Frank Hold his hands!

Berna Need it – need it!

Trish Got it! Yes!

Terry Please –!

Frank Pull – pull – pull!

> *George stops playing. Now Frank stands up in triumph, a portion of Terry's shirt held aloft.*

There!

Trish Well done, Frank.

Berna Now hang it up, Terry. (*to all*) Yes?

George Yes – yes!

Trish Hang it up there, Terry. Come on – be a sport!

> *Terry gets to his feet and pulls the remnant of his shirt together.*

Terry Happy now, are you?

Frank On the lifebelt stand. Has to be done in person.

Terry You're a shower of bastards – you know that.

> *He takes the piece of the shirt and hangs it up. They applaud.*

Berna Terry Martin Was Here.

Terry Satisfied?

Trish Wonderful!

Terry OK?

Frank You'll be remembered here for ever, Terry.

Terry Happy now? I hope you're all happy now.

Berna Don't be such a crank.

Frank Bit of fun, Terry. That's all.

Terry (*relenting*) Not a button left.

Frank Just passing the time – killing time.

Terry And I could have split my head on those stones!

Frank Just a bit of fun. (*He goes to one of his bags and produces a shirt.*)

Trish You look wonderful, Terry. Doesn't he?

Frank This should fit you.

Terry raises his hand in a pretended gesture of striking him.

And it's your colour.

Terry I like this now. I'm not going to part with it. Bastards . . .

The moment has passed. They finish tidying up. They look around the pier, now restored to what it was when they arrived.

Trish So . . .

Berna So . . .

They look like people at a station – some standing – some sitting – just waiting patiently to get away.

Trish Lovely harvest day, isn't it?

435

Berna What time is it now?

Frank Coming up to seven thirty.

Brief pause. Frank sees two stones a few feet away from the mound of stones. He picks one up and places it on top of the mound.

Simple domestic instincts . . .

He now picks up the second stone and places it on top of the mound.

(*to Terry*) At seven thirty in the morning the rage for the absolute isn't quite so consuming . . . The acceptance of what *is* . . .

Brief pause.

Angela He's out there somewhere, just below the surface.

Terry Who's that?

Angela His dancing porpoise.

Frank Damn right. Waiting for an audience.

Terry Not many audiences around here.

Frank Or maybe just searching for the other thirteen. Who's to say?

Short pause.

Trish Is he punctual?

Terry (*laughing*) Carlin?

Trish (*wearily*) God! Your driver – Charlie!

Terry He'll be on time. He's always on bloody time.

Short pause.

Trish (*to George*) Are you not going to put that into the case?

George No.

Trish What's got into you?

George I'm not finished playing.

Short pause. Angela is still by herself at the end of the pier.

Angela There was a city called Eleusis in Attica in ancient Greece; and every year at the end of summer, religious ceremonies were held there in honour of Demeter, the goddess of the harvest – what we would call a harvest festival. And they were known as the Eleusinian Mysteries.

Frank Off again!

Trish No more stories, Angela. Let's get back to real life.

Angela All we know about the ceremonies is that they began with a period of fasting; that there was a ritual purification in the sea; and that young people went through a ceremony of initiation. And there was music and dancing and drinking. And we know, too, that sacrifice was offered. And that's about all we know. Because the people who took part in the ceremonies vowed never to speak of what happened there. So that when the civilization came to an end it took the secrets of the Eleusinian Mysteries with it.

Frank What's your point – that they had bishops too? I'll tell you something; it's going to be another roaster of a day.

Brief pause.

Berna Play something for us, George.

437

George What?

Berna Whatever gives you pleasure.

George My pleasure . . . right . . .

He strikes a few chords as he wonders what he will play. Then suddenly:

Trish Shh! Listen! Listen!

Berna What is it?

Trish Stop! Quiet! Stop!

Frank Is it –?

Trish The minibus! Isn't it? Listen!

Frank I don't hear –

Berna It is! She's right!

Trish At last! At last!

Terry Told you he was bloody punctual.

They are all suddenly animated, excited, joyous. They pick up their belongings. They all talk at the same time.

Frank Good old Charlie!

Terry Whose is this?

Trish What new jokes will he have?

Angela Don't forget your sleeping-bag.

Berna We'll be home by lunchtime.

Angela Can you manage all that?

Frank You're sun-burned.

George Am I?

Frank Your forehead.

Trish The moment I get home – straight to bed!

Frank You're very lucky to have Charlie.

And gradually as the minibus gets closer, their chatter and their excitement die away. Now the minibus has arrived. The engine is switched off. Frank goes to the exit.

Good man, Charlie. With you in a moment. (*He now sees the tin of honey cake and picks it up.*) What's this?

Terry That's for Carlin.

Frank Like hell. I'm taking –

Terry Leave it, Frank.

Frank Sorry . . .

Nobody moves, they look around. Nobody speaks. Finally:

Trish Nice place all the same . . . Isn't it?

Frank Lovely.

Trish It really is, Terry.

Berna So peaceful.

Trish Lovely.

Frank Really peaceful.

Trish Wonderful.

Frank Wonderful.

Trish (*to George*) Isn't it wonderful?

George Yes.

Terry Angela's right: it was a mess, the whole thing.

Frank Terry –

439

Terry The least said . . . I just feel I've let you all down.

Frank Don't say another word. It was a great birthday party. We had a wonderful time.

Trish He's right, Terry. Terrific.

Frank Thank you. And we'll do it again some time. (*to all*) Agreed? (*to George*) Right, George?

   George spreads his hands and smiles.

Only this time I'll take Mr Carlin in hand and he'll do what he's supposed to do.

Trish And even though we don't make it out there –

Frank Of course we'll make it! Why wouldn't we make it?

Trish Well, at least now we know . . . it's there.

Frank (*calls*) 'Bye, Conall!

Trish (*calls*) 'Bye, Conall!

   Frank sings 'Aloha'.

Terry I should tell you –

Trish (*calls*) Be good, Conall!

Terry I should have said –

Frank Trish, my love, you're looking nowhere near it.

Trish What do you –?

   Frank turns her head to the right.

Frank Got it now?

Trish Ah.

Frank Still County Sligo.

Trish I know it's County Sligo, Frank.

Frank (*to all*) See? Nothing changes.

Angela (*to Terry*) You should have told us what?

Terry Nothing.

Angela What should you have told us?

Terry (*reluctantly*) What I said yesterday afternoon – this morning – I'm confused – when was it? – anyhow, when I told you I owned the island, that *is* true – well, partially true. I *have* taken an option on it. The option expires in a month. And I'm not going to pick it up.

Trish Now that's the best news I've heard all day! The moment you told that story about –

> *Terry holds up his hand to silence her.*

Terry I want to pick it up. Oh, yes. Trouble is – I haven't the money. The bookie business – concert promotion – the last few years have been disastrous. And I'm afraid – (*He laughs.*) – not to put a tooth in it – I'm broke.

Trish But, Terry, you –

Terry Things will pick up. The tide will turn. I'll rise again. Oh, yes, I'll rise again. (*to Berna*) That's why I didn't tell you I'd optioned it. Knew I'd lose it. (*to all*) Actually I didn't mean to tell anybody . . . Look at those solemn faces! (*He laughs.*) To own Oileán Draíochta for two whole months – wasn't that wonderful enough? Wasn't that a terrific secret to have? Anyway . . . One small thing. I'd be glad if you kept it to yourselves – that I'm broke. Don't want a hundred creditors descending on me.

Berna I'm sorry, Terry.

Terry So we'll come back again, will we? What d'you say?

Trish But, Terry, how can you –?

Terry When will we come back?

Frank Good God, Terry, how can you –?

Terry Next year? What about next year?

Frank If I'd known – if any of us had any idea you were –

Terry My birthday next year – right?

Frank And you've been doling out – day after day – month after –

Angela (*triumphantly*) Yes, we will! Next year – and the year after – and the year after that! Because we want to! Not out of need – out of desire! Not in expectation – but to attest, to affirm, to acknowledge – to shout Yes, Yes, Yes! Damn right we will, Terry! Yes – yes – yes!

Frank Twelve months' time – agreed?

Trish Agreed!

Frank Berna?

Berna Yes!

Frank George?

George Agreed!

Frank No more talk! Settled! (*calls*) 'Bye, Conall! 'Bye, lads. They're waving to us! Wave back to them!

> *Frank waves vigorously. Trish, George and Berna make smaller gestures.*

Trish 'Bye!

Frank (*calls*) Terry's birthday next year! And for a whole night!

> *They all join in, overlapping:*

442

Trish 'Bye, sheep!

George 'Bye.

Trish 'Bye, cattle.

Terry 'Bye, coloured birds.

Berna 'Bye, whin bush.

Frank 'Bye, bell.

Terry 'Bye, clothes on bushes.

Angela 'Bye, low hill.

George 'Bye.

Trish 'Bye, oak trees.

Angela 'Bye, apple trees.

Terry 'Bye, Conall.

All 'Bye . . . 'bye . . . 'bye . . .

Frank 'Bye, dancing dolphin . . . 'bye . . .

> *Still nobody moves. Now George plays in his 'sacred' style:*
> 'Come, my love, come, my boat lies low
> She lies high and dry on the O-hi-o
> Come, my love, come, come along with me
> And I'll take you back to Tennessee.'

Trish Charlie's waiting for us. Shouldn't we make a move?

> *But nobody does. Now Berna begins to hum with the song, beginning with the first verse:*

Berna (*hums*)
> 'Down by the cane-brake close by the mill
> There lived a blue-eyed girl and her name was Nancy
> Dill . . .'

George accompanies her. Now Terry hums with her:

Terry and Berna (*hum*)
'I told her that I loved her, I loved her very long
I'm going to serenade her and this will be my song . . .'

Now Trish and Frank join in the humming:

Terry, Berna, Trish and Frank
'Come, my love, come, my boat lies low
She lies high and dry on the O-hi-o
Come, my love, come, come along with me
And I'll take you back to Tennessee . . .'

They play/hum another verse and this time Angela joins them. And this continues to the end of the play.

Trish goes to the mound of stones. She walks around it once. Then she picks up a stone from the bottom of the mound and places it on the top. Then she walks around the mound a second time and again she places a stone on top. Then she goes to the lifebelt stand and lightly touches her votive offering. Then she goes to her belongings, picks them up and slowly moves off.

The moment Trish completes her first encircling Berna joins her. First she places the flowers Frank gave her at the foot of the stand. Then she does the ritual that Trish is doing. And this ceremony – encircling, lifting a stone, encircling, lifting a stone, touching the votive offering – is repeated by every character. Frank immediately behind Berna, Terry immediately after Frank. And when they finish they pick up their belongings and – still humming to George's accompaniment – move slowly off. Now only George and Angela are left. George stops playing. He looks at her and gestures towards the mound.

Angela You go ahead, George, I think I'll pass.

She watches him as he does the ritual. When he has

finished he stands beside her, puts his arm on hers. They take a last look round.

George Nice place.

Angela Nice place. (*She nods in agreement.*)

George You'll come back some day.

Angela I don't think –

George Yes, you will. Some day. And when you do, do it for me. No, no, I don't mean *for* me – just in memory of me.

She looks at him for a second. Then quickly, impetuously, she catches his head between her hands and kisses him. Then she breaks away from him, rushes to the stand, kisses her sun hat and hangs it resolutely on the very top of the stand.

Angela (*defiantly*) For you, George! For both of us!

She rushes back to him, takes his arm and begins singing 'Down by the Cane-brake' loudly, joyously, happily – and he accompanies her with comparable brio. The others (off) join in.
George and Angela exit. The engine starts up. The singing and the engine compete. Both sounds are encompassed by the silence and complete stillness and gradually surrender to it.

Acknowledgements

'The World is Waiting for the Sunrise' Copyright © 1919, Chappell Music Ltd, London. Reproduced by permission of International Music Publications Ltd.

'I Want to be Happy' Copyright © 1920, Harms Inc., USA, Warner Chappell Music Ltd, London. Reproduced by permission of International Music Publications Ltd.

'Jolly Good Company' Copyright © 1931, Campbell, Connelly & Co. Ltd, 8–9 Frith Street, London WIV 5TZ. Used by permission, all rights reserved.

'There I Was Waiting at the Church' Copyright © 1906. Reproduced by permission of Francis Day and Hunter Ltd, London WC2H OEA.

'Down in de Cane-brake' Copyright © 1928, Forster Music Pub Inc., USA. Reproduced by permission of Francis Day and Hunter Ltd, London WC2H OEA.

'Heavenly Sunshine' Copyright © 1970, Al Gallico Music Corp., USA. Reproduced by permission of EMI Music Publishing Ltd, London WC2H OEA.

Every effort has been made to contact all copyright holders of songs quoted in the text of this play. In case of any queries, please contact Curtis Brown Group Ltd, 4th Floor, Haymarket House, 28/29 Haymarket, London SWIY 4SP.

MOLLY SWEENEY

for Megan

Characters

Molly Sweeney
Frank Sweeney
Mr Rice

Molly Sweeney was first produced at the Gate Theatre, Dublin, on 9 August 1994, with the following cast:

Molly Catherine Byrne
Frank Mark Lambert
Mr Rice T. P. McKenna

Directed by Brian Friel

Tell all the Truth but tell it slant –
Success in Circuit lies
Too bright for our infirm Delight
The Truth's superb surprise
As Lightning to the Children eased
With explanation kind
The Truth must dazzle gradually
Or every man be blind –

Emily Dickinson

'Learning to see is not like learning a new language. It's like learning language for the first time.'

Denis Diderot

Act One

When the lights go up, we discover the three characters –
Molly Sweeney, Mr Rice, Frank Sweeney – on stage. All
three stay on stage for the entire play.

I suggest that each character inhabits his/her own
special acting area – Mr Rice stage left, Molly Sweeney
centre stage, Frank Sweeney stage right (left and right
from the point of view of the audience).

Molly Sweeney and Frank are in their late thirties/early
forties. Mr Rice is older.

Most people with impaired vision look and behave like
fully sighted people. The only evidence of their disability
is usually a certain vacancy in the eyes or the way the
head is held. Molly should indicate her disability in some
such subtle way. No canes, no groping, no dark glasses,
etc.

Molly By the time I was five years of age, my father had
taught me the names of dozens of flowers and herbs and
shrubs and trees. He was a judge and his work took him
all over the county. And every evening, when he got
home, after he'd had a few quick drinks, he'd pick me up
in his arms and carry me out to the walled garden.

'Tell me now,' he'd ask. 'Where precisely are we?'

'We're in your garden.'

'Oh, you're such a clever little missy!' And he'd pretend
to smack me.

'Exactly what part of my garden?'

'We're beside the stream.'

'Stream? Do you hear a stream? I don't. Try again.'

'We're under the lime tree.'

'I smell no lime tree. Sorry. Try again.'

'We're beside the sundial.'

'You're guessing. But you're right. And at the bottom of the pedestal there is a circle of petunias. There are about twenty of them all huddled together in one bed. They are – what? – seven inches tall. Some of them are blue-and-white, and some of them are pink, and a few have big, red, cheeky faces. Touch them.'

And he would bend over, holding me almost upside down, and I would have to count them and smell them and feel their velvet leaves and their sticky stems. Then he'd test me.

'Now, Molly. Tell me what you saw.'

'Petunias.'

'How many petunias did you see?'

'Twenty.'

'Colour?'

'Blue-and-white and pink and red.'

'Good. And what shape is their bed?'

'It's a circle.'

'Splendid. Passed with flying colours. You *are* a clever lady.'

And to have got it right for him and to hear the delight in his voice gave me such pleasure.

Then we'd move on to his herb bed and to his rose bed and to his ageratum and his irises and his azaleas and his sedum. And when we'd come to his nemophila, he always said the same thing.

'Nemophila are sometimes called Baby Blue Eyes. I know you can't see them but they have beautiful blue eyes. Just like you. You're my nemophila.'

And then we'd move on to the shrubs and the trees and we'd perform the same ritual of naming and counting and touching and smelling. Then, when our tour was ended, he'd kiss my right cheek and then my left cheek with that old-world formality with which he did everything; and I loved that because his whiskey breath made my head giddy for a second.

'Excellent!' he'd say. 'Excellent testimony! We'll adjourn until tomorrow.'

Then if Mother were away in hospital with her nerves, he and I would make our own meal. But if she were at home she'd appear at the front door – always in her headscarf and wellingtons – and she'd shout, 'Molly! Daddy! Dinner!' I never heard her call him anything but Daddy and the word always seemed to have a mocking edge. And he'd say to me, 'Even scholars must eat. Let us join your mother.'

And sometimes, just before we'd go into that huge, echoing house, sometimes he'd hug me to him and press his mouth against my ear and whisper with fierce urgency, 'I promise you, my darling, you aren't missing a lot; not a lot at all. Trust me.'

Of course I trusted him; completely. But late at night, listening to Mother and himself fighting their weary war downstairs and then hearing him grope his way unsteadily to bed, I'd wonder what he meant. And it was only when I was about the same age as he was then, it was only then that I thought – I thought perhaps I was beginning to understand what he meant. But that was many, many years later. And by then Mother and he were long dead and the old echoing house was gone. And I had been married to Frank for over two years. And by then, too, I had had the operation on the first eye.

Mr Rice The day he brought her to my house – the first time I saw them together – my immediate thought was: What an unlikely couple!

I had met him once before about a week earlier; by himself. He had called to ask would I see her, just to give an opinion, if only to confirm that nothing could be done for her. I suggested he phone the hospital and make an

appointment in the usual way. But of course he didn't.
And within two hours he was back at my door again with
an enormous folder of material that had to do with her
case and that he had compiled over the years and he'd be
happy to go through it with me there and then because
not only were the documents and reports and
photographs interesting in themselves but they would be
essential reading for someone like myself who was going
to take her case on.

Yes, an ebullient fellow; full of energy and enquiry and
the indiscriminate enthusiasms of the self-taught. And
convinced, as they usually are, that his own life story was
of compelling interest. He had worked for some
charitable organization in Nigeria. Kept goats on an
island off the Mayo coast and made cheese. Sold storage
batteries for those windmill things that produce electricity.
Endured three winters in Norway to ensure the well-being
of whales. That sort of thing. Worthy pursuits, no doubt.
And he was an agreeable fellow; oh, yes; perfectly
agreeable. Frank. That was his name. She was Molly.
Reminded me instantly of my wife, Maria. Perhaps the
way she held her head. A superficial resemblance.
Anyhow. Molly and Frank Sweeney.

I liked her. I liked her calm and her independence; the
confident way she shook my hand and found a seat for
herself with her white cane. And when she spoke of her
disability, there was no self-pity, no hint of resignation.
Yes, I liked her.

Her life, she insisted, was uneventful compared with
his. An only child. Father a judge. Mother in and out of
institutions all her days with nervous trouble. Brought up
by various housekeepers. For some reason she had never
been sent to a blind school. Said she didn't know why;
perhaps because her father thought he could handle the
situation best at home.

She had been blind since she was ten months old. She

wasn't totally sightless: she could distinguish between
light and dark; she could see the direction from which
light came; she could detect the shadow of Frank's hand
moving in front of her face. But for all practical purposes
she had no useful sight. Other ophthalmologists she had
been to over the years had all agreed that surgery would
not help. She had a full life and never felt at all deprived.
She was now forty-one, married just over two years, and
working as a massage therapist in a local health club.
Frank and she had met there and had married within a
month. They were fortunate they had her earnings to live
on because he was out of work at the moment.

She offered this information matter-of-factly. And as
she talked, he kept interrupting. 'She knows when I pass
my hand in front of her face. So there is some vision, isn't
there? So there is hope, isn't there, isn't there?' Perhaps, I
said. 'And if there is a chance, any chance, that she might
be able to see, we must take it, mustn't we? How can we
not take it? She has nothing to lose, has she? What has
she to lose? Nothing! Nothing!'

And she would wait without a trace of impatience until
he had finished and then she would go on. Yes, I liked her
at once.

His 'essential' folder. Across it he had written, typically,
Researched and Compiled by Frank C. Sweeney. The 'C'
stood for Constantine, I discovered. And it did have some
interest, the folder. Photographs of her cycling by herself
across a deserted beach. Results of tests she had
undergone years ago. A certificate for coming first in her
physiotherapy exams. Pictures of them on their
honeymoon in Stratford-on-Avon – his idea of self-
improvement, no doubt. Letters from two specialists she
had been to in her late teens. An article he had cut out of
a magazine about miraculous ophthalmological
techniques once practised in Tibet – or was it Mongolia?
Diplomas she had won in provincial swimming

championships. And remarkably – in his own furious
handwriting – remarkably, extracts from essays by various
philosophers on the relationship between vision and
knowledge, between seeing and understanding. A strange
fellow, indeed.

And when I talked to them on that first occasion I saw
them together in my house, I knew that she was there at
Frank's insistence, to please him, and not with any
expectation that I could help. And as I watched her sitting
there, erect in her seat and staring straight ahead, two
thoughts flitted across my mind. That her blindness was
his latest cause and that it would absorb him just as long
as his passion lasted. And then, I wondered, what then?
But perhaps that was too stern a judgement.

And the second and much less worthy thought I had
was this. No, not a thought; a phantom desire, a fantasy
in my head; absurd, bizarre, because I knew only the
barest outlines of her case, hadn't even examined her yet;
the thought, the bizarre thought that perhaps, perhaps –
up here in Donegal – not in Paris or Dallas or Vienna or
Milan – but perhaps up here in remote Ballybeg was I
about to be given – what is the vulgar parlance? – the
chance of a lifetime, the one-in-a-thousand opportunity
that can rescue a career – no, no, transform a career –
dare I say it, restore a reputation? And if that opportunity
were being offered to me and if after all these years I
could pull myself together and measure up to it, and if, oh
my God, if by some miracle pull it off perhaps . . . (*He
laughs in self-mockery.*)

Yes, I'm afraid so. People who live alone frequently
enjoy an opulent fantasy life.

Frank One of the most fascinating discoveries I made
when I was in the cheese business – well, perhaps not
fascinating, but interesting, definitely interesting – one of
the more interesting discoveries I made – this was long

before I met Molly – for three and a half years I had a
small goat farm on the island of Inis Beag off the Mayo
coast – no, no, not a farm for small goats – a farm for
ordinary goats – well, extraordinary goats as a matter of
fact because I imported two piebald Iranian goats – and I
can't tell you how complicated and expensive that whole
process was; and the reason I wanted them, the reason I
wanted Iranians, was that in all the research I had done
and according to all the experts they were reputed to give
the highest milk yield – untrue as it turned out – and
because their pelts were in great demand as wall coverings
in California – equally untrue, I'm afraid; and although
they bred very successfully – eventually I had a herd of
fourteen – they couldn't endure the Mayo winters with
the result that I had to keep them indoors and feed them
for six months of the year – in Mayo the winter lasts for
six months for God's sake – at least it did on Inis Beag.
And of course that threw my whole financial planning
into disarray. As you can imagine. And yes, as a matter of
interest, they are small animals, Iranian goats. And, as I
say, from Iran which, as you know, is an ancient
civilization in South West . . . Asia . . .

But I was telling you about – what? The interesting
discovery! Yes! Well, perhaps not an interesting discovery
in any general sense but certainly of great interest to
anybody who hopes to make cheese from the milk of
imported Iranian goats, not that there are thousands of
those people up and down the country! Anyhow –
anyhow – what I discovered was this. I had those goats
for three and half years, and even after all that time their
metabolism, their internal clock, stayed Iranian; never
adjusted to Irish time. Their system never made the
transition. They lived in a kind of perpetual jet-lag.

So what, you may ask. So for three and a half years I
had to get up to feed them at three in the morning my
time because that was 7.00 a.m. their time, their breakfast

time! And worse – worse – they couldn't be kept awake and consequently couldn't be milked after eight in the evening because that was midnight their time – and they were lying there, dead out, snoring! Bizarre! Some imprint in the genes remained indelible and immutable. I read a brilliant article once by a professor in an American magazine and he called this imprint an engram, from the Greek word meaning something that is etched, inscribed, on something. He said it accounts for the mind's strange ability to recognize instantly somebody we haven't seen for maybe thirty years. Then he appears. The sight of him connects with the imprint, the engram. And bingo – instant recognition!

Interesting word – engram. The only other time I heard it used was by Mr Rice, Molly's ophthalmologist. In that swanky accent of his – 'engram'. And he was born in the village of Kilmeedy in County Limerick for God's sake! I really never did warm to that man. No wonder his wife cleared off with another man. No, no, no, I don't mean that; I really don't mean that; that's a rotten thing to say; sorry; I shouldn't have said that. But I was talking about the word engram and how he pronounced it. That was before any of the operations, and he was explaining to Molly that if by some wonderful, miraculous good fortune her sight were restored, even partially restored, she would still have to learn to see and that would be an enormous and very difficult undertaking.

The way he explained it was this. She knew dozens of flowers; not to see; not by sight. She knew them only if she could touch them and smell them because those tactile engrams were implanted in her brain since she was a child. But if she weren't allowed to touch, to smell, she wouldn't know one flower from another; she wouldn't know a flower from a football. How could she?

And interestingly, interestingly this very same problem

was debated three hundred years ago by two philosophers, William Molyneux and his friend, John Locke. I came across this discussion in a Do-It-Yourself magazine of all places! Fascinating stuff, philosophy – absolutely fascinating. Anyhow – anyhow. If you are blind, said Molyneux – he was an Irishman by the way and in fact his wife was blind – if you are blind you can learn to distinguish between a cube and a sphere just by touching them, by feeling them. Right? Right. Now, supposing your vision is suddenly restored, will you be able – by sight alone, without touching, without feeling – will you be able to tell which object is the cube and which the sphere? Sorry, friend, said Locke – incidentally he went to Westminster School where he was flogged regularly – sorry, friend, you will not be able to tell which is which.

Then who comes along to join in the debate but another philosopher, George Berkeley, with his essay entitled *An Essay Towards a New Theory of Vision*. Another Irishman incidentally; Bishop Berkeley. And actually when I say along came the Bishop, his 'Essay' didn't appear until seventeen years after the discussion I told you about between Locke and Molyneux. Anyhow – anyhow. When the problem was put to the Lord Bishop, he came to the same conclusion as his friends. But he went even further. He said that there was no necessary connection *at all* between the tactile world – the world of touch – and the world of sight; and that any connection between the two could be established only by living, only by experience, only by learning the connection.

Which, indeed, is really what Rice said to Molly three hundred years later. That most of us are born with all five senses; and with all the information they give us, we build up a sight world from the day we are born – a world of objects and ideas and meanings. We aren't given that world, he said. We make it ourselves – through our experience, by our memory, by making categories, by interconnections. Now Molly had only ten months of sight and what she had seen in that time was probably forgotten. So, if her sight were restored, everything would have to be learned anew: she would have to *learn* to see. She would have to build up a whole repertory of visual engrams and then, then she would have to establish connections between these new imprints and the tactile engrams she already possessed. Put it another way: she would have to create a whole new world of her own.

How in God's name did I get into all that? The goats! Engrams! Three o'clock every bloody morning! I'll tell you something: three and a half years on that damned island and I lost four stone weight. And not an ounce of cheese – ever!

Not that it mattered, I suppose. I didn't go to Inis Beag to make my fortune. God knows why I went. God knows why I've spent my life at dozens of mad schemes. Crazy . . . Billy Hughes – Billy's an old pal of mine – Billy says I'm haunted for God's sake, always looking for . . . whatever . . .

Anyhow – anyhow. To go back for a second to our friend who knew what a cube was by touching it but couldn't identify it by sight alone. Rice talked a lot to Molly about all that stuff. He said neurologists had a word for people in that condition – seeing but not knowing, not recognizing, what it is they see. A word first used in this context by Freud, apparently. He said that people in that condition are called agnosic. Yes. Agnosic. Strange; because I always thought that word had to do with believing or not believing.

Molly I didn't like Mr Rice when I first met him. But I got to like him. I suppose because I trusted him. Frank never warmed to him. He was put off by his manner and the way he spoke. But I thought that for all his assurance there was something . . . unassured about him.

He was said to have been one of the most brilliant

ophthalmologists ever in the country. Worked in the top
eye hospitals all over the world – America, Japan,
Germany. Married a Swiss girl. They had two daughters.
Then she left him – according to the gossip; went off with
a colleague of his from New York. The daughters lived
with her parents in Geneva. For years after that there are
gaps in his story. Nobody seems to know what became of
him. They say that he had a breakdown; that he worked
as a labourer in Bolivia; that he ran a pub in Glasgow.
Anyhow he turned up here in Ballybeg and got a job in the
hospital and took a rented bungalow at the outskirts of
the town. He looked after himself in a sort of way. Walked
a bit. Did a lot of fly-fishing during the season – Frank
said he was beautiful to watch. People thought him a bit
prickly, a bit uppity, but that was probably because he
didn't mix much. I'm sure a brilliant man like that never
thought he'd end up in a Regional Hospital in the north-
west of Donegal. When I wondered what he looked like I
imagined a face with an expression of some bewilderment.

Maybe I liked him because of all the doctors who
examined me over the years he was the only one who
never quizzed me about what it felt like to be blind – I
suppose because he knew everything about it. The others
kept asking me what the idea of colour meant to me, or
the idea of space, or the notion of distance. You live in a
world of touch, a tactile world, they'd say. You depend
almost entirely on tactile perceptions, on knowing things
by feeling their shape. Tell us: How do you think your
world compares with the world the rest of us know, the
world you would share with us if you had visual
perception as well?

He never asked me questions like that. He did ask me
once did the idea, the possibility, of seeing excite me or
frighten me. It certainly excited Frank, I said. But why
should it be frightening? A stupid question, I know, he
said. Very stupid.

Why indeed should it be frightening? And how could I answer all those other questions? I know only my own world. I didn't think of it as a deprived world. Disadvantaged in some ways; of course it was. But at that stage I never thought of it as deprived. And Mr Rice knew that.

And how could I have told those other doctors how much pleasure my world offered me? From my work, from the radio, from walking, from music, from cycling. But especially from swimming. Oh I can't tell you the joy I got from swimming. I used to think – and I know this sounds silly – but I really did believe I got more pleasure, more delight, from swimming than sighted people can ever get. Just offering yourself to the experience – every pore open and eager for that world of pure sensation, of sensation alone – sensation that could not have been enhanced by sight – experience that existed only by touch and feel; and moving swiftly and rhythmically through that enfolding world; and the sense of such assurance, such liberation, such concordance with it . . . Oh I can't tell you the joy swimming gave me. I used to think that the other people in the pool with me, the sighted people, that in some way their pleasure was actually diminished because they could see, because seeing in some way qualified the sensation; and that if they only knew how full, how total my pleasure was, I used to tell myself that they must, they really must envy me.

Silly I suppose. Of course it was. I tried to explain how I felt to Mr Rice.

'I know what you mean,' he said.

And I think he did know.

Yes, maybe he was a bit pompous. And he could be sarcastic at times. And Frank said he didn't look at all bewildered; ever. But although I never saw my father's face, I imagine it never revealed any bewilderment either.

Mr Rice In the present state of medicine nothing can be done for people who are born blind, the clinically blind. Their retinas are totally insensitive to light and so are non-functional. There are no recorded cases of recovery from clinical blindness.

Molly Sweeney wasn't born blind. She was functionally blind and lived in a blind world for forty years. But she wasn't clinically blind: her retinas weren't totally insensitive to light. For God's sake how often did the husband, Mr Autodidact, tell me that she was aware of the shadow of his hand in front of her face?

So in theory, perhaps – purely theoretically – her case wasn't exactly hopeless. But I did make a point of giving her and her husband the only statistic available to us; and a dispiriting statistic it is. The number of cases known to us – of people who became blind shortly after birth and had their sight restored many years later – the number of cases over the past ten centuries is not more than twenty. Twenty people in a thousand years.

I know she believed me. I wasn't at all sure Frank Constantine did.

Anyhow, as a result of that first cursory examination in my home I decided to bring her into the clinic for tests.

Frank Well of course the moment Rice said in that uppity voice of his, 'In theory – in theory – in theory – perhaps in theory – perhaps – perhaps' – the first time Molly met him – after a few general questions, a very quick examination – ten o'clock in the morning in his house – I'll never forget it – the front room in the rented bungalow – no fire – the remains of last night's supper on a tray in the fireplace – teapot, crusts, cracked mug – well of course, goddamit, of course the head exploded! Just ex-ploded!

Molly was going to see! I knew it! For all his perhapses! Absolutely no doubt about it! A new world – a new life! A new life for both of us!

467

*Miracle of Molly Sweeney. Gift of sight restored to
middle-aged woman. 'I've been given a new world,' says
Mrs Sweeney.*

Unemployed husband cries openly.

And why not?

Oh my God . . .

Sight . . .

I saw an Austrian psychiatrist on the television one
night. Brilliant man. Brilliant lecture. He said that when
the mind is confronted by a situation of overwhelming
intensity – a moment of terror or ecstasy or tragedy – to
protect itself from overload, from overcharge, it switches
off and focuses on some trivial detail associated with the
experience.

And he was right. I know he was. Because that
morning in that front room in the chilly bungalow –
immediately after that moment of certainty, that
explosion in the head – my mind went numb; fused; and
all I could think of was that there was smell of fresh
whiskey off Rice's breath. And at ten o'clock in the
morning that seemed the most astonishing thing in the
world and I could barely stop myself from saying to
Molly, 'Do you not smell the whiskey off his breath? The
man's reeking of whiskey!'

Ridiculous . . .

Mr Rice Tests revealed that she had thick cataracts on
both eyes. But that wasn't the main problem. She also had
retinitis pigmentosa; as the name suggests, a discoloration
of the retina. She seemed to have no useful retinal
function. It wasn't at all surprising that other doctors had
been put off.

There were scars of old disease, too. But what was
encouraging – to put it at its very best – was that there
was no current, no active disease process. So that if I were
to decide to operate and if the operation were even

partially successful, her vision, however impaired, ought
to be stable for the rest of her life.

So in theory perhaps . . .

Frank On the morning of Tuesday, October 7, he
operated on the right eye to remove a cataract and
implant a new lens.

I was told not to visit her until the following day
because the eye would be bandaged for twenty-four hours
and she had to have as much rest and quiet as possible.
Naturally, of course . . .

And a wonderful thing happened that night when I was
at home by myself. I got a call from London; from a
friend I knew in Nigeria in the old days. Chap called
Winterman, Dick Winterman. Inviting me to set up and
supervise a food convoy to Ethiopia. Was I interested?

Of course I was interested. The first job I'd been offered
in months. But not now. How could I go now for God's
sake? Molly was on the verge of a new life. I had to be
with her now. Anyhow, as I told Dick, those rambling
days were over.

All the same it was nice to be remembered. And to be
remembered on that night – I thought that was a good
omen.

Mr Rice I'm ashamed to say that within a week I crossed
the frontier into the fantasy life again. The moment I
decided I was going to operate on Molly I had an impulse
– a dizzying, exuberant, overmastering, intoxicating
instinct to phone Roger Bloomstein in New York and
Hans Girder in Berlin and Hiroko Matoba in Kyoto –
even old Murnahan in Dublin – and tell them what I was
about to do. Yes, yes, especially old Murnahan in Dublin;
and say to him, 'Paddy Rice here, Professor. Of course
you remember him! You called him a rogue star once –
oh, yes, that caused a titter. Well, he works in a rundown
hospital in Donegal now. And I suspect, I think, I believe

469

for no good reason at all that Paddy Rice is on the trembling verge, Professor. He has a patient who has been blind for forty years. And do you know what? He is going to give her vision – the twenty-first recorded case in over a thousand years! And for the first time in her life – how does Saint Mark put it in the gospel? – for the first time in her life she will 'see men walking as if like trees'.

Delirium . . . hubris . . . the rogue star's token insurrection . . . a final, ridiculous flourish. For God's sake, a routine cataract operation?

Of course I made no calls. Instead I wrote to my daughters, Aisling and Helga in Geneva, and enclosed what money I could afford. Then to Maria, my ex-wife, in New York; yet another open-heart letter, full of candour and dreary honesty. I told her I was busy and in good spirits and involved in a new case that was unusual in some respects.

Then I made supper; had a few drinks; fell asleep in the armchair. I woke again at 4.00 a.m., my usual hour, and sat there waiting for a new day, and said to myself over and over again: Why the agitation over this case? You remove cataracts every day of the week, don't you? And isn't the self-taught husband right? (*angrily*) What has she to lose for Christ's sake? Nothing! Nothing at all!

Molly What a party we had the night before the operation! Three o'clock in the morning before we got the house cleared. Oh, God! And I had to be in the hospital for ten – fasting. Frank wanted to get a taxi but I said we should walk to get all that alcohol out of the system.

And it wasn't that we had organized anything that night. A few neighbours just dropped in to wish me luck; and then a few more; and then Frank said, 'Come on! This is beginning to feel like a wake!' and away he went to the off-licence and came back with a load of stuff.

Who was there? Tony and Betty from this side; with

Molly, their baby; they called her after me; she was just a
toddler then. And the Quinns from that side; Jack and
Mary. Jack wasn't drinking for some reason and Mary
certainly was; so that was a delicate situation. And old
Mr O'Neill from across the street; first time outside his
house since his wife, Louise, died three months before;
and Frank just took him by the arm and said he would
fall into a decline if he didn't pull himself together.
Anyhow, after two or three beers, what does Mr O'Neill
do? Up on top of the table and begins reciting 'A bunch of
the boys were whooping it up in the Malamute saloon' –
or whatever the right name is! Yes! Little timid Mr
O'Neill, the mourning widower! And he acted it out so
seriously. And of course we all began to snigger. And the
more we sniggered, the more melodramatic he became. So
that by the time he got to 'The woman that kissed him
and pinched his poke was the lady that's known as Lou' –
he always called Louise, his dead wife, Lou – well of
course by that time we were falling about. Oh, he was
furious. Sulked in the corner for ages. God!

Who else? Billy Hughes was there; an old bachelor
friend of Frank. Years ago Frank and he borrowed money
from the bank and bought forty beehives; but I gather
that didn't work out. And Dorothy and Joyce; they're
physiotherapists in the hospital. And Tom McLaughlin,
another of Frank's bachelor friends. He's a great fiddler,
Tom. And that was it. And of course Rita, Rita Cairns,
my oldest, my closest friend. She managed the health club
I was working in. Rita probably knows me better than
anybody.

There was a lot of joking that there were thirteen of us
if you counted the baby. And Billy Hughes, who was
already well tanked by the time he arrived, he suggested
that maybe Jack – from that side – maybe Jack would do
the decent and volunteer to leave since he was in a bad
mood and wasn't drinking anyway. And Mary, Jack's

wife, she said that was the brightest idea all evening. So that was an even trickier situation.

And at some point in the night – it must have been about two – I'm afraid I had a brainwave. Here we are, all friends together, having a great time; so shouldn't I phone Mr Rice and ask him to join us? Wasn't he a friend, too? And I made for the phone and dialled the number. But Frank, thank God, Frank pulled the phone out of my hand before he answered. Imagine the embarrassment that would have been!

Anyway we chatted and we played tapes and we sang and we drank. And Tony and Betty from this side, Molly's parents, they sang 'Anything You Can Do I Can Do Better' and there was so much tension between them you knew they weren't performing at all. And Dorothy and Joyce did their usual Laurel and Hardy imitation. And Billy Hughes, the bee-man, told some of his jokes that only Frank and he found funny. And as usual Rita, Rita Cairns, sang 'Oft in the Stilly Night', her party piece. That was my father's song, too. She has a sweet voice, really a child's voice, and she sings it beautifully. And as usual, when she had finished, so she tells me, she nodded her head and smiled and cried all at the same time. That's what she – 'The Shooting of Dan McGrew'! That's the title of Mr O'Neill's poem! Poor old Mr O'Neill. Somebody told me recently that he's in a hospice now.

And shortly after midnight – long before I had the brainwave to phone Mr Rice – Tom McLaughlin, Tom the fiddler, played 'The Lament for Limerick'! He played it softly, delicately. And suddenly, suddenly I felt utterly desolate. Maybe it was Rita singing, 'Oft in the Stilly Night' earlier. Or maybe it was because all that night nobody once mentioned the next day or how they thought the operation might go; and because nothing was said, maybe that made the occasion a bit unreal, a bit frantic.

Or maybe it was because I was afraid that if things turned out as Frank and Mr Rice hoped, I was afraid that I would never again know these people as I knew them now, with my own special knowledge of each of them, the distinctive sense each of them exuded for me; and knowing them differently, experiencing them differently, I wondered – I wondered would I ever be as close to them as I was now.

And then with sudden anger I thought: Why am I going for this operation? None of this is my choosing. Then why is this happening to me? I am being used. Of course I trust Frank. Of course I trust Mr Rice. But how can they know what they are taking away from me? How do they know what they are offering me? They don't. They can't. And have I anything to gain? Anything? Anything?

And then I knew, suddenly I knew why I was so desolate. It was the dread of exile, of being sent away. It was the desolation of homesickness.

And then a strange thing happened. As soon as Tom played the last note of 'The Lament for Limerick', I found myself on my feet in the middle of the sitting-room and calling, 'A hornpipe, Tom! A mad, fast hornpipe!' And the moment he began to play, I shouted – screamed, 'Now watch me! Just you watch me!' And in a rage of anger and defiance I danced a wild and furious dance round and round that room; then out to the hall; then round the kitchen; then back to the room again and round it a third time. Mad and wild and frenzied. But so adroit, so efficient. No timidity, no hesitations, no falterings. Not a glass overturned, not a shoulder brushed. Weaving between all those people, darting between chairs and stools and cushions and bottles and glasses with complete assurance, with absolute confidence. Until Frank said something to Tom and stopped him playing.

God knows how I didn't kill myself or injure somebody. Or indeed how long it lasted. But it must have been terrifying to watch because, when I stopped, the room was hushed.

Frank whispered something to me. I don't know what he said – I was suddenly lost and anxious and frightened. I remember calling, 'Rita? Where are you, Rita?'

'Here at the window,' she said. And I stumbled, groped my way to her and sat beside her. 'Come on, sweetie,' she said. 'We'll have none of that. You're not allowed to cry. I'm the only one that's allowed to give a performance and then cry.'

Mr Rice The night before I operated on Molly Sweeney I thought about that high summer in my thirty-second year. Cairo. Another lecture; another conference; another posh hotel. As usual we all met up: Roger Bloomstein from New York, Hans Girder from Berlin, Hiroko Matoba from Kyoto, myself. The meteors. The young turks. The four horsemen. Oslo last month. Helsinki next week. Paris the week after. That luminous, resplendent life. Those glowing, soaring careers.

Maria left the children with parents in Geneva and flew down to join us. Still wan and translucent after the birth of Helga. And so beautiful; my God, so beautiful. We had a dinner party for her the night she arrived. Roger was master-of-ceremonies. Toasted her with his usual elegance. Said she was our Venus – no, our Galatea. She smiled her secret smile and said each of us was her Icarus.

Insatiable years. Work. Airports. Dinners. Laughter. Operating theatres. Conferences. Gossip. Publications. The professional jealousies and the necessary vigilance. The relentless, devouring excitement. But above all, above all the hunger to accomplish, the greed for achievement.

Shards of those memories came back to me on the night before I operated on Molly Sweeney on Tuesday, October 7. I had had a few drinks. I had had a lot of drinks. The fire was dead. I was drifting in and out of sleep.

Then the phone rang; an anxious sound at two in the morning. By the time I had pulled myself together and got to it, it had stopped. Wrong number probably.

I had another drink and sat beside the dead fire and relived for the hundredth time that other phone-call. The small hours of the morning, too. In Cairo. That high summer of my thirty-second year.

It was Roger Bloomstein. Brilliant Roger. Treacherous Icarus. To tell me that Maria and he were at the airport and about to step on a plane for New York. They were deeply in love. They would be in touch in a few days. He was very sorry to have to tell me this. He hoped that in time I would see the situation from their point of view and come to understand it. And he hung up.

The mind was instantly paralysed. All I could think was: He's confusing seeing with understanding. Come on, Bloomstein. What's the matter with you? Seeing isn't understanding.

You know that! Don't talk rubbish, man!

And then ... and then ... oh, Jesus, Maria ...

Frank Just as I was about to step into bed that night – that same Tuesday night that Dick Winterman phoned – the night of the operation – I was on the point of stepping into bed when suddenly, suddenly I remembered: Ethiopia is Abyssinia! Abyssinia is Ethiopia! They're the same place! Ethiopia is the new name for the old Abyssinia! For God's sake only last year the *National Geographic* magazine had a brilliant article on it with all these stunning photographs. For God's sake I could write a book about Ethiopia! Absolutely *the* most interesting country in the world! Let me give you one fascinating fact about the name, the name Abyssinia. The name Abyssinia is derived from the word 'habesh'; and the word 'habesh' means mixed – on account of the varied nature of its peoples. But interestingly,

interestingly the people themselves always called themselves Ethiopians, never Abyssinians, because they considered the word Abyssinia and Abyssinians as derogatory – they didn't want to be thought of as mixed! So now the place is officially what the people themselves always called it – Ethiopia. Fascinating!

But of course I had to say no to Dick. As I said. Those rambling days were over. Molly was about to inherit a new world; and I had a sense – stupid, I know – I had a sense that maybe I was, too.

Pity to miss Abyssinia all the same – the one place in the whole world I've always dreamed of visiting; a phantom desire, a fantasy in the head. Pity to miss that.

You shouldn't have dangled it in front of me, Dick Winterman. Bloody, bloody heartbreaking.

Molly I remember so well the first day Frank came to the health club. That was the first time I'd met him. I was on a coffee-break. A Friday afternoon.

I had known of him for years of course. Rita Cairns and his friend Billy Hughes used to go out occasionally and I'd hear his name mentioned. She never said anything bad about him; but when his name came up, you got the feeling he was a bit . . . different.

Anyhow that Friday he came into the club and Rita introduced us and we chatted. And for the whole ten minutes of my coffee-break he gave me a talk about a feasibility study he was doing on the blueback salmon, know in Oregon as sockeye and in Alaska as redfish, and of his plan to introduce it to Irish salmon farmers because it has the lowest wastage rate in all canning factories where it is used.

When he left I said to Rita that I'd never met a more enthusiastic man in my life. And Rita said in her laconic way, 'Sweetie, who wants their enthusiasm focussed on bluebacks for God's sake?'

Anyhow, ten minutes after he left, the phone rang.
Could we meet that evening? Saturday? Sunday? What
about a walk, a meal, a concert? Just a chat?

I asked him to call me the following Friday.

I thought a lot about him that week. I suppose he was
the first man I really knew – apart from my father. And I
liked his energy. I liked his enthusiasm. I liked his passion.
Maybe what I really liked about him was that he was
everything my father wasn't.

Frank I spent a week in the library – the week after I first
met her – one full week immersing myself in books and
encyclopaedias and magazines and articles – anything,
everything I could find about eyes and vision and eye-
diseases and blindness.

Fascinating. I can't tell you – fascinating. I look out of
my bedroom window and at a single glance I see the front
garden and the road beyond and cars and buses and the
tennis-courts on the far side and people playing on them
and the hills beyond that. Everything – all those details
and dozens more – all seen in one immediate,
comprehensive perception. But Molly's world isn't
perceived instantly, comprehensively. She composes a
world from a sequence of impressions; one after the other,
in time. For example, she knows that this is a carving
knife because first she can feel the handle; then she can
feel this long blade; then this sharp edge. In sequence. In
time. What is this object? These are ears. This is a furry
body. Those are paws. That is a long tail. Ah, a cat! In
sequence. Sequentially.

Right? Right. Now a personal question. You are going
to ask this blind lady out for an evening. What would be
the ideal entertainment for somebody like her? A meal? A
concert? A walk? Maybe a swim? Billy Hughes says she's
a wonderful swimmer. (*He shakes his head slowly.*)

The week in the library pays off. Know the answer

instantly. Dancing. Take her dancing. With her disability the perfect, the absolutely perfect relaxation. Forget about space, distance, who's close, who's far, who's approaching. Forget about time. This is not a sequence of events. This is one continuous, delightful event. Nothing leads to nothing else. There is only now. There is nothing subsequent. I am your eyes, your ears, your location, your sense of space. Trust me.

Dancing. Obvious.

Straight into a phone-box and asked her would she come with me to the Hikers Club dance the following Saturday. It'll be small, I said; more like a party. What do you say?

Silence.

We'll ask Billy and Rita and we'll make it a foursome and we'll have our own table and our own fun.

Not a word.

Please, Molly.

In my heart of hearts I really didn't think she'd say yes. For God's sake why should she? Middle-aged. No skill. No job. No prospect of a job. Two rooms above Kelly's cake-shop. And not exactly Rudolf Valentino. And when she did speak, when she said very politely, 'Thank you, Frank. I'd love to go,' do you know what I said? 'All right then.' Bloody brilliant.

But I vowed to myself in that phone-box, I made a vow there and then that at the dance on Saturday night I wouldn't open the big mouth – big? – enormous for Christ's sake! – I wouldn't open it once all night, all week.

Talking of Valentino, in point of fact Valentino was no Adonis himself. Average height; average looks; mediocre talent. And if he hadn't died so young – in 1926 – he was only 31 – and in those mysterious circumstances that were never fully explained – he would never have become the cult figure the studios worked so hard to . . .

Anyhow . . .

Molly As usual Rita was wonderful. She washed my hair,
my bloody useless hair – I can do nothing with it – she
washed it in this special shampoo she concocted herself.
Then she pulled it all away back from my face and piled it
up, just here, and held it in place with her mother's silver
ornamental comb. And she gave me her black shoes and
her new woollen dress she'd just bought for her brother's
wedding.

'There's still something not right,' she said. 'You still
remind me of my Aunt Madge. Here – try these.' And she
whipped off her earrings and put them on me. 'Now we
have it,' she said. 'Bloody lethal. Francis Constantine,
you're a dead duck!'

Frank She had the time of her life. Knew she would. We
danced every dance. Sang every song at the top of our
voices. Ate an enormous supper. Even won a spot prize: a
tin of shortbread and a bottle of Albanian wine. The
samba, actually. I wasn't bad at the samba once.

Dancing. I knew. I explained the whole thing to her. She
had to agree. For God's sake she didn't have to say a
word – she just glowed.

Molly It was almost at the end of the night – we were
doing an old-time waltz – and suddenly he said to me,
'You are such a beautiful woman, Molly.'

Nobody had ever said anything like that to me before. I
was afraid I might cry. And before I could say a word, he
plunged on: 'Of course I know that the very idea of
appearance, of how things look, can't have much meaning
for you. I do understand that. And maybe at heart you're
a real philosophical sceptic because you question not only
the idea of appearance but probably the existence of
external reality itself. Do you, Molly?'

Honest to God . . . the second last dance at the Hikers
Club . . . a leisurely, old-time waltz . . .

And I knew that night that he would ask me to marry

him. Because he liked me – I knew he did. And because of
my blindness – oh, yes, that fascinated him. He couldn't
resist the different, the strange. I think he believed that
some elusive off-beat truth resided in the quirky, the off-
beat. I suppose that's what made him such a restless man.
Rita of course said it was inevitable he would propose to
me. 'All part of the same pattern, sweetie: bees – whales –
Iranian goats – Molly Sweeney.'

Maybe she was right.

And I knew, too, after that night in the Hikers Club,
that if he did ask me to marry him, for no very good
reason at all I would probably say yes.

Mr Rice The morning of the operation I stood at the
window of my office and watched them walk up the
hospital drive. It was a blustery morning, threatening
rain.

She didn't have her cane and she didn't hold his arm.
But she moved briskly with her usual confidence; her head
high; her face alert and eager. In her right hand she
carried a grey, overnight bag.

He was on her left. Now in the open air a smaller
presence in a shabby raincoat and cap; his hands clasped
behind his back; his eyes on the ground; his head bowed
slightly against the wind so that he looked . . . passive.
Not a trace of the assurance, the ebullience, that relentless
energy.

And I thought: Are they really such an unlikely couple?
And I wondered what hopes moved in them as they came
towards me. Were they modest? Reasonable?
Outrageous? Of course, of course they were outrageous.

And suddenly and passionately and with utter
selflessness I wanted nothing more in the world than that
their inordinate hopes would be fulfilled, that I could give
them their miracle. And I whispered to Hans Girder and
to Matoba and to Murnaghan and to Bloomstein – yes, to

Bloomstein, too! – to gather round me this morning and steady my unsteady hand and endow me with all their exquisite skills.

Because as I watched them approach the hospital that blustery morning, one head alert, one head bowed, I was suddenly full of anxiety for both of them. Because I was afraid – even though she was in the hands of the best team in the whole world to deliver her miracle, because she was in the hands of the best team in the whole world – I was fearful, I suddenly knew that that courageous woman had everything, everything to lose.

Act Two

Molly The morning the bandages were to be removed a staff nurse spent half-an-hour preparing me for Mr Rice. It wasn't really her job, she told me; but this was my big day and I had to look my best and she was happy to do it.

So she sponged my face and hands. She made me clean my teeth again. She wondered did I use lipstick – maybe just for today? She did the best she could with my hair, God help her. She looked at my fingernails and suggested that a touch of clear varnish would be nice. She straightened the bow at the front of my nightdress and adjusted the collar of my dressing-gown. She put a dab of her own very special perfume on each of my wrists – she got it from a cousin in Paris. Then she stood back and surveyed me and said,

'Now. That's better. You'll find that from now on – if everything goes well of course – you'll find that you'll become very aware of your appearance. They all do for some reason. Don't be nervous. You look just lovely. He'll be here any minute now.'

I asked her where the bathroom was.

'At the end of the corridor. Last door on the right. I'll bring you.'

'No,' I said. 'I'll find it.'

I didn't need to go to the bathroom. I just wanted to take perhaps a last walk; in my own world; by myself.

I don't know what I expected when the bandages would be removed. I think maybe I didn't allow myself any expectations. I knew that in his heart Frank believed that somehow, miraculously, I would be given the perfect vision that sighted people have, even though Mr Rice had told us again and again that my eyes weren't capable of that vision. And I knew what Mr Rice hoped for: that I would have partial sight. 'That would be a total success for me' is what he said. But I'm sure he meant it would be great for all of us.

As for myself, if I had any hope, I suppose it was that neither Frank nor Mr Rice would be too disappointed because it had all become so important for them.

No, that's not accurate either. Yes, I did want to see. For God's sake of course I wanted to see. But that wasn't an expectation, not even a mad hope. If there was a phantom desire, a fantasy in my head, it was this. That perhaps by some means I might be afforded a brief excursion to this land of vision; not to live there – just to visit. And during my stay to devour it again and again with greedy, ravenous eyes. To gorge on all those luminous sights and wonderful spectacles until I knew every detail intimately and utterly – every ocean, every leaf, every field, every star, every tiny flower. And then, oh yes, then to return home to my own world with all that rare understanding within me for ever.

No, that wasn't even a phantom desire. Just a stupid fantasy. And it came into my head again when that poor nurse was trying to prettify me for Mr Rice. And I thought to myself: It's like being back at school – I'm getting dressed up for the annual excursion.

When Mr Rice did arrive, even before he touched me, I knew by his quick, shallow breathing that he was far more nervous than I was. And then as he took off the bandages his hands trembled and fumbled.

'There we are,' he said. 'All off. How does that feel?'

'Fine,' I said. Even though I felt nothing. Were all the bandages off?

'Now, Molly. In your own time. Tell me what you see.'

Nothing. Nothing at all. Then out of the void a blur; a haze; a body of mist; a confusion of light, colour, movement. It had no meaning.

'Well?' he said. 'Anything? Anything at all?'

I thought: Don't panic; a voice comes from a face; that blur is his face; look at him.

'Well? Anything?'

Something moving; large; white. The nurse? And lines, black lines, vertical lines. The bed? The door?

'Anything, Molly?' A bright light that hurt. The window maybe?

'I'm holding my hand before your eyes, Molly. Can you see it?'

A reddish blob in front of my face; rotating; liquefying; pulsating. Keep calm. Concentrate.

'Can you see my hand, Molly?'

'I think so . . . I'm not sure . . .'

'Now I'm moving my hand slowly.'

'Yes . . . yes . . .'

'Do you see my hand moving?'

'Yes . . .'

'What way is it moving?'

'Yes . . . I do see it . . . up and down . . . up and down . . . Yes! I see it! I do! Yes! Moving up and down! Yes-yes-yes!'

'Splendid!' he said. 'Absolutely splendid! You are a clever lady!'

And there was such delight in his voice. And my head was suddenly giddy. And I thought for a moment – for a moment I thought I was going to faint.

Frank There was some mix-up about what time the bandages were to be removed. At least I was confused. For some reason I got it into my head that they were to be taken off at eight in the morning, October 8, the day after the operation. A Wednesday, I remember, because I was doing a crash-course in speed-reading and I had to switch from the morning to the afternoon class for that day.

So; eight o'clock sharp; there I was sitting in the hospital, all dickied up – the good suit, the shoes polished, the clean shirt, the new tie, and with my bunch of flowers, waiting to be summoned to Molly's ward.

The call finally did come – at a quarter to twelve. Ward 10. Room 17. And of course by then I knew the operation was a disaster.

Knocked. Went in. Rice was there. And a staff nurse, a tiny little woman. And an Indian man – the anaesthetist, I think. The moment I entered he rushed out without saying a word.

And Molly. Sitting very straight in a white chair beside her bed. Her hair pulled away back from her face and piled up just here. Wearing a lime-green dressing-gown that Rita Cairns had lent her and the blue slippers I got her for her last birthday.

There was a small bruise mark below her right eye.

I thought: How young she looks, and so beautiful, so very beautiful.

'There she is,' said Rice. 'How does she look?'

'She looks well.'

'Well? She looks wonderful! And why not? Everything went brilliantly! A complete success! A dream!'

He was so excited, there was no trace of the posh accent. And he bounced up and down on the balls of his feet. And he took my hand and shook it as if he were congratulating me. And the tiny staff nurse laughed and said 'Brilliant! Brilliant!' and in her excitement knocked the chart off the end of the bed and then laughed even more.

'Speak to her!' said Rice. 'Say something!'

'How are you?' I said to Molly.

'How do I look?'

'You look great.'

'Do you like my black eye?'

'I didn't notice it,' I said.

'I'm feeling great,' she said. 'Really. But what about you?'

'What do you mean?'

'Did you manage all right on your own last night?'

I suppose at that moment and in those circumstances it did sound a bit funny.

Anyhow Rice laughed out loud and of course the staff nurse; and then Molly and I had to laugh, too. In relief, I suppose, really . . .

Then Rice said to me,

'Aren't you going to give the lady her flowers?'

'Sorry,' I said. 'I got Rita to choose them. She said they're your favourite.'

Could she see them? I didn't know what to do. Should I take her hand and put the flowers into it?

I held them in front of her. She reached out confidently and took them from me.

'They're lovely,' she said. 'Thank you. Lovely.'

And she held them at arm's length, directly in front of her face, and turned them round. Suddenly Rice said,

'What colour are they, Molly?'

She didn't hesitate at all.

'They're blue,' she said. 'Aren't they blue?'

'They certainly are! And the paper?' Rice asked. 'What colour is the wrapping paper?'

'Is it . . . yellow?'

'Yes! So you know some colours! Excellent! Really excellent!'

And the staff nurse clapped with delight.

'Now – a really hard question, and I'm not sure I know the answer to it myself. What sort of flowers are they?'

She brought them right up to her face. She turned them upside down. She held them at arm's length again. She stared at them – peered at them really – for what seemed an age. I knew how anxious she was by the way her mouth was working.

'Well, Molly? Do you know what they are?'

We waited. Another long silence. Then suddenly she

closed her eyes shut tight. She brought the flowers right
up against her face and inhaled in quick gulps and at the
same time, with her free hand, swiftly, deftly felt the stems
and the leaves and the blossoms. Then with her eyes still
shut tight she called out desperately, defiantly,

'They're cornflowers! That's what they are!
Cornflowers! Blue cornflowers! Centaurea!'

Then for maybe half-a-minute she cried. Sobbed really.

The staff nurse looked uneasily at Rice. He held up his
hand.

'Cornflowers, indeed. Splendid,' he said very softly.
'Excellent. It has been a heady day. But we're really on
our way now, aren't we?'

I went back to the hospital again that night after my
class. She was in buoyant form. I never saw her so
animated.

'I can see, Frank!' she kept saying. 'Do you hear me? – I
can see!' Mr Rice was a genius! Wasn't it all wonderful?
The nurses were angels! Wasn't I thrilled? She loved my
red tie – it was red, wasn't it? And everybody was so kind.
Dorothy and Joyce brought those chocolates during their
lunch-break. And old Mr O'Neill sent that Get Well card
– there – look – on the window-sill. And didn't the
flowers look beautiful in that pink vase? She would have
the operation on the left eye just as soon as Mr Rice
would agree. And then, Frank, and then and then and
then and then – oh, God, what then!

I was so happy, so happy for her. Couldn't have been
happier for God's sake.

But just as on that first morning in Rice's bungalow
when the only thing my mind could focus on was the
smell of fresh whiskey off his breath, now all I could
think of was some – some – some absurd scrap of
information a Norwegian fisherman told me about the
eyes of whales.

Whales for God's sake!

487

Stupid information. Useless, off-beat information. Stupid, useless, quirky mind . . .

Molly was still in full flight when a nurse came in and said that visiting time was long over and that Mrs Sweeney needed all her strength to face tomorrow.

'How do I look?'

'Great,' I said.

'Really, Frank?'

'Honestly. Wonderful.'

'Black eye and all?'

'You wouldn't notice it,' I said.

She caught my hand.

'Do you think . . .?'

'Do I think what?'

'Do you think I look pretty, Frank?'

'You look beautiful,' I said. 'Just beautiful.'

'Thank you.'

I kissed her on the forehead and, as I said good night to her, she gazed intently at my face as if she were trying to read it. Her eyes were bright; unnaturally bright; burnished. And her expression was open and joyous. But as I said good night I had a feeling she wasn't as joyous as she looked.

Mr Rice When I look back over my working life I suppose I must have done thousands of operations. Sorry – performed. Bloomstein always corrected me on that: 'Come on, you bloody bogman! We're not mechanics. We're artists. We perform.' (*He shrugs his shoulders in dismissal.*)

And of those thousands I wonder how many I'll remember.

I'll remember Dubai. An Arab gentleman whose left eye had been almost pecked out by one of his peregrines and who sent his private jet to New York for Hans Girder and myself. The eye was saved, really because Girder was a magician. And we spent a week in a palace of marble and gold and played poker with the crew of the jet and lost every penny of the ransom we had just earned.

And I'll remember a city called Frankfort in Kentucky; and an elderly lady called Busty Butterfly who had been blinded in a gas explosion. Hiroko Matoba and I 'performed' that operation. A tricky one, but he and I always worked well together. And Busty Butterfly was so grateful that she wanted me to have her best racehorse and little Hiroko to marry her.

And I'll remember Ballybeg. Of course I'll remember Ballybeg. And the courageous Molly Sweeney. And I'll remember it not because of the operation – the operation wasn't all that complex; nor because the circumstances were special; nor indeed because a woman who had been blind for over forty years got her sight back. Yes, yes, yes, I'll remember it for all those reasons. Of course I will. But the core, the very heart, of the memory will be something different, something altogether different.

Perhaps I should explain that after that high summer of my thirty-second year – that episode in Cairo – the dinner party for Maria – Bloomstein's phone-call – all that tawdry drama – my life no longer . . . cohered. I withdrew from medicine, from friendships, from all the consolations of work and the familiar; and for seven years and seven months – sounds like a fairy tale I used to read to Aisling – I subsided into a terrible darkness . . .

But I was talking of Molly's operation and my memory of that. And the core of that memory is this. That for seventy-five minutes in the theatre on that blustery October morning, the darkness miraculously lifted, and I performed – I watched myself do it – I performed so assuredly and with such skill, so elegantly, so efficiently, so economically – yes, yes, yes, of course it sounds vain – vanity has nothing to do with it – but suddenly, miraculously, all the gifts, all the gifts were mine again,

abundantly mine, joyously mine; and on that blustery
October morning I had such a feeling of mastery and –
how can I put it? – such a sense of playfulness for God's
sake that I knew I was restored. No, no, no, not fully
restored. Never fully restored. But a sense that a practical
restoration, perhaps a restoration to something truer –
that was possible. Yes, maybe that was possible . . .

Yes, I'll remember Ballybeg. And when I left that dreary
little place, that's the memory I took away with me. The
place where I restored her sight to Molly Sweeney. Where
the terrible darkness lifted. Where the shaft of light
glanced off me again.

Molly Mr Rice said he couldn't have been more pleased
with my progress. He called me his Miracle Molly. I liked
him a lot more as the weeks passed.

And as usual Rita was wonderful. She let me off work
early every Monday, Wednesday and Friday. And I'd
dress up in this new coat I'd bought – a mad splurge to
keep the spirits up – brilliant scarlet with a matching
beret – Rita said I could be seen from miles away, like a
distress signal – anyhow in all my new style I'd walk to
the hospital on those three afternoons – without my
cane! – and sometimes that was scary, I can tell you. And
Mr Rice would examine me and say, 'Splendid, Molly!
Splendid!' And then he'd pass me on to a
psychotherapist, Mrs Wallace, a beautiful looking young
woman according to Frank, and I'd do all sorts of tests
with her. And then she'd pass me on to George, her
husband, for more tests – he was a behavioural
psychologist, if you don't mind, a real genius apparently
– the pair of them were writing a book on me. And then
I'd go back to Mr Rice again and he'd say 'Splendid!'
again. And then I'd walk home – still no cane! – and
have Frank's tea waiting for him when he'd get back
from the library.

I can't tell you how kind Frank was to me, how patient he was. As soon as tea was over, he'd sit at the top of the table and he'd put me at the bottom and he'd begin my lesson.

He'd put something in front of me – maybe a bowl of fruit – and he'd say,

'What have I got in my hand?'

'A piece of fruit.'

'What sort of fruit?'

'An orange, Frank. I know the colour, don't I?'

'Very clever. Now, what's this?'

'It's a pear.'

'You're guessing.'

'Let me touch it.'

'Not allowed. You already have your tactical engrams. We've got to build up a repertory of visual engrams to connect with them.'

And I'd say, 'For God's sake stop showing off your posh new words, Frank. It's a banana.'

'Sorry. Try again.'

'It's a peach. Right?'

'Splendid!' he'd say in Mr Rice's accent. 'It certainly is a peach. Now, what's this?'

And he'd move on to knives and forks, or shoes and slippers, or all the bits and pieces on the mantelpiece for maybe another hour or more. Every night. Seven nights a week.

Oh, yes, Frank couldn't have been kinder to me.

Rita, too. Even kinder. Even more patient.

And all my customers at the health club, the ones who had massages regularly, they sent me a huge bouquet of pink-and-white tulips. And the club I used to swim with, they sent me a beautiful gardening book. God knows what they thought – that I'd now be able to pick it up and read it? But everyone was great, just great.

Oh, yes, I lived in a very exciting world for those first

weeks after the operation. Not at all like that silly world I wanted to visit and devour – none of that nonsense.

No, the world that I now saw – half-saw, peered at really – it was a world of wonder and surprise and delight. Oh, yes; wonderful, surprising, delightful. And joy – such joy, small unexpected joys that came in such profusion and passed so quickly that there was never enough time to savour them.

But it was a very foreign world, too. And disquieting; even alarming. Every shape an apparition, a spectre that appeared suddenly from nowhere and challenged you. And all that movement – nothing ever still – everything in motion all the time; and every movement unexpected, somehow threatening. Even the sudden sparrows in the garden, they seemed aggressive, dangerous.

So that after a time the mind could absorb no more sensation. Just one more colour – light – movement – ghostly shape – and suddenly the head imploded and the hands shook and the heart melted with panic. And the only escape – the only way to live – was to sit absolutely still; and shut the eyes tight; and immerse yourself in darkness; and wait. Then when the hands were still and the heart quiet, slowly open the eyes again. And emerge. And try to find the courage to face it all once more.

I tried to explain to Frank once how – I suppose how *terrifying* it all was. But naturally, naturally he was far more concerned with teaching me practical things. And one day when I mentioned to Mr Rice that I didn't think I'd find things as unnerving as I did, he said in a very icy voice,

'And what sort of world did you expect, Mrs Sweeney?'

Yes, it was a strange time. An exciting time, too – oh, yes, exciting. But so strange. And during those weeks after the operation I found myself thinking more and more about my mother and father, but especially about my mother and what it must have been like for her living in that huge, echoing house.

Mr Rice I operated on the second eye, the left eye, six weeks after the first operation. I had hoped it might have been a healthier eye. But when the cataract was removed, we found a retina much the same as in the right: traces of pigmentosa, scarred macula, areas atrophied. However, with both eyes functioning to some degree, her visual field was larger and she fixated better. She could now see from a medical point of view. From a psychological point of view she was still blind. In other words she now had to learn to see.

Frank As we got closer to the end of that year, it was quite clear that Molly was changing – had changed. And one of the most fascinating insights into the state of her mind at that time was given to me by Jean Wallace, the psychotherapist; very interesting woman; brilliant actually; married to George, a behavioural psychologist, a second-rater if you ask me; and what a bore – what a bore! Do you know what that man did? Lectured me one day for over an hour on cheese-making if you don't mind! Anyhow – anyhow – the two of them – the Wallaces – they were doing this book on Molly; a sort of documentation of her 'case-history' from early sight to life-long blindness to sight restored to . . . whatever. And the way Jean explained Molly's condition to me was this.

All of us live on a swing, she said. And the swing normally moves smoothly and evenly across a narrow range of the usual emotions. Then we have a crisis in our life; so that instead of moving evenly from, say, feeling sort of happy to feeling sort of miserable, we now swing from elation to despair, from unimaginable delight to utter wretchedness.

The word she used was 'delivered' to show how passive we are in this terrifying game: We are delivered into one emotional state – snatched away from it – delivered into the opposite emotional state. And we can't help ourselves.

We can't escape. Until eventually we can endure no more abuse – become incapable of experiencing anything, feeling anything at all.

That's how Jean Wallace explained Molly's behaviour to me. Very interesting woman. Brilliant actually. And beautiful, too. Oh, yes, all the gifts. And what she said helped me to understand Molly's extraordinary behaviour – difficult behaviour – yes, goddamit, very difficult behaviour over those weeks leading up to Christmas.

For example – for example. One day, out of the blue, a Friday evening in December, five o'clock, I'm about to go to the Hikers Club, and she says, 'I feel like a swim, Frank. Let's go for a swim now.'

At this stage I'm beginning to recognize the symptoms: the defiant smile, the excessive enthusiasm, some reckless, dangerous proposal. 'Fine. Fine,' I say. Even though it's pitch dark and raining. So we'll go to the swimming-pool? Oh, no. She wants to swim in the sea. And not only swim in the sea on a wet Friday night in December, but she wants to go out to the rocks at the far end of Tramore and she wants to climb up on top of Napoleon Rock as we call it locally – it's the highest rock there, a cliff really – and I'm to tell her if the tide is in or out and how close are the small rocks in the sea below and how deep the water is because she's going to dive – to dive for God's sake – the eighty feet from the top of Napoleon down into the Atlantic ocean.

'And why not, Frank? Why not for God's sake?'

Oh, yes, an enormous change. Something extra-ordinary about all that.

Then there was the night I watched her through the bedroom door. She was sitting at her dressing-table, in front of the mirror, trying her hair in different ways. When she would have it in a certain way, she'd lean close to the mirror and peer into it and turn her head from side to side. But you knew she couldn't read her reflection, could scarcely even see it. Then she would try the hair in a different style and she'd lean into the mirror again until her face was almost touching it and again she'd turn first to one side and then the other. And you knew that all she saw was a blur.

Then after about half-a-dozen attempts she stood up and came to the door – it was then I could see she was crying – and she switched off the light. Then she went back to the dressing-table and sat down again; in the dark; for maybe an hour; sat there and gazed listlessly at the black mirror.

Yes, she did dive into the Atlantic from the top of Napoleon Rock; first time in her life. Difficult times. Oh, I can't tell you. Difficult times for all of us.

Mr Rice The dangerous period for Molly came – as it does for all patients – when the first delight and excitement at having vision have died away. The old world with its routines, all the consolations of work and the familiar, is gone for ever. A sighted world – a partially sighted world, for that is the best it will ever be – is available. But to compose it, to put it together, demands effort and concentration and patience that are almost superhuman.

So the question she had to ask herself was: How much do I want this world? And am I prepared to make that enormous effort to get it?

Frank Then there was a new development – as if she hadn't enough troubles already. A frightening new development. She began getting spells of dizziness when everything seemed in a thick fog, all external reality became just a haze. This would hit her for no reason at all – at work, or walking home, or in the house; and it would last for an hour, maybe several hours.

Rice had no explanation for it. But you could see he was concerned.

'It's called "gnosis",' he said.
'How do you spell that?'
'G-n-o-s-i-s.'
'And what is it?'
'It's a condition of impaired vision, Mr Sweeney.'
He really was a right little bastard at times.

Anyhow, I looked it up in the library, and interestingly, interestingly I could find no reference at all to a medical condition called 'gnosis'. But according to the dictionary the word meant a mystical knowledge, a knowledge of spiritual things! And my first thought was: Good old Molly! Molly's full of mystical knowledge! God forgive me; I really didn't mean to be so cheap.

I meant to tell Rice about *that* meaning of the word the next time I met him – just to bring him down a peg. But it slipped my mind. I suppose because the condition disappeared as suddenly as it appeared. And anyway she had so many troubles at that stage that my skirmishes with Rice didn't matter any more.

Molly Tests – tests – tests – tests – tests! Between Mr Rice and Jean Wallace and George Wallace and indeed Frank himself I must have spent months and months being analysed and answering questions and identifying drawings and making sketches. And, God, those damned tests with photographs and lights and objects – those endless tricks and illusions and distortions – the Zöllner illusion, the Ames distorting room, the Staircase illusion, the Müller-Lyer illusion. And they never told you if you had passed or failed so you always assumed you failed. Such peace – such peace when they were all finished.

I stopped at the florist one evening to get something for Tony and Betty from this side – what was this side; Molly's father and mother. For their wedding anniversary. And I spotted this little pot of flowers, like large butter-cups, about six inches tall, with blue petals and what seemed to me a whitish centre. I thought I recognized them but I wasn't quite sure. And I wouldn't allow myself to touch them.

'I'll take these,' I said to the man.

'Pretty, aren't they?' he said. 'Just in from Holland this morning. And do you know what? – I can't remember what they're called. Do you know?'

'They're nemophila.'

'Are they?'

'Yes,' I said. 'Feel the leaves. They should be dry and feathery.'

'You're right,' he said. 'That's what they are. They have another name, haven't they?'

'Baby Blue Eyes,' I said.

'That's it! I'd forgotten that. Getting too old for this job.'

Yes, that gave me some pleasure. One silly little victory. And when I took them home and held them up to my face and looked closely at them, they weren't nearly as pretty as buttercups. Weren't pretty at all. Couldn't give that as a present next door.

Frank It was the clever Jean Wallace who spotted the distress signals first. She said to me: 'We should be seeing a renaissance of personality at this point. Because if that doesn't take place – and it's not – then you can expect a withdrawal.'

And she was right. That's what's happened. Molly just . . . withdrew.

Then in the middle of February she lost her job in the health club. And now Rita was no longer a friend. And that was so unfair – Rita kept making allowances for her long after any other boss would have got rid of her; turning in late; leaving early; maybe not even making an appearance for two or three days. Just sitting alone in her bedroom with her eyes shut, maybe listening to the radio, maybe just sitting there in silence.

I made a last effort on the first of March. I took her new scarlet coat out of the wardrobe and I said, 'Come on, girl! Enough of this. We're going for a long walk on Tramore beach. Then we'll have a drink in Moriarity's. Then we'll have dinner in that new Chinese place. Right? Right!' And I left the coat at the foot of her bed.

And that's where it lay for weeks. And weeks. In fact she never wore it out again.

And at that point I had come to the end of my tether. There seemed to be nothing more I could do.

Mr Rice In those last few months a new condition appeared. She began showing symptoms of a condition known as blindsight. This is a physiological condition, not psychological. On those occasions she claimed she could see nothing, absolutely nothing at all. And indeed she was telling the truth. But even as she said this, she behaved as if she could see – reach for her purse, avoid a chair that was in her way, lift a book and hand it to you. She *was* indeed receiving visual signals and she *was* indeed responding to them. But because of a malfunction in part of the cerebral cortex none of this perception reached her consciousness. She was totally unconscious of seeing anything at all.

In other words she *had* vision – but a vision that was utterly useless to her.

Blindsight . . . curious word . . .

I remember in Cleveland once, Bloomstein and Maria and I were in a restaurant and when Maria left the table Bloomstein said to me,

'Beautiful lady. You *do* know that?'

'I know,' I said.

'Do you really?'

I said of course I did.

'That's not how you behave,' he said. 'You behave like a man with blindsight.'

Frank We were in the pub this night, Billy Hughes and myself, just sitting and chatting about – yes! I remember what we were talking about! An idea Billy had of recycling old tea-leaves and turning them into a substitute for tobacco. We should have followed that up.

Anyhow – anyhow, this man comes up to me in the bar, says he's a journalist from a Dublin paper, asks would I be interested in giving him the full story about Molly.

He seemed a decent man. I talked to him for maybe an hour at most. Of course it was stupid. And I really didn't do it for the bloody money.

Jack from next door spotted the piece and brought it in. *Miracle Cure False Dawn. Molly sulks in darkness. Husband drowns sorrow in pub.*

Of course she heard about it – God knows how. And now I was as bad as all the others: I had let her down, too.

Molly During all those years when my mother was in the hospital with her nerves my father brought me to visit her only three times. Maybe that was her choice. Or his. I never knew.

But I have a vivid memory of each of those three visits.

One of the voice of a youngish woman. My father and mother are in her ward, surrounded by a screen, fighting as usual, and I'm standing outside in the huge echoey corridor. And I can hear a young woman sobbing at the far end of the corridor. More lamenting than sobbing. And even though a lot of people are passing along that corridor I remember wondering why nobody paid any attention to her. And for some reason the sound of that lamentation stayed with me.

And I remember another patient, an old man, leaning over me and enveloping me in the smell of snuff. He slipped a coin into my hand and said, 'Go out and buy us a fancy new car, son, and the two of us will drive away to beautiful Fethard-on-Sea.' And he laughed. He had given me a shilling.

And the third memory is of my mother sitting on the side of her bed, shouting at my father, screaming at him, 'She should be at a blind school! You know she should! But you know the real reason you won't send her? Not because you haven't the money. Because you want to punish me.'

I didn't tell Mr Rice that story when he first asked me about my childhood. Out of loyalty to Father, maybe. Maybe out of loyalty to Mother, too.

Anyhow those memories came into my head the other day. I can't have been more than six or seven at the time.

Mr Rice In those last few months it was hard to recognize the woman who had first come to my house. The confident way she shook my hand. Her calm and her independence. The way she held her head.

How self-sufficient she had been then – her home, her job, her friends, her swimming; so naturally, so easily experiencing her world with her hands alone.

And we had once asked so glibly: What has she to lose?

Molly In those last few months I was seeing less and less. I was living in the hospital then, Mother's old hospital. And what was strange was that there were times when I didn't know if the things I did see were real or was I imagining them. I seemed to be living on a borderline between fantasy and reality.

Yes, that was a strange state. Anxious at first; oh, very anxious. Because it meant that I couldn't trust any more what sight I still had. It was no longer trustworthy.

But as time went on that anxiety receded; seemed to be a silly anxiety. Not that I began trusting my eyes again. Just that trying to discriminate, to distinguish between what might be real and what might be imagined, being guided by what Father used to call 'excellent testimony' – that didn't seem to matter all that much, seemed to matter less and less. And for some reason the less it mattered, the more I thought I could see.

Mr Rice In those last few months – she was living in the psychiatric hospital at that point – I knew I had lost contact with her. She had moved away from us all. She wasn't in her old blind world – she was exiled from that. And the sighted world, which she had never found hospitable, wasn't available to her any more.

My sense was that she was trying to compose another life that was neither sighted nor unsighted, somewhere she hoped was beyond disappointment; somewhere, she hoped, without expectation.

Frank The last time I saw Rice was on the following Easter Sunday; April 7; six months to the day after the first operation. Fishing on a lake called Lough Anna away up in the hills. Billy Hughes spotted him first.

'Isn't that your friend, Mr Rice? Wave to him, man!'

And what were Billy and I doing up there in the wilds? Embarrassing. But I'll explain.

Ballybeg got its water supply from Lough Anna and in the summer, when the lake was low, from two small adjoining lakes. So to make the supply more efficient it was decided that at the end of April the two small lakes would be emptied into Lough Anna and it would become the sole reservoir for the town. That would raise the water-level of Anna by fifteen feet and of course ruin the trout fishing there – not that that worried them. So in fact that Easter Sunday would have been Rice's last time to fish there. But he probably knew that because Anna was his favourite lake; he was up there every chance he got; and he had told me once that he had thought of putting a boat on it. Anyhow – anyhow.

Billy Hughes and his crazy scheme. He had heard that there was a pair of badgers in a sett at the edge of the lake. When Anna was flooded in three weeks' time, they would be drowned. They would have to be moved. Would I help him?

Move two badgers! Wonderful! So why did I go with him? Partly to humour the eejit. But really, I suppose, really because that would be our last day together, that Easter Sunday.

And that's how we spent it – digging two bloody badgers out of their sett. Dug for two-and-a-half hours. Then flung old fishing nets over them to immobilize them. Then lifted them into two wheelbarrows. Then hauled those wheelbarrows along a sheep track up the side of the mountain – and each of those brutes weighed at least thirty pounds – so that we were hauling half-a-hundred-weight of bloody badger-meat up an almost vertical mountainside. And then – listen to this – the greatest lunacy of all – then tried to force them into an old, abandoned sett half-way up the mountain! Brilliant Billy Hughes!

Because of course the moment we cut them out of the nets and tried to push them down the new hole, well naturally they went wild; bit Billy's ankle and damn near fractured my arm; and then went careering down the hillside in a mad panic, trailing bits of net behind them. And because they can't see too well in daylight or maybe because they're half-blind anyway, stumbling into bushes and banging into rocks and bumping into each other and sliding and rolling and tumbling all over the place. And where did they head for? Of course – of course – straight back to the old sett at the edge of the water – the one we'd destroyed with all our digging!

Well, what could you do but laugh? Hands blistered, bleeding ankle, sore arm, filthy clothes. Flung ourselves on the heather and laughed until our sides hurt. And then

Billy turned to me and said very formally, 'Happy Easter, Frank' and it seemed the funniest thing in the world and off we went again. What an eejit that man was!

Rice joined us when we were putting the wheelbarrows into the back of Billy's van.

'I was watching you from the far side,' he said. 'What in God's name were you doing?'

Billy told him.

'Good heavens!' he said, posh as ever. 'A splendid idea. Always a man for the noble pursuit, Frank.'

The bastard couldn't resist it, I knew. But for some reason he didn't anger me that day; didn't even annoy me. Maybe because his fishing outfit was a couple of sizes too big for him and in those baggy trousers he looked a bit like a circus clown. Maybe because at that moment, after that fiasco with the badgers, standing on that shore that would be gone in a few weeks' time, none of the three of us – Billy, Rice, myself – none of the three of us seemed such big shots at that moment. Or maybe he didn't annoy me that Easter Sunday afternoon because I knew I'd probably never see him again. I was heading off to Ethiopia in the morning.

We left the van outside Billy's flat and he walked me part of the way home.

When we got to the courthouse I said he'd come far enough: we'd part here. I hoped he'd get work. I hoped he'd meet some decent woman who'd marry him and beat some sense into him. And I'd be back home soon, very soon, the moment I'd sorted out the economy of Ethiopia . . . The usual stuff.

Then we hugged quickly and he walked away and I looked after him and watched his straight back and the quirky way he threw out his left leg as he walked and I thought, my God, I thought how much I'm going to miss that bloody man.

And when he disappeared round the corner of the

courthouse, I thought, too – I thought, too – Abyssinia for Christ's sake – or whatever it's called – Ethiopia – Abyssinia – whatever it's called – who cares what it's called – who gives a damn – who in his right mind wants to go there for Christ's sake? Not you. You certainly don't. Then why don't you stay where you are for Christ's sake? What are you looking for?

Oh, Jesus . . .

Mr Rice Roger Bloomstein was killed in an air-crash on the evening of the Fourth of July. He was flying his plane from New York to Cape Cod where Maria and he had rented a house for the summer. An eyewitness said the engine stopped suddenly, and for a couple of seconds the plane seemed to sit suspended in the sky, golden and glittering in the setting sun, and then plummeted into the sea just south of Martha's Vineyard.

The body was never recovered.

I went to New York for the memorial service the following month. Hiroko Matoba couldn't come: he had had a massive heart attack the previous week. So of the four horsemen, the brilliant meteors, there were only the two of us: Hans, now the internationally famous Herr Girder, silver-haired, sleek, smiling; and myself, seedy, I knew, after a bad flight and too much whiskey.

Girder asked about Molly. He had read an article George Wallace had written about 'Mrs M' in the *Journal of Psychology*. The enquiry sounded casual but the smiling eyes couldn't conceal the vigilance. So the vigilance was still necessary despite the success, maybe more necessary because of the success.

'Lucky Paddy Rice,' he said. 'The chance of a lifetime. Fell on your feet again.'

'Not as lucky as you, Hans.'

'But it didn't end happily for the lady?'

''Fraid not,' I said.

'Too bad. No happy endings. So she is totally sightless now?'

'Totally.'

'And mentally?'

'Good days – bad days,' I said.

'But she won't survive?'

'Who's to say?' I said.

'No, no. They don't survive. That's the pattern. But they'll insist on having the operation, won't they? And who's to dissuade them?'

'Let me get you a drink,' I said and I walked away.

I watched Maria during the service. Her beauty had always been chameleon. She had an instinctive beauty for every occasion. And today with her drained face and her dazed eyes and that fragile body, today she was utterly vulnerable, and at the same time, within her devastation, wholly intact and untouchable. I had never seen her more beautiful.

When the service was over she came to me and thanked me for coming. We talked about Aisling and Helga. They were having a great time with her parents in Geneva; they loved it there and her parents spoiled them; they weren't good at answering letters but they liked getting mine even though they were a bit scrappy. They were happy girls, she said.

Neither of us spoke Roger's name.

Then she took my hand and kissed it and held it briefly against her cheek. It was a loving gesture. But for all its tenderness, because of its tenderness, I knew she was saying a final goodbye to me.

As soon as I got back to Ballybeg I resigned from the hospital and set about gathering whatever belongings I had. The bungalow was rented, never more than a lodging. So the moving out was simple – some clothes, a few books, the fishing rods. Pity to leave the lakes at that time of year. But the lake I enjoyed most – a lake I had grown to love – it had been destroyed by flooding. So it was all no great upheaval.

I called on Molly the night before I left. The nurse said she was very frail. But she could last for ever or she could slip away tonight. 'It's up to herself,' she said. 'But a lovely woman. No trouble at all. If they were all as nice and quiet . . .'

She was sleeping and I didn't waken her. Propped up against the pillows; her mouth open; her breathing shallow; a scarlet coat draped around her shoulders; the wayward hair that had given her so much trouble now contained in a net.

And looking down at her I remembered – was it all less than a year ago? – I had a quick memory of the first time I saw her in my house, and the phantom desire, the insane fantasy that crossed my mind that day: Was this the chance of a lifetime that might pull my life together, rescue a career, restore a reputation? Dear God, that opulent fantasy life . . .

And looking down at her – the face relaxed, that wayward hair contained in a net – I thought how I had failed her. Of course I had failed her. But at least, at least for a short time she did see men 'walking as if like trees'. And I think, perhaps, yes I think she understood more than any of us what she did see.

Molly When I first went to Mr Rice I remember him asking me was I able to distinguish between light and dark and what direction light came from. And I remember thinking: Oh my God, he's asking you profound questions about good and evil and about the source of knowledge and about big mystical issues! Careful! Don't make a fool of yourself! And of course all the poor man wanted to know was how much vision I had. And I could answer him easily now: I can't distinguish between light and dark, nor the direction from which light comes, and I certainly

wouldn't see the shadow of Frank's hand in front of my
face. Yes, that's all long gone. Even the world of touch has
shrunk. No, not that it has shrunk; just that I seem to
need much less of it now. And after all that anxiety and
drudgery we went through with engrams and the need to
establish connections between visual and tactile engrams
and synchronizing sensations of touch and sight and
composing a whole new world. But I suppose all that had
to be attempted.

I like this hospital. The staff are friendly. And I have
loads of visitors. Tony and Betty and baby Molly from
this side – well, what used to be this side. They light an
odd fire in the house, too, to keep it aired for Frank. And
Mary from that side. She hasn't told me yet but I'm afraid
Jack has cleared off. And Billy Hughes; out of loyalty to
Frank; every Sunday in life, God help me; God help *him*.
And Rita. Of course, Rita. We never talk about the row
we had. That's all in the past. I love her visits: she has all
the gossip from the club. Next time she's here I must ask
her to sing 'Oft in the Stilly Night' for me. And no crying
at the end!

And old Mr O'Neill! Yes! Dan McGrew himself! And
Louise – Lou – his wife! Last Wednesday she appeared in
a crazy green cloche hat and deep purple gloves up to here
(*elbow*) and eyeshadow half-way down her cheek and a
shocking black woollen dress that scarcely covered her
bum! Honestly! He was looking just wonderful; not a day
over forty. And he stood in the middle of the ward and
did the whole thing for me – 'A bunch of the boys were
whooping it up in the Malamute saloon'. And Lou gazing
at him in admiration and glancing at us as if to say, 'Isn't
he just the greatest thing ever?' And he was – he was! Oh,
that gave my heart a great lift.

And yesterday I got a letter, twenty-seven pages long.
Frank – who else? It took the nurse an hour to read it to
me. Ethiopia is paradise. The people are heroes. The

climate is hell. The relief workers are completely
dedicated. Never in his life has he felt so committed, so
passionate, so fulfilled. And they have a special bee out
there, the African bee, that produces twice as much honey
as our bees and is immune to all known bee diseases and
even though it has an aggressive nature he is convinced it
would do particularly well in Ireland. Maybe in Leitrim.
And in his very limited spare time he has taken up
philosophy. It is fascinating stuff. There is a man called
Aristotle that he thinks highly of. I should read him, he
says. And he sent a money order for two pounds and he'll
write again soon.

Mother comes in occasionally; in her pale blue
headscarf and muddy wellingtons. Nobody pays much
attention to her. She just wanders through the wards. She
spent so much time here herself, I suppose she has an
affection for the place. She doesn't talk much – she never
did. But when she sits uneasily on the edge of my bed, as
if she were waiting to be summoned, her face always
frozen in that nervous half-smile, I think I know her
better than I ever knew her and I begin to love her all over
again.

Mr Rice came to see me one night before he went away.

I was propped up in bed, drifting in and out of sleep,
and he stood swaying at the side of the bed for maybe five
minutes, just gazing at me. I kept my eyes closed. Then he
took both my hands in his and said, 'I'm sorry, Molly
Sweeney. I'm so sorry.'

And off he went.

I suppose it was mean of me to pretend I was asleep.
But the smell of whiskey was suffocating; and the night
nurse told me that on his way out the front door he
almost fell down the stone steps.

And sometimes Father drops in on his way from court.
And we do imaginary tours of the walled garden and
compete with each other in the number of flowers and

shrubs each of us can identify. I asked him once why he
had never sent me to a school for the blind. And as soon
as I asked him I knew I sounded as if I was angry about it,
as if I wanted to catch him out. But he wasn't at all
disturbed. The answer was simple, he said. Mother wasn't
well; and when she wasn't in hospital she needed my
company at home. But even though I couldn't see the
expression on his face, his voice was lying. The truth of
the matter was he was always mean with money; he
wouldn't pay the blind school fees.

And once – just once – I thought maybe I heard the
youngish woman sobbing quietly at the far end of the
corridor, more lamenting than sobbing. But I wasn't sure.
And when I asked the nurse, she said I must have
imagined it; there was nobody like that on our floor. And
of course my little old snuff man must be dead years ago –
the man who wanted us to drive to beautiful Fethard-on-
Sea. He gave me a shilling, I remember; a lot of money in
those days.

I think I see nothing at all now. But I'm not absolutely
sure of that. Anyhow my borderline country is where I
live now. I'm at home there. Well . . . at ease there. It
certainly doesn't worry me any more that what I think I
see may be fantasy or indeed what I take to be imagined
may very well be real – what's Frank's term? – external
reality. Real – imagined – fact – fiction – fantasy – reality
– there it seems to be. And it seems to be all right.

And why should I question any of it any more?